ARTHASHASTRA

Kautilya (c. 370–283 BCE) was an ancient Indian polymath, strategist and statesman. Born in Magadha, India, he served as chief advisor to Emperor Chandragupta Maurya, founder of the Mauryan Empire.

Kautilya's seminal work, *Arthashastra*, remains a foundational text on politics, economics and statecraft. His innovative ideas on governance, diplomacy and warfare continue to influence scholars and policymakers worldwide.

ARTHASHASTRA

KAUTILYA

Om Books International

This edition first published in 2025 by

Om Books International

Corporate and Editorial Office
A-12, Sector 64, Noida 201 301
Uttar Pradesh, India
Phone: +91 120 477 4100
Email: editorial@ombooks.com
Website: www.ombooksinternational.com

Sales Office
107, Ansari Road, Darya Ganj,
New Delhi 110 002, India
Phone: +91 11 4000 9000
Email: sales@ombooks.com
Website: www.ombooks.com

ISBN: 978-81-960435-8-2

Printed in India

10 9 8 7 6 5 4 3 2 1

Contents

Book I

Concerning Discipline

Chapter 1 and 2

THE LIFE OF A KING AND THE END OF SCIENCES

Determination of the place of Anvikshaki

ANVIKSHAKI, the triple Vedas (*Trayi*), *Varta* (agriculture, cattle breeding and trade), and *Dandaniti* (science of government) are what are called the four sciences.

The school of Manu (*Manava*) hold that there are only three sciences: the triple Vedas, *Varta* and the science of government, in as much as the science of *Anvikshaki* is nothing but a special branch of the Vedas.

The school of Brihaspati say that there are only two sciences: *Varta* and the science of government, inasmuch as the triple Vedas are merely an abridgment (*Samvarana*, pretext?) for a man experienced in affairs temporal (*Lokayatravidah*).

The school of Usanas declare that there is only one science, and that is the science of government; for, they say, it is in that science that all other sciences have their origin and end.

But Kautilya holds that four and only four are the sciences; wherefore it is from these sciences that all that concerns righteousness and wealth is learnt, therefore they are so called.

Anvikshaki comprises the philosophy of *Sankhya*, *Yoga*, and *Lokayata* (Atheism?).

Righteous and unrighteous acts (*Dharmadharmau*) are learnt from the triple Vedas; wealth and non-wealth from *Varta*; the expedient and the inexpedient (*Nyayanyayau*), as well as potency and impotency (*Balabale*) from the science of government.

When seen in the light of these sciences, the science of *Anvikshaki* is most beneficial to the world, keeps the mind steady and firm in weal and woe alike, and bestows excellence of foresight, speech and action.

Light to all kinds of knowledge, easy means to accomplish all kinds of acts and receptacle of all kinds of virtues, is the science of *Anvikshaki* ever held to be.

[Thus end Chapters 1 and 2, 'Determination of the Place of Anvikshaki', among Sciences in Book I, 'Concerning Discipline', of the Arthashastra of Kautilya.]

Chapter 3

THE END OF SCIENCES

Determination of the place of the Triple Vedas

THE three Vedas, Sama, Rik and Yajus, constitute the triple Vedas. These together with Atharvaveda and the Itihasaveda are (known as) the Vedas. Siksha (Phonetics), Kalpa (ceremonial injunctions), Vyakarana (grammar), Nirukta (glossarial explanation of obscure Vedic terms), *Chandas* (Prosody), and Astronomy form the *Angas*.

As the triple Vedas definitely determine the respective duties of the four castes and of the four orders of religious life, they are the most useful.

The duty of the Brahman is study, teaching, performance of sacrifice, officiating in others' sacrificial performance and the giving and receiving of gifts.

That of a Kshatriya is study, performance of sacrifice, giving gifts, military occupation, and protection of life.

That of a Vaisya is study, performance of sacrifice, giving gifts, agriculture, cattle breeding, and trade.

That of a Sudra is the serving of twice-born (*dvijati*), agriculture, cattle breeding, and trade (*varta*), the profession of artisans and court bards (*karukusilavakarma*).

The duty of a householder is earning livelihood by his own profession, marriage among his equals of different ancestral Rishis, intercourse with his wedded wife after her monthly ablution, gifts to gods, ancestors, guests and servants, and the eating of the remainder.

That of a student (*Brahmacharin*) is learning the Vedas, fire worship, ablution, living by begging, and devotion to his teacher even at the cost of his own life, or in the absence of his teacher, to the teacher's son, or to an elder classmate.

That of a *Vanaprastha* (forest-recluse) is observance of chastity, sleeping on the bare ground, keeping twisted locks, wearing deer skin, fire worship, ablution, worship of gods, ancestors and guests, and living upon foodstuff procurable in forests.

That of an ascetic retired from the world (*Parivrajaka*) is complete control of the organs of sense, abstaining from all kinds of work, disowning money, keeping from society, begging in many places, dwelling in forests, and purity both internal and external.

Harmlessness, truthfulness, purity, freedom from spite, abstinence from cruelty, and forgiveness are duties common to all.

The observance of one's own duty leads one to *Svarga* and infinite bliss (*Anantya*). When it is violated, the world will come to an end owing to confusion of castes and duties.

Hence the king shall never allow people to swerve from their duties; for whoever upholds his own duty, ever adhering to the customs of the *Arya*s, and following the rules of caste and divisions of religious life, will surely be happy both here and hereafter. For the world, when maintained in accordance with injunctions of the triple Vedas, will surely progress, but never perish.

[Thus ends Chapter 3, 'Determination of the place of the Triple Vedas', among Sciences in Book I, 'Concerning Discipline', of the Arthashastra of Kautilya.]

Chapter 4

THE END OF SCIENCES

Varta and Dandaniti

AGRICULTURE, cattle breeding and trade constitute *Varta*. It is most useful in that it brings in grains, cattle, gold, forest produce (*kupya*), and free labour (*vishti*). It is by means of the treasury and the army obtained solely through *Varta* that the king can hold under his control both his and his enemy's party.

That sceptre on which the well-being and progress of the sciences of *Anvikshaki*, the triple Vedas, and *Varta* depend is known as *Danda* (punishment). That which treats of *Danda* is the law of punishment or science of government (*dandaniti*).

It is a means to make acquisitions, to keep them secure, to improve them, and to distribute among the deserved the profits of improvement. It is on this science of government that the course of the progress of the world depends.

'Hence', says my teacher, 'whoever is desirous of the progress of the world shall ever hold the sceptre raised (*udyatadanda*). Never can there be a better instrument than the sceptre to bring people under control'.

'No,' says Kautilya; for whoever imposes severe punishment becomes repulsive to the people; while he who awards mild punishment becomes contemptible. But whoever imposes punishment as deserved becomes respectable. For punishment (*danda*) when awarded with due consideration, makes the people devoted to righteousness and to works productive of wealth and enjoyment; while punishment, when ill-awarded under the influence of greed and anger or owing to ignorance, excites fury even among hermits and ascetics dwelling in forests, not to speak of householders.

But when the law of punishment is kept in abeyance, it gives rise to such disorder as is implied in the proverb of fishes (*matsyanyayamudbhavayati*); for in the absence of a magistrate (*dandadharabhave*), the strong will swallow the weak; but under his protection, the weak resist the strong.

This people (*loka*) consisting of four castes and four orders of religious life, when governed by the king with his sceptre, will keep to their respective paths, ever devotedly adhering to their respective duties and occupations.

[Thus ends Chapter 4, 'Determination of the Place of Varta and of Dandaniti', among Sciences in Book I, 'Concerning Discipline', of the Arthashastra of Kautilya. 'The End of Sciences' is completed.]

Chapter 5

ASSOCIATION WITH THE AGED

HENCE the (first) three sciences (out of the four) are dependent for their well-being on the science of government. *Danda*, punishment, which alone can procure safety and security of life is, in its turn, dependent on discipline (*vinaya*).

Discipline is of two kinds: artificial and natural; for instruction (*kriya*) can render only a docile being conformable to the rules of discipline, and not an undocile being (*adravyam*). The study of sciences can tame only those who are possessed of such mental faculties as obedience, hearing, grasping, retentive memory, discrimination, inference and deliberation, but not others devoid of such faculties.

Sciences shall be studied and their precepts strictly observed under the authority of specialist teachers.

Having undergone the ceremony of tonsure, the student shall learn the alphabet (*lipi*) and arithmetic. After investiture with sacred thread, he shall study the triple Vedas, the science of Anvikshaki under teachers of acknowledged authority (*sishta*), the science of *Varta* under government superintendents, and the science of *Dandaniti* under theoretical and practical politicians (*vaktriprayoktribhyah*).

He (the prince) shall observe celibacy till he becomes sixteen years old. Then he shall observe the ceremony of tonsure (*godana*) and marry.

In view of maintaining efficient discipline, he shall ever and invariably keep company with aged professors of sciences in whom alone discipline has its firm root.

He shall spend the forenoon in receiving lessons in military arts concerning elephants, horses, chariots and weapons, and the afternoon in hearing the Itihasa.

Purana, *Itivritta* (history), *Akhyayika* (tales), *Udaharana* (illustrative stories), Dharmasastra, and Arthashastra are (known by the name) Itihasa.

During the rest of the day and night, he shall not only receive new lessons and revise old lessons, but also hear over and again what has not been clearly understood.

For from hearing (*sutra*) ensues knowledge; from knowledge steady application (*yoga*) is possible; and from application self-possession (*atmavatta*) is possible. This is what is meant by efficiency of learning (*vidyasamarthyam*).

The king who is well educated and disciplined in sciences, devoted to good government of his subjects, and bent on doing good to all people will enjoy the earth unopposed.

[Thus ends Chapter 5, 'Association with the Aged', in Book I, 'Concerning Discipline', of the Arthashastra of Kautilya.]

Chapter 6

RESTRAINT OF THE ORGANS OF SENSE

The Shaking Off of the Aggregate of the Six Enemies

RESTRAINT of the organs of sense, on which success in study and discipline depends can be enforced by abandoning lust, anger, greed, vanity (*mana*), haughtiness (*mada*), and overjoy (*harsha*).

Absence of discrepancy (*avipratipatti*) in the perception of sound, touch, colour, flavour and scent by means of the ear, the skin, the eyes, the tongue, and the nose, is what is meant by the restraint of the organs of sense. Strict observance of the precepts of sciences also means the same; for the sole aim of all the sciences is nothing but restraint of the organs of sense.

Whosoever is of reverse character, whoever has not his organs of sense under his control, will soon perish, though possessed of the whole earth bounded by the four quarters.

For example: Bhoja, known also by the name *Dandakya*, making a lascivious attempt on a Brahman maiden, perished along with his kingdom and relations;

So also Karala, the Vaideha. Likewise Janamejaya under the influence of anger against Brahmans, as well as Talajangha against the family of Bhrigus.

Aila in his attempt under the influence of greed to make exactions from Brahmans, as well as Ajabindu, the Sauvira (in a similar attempt);

Ravana unwilling under the influence of vanity to restore a stranger's wife, as well as Duryodhana to part with a portion of his kingdom; Dambhodbhava as well as Arjuna of Haihaya dynasty being so haughty as to despise all people;

Vatapi in his attempt under the influence of overjoy to attack Agastya, as well as the corporation of the Vrishnis in their attempt against Dvaipayana.

Thus these and several other kings, falling prey to the aggregate of the six enemies and having failed to restrain their organs of sense, perished together with their kingdom and relations. Nabhaga, having driven out the aggregate of the six enemies, as well as Ambarisha of Jamadagnya famous for his restraint of the organs of sense, long enjoyed the earth.

[Thus ends Chapter 6, 'The Shaking Off of the Aggregate of the Six Enemies', in the section of the 'Restraint Of the Organs of Sense', in Book I, 'Concerning Discipline', of the Arthashastra of Kautilya.]

Chapter 7

RESTRAINT OF THE ORGANS OF SENSE

The Life of a Saintly King

HENCE by overthrowing the aggregate of the six enemies, he shall restrain the organs of sense; acquire wisdom by keeping company with the aged; see through his spies; establish safety and security by being ever active; maintain his subjects in the observance of their respective duties by exercising authority; keep up his personal discipline by receiving lessons in the sciences; and endear himself to the people by bringing them in contact with wealth and doing good to them.

Thus, with his organs of sense under his control, he shall keep away from hurting the women and property of others; avoid not only lustfulness, even in dream, but also falsehood, haughtiness and evil proclivities; and keep away from unrighteous and uneconomical transactions.

Not violating righteousness and economy, he shall enjoy his desires. He shall never be devoid of happiness. He may enjoy in an equal degree the three pursuits of life—charity, wealth and desire, which are inter-dependent upon each other. Anyone of these three, when enjoyed to an excess, hurts not only the other two, but also itself.

Kautilya holds that wealth and wealth alone is important, inasmuch as charity and desire depend upon wealth for their realization.

Those teachers and ministers who keep him from falling a prey to dangers, and who, by striking the hours of the day as determined by measuring shadows (*chhayanalikapratodena*) warn him of his careless proceedings even in secret shall invariably be respected.

Sovereignty (*rajatva*) is possible only with assistance. A single wheel can never move. Hence he shall employ ministers and hear their opinion.

[Thus ends Chapter 7, 'The Life of a Saintly King' in the section of the 'Restraint of the Organs of Sense', in Book I, 'Concerning Discipline', of the Arthashastra of Kautilya; 'Restraint of the Organs of Sense' is completed.]

Chapter 8

CREATION OF MINISTERS

'THE king,' says Bharadvaja, 'shall employ his classmates as his ministers; for they can be trusted by him inasmuch as he has personal knowledge of their honesty and capacity'.

'No,' says Visalaksha, 'for, as they have been his playmates as well, they would despise him. But he shall employ as ministers those whose secrets, possessed of in common, are well known to him. Possessed of habits and defects in common. with the king, they would never hurt him lest he would betray their secrets.'

'Common is this fear,' says Parasara, 'for under the fear of betrayal of his own secrets, the king may also follow them in their good and bad acts.'

'Under the control of as many persons as are made aware by the king of his own secrets, might he place himself in all humility by that disclosure. Hence he shall employ as ministers those who have proved faithful to him under difficulties fatal to life and are of tried devotion.'

'No,' says Pisuna, 'for this is devotion, but not intelligence (*buddhigunah*). He shall appoint as ministers those who, when employed as financial matters, show as much as, or more than, the fixed revenue, and are thus of tried ability.'

'No,' says Kaunapadanta, 'for such persons are devoid of other ministerial qualifications; he shall, therefore, employ as ministers those whose fathers and grandfathers had been ministers before; such persons, by virtue of their knowledge of past events and of an established relationship with the king, will, though offended, never desert him; for such faithfulness is seen even among dumb animals; cows, for example, stand aside from strange cows and ever keep company with accustomed herds.'

'No,' says Vatavyadhi, 'for such persons, having acquired complete dominion over the king, begin to play themselves as the king. Hence he shall employ as ministers such new persons as are proficient in the science of polity. It is such new persons who will regard the king as the real sceptre-bearer (*dandadhara*) and dare not offend him'.

'No,' says the son of Bahudanti (a woman), 'for a man possessed of only theoretical knowledge and having no experience of practical politics is likely to commit serious blunders when engaged in actual work. Hence he shall employ as ministers such as are born of high family and possessed of wisdom, purity of purpose, bravery and loyal feelings inasmuch as ministerial appointments shall purely depend on qualifications.'

'This,' says Kautilya, 'is satisfactory in all respects; for a man's ability is inferred from his capacity shown in work. And in accordance in difference with the working capacity.'

Having divided the spheres of their powers and having definitely taken into consideration the place and time where and when they have to work, such persons shall be employed not as councillors (*mantrinah*) but as ministerial officers (*amatyah*).

[Thus ends Chapter 8, 'Creation of Ministers', in Book I, 'Concerning Discipline', of the Arthashastra of Kautilya.]

Chapter 9

THE CREATION OF COUNCILLORS AND PRIESTS

NATIVE, born of high family, influential, well trained in arts, possessed of foresight, wise, of strong memory, bold, eloquent, skilful, intelligent, possessed of enthusiasm, dignity and endurance, pure in character, affable, firm in loyal devotion, endowed with excellent conduct, strength, health and bravery, free from procrastination and ficklemindedness, affectionate, and free from such qualities as excite hatred and enmity—these are the qualifications of a ministerial officer (*amatyasampat*).

Such as are possessed of one half or one quarter of the above qualifications come under middle and low ranks.

Of these qualifications, native birth and influential position shall be ascertained from reliable persons; educational qualifications (*silpa*) from professors of equal learning; theoretical and practical knowledge, foresight, retentive memory, and affability shall be tested from successful application in works; eloquence, skilfullness and flashing intelligence from power shown in narrating stories (*kathayogeshu*, i.e., in conversation); endurance, enthusiasm and bravery in troubles; purity of life, friendly disposition and loyal devotion by frequent association; conduct, strength, health, dignity, and freedom from indolence and ficklemindedness shall be ascertained from their intimate friends; and affectionate and philanthrophic nature by personal experience.

The works of a king may be visible, invisible (*paroksha*) and inferential.

That which he sees is visible; and that which he is taught by another is invisible; and inference of the nature of what is not accomplished from what is accomplished is inferential.

As works do not happen to be simultaneous, are various in form, and pertain to distant and different localities, the king shall, in view of being abreast of time and place, depute his ministers to carry them out. Such is the work of ministers.

Him whose family and character are highly spoken of, who is well educated in the Vedas and the six Angas, is skilful in reading portents providential or accidental, is well versed in the science of government, and who is obedient and who can prevent calamities providential or human by performing such expiatory rites as are prescribed in the Atharvaveda, the king shall employ as high priest. As a student his teacher, a son his father, and a servant his master, the king shall follow him.

That *Kshatriya* breed which is brought up by Brahmans, is charmed with the counsels of good councillors, and which faithfully follows the precepts of the *sastras* becomes invincible and attains success, though unaided with weapons.

[Thus ends Chapter 9, 'Creation of Councillors and Priests', in Book I 'Concerning Discipline', of the Arthashastra of Kautilya.]

Chapter 10

ASCERTAINING BY TEMPTATIONS PURITY OR IMPURITY IN THE CHARACTER OF MINISTERS

ASSISTED by his prime minister (*mantri*) and his high priest, the king shall, by offering temptations, examine the character of ministers (*amatya*) appointed in government departments of ordinary nature.

The king shall dismiss a priest who, when ordered, refuses to teach the Vedas to an outcaste person or to officiate in a sacrificial performance (apparently) undertaken by an outcaste person (*ayajya*).

Then the dismissed priest shall, through the medium of spies under the guise of classmates (*satri*), instigate each minister one after another, saying on oath, 'This king is unrighteous; well let us set up in his place another king who is righteous, or who is born of the same family as of this king, or who is kept imprisoned, or a neighbouring king of his family and of self-sufficiency (*ekapragraha*), or a wild chief (*atavika*), or an upstart (*aupapadika*); this attempt is to the liking of all of us; what dost thou think?'

If anyone or all of the ministers refuse to acquiesce in such a measure, he or they shall be considered pure. This is what is called religious allurement.

A commander of the army, dismissed from service for receiving condemnable things (*asatpragraha*) may, through the agency of spies under the guise of classmates (*satri*), incite each minister to murder the king in view of acquiring immense wealth, each minister being asked, 'This attempt is to the liking of all of us; what dost thou think?'

If they refuse to agree, they are to be considered pure. This is what is termed monetary allurement.

A woman spy under the guise of an ascetic and highly esteemed in the harem of the king may allure each prime minister (*mahamatya*) one after another, saying, 'The queen is enamoured of thee and has made arrangements for thy entrance into her chamber; besides this, there is also the certainty of large acquisitions of wealth.'

If they discard the proposal, they are pure. This is what is styled love allurement.

With the intention of sailing on a commercial vessel (*prahavananimittam*), a minister may induce all other ministers to follow him. Apprehensive of danger, the king may arrest them all. A spy under the guise of a fraudulent disciple, pretending to have suffered imprisonment may incite each of the ministers thus deprived of wealth and rank, saying, 'The king has betaken himself to an unwise course; well, having murdered him, let us put another in his stead. We all like this; what dost thou think?'

If they refuse to agree, they are pure. This is what is termed allurement under fear.

Of these tried ministers, those whose character has been tested under religious allurements shall be employed in civil and criminal courts (*dharmasthaniyakantaka sodhaneshu*); those whose purity has been tested under monetary allurements shall be employed in the work of a revenue collector and chamberlain; those who have been tried under love allurements shall be appointed to superintend the pleasure grounds (*vihara*) both external and internal; those who have been tested by allurements under fear shall be appointed to immediate service; and those whose character has been tested under all kinds of allurements shall be employed as prime ministers (*mantrinah*), while those who are proved impure under one or all of these allurements shall be appointed in mines, timber and elephant forests, and manufactories.

Teachers have decided that in accordance with ascertained purity, the king shall employ in corresponding works those ministers whose character has been tested under the three pursuits of life—religion, wealth and love—and under fear.

Never, in the view of Kautilya, shall the king make himself or his queen an object (*laksham*, butt) of testing the character of his councillors, nor shall he vitiate the pure like water with poison.

Sometimes the prescribed medicine may fail to reach the person of moral disease; the mind of the valiant, though naturally kept steadfast, may not, when once vitiated and repelled under the four kinds of allurements, return to and recover its original form.

Hence having set up an external object as the butt for all the four kinds of allurements, the king shall, through the agency of spies (*satri*), find out the pure or impure character of his ministers (*amatya*).

[Thus ends Chapter 10, 'Ascertaining by Temptations Purity or Impurity in the Character of Ministers', in Book I, 'Concerning Discipline', of the Arthashastra of Kautilya.]

Chapter 11

THE INSTITUTION OF SPIES

ASSISTED by the council of his ministers tried under espionage, the king shall proceed to create spies under the guise of a fraudulent disciple (*kapatikachatra*), a recluse (*udasthita*), a householder (*grihapaitika*), a merchant (*vaidehaka*), an ascetic practising austerities (*tapasa*), a classmate or a colleague (*satri*), a firebrand (*tikshna*), a poisoner (*rasada*) and a mendicant woman (*bhikshuki*).

A skilful person capable of guessing the mind of others is a fraudulent disciple. Having encouraged such a spy with honour and money rewards, the minister shall tell him, 'Sworn to the king and myself, thou shalt inform us of whatever wickedness thou findest in others.'

One who is initiated in asceticism and is possessed of foresight and pure character is a recluse. This spy, provided with much money and many disciples, shall carry on agriculture, cattle rearing, and trade (*vartakarma*) on the lands allotted to him for the purpose. Out of the produce and profits thus acquired, he shall provide all ascetics with subsistence, clothing and lodging, and send on espionage such among those under his protection as are desirous to earn a livelihood (*vrittikama*), ordering each of them to detect a particular kind of crime committed in connection with the king's wealth and to report on it when they come to receive their subsistence and wages. All the ascetics (under the recluse) shall severally send their followers on similar errands.

A cultivator, fallen from his profession, but possessed of foresight and pure character is termed a householder spy. This spy shall carry on the cultivation of lands allotted to him for the purpose, and maintain cultivators, etc., as before.

A trader, fallen from his profession, but possessed of foresight and pure character, is a merchant spy. This spy shall carry on the manufacture of merchandise on lands allotted to him for the purpose, etc., as before.

A man with shaved head (*munda*) or braided hair (*jatila*) and desirous to earn livelihood is a spy under the guise of an ascetic practising austerities. Such a spy surrounded by a host of disciples with shaved head or braided hair may take his abode in the suburbs of a city, and pretend as a person barely living on a handful of vegetables or meadow grass (*yavasamushti*) taken once in the interval of a month or two, but he may take in secret his favourite foodstuff (*gudhamishtamaharam*).

Merchant spies pretending to be his disciples may worship him as one possessed of preternatural powers. His other disciples may widely proclaim that 'this ascetic is an accomplished expert of preternatural powers'.

Regarding those persons who, desirous of knowing their future, throng to him, he may, through palmistry, foretell such future events as he can ascertain by the nods and signs of his disciples (*angavidyaya sishyasanjnabhischa*) concerning the works of highborn people of the country, viz., small profits, destruction by fire, fear from robbers, the execution of the seditious, rewards for the good, forecast of foreign affairs (*videsa pravrittivijnanam*), saying, 'This will happen to-day, that to-morrow, and that this king will do.' Such assertions of the ascetic his disciples shall corroborate (by adducing facts and figures).

He shall also foretell not only the rewards which persons possessed of foresight, eloquence and bravery are likely to receive at the hands of the king, but also probable changes in the appointments of ministers.

The king's minister shall direct his affairs in conformity to the forecast made by the ascetic. He shall appease with offer of wealth and honour those who have had some well-known cause to be disaffected, and impose punishments in secret on those who are for no reason disaffected or who are plotting against the king.

Honoured by the king with awards of money and titles, these five institutes of espionage (*samstha*) shall ascertain the purity of character of the king's servants.

[Thus ends Chapter 11, 'The Institution of Spies', in Book I, 'Concerning Discipline', of the Arthashastra of Kautilya.]

Chapter 12

INSTITUTION OF SPIES

Creation of Wandering Spies

THOSE orphans (*asambandhinah*) who are to be necessarily fed by the state and are put to study science, palmistry (*angavidya*), sorcery (*mayagata*), the duties of the various orders of religious life, legerdemain (*jambhakavidya*), and the reading of omens and augury (*antara-chakra*), are classmate spies or spies learning by social intercourse (*samsargavidyasatrinah*).

Such brave desperados of the country who, reckless of their own life, confront elephants or tigers in fight mainly for the purpose of earning money are termed firebrands or fiery spies (*tikshna*).

Those who have no trace of filial affection left in them and who are very cruel and indolent are poisoners (*rasada*).

A poor widow of Brahman caste, very clever, and desirous to earn her livelihood is a woman ascetic (*parivrajika*). Honoured in the king's harem, such a woman shall frequent the residences of the king's prime ministers (*mahamatyakulani*).

The same rule shall apply to women with shaved head (*munda*), as well as to those of Sudra caste. All these are wandering spies (*sancharah*).

Of these spies, those who are of good family, loyal, reliable, well trained in the art of putting on disguises appropriate to countries and trades, and possessed of knowledge of many languages and arts shall be sent by the king to espy in his own country the movements of his ministers, priests, commanders of the army, the heir apparent, the doorkeepers, the officer in charge of the harem, the magistrate (*prasastri*), the collector general (*samahartri*), the chamberlain (*sannidhatri*), the commissioner (*pradeshtri*), the city constable (*nayaka*), the officer in charge of the city (*paura*), the superintendent of transactions (*vyavaharika*), the superintendent of manufactories (*karmantika*), the assembly of councillors (*mantriparishad*), heads of departments (*adhyakshah*), the commissary general (*dandapala*), and officers in charge of fortifications, boundaries and wild tracts.

Fiery spies, such as are employed to hold the royal umbrella, vase, fan and shoes, or to attend at the throne, chariot and conveyance shall espy the public character (*bahyam charam*) of these (officers).

Classmate spies shall convey this information (i.e., that gathered by the fiery spies) to the institutes of espionage (*samsthasvarpayeyuh*).

Poisoners such as a sauce-maker (*suda*), a cook (*aralika*), procurer of water for bathing (*snapaka*) shampooer, the spreader of bed (*astaraka*), a barber (*kalpaka*), toilet-maker (*prasadhaka*), a water-servant; servants such as have taken the appearance of a humpbacked person, a dwarf, a pigmy (*kirata*), the dumb, the deaf, the idiot, the blind; artisans such as actors, dancers, singers, players on musical instruments, buffoons, and a bard; as well as women shall espy the private character of these officers.

A mendicant woman shall convey this information to the institute of espionage.

The immediate officers of the institutes of espionage (*samsthanamantevasinah*) shall by making use of signs or writing (*samjnalipibhih*) set their own spies in motion (to ascertain the validity of the information).

Neither the institutes of espionage nor they (the wandering spies) shall know each other.

If a mendicant woman is stopped at the entrance, the line of doorkeepers, spies under the guise of father and mother (*matapitri vyanjanah*), women artisans, court bards, or prostitutes shall, under the pretext of taking in musical instruments, or through cipher-writing (*gudhalekhya*), or by means of signs, convey the information to its destined place (*charam nirhareyuh*).

(Spies of the institutes of espionage) may suddenly go out under the pretext of long-standing disease, or lunacy, or by setting fire (to something) or by administering poison (to someone).

When the information thus received from these three different sources is exactly of the same version, it shall be held reliable. If they (the three sources) frequently differ, the spies concerned shall either be punished in secret or dismissed. Those spies who are referred to in Book IV, 'Removal of Thorns', shall receive their salaries from those kings (*para*, i.e., foreign) with whom they live as servants; but when they aid both the states in the work of catching hold of robbers, they shall become recipients of salaries from both the states (*ubhayavetanah*).

Those whose sons and wives are kept (as hostages) shall be made recipients of salaries from two states and considered as under the mission of enemies. Purity of character of such persons shall be ascertained through persons of similar profession.

Thus with regard to kings who are inimical, friendly, intermediate, of low rank, or neutral, and with regard to their eighteen government departments (*ashtaldasa tirtha*), spies shall be set in motion.

The humpbacked, the dwarf, the eunuch, women of accomplishments, the dumb, and various grades of *mleccha* caste shall be spies inside their houses.

Merchant spies inside forts; saints and ascetics in the suburbs of forts; the cultivator and the recluse in country parts; herdsmen in the boundaries of the country; in forests, forest-dwellers, *sramana*s and chiefs of wild tribes shall be stationed to ascertain the movements of enemies. All these spies shall be very quick in the dispatch of their work.

Spies set up by foreign kings shall also be found out by local spies; spies by spies of like profession. It is the institutes of espionage, secret or avowed, that set spies in motion.

Those chiefs whose inimical design has been found out by spies supporting the king's cause shall, in view of affording opportunity to detect the spies of foreign kings, be made to live on the boundaries of the state.

[Thus ends Chapter 12, 'Creation of Wandering Spies', in the section of 'The Institution of Spies', in Book I, 'Concerning Discipline', of the Arthashastra of Kautilya.]

Chapter 13

PROTECTION OF PARTIES FOR OR AGAINST ONE'S OWN CAUSE IN ONE'S OWN STATE

HAVING set up spies over his prime ministers (*mahamatyra*), the king shall proceed to espy both citizens and country people.

Classmate spies (*satri*) formed as opposing factions shall carry on disputations in places of pilgrimage (*tirtha*), in assemblies, houses, corporations (*puga*), and amid congregations of people. One spy may say:

'This king is said to be endowed with all desirable qualities; he seems to be a stranger to such tendencies as would lead him to oppress citizens and country people by levying heavy fines and taxes'.

Against those who seem to commend this opinion, another spy may interrupt the speaker and say:

'People suffering from anarchy as illustrated by the proverbial tendency of a large fish swallowing a small one (*matsyanyayabhibhutah prajah*), first elected Manu, the Vaivasvata, to be their king; and allotted one-sixth of the grains grown and one-tenth of merchandise as sovereign dues. Fed by this payment, kings took upon themselves the responsibility of maintaining the safety and security of their subjects (*yogakshemavahah*), and of being answerable for the sins of their subjects when the principle of levying just punishments and taxes has been violated. Hence hermits too provide the king with one-sixth of the grains gleaned by them, thinking that 'it is a tax payable to him who protects us'. It is the king in whom the duties of both Indra (the rewarder) and Yama (the punisher) are blended, and he is a visible dispenser of punishments and rewards (*heda-prasada*); whoever disregards kings will be visited with divine punishments too. Hence kings shall never be despised.'

Thus treacherous opponents of sovereignty shall be silenced.

Spies shall also know the rumours prevalent in the state. Spies with shaved heads or braided hair shall ascertain whether there prevails content or discontent among those who live upon the grains, cattle, and gold of the king, among those who supply the same (to the king) in weal or woe, those who keep under restraint a disaffected relative of the king or a rebellious district, as well as those who drive away an invading enemy or a wild tribe. The greater the contentment of such persons, the more shall be the honour shown to them; while those who are disaffected shall be ingratiated by rewards or conciliation; or dissension may be sown among them so that they may alienate themselves from each other, from a neighbouring enemy, from a wild tribe, or from a banished or imprisoned prince. Failing this measure, they may be so employed in collecting fines and taxes as to incur the displeasure of the people. Those who are inebriated with feelings of enmity may be put down by punishment in secret or by making them incur the displeasure of the whole country. Or having taken the sons and wives of such treacherous persons under state protection, they may be made to live in mines, lest they afford shelter to enemies.

Those that are angry, those that are greedy, those that are alarmed, as well as those that despise the king are the instruments of enemies. Spies under the guise of astrologers and tellers of omens and augury shall ascertain the relationship of such persons with each other and with foreign kings.

Honours and rewards shall be conferred upon those that are contented, while those that are disaffected shall be brought round by conciliation, by gifts, or by sowing dissension, or by punishment.

Thus in his own state a wise king shall guard factions among his people, friendly or hostile, powerful or powerless, against the intrigue of foreign kings.

[Thus ends Chapter 13, 'Protection of Parties for or against One's Own Cause in One's Own State', in Book I, 'Concerning Discipline', of the Arthashastra of Kautilya.]

Chapter 14

WINNING OVER FACTIONS FOR OR AGAINST AN ENEMY'S CAUSE IN AN ENEMY'S STATE

PROTECTION of parties for or against one's own cause in one's own state has been dealt with. Similar measures in connection with parties in a foreign state are to be treated of. Those who are deluded with false promise of large rewards; those of whom one party, though equally skilful as another party in artistic work or in turning out productive or beneficial works, is slighted by bestowing larger rewards on its rival party; those who are harassed by courtiers (*vallabhavaruddhah*); those who are invited to be slighted; those who are harassed by banishment; those who, in spite of their large outlay of money, have failed in their undertakings; those who are prevented from the exercise of their rights or from taking possession of their inheritance; those who have fallen from their rank and honours in government service; those who are shoved to the corner by their own kinsmen; those whose women are violently assaulted; those who are thrown in jail; those who are punished in secret; those who are warned of their misdeeds; those whose property has been wholly confiscated; those who have long suffered from imprisonment; those whose relatives are banished—all these come under the group of provoked persons.

He who has fallen a victim to misfortune by his own misdeeds; he who is offended (by the king); he whose sinful deeds are brought to light; he who is alarmed at the award of punishment on a man of like guilt; he whose lands have been confiscated; he whose rebellious spirit is put down by coercive measures; he who, as a superintendent of all government departments, has suddenly amassed a large amount of wealth; he who, as a relative of such a rich man, aspires to inherit his wealth; he who is disliked by the king; and he who hates the king—all these come under the group of persons alarmed.

He who is impoverished; he who has lost much wealth; he who is niggardly; he who is addicted to evil propensities; and he who is engaged in dangerous transactions—all these constitute the group of ambitious persons. He who is self-sufficient; he who is fond of honours; he who is intolerant of his rival's honour; he who is esteemed low; he who is of a fiery spirit; he who is foolhardy as well as he who is not content with what he has been enjoying—all these come under the group of haughty persons.

Of these, he who clings to a particular faction shall be so deluded by spies with shaved head or braided hair as to believe that he is intriguing with that party. Partisans under provocation, for example, may be won over by telling that 'just as an elephant in rut and mounted over by a driver under intoxication tramples under its foot whatever it comes across, so this king, dispossessed of the eye of science, blindly attempts to oppress both citizens and country people; it is possible to restrain him by setting up a rival elephant against him; so have forbearance enough (to wait)'.

Likewise alarmed persons may be won over by telling that 'just as a hidden snake bites and emits poison over whatever alarms it, so this king, apprehensive of danger from thee, will ere long emit the poison of his resentment on thee; so thou mayest better go elsewhere'.

Similarly, ambitious persons may be won over by telling that 'just as a cow reared by dog-keepers gives milk to dogs, but not to Brahmans, so this king gives milk (rewards) to those who are devoid of valour, foresight, eloquence and bravery, but not to those who are possessed of noble character; so the other king who is possessed of power to discriminate men from men may be courted'.

In like manner haughty persons may be won over by telling that 'just as a reservoir of water belonging to *Chandalas* is serviceable only to *Chandalas*, but not to others, so this king of low birth confers his patronage only on low-born people, but not on Aryas like thee; so the other king who is possessed of power to distinguish between men and men may be courted'.

All these disaffected persons, when acquiescing to the above proposals, may be made under a solemn compact (*panakarmana*) to form a combination together with the spies to achieve their end.

Likewise friends of a foreign king may also be won over by means of persuation and rewards, while implacable enemies may be brought round by sowing dissensions, by threats, and by pointing out the defects of their master.

[Thus ends Chapter 14, 'Winning over Factions for or against an Enemy's Cause in an Enemy's State', in Book I, 'Concerning Discipline', of the Arthashastra of Kautilya.]

Chapter 15

THE BUSINESS OF COUNCIL MEETING

HAVING gained a firm hold on the affection of both local and foreign parties both in his own and enemy's state, the king shall proceed to think of administrative measures.

All kinds of administrative measures are preceded by deliberations in a well-formed council. The subject matter of a council shall be entirely secret and deliberations in it shall be so carried that even birds cannot see them; for it is said that the secrecy of counsels was divulged by parrots, minas, dogs and other low creatures of mean birth. Hence without providing himself with sufficient safeguard against disclosure, he shall never enter into deliberations in a council.

Whoever discloses counsels shall be torn to pieces. The disclosure of counsels may be detected by observing changes in the attitude and countenance of envoys, ministers and masters. Change in conduct is change in attitude (*ingitamanyathavrittih*); and observation of physical appearance is countenance (*akritigrahanamakarah*).

Maintenance of the secrecy of a council matter, and keeping guard over officers that have taken part in the deliberation over it (shall be strictly observed) till the time of starting the work so considered approaches.

Carelessness, intoxication, talking in sleep, love and other evil habits of councillors are the causes of the betrayal of counsels.

Whoever is of hidden nature or is disregarded will disclose counsels. Hence steps shall be taken to safeguard counsels against such dangers. Disclosure of counsels is advantageous to persons other than the king and his officers.

'Hence,' says Bharadvaja, 'the king shall singly deliberate over secret matters; for ministers have their own ministers, and these latter some of their own; this kind of successive line of ministers tends to the disclosure of counsels.'

'Hence no outside person shall know anything of the work which the king has in view. Only those who are employed to carry it out shall know it either when it is begun or when accomplished'. 'No deliberation,' says Visalaksha, 'made by a single person will be successful; the nature of the work which a sovereign has to do is to be inferred from the consideration of both the visible and invisible causes. The perception of what is not or cannot be seen, the conclusive decision of whatever is seen, the clearance of doubts as to whatever is susceptible of two opinions, and the inference of the whole when only a part is seen—all this is possible of decision only by ministers. Hence he shall sit at deliberation with persons of wide intellect.

He shall despise none, but hear the opinions of all. A wise man shall make use of even a child's sensible utterance.

'This is,' says Parasara, 'ascertaining the opinions of others, but not keeping counsels. He shall ask his ministers for their opinion, on a work similar to the one he has in view, telling them that "this is the work; it happened thus; what is to be done if it will turn out thus"; and he shall do as they decide. If it is done thus, both the ascertainment of opinions and maintenance of secrecy can be attained.'

'Not so,' says Pisuna, 'for ministers, when called for their opinions regarding a distant undertaking, or an accomplished or an unaccomplished work, either approach the subject with indifference or give their opinions half-heartedly. This is a serious defect. Hence he shall consult such persons as are believed to be capable of giving decisive opinion regarding those works about which he seeks for advice. If he consults thus, he can secure good advice as well as secrecy of counsel'.

'Not so,' says Kautilya, 'for this (kind of seeking for advice) is infinite and endless. He shall consult three or four ministers. Consultation with a single (minister) may not lead to any definite conclusion in cases of complicated issues. A single minister proceeds wilfully and without restraint. In deliberating with two ministers, the king may be overpowered by their combined action, or imperilled by their mutual dissension. But with three or four ministers he will not come to any serious grief, but will arrive at satisfactory results. With ministers more than four in number, he will have to come to a decision after a good deal of trouble; nor will secrecy of counsel be maintained without much trouble. In accordance with the requirements of place, time and nature of the work in view, he may, as he deems it proper, deliberate with one or two ministers or by himself.

Means to carry out works, command of plenty of men and wealth, allotment of time and place, remedies against dangers, and final success are the five constituents of every council deliberation.

The king may ask his ministers for their opinion either individually or collectively, and ascertain their ability by judging over the reasons they assign for their opinions.

He shall lose no time when the opportunity waited for arrives; nor shall he sit long at consultation with those whose parties he intends to hurt.

The school of Manu says that the assembly of ministers (*mantriparishad*) shall be made to consist of twelve members. The school of Brihaspathi says that it shall consist of sixteen members.

The school of Usanas says that it shall consist of twenty members. But Kautilya holds that it shall consist of as many members as the needs of his dominion require (*yathasamarthyam*).

Those ministers shall have to consider all that concerns the parties of both the king and his enemy. They shall also set themselves to start the work that is not yet begun, to complete what has been begun, to improve what has been accomplished, and to enforce strict obedience to orders (*niyogasampadam*).

He shall supervise works in company with his officers that are near (*asannaih*); and consult by sending writs (*patrasampreshanena*) those that are (not) near (*asanna*). One thousand sages form Indra's assembly of ministers (*mantriparishad*). They are his eyes. Hence he is called thousand-eyed though he possesses only two eyes.

In works of emergency, he shall call both his ministers and the assembly of ministers (*mantrino mantriparishadam cha*), and tell them of the same. He shall do whatever the majority (*bhuyishthah*) of the members suggest or whatever course of action leading to success (*karyasiddhikaram va*) they point out. And while doing any work, none of his enemies (*pare*) shall know his secret, but he shall know the weak points of his enemy. Like a tortoise he shall draw in his limbs that are stretched out. Just as balls of meal offered to ancestors by a person not learned in the Vedas are unfit to be eaten by wise men, so whoever is not well versed in sciences shall be unfit to hear of council deliberations.

[Thus ends Chapter 15, 'The Business of Council-meeting', in Book I, 'Concerning Discipline', of the Arthashastra of Kautilya.]

Chapter 16

THE MISSION OF ENVOYS

WHOEVER has succeeded as a councillor is an envoy. Whoever possesses ministerial qualifications is a charge-d'affaires (*nisrishtarthah*).

Whoever possesses the same qualifications less by one quarter is an agent entrusted with a definite mission (*parimitarthah*).

Whoever possesses the same qualifications less by one half is a conveyer of royal writs (*sasanaharah*).

Having made excellent arrangements for carriage, conveyance, servants and subsistence, he (an envoy) shall start on his mission, thinking that 'the enemy shall be told thus: the enemy (*para*) will say, thus; this shall be the reply to him; and thus he shall be imposed upon'.

The envoy shall make friendship with the enemy's officers such as those in charge of wild tracts, of boundaries, of cities, and of country parts. He shall also contrast the military stations, sinews of war, and strongholds of the enemy with those of his own master. He shall ascertain the size and area of forts and of the state, as well as strongholds of precious things and assailable and unassailable points.

Having obtained permission, he shall enter into the capital of the enemy and state the object of the mission as exactly as entrusted to him even at the cost of his own life.

Brightness in the tone, face and eyes of the enemy; respectful reception of the mission; enquiry about the health of friends; taking part in the narration of virtues; giving a seat close to the throne; respectful treatment of the envoy; remembrance of friends; closing the mission with satisfaction—all these shall be noted as indicating the good graces of the enemy and the reverse his displeasure.

A displeased enemy maybe told:

'Messengers are the mouthpieces of kings, not only of thyself, but of all; hence messengers who, in the face of weapons raised against them, have to express their mission as exactly as they are entrusted with do not, though outcasts, deserve death; where is then reason to put messengers of Brahman caste to death? This is another's speech. This (i.e., delivery of that speech verbatim) is the duty of messengers.'

Not puffed up with the respects shown to him, he shall stay there till he is allowed to depart. He shall not care for the mightiness of the enemy; shall strictly avoid women and liquor; shall take bed single; for it is well known that the intentions of envoys are ascertained while they are asleep or under the influence of liquor.

He shall, through the agency of ascetic and merchant spies or through their disciples or through spies under the disguise of physicians, and heretics, or through recipients of salaries from two states (*ubhayavetana*), ascertain the nature of the intrigue prevalent among parties favourably disposed to his own master, as well as the conspiracy of hostile factions, and understand the loyalty or disloyalty of the people to the enemy besides any assailable points.

If there is no possibility of carrying on any such conversation (conversation with the people regarding their loyalty), he may try to gather such information by observing the talk of beggars, intoxicated and insane persons or of persons babbling in sleep, or by observing the signs made in places of pilgrimage and temples or by deciphering paintings and secret writings (*chitra-gudha-lekhya-samjna-bhih*).

Whatever information he thus gathers he shall try to test by intrigues.

He shall not check the estimate which the enemy makes of the elements of sovereignty of his own master; but he shall only say in reply, 'All is known to thee'. Nor shall he disclose the means employed (by his master) to achieve an end in view.

If he has not succeeded in his mission, but is still detained, he shall proceed to infer thus:

Whether seeing the imminent danger into which my master is likely to fall and desirous of averting his own danger; whether in view of inciting against my master an enemy threatening in the rear or a king whose dominion in the rear is separated by other intervening states; whether in view of causing internal rebellion in my master's state, or of inciting a wild chief (*atavika*) against my master; whether in view of destroying my master by employing a friend or a king whose dominion stretches out in the rear of my master's state (*akranda*); whether with the intention of averting the internal trouble in his own state or of preventing a foreign invasion or the inroads of a wild chief; whether in view of causing the approaching time of my master's expedition to lapse; whether with the desire of collecting raw materials and merchandise, or of repairing his fortifications, or of recruiting a strong army capable to fight; whether waiting for the time and opportunity necessary for the complete training of his own army; or whether in view of making a desirable alliance in order to avert the present contempt brought about by his own carelessness, this king detains me thus?

Then he may stay or get out as he deems it desirable; or he may demand a speedy settlement of his mission.

Or having intimated an unfavourable order (*sasana*) to the enemy, and pretending apprehension of imprisonment or death, he may return even without permission; otherwise he may be punished.

Transmission of missions, maintenance of treaties, issue of ultimatum (*pratapa*), gaining of friends, intrigue, sowing dissension among friends, fetching secret force; carrying away by stealth relatives and gems, gathering information about the movements of spies, bravery, breaking of treaties of peace, winning over the favour of the envoy and government officers of the enemy—these are the duties of an envoy (*duta*).

The king shall employ his own envoys to carry on works of the above description, and guard himself against (the mischief of) foreign envoys by employing counter envoys, spies, and visible and invisible watchmen.

[Thus ends Chapter 16, 'The Mission of Envoys', in Book I, 'Concerning Discipline', of the Arthashastra of Kautilya.]

Chapter 17

PROTECTION OF PRINCES

HAVING secured his own personal safety first from his wives and sons, the king can be in a position to maintain the security of his kingdom against immediate enemies as well as foreign kings.

We shall treat 'Protection of Wives' in connection with 'Duties towards the Harem'.

Ever since the birth of princes, the king shall take special care of them.

'For,' says Bharadvaja, 'princes like crabs have a notorious tendency of eating up their begetter. When they are wanting in.'

'This is,' says Visalaksha, 'cruelty, destruction of fortune, and extirpation of the seed of the race of Kshatriyas. Hence it is better to keep them under guard in a definite place.'

'This,' says the school of Parasara, 'is akin to the fear from a lurking snake (*ahibhayam*); for a prince may think that apprehensive of danger, his father has locked him up, and may attempt to put his own father on his lap. Hence it is better to keep a prince under the custody of boundary guards or inside a fort.'

'This,' says Pisuna, 'is akin to the fear (from a wolf in the midst) of a flock of sheep (*aurabhrakam bhayam*); for after understanding the cause of his rustication, he may avail himself of the opportunity to make an alliance with the boundary guards (against his father). Hence it is better to throw him inside a fort belonging to a foreign king far away from his own state.'

'This', says Kaunapadanta, 'is akin to the position of a calf (*vatsasthanam*); for just as a man milks a cow with the help of its calf, so the foreign king may milk (reduce) the prince's father. Hence it is better to make a prince live with his maternal relations.'

'This,' says Vatavyadhi 'is akin to the position of a flag (*dhvajasthanametat*): for as in the case of Aditi and Kausika, the prince's maternal relations may, unfurling this flag, go on begging. Hence princes may be suffered to dissipate their lives by sensual excesses (*gramyadharma*) inasmuch as revelling sons do not dislike their indulgent father.'

'This,' says Kautilya, 'is death in life; for no sooner is a royal family with a prince or princes given to dissipation attacked, than it perishes like a worm-eaten piece of wood. Hence when the queen attains the age favourable for procreation, priests shall offer to Indra and Brihaspati the requisite oblations. When she is big with a child, the king shall observe the instructions of midwifery with regard to gestation and delivery. After delivery, the priests shall perform the prescribed purificatory ceremonials. When the prince attains the necessary age, adepts shall train him under proper discipline.'

'Anyone of the classmate spies,' say (politicians known as) *Ambhiyas*, 'may allure the prince towards hunting, gambling, liquor and women, and instigate him to attack his own father and snatch the reins of government in his own hands. Another spy shall prevent him from such acts.'

'There can be,' says Kautilya, 'no greater crime or sin than making wicked impressions on an innocent mind; just as a fresh object is stained with whatever it is brought in close association, so a prince with fresh mind is apt to regard as scientific injunctions all that he is told of. Hence he shall be taught only of righteousness and of wealth (*artha*), but not of unrighteousness and of non-wealth. Classmate spies shall be so courteous towards him as to say, "Thine are we". When, under the temptation of youth, he turns his eye towards women, impure women under the disguise of Aryas shall, at night and in lonely places, terrify him; when fond of liquor, he shall be terrified by making him drink such liquor as is adulterated with narcotics (*yogapana*); when fond of gambling, he shall be terrified by spies under the disguise of fraudulent persons; when fond of hunting, he shall be terrified by spies under the disguise of highway robbers; and when desirous of attacking his own father, he shall, under the pretence of compliance, be gradually persuaded of the evil consequences of such attempts, by telling: "A king is not made by a mere wish; failure of thy attempt will bring about thy own death; success makes thee fall into hell and causes the people to lament (for thy father) and destroy the only clod (*ekaloshtavadhascha*, i.e., thyself)".'

When a king has an only son who is either devoid of worldly pleasures or is a favourite child, the king may keep him under chains. If a king has many sons, he may send some of them to where there is no heir apparent, nor a child either just born or in the embryo.

When a prince is possessed of good and amicable qualities, he may be made the commander-in-chief or installed as heir apparent.

Sons are of three kinds: those of sharp intelligence; those of stagnant intelligence; and those of perverted mind.

Whoever carries into practice whatever he is taught concerning righteousness and wealth is one of sharp intelligence; whoever never carries into practice the good instructions he has imbibed is one of stagnant intelligence; and whoever entangles himself in dangers and hates righteousness and wealth is one of perverted mind.

If a king has an only son (of the last type), attempts shall be made to procreating a son to him; or sons may be begotten on his daughters.

When a king is too old or diseased (to beget sons), he may appoint a maternal relation or a blood relation (*kulya*) of his or anyone of his neighbouring kings possessed of good and amicable qualities to sow the seed in his own field (*kshetrebijam*, i.e., to beget a son on his wife.)

But never shall a wicked and an only son be installed on the royal throne.

A royal father who is the only prop for many (people) shall be favourably disposed towards his son. Except in dangers, sovereignty falling to the lot of the eldest (son) is always respected. Sovereignty may (sometimes) be the property of a clan; for the corporation of clans is invincible in its nature and being free from the calamities of anarchy, can have a permanent existence on earth.

[Thus ends Chapter 17, 'Protection of Princes', in Book I, 'Concerning Discipline', of the Arthashastra of Kautilya.]

Chapter 18

THE CONDUCT OF A PRINCE KEPT UNDER RESTRAINT AND THE TREATMENT OF A RESTRAINED PRINCE

A PRINCE, though put to troubles and employed in an unequal task, shall yet faithfully follow his father unless that task costs his life, enrages the people, or causes any other serious calamities. If he is employed in a good or meritorious work, he shall try to win the good graces of the superintendent of that work, carry the work to a profitable end beyond expectation, and present his father with the proportional profit derived from that work as well as with the excessive profit due to his skill. If the king is not still pleased with him and shows undue partiality to another prince and other wives, he may request the king to permit him for a forest life.

Or if he apprehends imprisonment or death, he may seek refuge under a neighbouring king who is known to be righteous, charitable, truthful, and not given to cunning, but also welcomes and respects guests of good character. Residing therein he may provide himself with men and money, contract marriage connection with influential personages, and not only make alliance with wild tribes, but win over the parties (in his father's state).

Or moving alone, he may earn his livelihood by working in gold mines or ruby mines or by manufacturing gold and silver ornaments or any other commercial commodities. Having acquired close intimacy with heretics (*pashanda*), rich widows, or merchants carrying on ocean traffic, he may, by making use of poison (*madanarasa*), rob them of their wealth as well as the wealth of gods unless the latter is enjoyable by Brahmans learned in the Vedas. Or he may adopt such measures as are employed to capture the villages of a foreign king. Or he may proceed (against his father) with the help of the servants of his mother.

Or having disguised himself as a painter, a carpenter, court bard, a physician, a buffoon, or a heretic, and assisted by spies under similar disguise, he may, when opportunity affords itself, present himself armed with weapons and poison before the king, and address him:

'I am the heir apparent; it does not become thee to enjoy the state alone when it is enjoyable by both of us, or when others justly desire such enjoyment; I ought not to be kept away by awarding an allowance of double the subsistence and salary.'

These are the measures that a prince kept under restraint has to take.

Spies or his mother, natural or adoptive, may reconcile an heir apparent under restraint and bring him to the court.

Or secret emissaries armed with weapons and poison may kill an abandoned prince. If he is not abandoned, he may be caught hold of at night by employing women equal to the occasion, or by making use of liquor, or on the occasion of hunting, and brought back (to the court).

When thus brought back, he shall be conciliated by the king with promise of sovereignty 'after me' (i.e., after the king's death), and kept under guard, in a definite locality. Or if the king has many sons, an unruly prince may be banished.

[Thus ends Chapter 18, 'The Conduct of a Prince Kept under Restraint and the Treatment of a Restrained Prince', in Book I, 'Concerning Discipline', of the Arthashastra of Kautilya.]

Chapter 19

THE DUTIES OF A KING

IF a king is energetic, his subjects will be equally energetic. If he is reckless, they will not only be reckless likewise, but also eat into his works. Besides, a reckless king will easily fall into the hands of his enemies. Hence the king shall ever be wakeful.

He shall divide both the day and the night into eight *nalika*s (1½ hours), or according to the length of the shadow (cast by a gnomon standing in the sun): the shadow of three *purusha*s (36 *angula*s or inches), of one *purusha* (12 inches), of four *angula*s (4 inches), and absence of shadow denoting midday are the four one-eighth divisions of the forenoon; like divisions (in the reverse order) in the afternoon.

Of these divisions, during the first one-eighth part of the day, he shall post watchmen and attend to the accounts of receipts and expenditure; during the second part, he shall look to the affairs of both citizens and country people; during the third, he shall not only bathe and dine, but also study; during the fourth, he shall not only receive revenue in gold (*hiranya*), but also attend to the appointments of superintendents; during the fifth, he shall correspond in writs (*patrasampreshanena*) with the assembly of his ministers, and receive the secret information gathered by his spies; during the sixth, he may engage himself in his favourite amusements or in self-deliberation; during the seventh, he shall superintend elephants, horses, chariots and infantry, and during the eighth part, he shall consider various plans of military operations with his commander-in-chief.

At the close of the day, he shall observe the evening prayer (*sandhya*).

During the first one-eighth part of the night, he shall receive secret emissaries; during the second, he shall attend to bathing and supper and study; during the third, he shall enter the bedchamber amid the sound of trumpets and enjoy sleep during the fourth and fifth parts; having been awakened by the sound of trumpets during the sixth part, he shall recall to his mind the injunctions of sciences as well as the day's duties; during the seventh, he shall sit considering administrative measures and send out spies; and during the eighth division of the night, he shall receive benedictions from sacrificial priests, teachers, and the high priest, and having seen his physician, chief cook and astrologer, and having saluted both a cow with its calf and a bull by circumambulating round them, he shall get into his court.

Or in conformity to his capacity, he may alter the timetable and attend to his duties.

When in the court, he shall never cause his petitioners to wait at the door, for when a king makes himself inaccessible to his people and entrusts his work to his immediate officers, he may be sure to engender confusion in business, and to cause thereby public disaffection, and himself a prey to his enemies.

He shall, therefore, personally attend to the business of gods, of heretics, of Brahmans learned in the Vedas, of cattle, of sacred places, of minors, the aged, the afflicted, and the helpless, and of women—all this in order (of enumeration) or according to the urgency or pressure of those works.

All urgent calls he shall hear at once, but never put off; for when postponed, they will prove too hard or impossible to accomplish.

Having seated himself in the room where the sacred fire has been kept, he shall attend to the business of physicians and ascetics practising austerities; and that in company with his high priest and teacher and after preliminary salutation (to the petitioners).

Accompanied by persons proficient in the three sciences (*trividya*) but not alone lest the petitioners be offended, he shall look to the business of those who are practising austerities, as well as of those who are experts in witchcraft and *yoga*.

Of a king, the religious vow is his readiness to action; satisfactory discharge of duties is his performance of sacrifice; equal attention to all is the offer of fees and ablution towards consecration.

In the happiness of his subjects lies his happiness; in their welfare his welfare; whatever pleases himself he shall not consider as good, but whatever pleases his subjects he shall consider as good.

Hence the king shall ever be active and discharge his duties; the root of wealth is activity, and of evil its reverse.

In the absence of activity acquisitions present and to come will perish; by activity he can achieve both his desired ends and abundance of wealth.

[Thus ends Chapter 19, 'The Duties of a King', in Book I. 'Concerning Discipline', of the Arthashastra of Kautilya.]

Chapter 20

DUTY TOWARDS THE HAREM

ON a site naturally best fitted for the purpose, the king shall construct his harem consisting of many compartments, one within the other, enclosed by a parapet and a ditch, and provided with a door.

He shall construct his own residential palace after the model of his treasury house; or he may have his residential abode in the centre of the delusive chamber (*mohanagriha*), provided with secret passages made into the walls; or in an underground chamber provided with the figures of goddesses and of altars (*chaitya*) carved on the wooden door frame, and connected with many underground passages for exit; or in an upper storey provided with a staircase hidden in a wall, with a passage for exit made in a hollow pillar, the whole building being so constructed with mechanical contrivance as to be caused to fall down when necessary.

Or considering the danger from his own classmates (*sahadhyayi*), such contrivances as the above, mainly intended as safeguards against danger, may be made on occasions of danger or otherwise as he deems fit.

No other kind of fire can burn that harem which is thrice circumambulated from right to left by a fire of human make (*manushyenagnina*); nor can there be kindled any other fire. Nor can fire destroy that harem the walls of which are made of mud mixed with ashes produced by lightning, and wetted in hail water (*karaka-vari*).

Poisonous snakes will not dare to enter into such buildings as are provided with *jivanti* (*faederia faetida*), *sveta* (*Aconitum ferox*), *mushkakapushpa* (?), and *vandaka* (*Epidendrum tesselatum*), and as are protected by the branches of *pejata* (?) and of *asvattha* (*Ficus religiosa*).

Cats, peacocks, mangooses, and the spotted deer eat up snakes.

Parrots, minas (*sarika*), and Malbar birds (*bhringaraja*) shriek when they perceive the smell of snake poison.

The heron (*crauncha*) swoons in the vicinity of poison; the pheasant (*jivanjivaka*) feels distress; the youthful cuckoo (*mattakokila*) dies; the eyes of partridge (*chakora*) are reddened.

Thus remedies shall be applied against fire and poison.

On one side in the rear of the harem, there shall be made, for the residence of women, compartments provided not only with all kinds of medicines useful in midwifery and diseases, but also with well-known pot-herbs (*prakhyatasamsthavriksha*), and a water reservoir; outside these compartments, the residences of princes and princesses; in front (of the latter building), the toilet ground (*alankara bhumi*), the council ground (*mantrabhumi*), the court, and the offices of the heir apparent and of superintendents.

In the intervening places between two compartments, the army of the officer in charge of the harem shall be stationed.

When in the interior of the harem, the king shall see the queen only when her personal purity is vouchsafed by an old maidservant. He shall not touch any woman (unless he is apprised of her personal purity); for hidden in the queen's chamber, his own brother slew king Bhadrasena; hiding himself under the bed of his mother, the son killed king Karusa; mixing fried rice with poison, as though with honey, his own queen poisoned Kasiraja; with an anklet painted with poison, his own queen killed Vairantya; with a gem of her zone bedaubed with poison, his own queen killed Sauvira; with a looking glass painted with poison, his own queen killed Jalutha; and with a weapon hidden under her tuft of hair, his own queen slew Viduratha.

Hence the king shall always be careful to avoid such lurking dangers. He shall keep away his wives from the society of ascetics with shaved head or braided hair, of buffoons, and of outside prostitutes (*dasi*). Nor shall women of high birth have occasion to see his wives except appointed midwives.

Prostitutes (*rupajiva*) with personal cleanliness effected by fresh bath and with fresh garments and ornaments shall attend the harem.

Eighty men and fifty women under the guise of fathers and mothers, and aged persons, and eunuchs shall not only ascertain purity and impurity in the life of the inmates of the harem, but also so regulate the affairs as to be conducive to the happiness of the king.

Every person in the harem shall live in the place assigned to him, and shall never move to the place assigned to others. No one of the harem shall at any time keep company with any outsider.

The passage of all kinds of commodities from or into the harem shall be restricted and shall, after careful examination, be allowed to reach their destination either inside or outside the harem as indicated by the seal mark (*mudra*).

[Thus ends Chapter 20, 'Duty Towards the Harem', in Book I, 'Concerning Discipline', of the Arthashastra of Kautilya.]

Chapter 21

PERSONAL SAFETY

ON getting up from the bed, the king shall be received by troops of women armed with bows. In the second compartment, he shall be received by the *kanchuki* (presenter of the king's coat), the *ushnisi* (presenter of king's headdress), aged persons, and other harem attendants.

In the third compartment, he shall be received by crooked and dwarfish persons; in the fourth, by prime ministers, kinsmen, and doorkeepers with barbed missiles in their hand.

The king shall employ as his personal attendants those whose fathers and grandfathers had been royal servants, those who bear close relationship to the king, those who are well trained and loyal, and those who have rendered good service.

Neither foreigners, nor those who have earned neither rewards nor honour by rendering good service, nor even natives found engaged in inimical works shall form the bodyguard of the king or the troops of the officers in charge of the harem.

In a well-guarded locality, the head cook (*mahanasika*) shall supervise the preparation of varieties of relishing dishes. The king shall partake of such fresh dishes after making an oblation out of them first to the fire and then to birds.

When the flame and the smoke turn blue and crackle, and when birds (that eat the oblation) die, presence of poison (in the dish) shall be inferred. When the vapour arising from cooked rice possesses the colour of the neck of a peacock, and appears chill as if suddenly cooled, when vegetables possess an unnatural colour, and are watery and hardened, and appear to have suddenly turned dry, being possessed of broken layers of blackish foam, and being devoid of smell, touch and taste natural to them; when utensils reflect light either more or less than usual, and are covered with a layer of foam at their edges; when any liquid preparation possesses streaks on its surface; when milk bears a bluish streak in the centre of its surface; when liquor and water possess reddish streaks; when curd is marked with black and dark streaks, and honey with white streaks; when watery things appear parched as if overcooked and look blue and swollen; when dry things have shrinked and changed in their colour; when hard things appear soft, and soft things hard; when minute animalculae die in the vicinity of the dishes; when carpets and curtains possess blackish circular spots, with their threads and hair fallen off; when metallic vessels set with gems appear tarnished as though by roasting, and have lost their polish, colour, shine, and softness of touch, presence of poison shall be inferred.

As to the person who has administered poison, the marks are parched and dry mouth; hesitation in speaking; heavy perspiration; yawning; too much bodily tremor; frequent tumbling; evasion of speech; carelessness in work; and unwillingness to keep to the place assigned to him.

Hence physicians and experts capable of detecting poison shall ever attend upon the king.

Having taken out from the storeroom of medicines that medicine the purity of which has been proved by experiment, and having himself together with the decoctioner and the purveyor (*pachaka* and *poshaka*) tasted it, the physician shall hand over the medicine to the king. The same rule shall apply to liquor and other beverages.

Having cleaned their person and hands by fresh bath and put on newly washed garment, servants in charge of dresses and toilets shall serve the king with dresses and toilets received under seal from the officer in charge of the harem.

Prostitutes shall do the duty of bathroom servants, shampooers, bedding-room servants, washermen, and flower garland makers. While presenting to the king water, scents, fragrant powders, dress and garlands, servants along with the above prostitutes shall first touch these things by their eyes, arms and breast.

The same rule shall apply to whatever has been received from an outside person.

Musicians shall entertain the king with those kinds of amusements in which weapons, fire and poison are not made use of. Musical instruments as well as the ornaments of horses, chariots and elephants shall invariably be kept inside (the harem).

The king shall mount over chariots or beasts of burden only when they are first mounted over by his hereditary driver or rider.

He shall get into a boat only when it is piloted by a trustworthy sailor and is conjoined to a second boat. He shall never sail on any ship which had once been weatherbeaten; and (while boating on a good ship) his army shall all the while stand on the bank or the shore.

He shall get into such water as is free from large fishes (*matsya*) and crocodiles. He shall ramble only in such forests as are freed from snakes and crocodiles (*graha*).

With a view of acquiring efficiency in the skill of shooting arrows at moving objects, he shall engage himself in sports in such forests as are cleared by hunters and hound-keepers from the fear of highway robbers, snakes and enemies.

Attended by trustworthy bodyguard armed with weapons, he shall give interview to saints and ascetics. Surrounded by his assembly of minsters, he shall receive the envoys of foreign states.

Attired in military dress and having mounted a horse, a chariot or an elephant, he shall go and see his army equipped in military array.

On the occaision of going out of, and coming into (the capital), the king's road shall on both sides be well guarded by staff-bearers and freed from the presence of armed persons, ascetics and the cripple (*vyanga*).

He shall go to witness festive trains, fairs (*yatra*), procession or sacrificial performances only when they are policed by bands of 'The Ten Communities'. (*dasavargikadhishthitani*).

Just as he attends to the personal safety of others through the agency of spies, so a wise king shall also take care to secure his person from external dangers.

[Thus ends Chapter 21, 'Personal Safety', in Book I, 'Concerning Discipline', of the Arthashastra of Kautilya. With this, Book I, 'Concerning Discipline' of the Arthashastra of Kautilya has ended.]

Book II

The Duties of Government Superintendents

Chapter 1

FORMATION OF VILLAGES

EITHER by inducing foreigners to immigrate (*paradesapravahanena*) or by causing the thickly populated centres of his own kingdom to send forth the excessive population (*svadesabhishyandavamanena va*), the king may construct villages either on new sites or on old ruins (*bhutapurvama va*).

Villages consisting each of not less than a hundred families and of not more than five hundred families of agricultural people of Sudra caste, with boundaries extending as far as a *krosa* (2,250 yards.) or two, and capable of protecting each other shall be formed. Boundaries shall be denoted by a river, a mountain, forests, bulbous plants (*grishti*), caves, artificial buildings (*setubandha*), or by trees such as *salmali* (silk cotton tree), sami (*Acacia suma*), and *kshiravriksha* (milky trees).

There shall be set up a *sthaniya* (a fortress of that name) in the centre of eight-hundred villages, a *dronamukha* in the centre of four hundred villages, a *kharvatika* in the centre of two hundred villages and *sangrahana* in the midst of a collection of ten villages.

There shall be constructed in the extremities of the kingdom forts manned by boundary guards (*antapala*) whose duty shall be to guard the entrances into the kingdom. The interior of the kingdom shall be watched by trap-keepers (*vagurika*), archers (*sabara*), hunters (*pulinda*), chandalas and wild tribes (*aranyachara*).

Those who perform sacrifices (*ritvik*), spiritual guides, priests, and those learned in the Vedas shall be granted Brahmadaya lands yielding sufficient produce and exempted from taxes and fines (*adandkarani*).

Superintendents, accountants, Gopas, Sthanikas, veterinary surgeons (*anikastha*), physicians, horse trainers, and messengers shall also be endowed with lands which they shall have no right to alienate by sale or mortgage.

Lands prepared for cultivation shall be given to tax payers (*karada*) only for life (*ekapurushikani*).

Unprepared lands shall not be taken away from those who are preparing them for cultivation.

Lands may be confiscated from those who do not cultivate them; and given to others; or they may be cultivated by village labourers (*gramabhritaka*) and traders (*vaidehaka*), lest those owners who do not properly cultivate them pay less (to the government). If cultivators pay their taxes easily, they may be favourably supplied with grains, cattle and money.

The king shall bestow on cultivators only such favour and remission (*anugrahapariharau*) as will tend to swell the treasury, and shall avoid such as will deplete it.

A king with depleted treasury will eat into the very vitality of both citizens and country people. Either on the occasion of opening new settlements or on any other emergent occasions, remission of taxes shall be made.

He shall regard with fatherly kindness those who have passed the period of remission of taxes.

He shall carry on mining operations and manufactures, exploit timber and elephant forests, offer facilities for cattle breeding and commerce, construct roads for traffic both by land and water, and set up market towns (*panyapattana*).

He shall also construct reservoirs (*setu*) filled with water either perennial or drawn from some other source. Or he may provide with sites, roads, timber, and other necessary things to those who construct reservoirs of their own accord. Likewise in the construction of places of pilgrimage (*punyasthana*) and of groves.

Whoever stays away from any kind of cooperative construction (*sambhuya setubhandhat*) shall send his servants and bullocks to carry on his work, shall have a share in the expenditure, but shall have no claim to the profit.

The king shall exercise his right of ownership (*swamyam*) with regard to fishing, ferrying and trading in vegetables (*haritapanya*) in reservoirs or lakes (*setushu*).

Those who do not heed the claims of their slaves (*dasa*), hirelings (*ahitaka*), and relatives shall be taught their duty.

The king shall provide the orphans (*bala*), the aged, the infirm, the afflicted, and the helpless with maintenance. He shall also provide subsistence to helpless women when they are carrying and also to the children they give birth to.

Elders among the villagers shall improve the property of bereaved minors till the latter attain their age; so also the property of gods.

When a capable person other than an apostate (*patita*) or minor brothers, sisters, or widowed girls (*kanya vidhavascha*), he or she shall be punished with a fine of twelve panas.

When, without making provision for the maintenance of his wife and sons, any person embraces ascetism, he shall be punished with the first amercement; likewise any person who converts a woman to ascetism (*pravrajayatah*).

Whoever has passed the age of copulation may become an ascetic after distributing the properties of his own acquisition (among his sons); otherwise, he will be punished.

No ascetic other than a *vanaprastha* (forest hermit), no company other than the one of local birth (*sajatadanyassanghah*), and no guilds of any kind other than local cooperative guilds (*samutthayikadanyassamayanubandhah*) shall find entrance into the villages of the kingdom. Nor shall there be in villages buildings (*salah*) intended for sports and plays. Nor, in view of procuring money, free labour, commodities, grains, and liquids in plenty, shall actors, dancers, singers, drummers, buffoons (*vagjivana*), and bards (*kusilava*) make any disturbance to the work of the villagers; for helpless villagers are always dependent and bent upon their fields.

The king shall avoid taking possession of any country which is liable to the inroads of enemies and wild tribes and which is harassed by frequent visitations of famine and pestilence. He shall also keep away from expensive sports.

He shall protect agriculture from the molestation of oppressive fines, free labour, and taxes (*dandavishtikarabadhaih*); herds of cattle from thieves, tigers, poisonous creatures and cattle disease. He shall not only clear roads of traffic from the molestations of courtiers (*vallabha*), of workmen (*karmika*), of robbers, and of boundary guards, but also keep them from being destroyed by herds of cattle.

Thus the king shall not only keep in good repair timber and elephant forests, buildings, and mines created in the past, but also set up new ones.

[Thus ends Chapter 1, 'Formation of Villages', in Book II, 'The Duties of Government Superintendents', of the Arthashastra of Kautilya. End of twenty-second chapter from the beginning.]

Chapter 2

DIVISION OF LAND

THE king shall make provision for pasture grounds on uncultivable tracts.

Brahmans shall be provided with forests for *soma* plantation, for religious learning, and for the performance of penance, such forests being rendered safe from the dangers from animate or inanimate objects, and being named after the tribal name (*gotra*) of the Brahmans resident therein.

A forest as extensive as the above, provided with only one entrance rendered inaccessible by the construction of ditches all round, with plantations of delicious fruit trees, bushes, bowers, and thornless trees, with an expansive lake of water full of harmless animals, and with tigers (*vyala*), beasts of prey (*margayuka*), male and female elephants, young elephants, and bisons—all deprived of their claws and teeth—shall be formed for the king's sports.

On the extreme limit of the country or in any other suitable locality, another game forest with game beasts, open to all, shall also be made. In view of procuring all kinds of forest produce described elsewhere, one or several forests shall be specially reserved.

Manufactories to prepare commodities from forest produce shall also be set up.

Wild tracts shall be separated from timber forests. In the extreme limit of the country, elephant forests, separated from wild tracts, shall be formed.

The superintendent of forests with his retinue of forest guards shall not only maintain the upkeep of the forests, but also acquaint himself with all passages for entrance into, or exit from such of them as are mountainous or boggy or contain rivers or lakes.

Whoever kills an elephant shall be put to death.

Whoever brings in the pair of tusks of an elephant, dead from natural causes, shall receive a reward of four-and-a-half panas.

Guards of elephant forests, assisted by those who rear elephants, those who enchain the legs of elephants, those who guard the boundaries, those who live in forests, as well as by those who nurse elephants, shall, with the help of five or seven female elephants to help in tethering wild ones, trace the whereabouts of herds of elephants by following the course of urine and dungs left by elephants and along forest tracts covered over with branches of *bhallataki* (*Semicarpus anacardium*), and by observing the spots where elephants slept or sat before or left dungs, or where they had just destroyed the banks of rivers or lakes. They shall also precisely ascertain whether any mark is due to the movements of elephants in herds, of an elephant roaming single, of a stray elephant, of a leader of herds, of a tusker, of a rogue elephant, of an elephant in rut, of a young elephant, or of an elephant that has escaped from the cage.

Experts in catching elephants shall follow the instructions given to them by the elephant doctor (*anikastha*) and catch such elephants as are possessed of auspicious characteristics and good character.

The victory of kings (in battles) depends mainly upon elephants; for elephants, being of large bodily frame, are capable not only to destroy the arrayed army of an enemy, his fortifications and encampments, but also to undertake works that are dangerous to life.

Elephants bred in countries, such as Kalinga, Anga, Karusa, and the East are the best; those of the Dasarna and Western countries are of middle quality; and those of Saurashtra and Panchajana countries are of low quality. The might and energy of all can, however, be improved by suitable training.

[Thus ends Chapter 2, 'Division of Land', in Book II, 'The Duties of Government Superintendents', of the Arthashastra of Kautilya. End of twenty-third chapter from the beginning.]

Chapter 3

CONSTRUCTION OF FORTS

ON all the four quarters of the boundaries of the kingdom, defensive fortifications against an enemy in war shall be constructed on grounds best fitted for the purpose: a water fortification (*audaka*) such as an island in the midst of a river, or a plain surrounded by low ground; a mountainous fortification (*parvata*) such as a rocky tract or a cave; a desert (*dhanvana*) such as a wild tract devoid of water and overgrown with thicket growing in barren soil; or a forest fortification (*vanadurga*) full of wagtail (*khajana*), water and thickets.

Of these, water and mountain fortifications are best suited to defend populous centres; and desert and forest fortifications are habitations in wilderness (*atavisthanam*).

Or with ready preparations for flight the king may have his fortified capital (*sthaniya*) as the seat of his sovereignty (*samudayasthanam*) in the centre of his kingdom. In a locality naturally best fitted for the purpose, such as the bank of the confluence of rivers, a deep pool of perennial water, or of a lake or tank, a fort, circular, rectangular, or square in form, surrounded with an artificial canal of water, and connected with both land and water paths (may be constructed).

Round this fort, three ditches with an intermediate space of one danda (6 ft) from each other, fourteen, twelve and ten dandas respectively in width, with depth less by one quarter or by one half of their width, square at their bottom and one-third as wide as at their top, with sides built of stones or bricks, filled with perennial flowing water or with water drawn from some other source, and possessing crocodiles and lotus plants shall be constructed.

At a distance of four dandas (24 ft) from the (innermost) ditch, a rampart six dandas high and twice as much broad shall be erected by heaping mud upwards and by making it square at the bottom, oval at the centre pressed by the trampling of elephants and bulls, and planted with thorny and poisonous plants in bushes. Gaps in the rampart shall be filled up with fresh earth.

Above the rampart, parapets in odd or even numbers and with an intermediate space of from 12 to 24 *hasta*s from each other shall be built of bricks and raised to a height of twice their breadth. The passage for chariots shall be made of trunks of palm trees or of broad and thick slabs of stones with spheres like the head of a monkey carved on their surface; but never of wood as fire finds a happy abode in it.

Towers, square throughout and with moveable staircase or ladder equal to its height, shall also be constructed.

In the intermediate space measuring thirty dandas between two towers, there shall be formed a broad street in two compartments covered over with a roof and two-and-a-half times as long as it is broad.

Between the tower and the broad street there shall be constructed an Indrakosa which is made up of covering pieces of wooden planks affording seats for three archers.

There shall also be made a road for gods which shall measure two hastas inside (the towers ?), four times as much by the sides, and eight hastas along the parapet.

Paths (*charya*, to ascend the parapet ?) as broad as a danda (6 ft) or two shall also be made.

In an unassailable part (of the rampart), a passage for flight (*pradhavitikam*), and a door for exit (*nishkuradwaram*) shall be made.

Outside the rampart, passages for movements shall be closed by forming obstructions such as a knee-breaker (*janubhanjani*), a trident, mounds of earth, pits, wreaths of thorns, instruments made like the tail of a snake, palm leaf, triangle, and of dog's teeth, rods, ditches filled with thorns and covered with sand, frying pans and water pools.

Having made on both sides of the rampart a circular hole of a danda-and-a-half in diametre, an entrance gate (to the fort) one-sixth as broad as the width of the street shall be fixed.

A square (*chaturasra*) is formed by successive addition of one danda up to eight dandas commencing from five, or in the proportion, one-sixth of the length up to one-eighth.

The rise in level (*talotsedhah*) shall be made by successive addition of one hasta up to 18 hastas commencing from 15 hastas.

In fixing a pillar, six parts are to form its height, on the floor, twice as much (12 parts) to be entered into the ground, and one-fourth for its capital.

Of the first floor, five parts (are to be taken) for the formation of a hall (*sala*), a well, and a boundary house; two-tenths of it for the formation of two platforms opposite to each other (*pratimanchau*); an upper storey twice as high as its width; carvings of images; an uppermost storey, half or three-fourths as broad as the first floor; side walls built of bricks; on the left side, a staircase circumambulating from left to right; on the right, a secret staircase hidden in the wall; a top support of ornamental arches (*toranasirah*) projecting as far as two hastas; two door panels, (each) occupying three-fourths of the space; two and two cross-bars (*parigha*, to fasten the door); an iron bolt (*indrakila*) as long as an *aratni* (24 *angulas*); a boundary gate (*anidvaram*) five hastas in width; four beams to shut the door against elephants; and turrets (*hastinakha*) (outside the rampart) raised up to the height of the face of a man, removable or irremovable, or made of earth in places devoid of water.

A turret above the gate and starting from the top of the parapet shall be constructed, its front resembling an alligator up to three-fourths of its height.

In the centre of the parapets, there shall be constructed a deep lotus pool; a rectangular building of four compartments, one within the other; an abode of the Goddess Kumiri (*Kumaripuram*), having its external area one-and-a-half times as broad as that of its innermost room; a circular building with an archway; and in accordance with available space and materials, there shall also be constructed canals (*kulya*) to hold weapons and three times as long as broad.

In those canals, there shall be collected stones, spades (*kuddala*), axes (*kuthari*), varieties of staffs, cudgel (*musrinthi*), hammers (*mudgara*), clubs, discus, machines (*yantra*), and such weapons as can destroy a hundred persons at once (*sataghni*), together with spears, tridents, bamboo sticks with pointed edges made of iron, camel-necks, explosives (*agnisamyogas*), and whatever else can be devised and formed from available materials.

[Thus ends Chapter 3, 'Construction of Forts', in Book II, 'The Duties of Government Superintendents', of the Arthashastra of Kautilya. End of twenty-fourth chapter from the beginning.]

Chapter 4

BUILDINGS WITHIN THE FORT

DEMARCATION of the ground inside the fort shall be made first by opening three royal roads from west to east and three from south to north.

The fort shall contain twelve gates, provided with both a land and waterway kept secret.

Chariot roads, royal roads, and roads leading to dronamukha, sthaniya, country parts, and pasture grounds shall each be four dandas (24 ft) in width.

Roads leading to sayoniya (?), military stations (*vyuha*), burial or cremation grounds, and to villages shall be eight dandas in width.

Roads to gardens, groves and forests shall be four dandas.

Roads leading to elephant forests shall be two dandas.

Roads for chariots shall be five *aratnis* (7½ ft). Roads for cattle shall measure four *aratnis*; and roads for minor quadrupeds and men two aratnis.

Royal buildings shall be constructed on strong grounds.

In the midst of the houses of the people of all the four castes and to the north from the centre of the ground inside the fort, the king's palace, facing either the north or the east shall, as described elsewhere (Chapter 20, Book I), be constructed occupying one-ninth of the whole site inside the fort.

Royal teachers, priests, sacrificial place, water reservoir and ministers shall occupy sites east by north to the palace.

Royal kitchen, elephant stables, and the storehouse shall be situated on sites east by south.

On the eastern side, merchants trading in scents, garlands, grains, and liquids, together with expert artisans and the people of Kshatriya caste shall have their habitations.

The treasury, the accountant's office, and various manufactories (*karmanishadyascha*) shall be situated on sites south by east.

The storehouse of forest produce and the arsenal shall be constructed on sites south by west.

To the south, the superintendents of the city, of commerce, of manufactories, and of the army as well as those who trade in cooked rice, liquor, and flesh, besides prostitutes, musicians and the people of Vaisya caste shall live.

To the west by south, stables of asses, camels, and working house.

To the west by north, stables of conveyances and chariots.

To the west, artisans manufacturing worsted threads, cotton threads, bamboo mats, skins, armours, weapons and gloves as well as the people of Sudra caste shall have their dwellings.

To the north by west, shops and hospitals.

To the north by east, the treasury and the stables of cows and horses.

To the north, the royal tutelary deity of the city, ironsmiths, artisans working on precious stones, as well as Brahmans shall reside.

In the several corners, guilds and corporations of workmen shall reside.

In the centre of the city, the apartments of gods such as Aparajita, Apratihata, Jayanta, Vaijayanta, Siva, Vaisravana, Asvina (divine physicians), and the honourable liquor house (*Sri-madiragriham*), shall be situated.

In the corners, the guardian deities of the ground shall be appropriately set up.

Likewise the principal gates such as Brahma, Aindra, Yamya and Sainapatya shall be constructed; and at a distance of 100 bows (*dhanus*, i.e., 108 *angulas*) from the ditch (on the counterscarp side), places of worship and pilgrimage, groves and buildings shall be constructed.

Guardian deities of all quarters shall also be set up in quarters appropriate to them.

Either to the north or the east, burial or cremation grounds shall be situated; but that of the people of the highest caste shall be to the south (of the city). Violation of this rule shall be punished with the first amercement.

Heretics and Chandalas shall live beyond the burial grounds. Families of workmen may in any other way be provided with sites befitting with their occupation and fieldwork. Besides working in flower gardens, fruit gardens, vegetable gardens, and paddy fields allotted to them, they (families) shall collect grains and merchandise in abundance as authorized.

There shall be a water well for every ten houses. Oils, grains, sugar, salt, medicinal articles, dry or fresh vegetables, meadow grass, dried flesh, haystock, firewood, metals, skins, charcoal, tendons (*snayu*), poison, horns, bamboo, fibrous garments, strong timber, weapons, armour and stones shall also be stored (in the fort) in such quantities as can be enjoyed for years together without feeling any want. Of such collection, old things shall be replaced by new ones when received.

Elephants, cavalry, chariots and infantry shall each be officered with many chiefs inasmuch as chiefs, when many, are under the fear of betrayal from each other and scarcely liable to the insinuations and intrigues of an enemy.

The same rule shall hold good with the appointment of boundary guards, and repairers of fortifications.

Never shall *bahirikas* who are dangerous to the well-being of cities and countries be kept in forts. They may either be thrown in country parts or compelled to pay taxes.

[Thus ends Chapter 4, 'Buildings within the Fort', in Book II, 'The Duties of the Government Superintendents', of the Arthashastra of Kautilya. End of twenty-fifth chapter from the beginning.]

Chapter 5

THE DUTIES OF THE CHAMBERLAIN

THE chamberlain (*sannidhata,* one who ever attends upon the king) shall see to the construction of the treasury house, trading house, the storehouse of grains, the storehouse of forest produce, the armoury and the jail.

Having dug up a square well not too deep to be moist with water, having paved both the bottom and the sides with slabs of stone, he shall, by using strong timber, construct in that well a cage-like underground chamber of three storeys high, the topmost being on a level with the surface of the ground, with many compartments of various design, with floor plastered with small stones, with one door, with a movable staircase, and solemnized with the presence of the guardian deity.

Above this chamber, the treasury house closed on both sides, with projecting roofs and extensively opening into the storehouse shall be built of bricks.

He may employ outcast men (*abhityakta purusha*) to build at the extreme boundary of the kingdom a palacious mansion to hold substantial treasure against dangers and calamities.

The trading house shall be a quadrangle enclosed by four buildings with one door, with pillars built of burnt bricks, with many compartments, and with a row of pillars on both sides kept apart.

The storehouse shall consist of many spacious rooms and enclose within itself the storehouse of forest produce separated from it by means of wall and connected with both the underground chamber and the armoury.

The court (*dharmasthiya*) and the office of the ministers (*mahamatriya*) shall be built in a separate locality.

Provided with separate accommodation for men and women kept apart and with many compartments well guarded, a jail shall also be constructed.

All these buildings shall be provided with halls (*sala*) pits (*khata*—privy [?]), water well, bathroom, remedies against fire and poison, with cats, mangooses, and with necessary means to worship the guardian gods appropriate to each.

In (front of) the storehouse a bowl (*kunda*) with its mouth as wide as an *aratni* (24 *angulas*) shall be set up as rain gauge (*varshamana*).

Assisted by experts having necessary qualifications and provided with tools and instruments, the chamberlain shall attend to the business of receiving gems either old or new, as well as raw materials of superior or inferior value.

In cases of deception in gems, both the deceiver and the abettor shall be punished with the highest amercement; in the case of superior commodities, they shall be punished with the middlemost amercement; and in that of commodities of inferior value, they shall be compelled not only to restore the same, but also pay a fine equal to the value of the articles.

He shall receive only such gold coins as have been declared to be pure by the examiner of coins.

Counterfeit coins shall be cut into pieces.

Whoever brings in counterfeit coins shall be punished with the first amercement. Grains pure and fresh shall be received in full measures; otherwise a fine of twice the value of the grains shall be imposed.

The same rule shall hold good with the receipt of merchandise, raw materials and weapons.

In all departments, whoever, whether as an officer (*yukta*), a clerk (*upayukta*) or a servant (*tatpurusha*), misappropriates sums from one to four panas or any other valuable things shall be punished with the first, middlemost, and highest amercements and death, respectively.

If the officer who is in charge of the treasury causes loss in money, he shall be whipped (*ghatah*), while his abettors shall receive half the punishment; if the loss is due to ignorance, he shall be censured.

If, with the intention of giving a hint, robbers are frightened (by the guards), (the latter) shall be tortured to death.

Hence assisted by trustworthy persons, the chamberlain shall attend to the business of revenue collection.

He shall have so thorough a knowledge of both external and internal incomes running even for a hundred years that, when questioned, he can point out without hesitation the exact amount of net balance that remains after expenditure has been met with.

[Thus ends Chapter 5, 'The Duties of the Chamberlain', in Book II, 'The Duties of the Government Superintendents', of the Arthashastra of Kautilya. End of twenty-sixth chapter from the beginning.]

Chapter 6

THE BUSINESS OF COLLECTION OF REVENUE BY THE COLLECTOR GENERAL

THE collector general shall attend to (the collection of revenue from) forts (*durga*), country parts (*rashtra*), mines (*khani*), buildings and gardens (*setu*), forests (*vana*), herds of cattle (*vraja*), and roads of traffic (*vanikpatha*).

Tolls, fines, weights and measures, the town clerk (*nagaraka*), the superintendent of coinage (*lakshanadhyakshah*), the superintendent of seals and passports, liquor, slaughter of animals, threads, oils, ghee, sugar (*kshara*), the state goldsmith (*sauvarnika*), the warehouse of merchandise, the prostitute, gambling, building sites (*vastuka*), the corporation of artisans and handicrafts-men (*karusilpiganah*), the superintendent of gods, and taxes collected at the gates and from the people (known as) *bahirika*s come under the head of forts.

Produce from crown lands (*sita*), portion of produce payable to the government (*bhaga*), religious taxes (*bali*), taxes paid in money (*kara*), merchants, the superintendent of rivers, ferries, boats, and ships, towns, pasture grounds, road cess (*vartani*), ropes (*rajju*) and ropes to bind thieves (*chorarajju*) come under the head of country parts.

Gold, silver, diamonds, gems, pearls, corals, conch shells, metals (*loha*), salt and other minerals extracted from plains and mountain slopes come under the head of mines.

Flower gardens, fruit gardens, vegetable gardens, wet fields, and fields where crops are grown by sowing roots for seeds (*mulavapah*, i.e., sugar-cane crops, etc.) come under *setu*.

Game forests, timber forests, and elephant forests are forests.

Cows, buffaloes, goats, sheep, asses, camels, horses and mules come under the head of herds.

Land and waterways are the roads of traffic.

All these form the body of income (*ayasariram*).

Capital (*mula*), share (*bhaga*), premia (*vyaji*), *parigha* (?) fixed taxes (*klripta*), premia on coins (*rupika*), and fixed fines (*atyaya*) are the several forms of revenue (*ayamukha*, i.e., the mouth from which income is to issue).

The chanting of auspicious hymns during the worship of gods and ancestors, and on the occasion of giving gifts, the harem, the kitchen, the establishment of messengers, the storehouse, the armoury, the warehouse, the storehouse of raw materials, manufactories (*karmanta*), free labourers (*vishti*), maintenance of infantry, cavalry, chariots, and elephants, herds of cows, the museum of beasts, deer, birds, and snakes, and storage of firewood and fodder constitute the body of expenditure (*vyayasariram*).

The royal year, the month, the *paksha*, the day, the dawn (*vyushta*), the third and seventh *paksha*s of (the seasons such as) the rainy season, the winter season, and the summer short of their days, the rest complete, and a separate intercalary month are (the divisions of time).

He shall also pay attention to the work in hand (*karaniya*), the work accomplished (*siddham*), part of a work in hand (*sesha*), receipts, expenditure and net balance.

The business of upkeeping the government (*samsthanam*), the routine work (*pracharah*), the collection of necessaries of life, the collection and audit of all kinds of revenue—these constitute the work in hand.

That which has been credited to the treasury; that which has been taken by the king; that which has been spent in connection with the capital city not entered (into the register) or continued from year before last, the royal command dictated or orally intimated to be entered (into the register)—all these constitute the work accomplished.

Preparation of plans for profitable works, balance of fines due, demand for arrears of revenue kept in abeyance, and examination of accounts—these constitute what is called part of a work in hand which may be of little or no value.

Receipts may be (1) current, (2) last balance, and (3) accidental (*anyajatah*, received from external source). What is received day after day is termed current (*vartamana*).

Whatever has been brought forward from year before last, whatever is in the hands of others, and whatever has changed hands is termed last balance (*puryushita*).

Whatever has been lost and forgotten (by others), fines levied from government servants, marginal revenue (*parsva*), compensation levied for any damage (*parihinikam*), presentations to the king, the property of those who have fallen victims to epidemics (*damaragatakasvam*) leaving no sons, and treasure troves—all these constitute accidental receipts.

Investment of capital (*vikshepa*), the relics of a wrecked undertaking, and the savings from an estimated outlay are the means to check expenditure (*vyayapratyayah*).

The rise in price of merchandise due to the use of different weights and measures in selling is termed *vyaji*; the enhancement of price due to bidding among buyers is also another source of profit. Expenditure is of two kinds—daily expenditure and profitable expenditure.

What is continued every day is daily.

Whatever is earned once in a *paksha*, a month or a year is termed profit.

Whatever is spent on these two heads is termed as daily expenditure and profitable expenditure respectively.

That which remains after deducting all the expenditure already incurred and excluding all revenue to be realized is net balance (*nivi*) which may have been either just realized or brought forward.

Thus a wise collector general shall conduct the work of revenue collection, increasing the income and decreasing the expenditure.

[Thus ends Chapter 6, 'The Business of Collection of Revenue by the Collector General', in Book II, 'The Duties of Government Superintendents', of the Arthashastra of Kautilya. End of the twenty-seventh chapter from the beginning.]

Chapter 7

THE BUSINESS OF KEEPING UP ACCOUNTS IN THE OFFICE OF ACCOUNTANTS

THE superintendent of accounts shall have the accountant's office constructed with its door facing either the north or the east, with seats (for clerks) kept apart and with shelves of account books well arranged.

Therein the number of several departments; the description of the work carried on and of the results realized in several manufactories (*karmanta*); the amount of profit, loss, expenditure, delayed earnings, the amount of *vyaji* (premia in kind or cash) realized—the status of government agency employed, the amount of wages paid, the number of free labourers engaged (*vishti*) pertaining to the investment of capital on any work; likewise in the case of gems and commodities of superior or inferior value, the rate of their price, the rate of their barter, the counterweights (*pratimana*) used in weighing them, their number, their weight, and their cubical measure; the history of customs, professions, and transactions of countries, villages, families, and corporations; the gains in the form of gifts to the king's courtiers, their title to possess and enjoy lands, remission of taxes allowed to them, and payment of provisions and salaries to them; the gains to the wives and sons of the king in gems, lands, prerogatives, and provisions made to remedy evil portents; the treaties with, issues of ultimatum to, and payments of tribute from or to, friendly or inimical kings—all these shall be regularly entered in prescribed registers.

From these books the superintendent shall furnish the accounts as to the forms of work in hand, of works accomplished, of part of works in hand, of receipts, of expenditure, of net balance, and of tasks to be undertaken in each of the several departments.

To supervise works of high, middling and low description, superintendents with corresponding qualifications shall be employed.

The king will have to suffer in the end if he curtails the fixed amount of expenditure on profitable works.

(When a man engaged by government for any work absents himself), his sureties who conjointly received (wages?) from the government, or his sons, brothers, wives, daughters or servants living upon his work shall bear the loss caused to the government.

The work of 354 days and nights is a year. Such a work shall be paid for more or less in proportion to its quantity at the end of the month, *Ashadha* (about the middle of July). (The work during) the intercalary month shall be (separately) calculated.

A government officer, not caring to know the information gathered by espionage and neglecting to supervise the despatch of work in his own department as regulated, may occasion loss of revenue to the government owing to his ignorance, or owing to his idleness when he is too weak to endure the trouble of activity, or due to inadvertence in perceiving sound and other objects of sense, or by being timid when he is afraid of clamour, unrighteousness, and untoward results, or owing to selfish desire when he is favourably disposed towards those who are desirous to achieve their own selfish ends, or by cruelty due to anger, or by lack of dignity when he is surrounded by a host of learned and needy sycophants, or by making use of false balance, false measures and false calculation owing to greediness.

The school of Manu holds that a fine equal to the loss of revenue and multiplied by the serial number of the circumstances of the guilt just narrated in order shall be imposed upon him.

The school of Parasara hold that the fine in all the cases shall be eight times the amount lost.

The school of Brihaspati says that it shall be ten times the amount. The school of Usanas says that it shall be twenty times the amount.

But Kautilya says that it shall be proportional to the guilt. Accounts shall be submitted in the month of *Ashadha*.

When they (the accountants of different districts) present themselves with sealed books, commodities and net revenue, they shall all be kept apart in one place so that they cannot carry on conversation with each other. Having heard from them the totals of receipts, expenditure and net revenue, the net amount shall be received.

By how much the superintendent of a department augments the net total of its revenue either by increasing anyone of the items of its receipts or by decreasing anyone of the items of expenditure, he shall be rewarded eight times that amount. But when it is reversed (i.e., when the net total is decreased), the award shall also be reversed (i.e., he shall be made to pay eight times the decrease).

Those accountants who do not present themselves in time or do not produce their account books along with the net revenue shall be fined ten times the amount due from them.

When a superintendent of accounts (*karanika*) does not at once proceed to receive and check the accounts when the clerks (*karmika*) are ready, he shall be punished with the first amercement. In the reverse case (i.e., when the clerks are not ready), the clerks shall be punished with double the first amercement.

All the ministers (*mahamaras*) shall together narrate the whole of the actual accounts pertaining to each department. Whoever of these (ministers or clerks ?) is of undivided counsel or keeps himself aloof, or utters falsehood shall be punished with the highest amercement.

When an accountant has not prepared the table of daily accounts (*akritahorupaharam*), he may be given a month more (for its preparation). After the lapse of one month he shall be fined at the rate of 200 *panas* for each month (during which he delays the accounts).

If an accountant has to write only a small portion of the accounts pertaining to net revenue, he may be allowed five nights to prepare it.

Then the table of daily accounts submitted by him along with the net revenue shall be checked with reference to the regulated forms of righteous transactions and precedents and by applying such arithmetical processes as addition, subtraction, inference and by espionage. It shall also be verified with reference to (such divisions of time as) days, five nights, *pakshas*, months, four months, and the year.

The receipt shall be verified with reference to the place and time pertaining to them, the form of their collection (i.e., capital, share), the amount of the present and past produce, the person who has paid it, the person who caused its payment, the officer who fixed the amount payable, and the officer who received it. The expenditure shall be verified with reference to the cause of the profit from any source in the place and time pertaining to each item, the amount payable, the amount paid, the person who ordered the collection, the person who remitted the same, the person who delivered it, and the person who finally received it.

Likewise the net revenue shall be verified with reference to the place, time, and source pertaining to it, its standard of fineness and quantity, and the persons who are employed to guard the deposits and magazines (of grains, etc.).

When an officer (*karanika*) does not facilitate or prevents the execution of the king's order, or renders the receipts and expenditure otherwise than prescribed, he shall be punished with the first amercement.

Any clerk who violates or deviates from the prescribed form of writing accounts, enters what is unknown to him, or makes double or treble entries (*punaruktam*) shall be fined 12 *panas*.

He who scrapes off the net total shall be doubly punished. He who eats it up shall be fined eight times. He who causes loss of revenue shall not only pay a fine equal to five times the amount lost (*panchabandha*), but also make good the loss. In case of uttering a lie, the punishment levied for theft shall be imposed. (When an entry lost or omitted) is made later or is made to appear as forgotten, but added later on recollection, the punishment shall be double the above.

The king shall forgive an offence when it is trifling, have satisfaction even when the revenue is scanty, and honour with rewards (*pragraha*) such of his superintendents as are of immense benefit to him.

[Thus ends Chapter 7, 'The Business of Keeping up the Accounts in the Office of Accountants', in Book II, 'The Duties of Government Superintendents', of the Arthashastra of Kautilya. End of twenty-eighth chapter from the beginning.]

Chapter 8

DETECTION OF WHAT IS EMBEZZLED BY GOVERNMENT SERVANTS OUT OF STATE REVENUE

ALL undertakings depend upon finance. Hence foremost attention shall be paid to the treasury.

Public prosperity (*pracharasamriddhih*), rewards for good conduct (*charitranugrahah*), capture of thieves, dispensing with (the service of too many) government servants, abundance of harvest, prosperity of commerce, absence of troubles and calamities (*upasargapramokshah*), diminution of remission of taxes, and income in gold (*hiranyopayanam*) are all conducive to financial prosperity.

Obstruction (*pratibandha*), loan (*prayoga*), trading (*vyavahara*), fabrication of accounts (*avastara*), causing the loss of revenue (*parihapana*), self-enjoyment (*upabhoga*), barter (*parivartana*), and defalcation (*apahara*) are the causes that tend to deplete the treasury.

Failure to start an undertaking or to realize its results, or to credit its profits (to the treasury) is known as obstruction. Herein a fine of ten times the amount in question shall be imposed.

Lending the money of the treasury on periodical interest is a loan.

Carrying on trade by making use of government money is trading.

These two acts shall be punished with a fine of twice the profit earned.

Whoever makes as unripe the ripe time or as ripe the unripe time (of revenue collection) is guilty of fabrication. Herein a fine of ten times the amount (*dasabandha*) shall be imposed.

Whoever lessens a fixed amount of income or enhances the expenditure is guilty of causing the loss of revenue. Herein a fine of four times the loss shall be imposed.

Whoever enjoys himself or causes others to enjoy whatever belongs to the king is guilty of self-enjoyment. Herein death sentence shall be passed for enjoying gems, middle-most amercement for enjoying valuable articles, and restoration of the articles together with a fine equal to their value shall be the punishment for enjoying articles of inferior value.

The act of exchanging government articles for (similar) articles of others is barter. This offence is explained by self-enjoyment.

Whoever does not take into the treasury the fixed amount of revenue collected, or does not spend what is ordered to be spent, or misrepresents the net revenue collected is guilty of defalcation of government money. Herein a fine of twelve times the amount shall be imposed.

There are about forty ways of embezzlement: what is realized earlier is entered later on; what is realized later is entered earlier; what ought to be realized is not realized; what is hard to realize is shown as realized; what is collected is shown as not collected; what has not been collected is shown as collected; what is collected in part is entered as collected in full; what is collected in full is entered as collected in part; what is collected is of one sort, while what is entered is of another sort; what is realized from one source is shown as realized from another; what is payable is not paid; what is not payable is paid; not paid in time; paid untimely; small gifts made large gifts; large gifts made small gifts; what is gifted is of one sort while what is entered is of another; the real donee is one while the person entered (in the register) as donee is another; what has been taken into (the treasury) is removed while what has not been credited to it is shown as credited; raw materials that are not paid for are entered, while those that are paid for are not entered; an aggregate is scattered in pieces; scattered items are converted into an aggregate; commodities of greater value are bartered for those of small value; what is of smaller value is bartered for one of greater value; price of commodities enhanced; price of commodities lowered; number of nights increased; number of nights decreased; the year not in harmony with its months; the month not in harmony with its days; inconsistency in the transactions carried on with personal supervision (*samagamavishanah*); misrepresentation of the source of income; inconsistency in giving charities; incongruity in representing the work turned out; inconsistency in dealing with fixed items; misrepresentation of test marks or the standard of fineness (of gold and silver); misrepresentation of prices of commodities; making use of false weights and measures; deception in counting articles; and making use of false cubic measures such as *bhajan*—these are the several ways of embezzlement.

Under the above circumstances, the persons concerned such as the treasurer (*nidhayaka*), the prescriber (*nibandhaka*), the receiver (*pratigrahaka*), the payer (*dayaka*), the person who caused the payment (dapaka), the ministerial servants of the officer (*mantri-vaiyavrityakara*) shall each be separately examined. If anyone of these tells a lie, he shall receive the same punishment as the chief officer, (*yukta*) who committed the offence.

A proclamation in public (*prachara*) shall be made to the effect: 'Whoever has suffered at the hands of this offender may make their grievances known to the king.'

Those who respond to the call shall receive such compensation as is equal to the loss they have sustained.

When there are a number of offences in which a single officer is involved, and when his being guilty of *parokta* in anyone of those charges has been established, he shall be answerable for all those offences. Otherwise (i.e., when it is not established), he shall be tried for each of the charges.

When a government servant has been proved to be guilty of having misappropriated part of a large sum in question, he shall be answerable for the whole.

Any informant (*suchaka*) who supplies information about embezzlement just under perpetration shall, if he succeeds in proving it, get as reward one-sixth of the amount in question; if he happens to be a government servant (*bhritaka*), he shall get for the same act one-twelfth of the amount.

If an informant succeeds in proving only a part of a big embezzlement, he shall, nevertheless, get the prescribed share of the part of the embezzled amount proved. An informant who fails to prove (his assertion) shall be liable to monetary or corporal punishment, and shall never be acquitted.

When the charge is proved, the informant may impute the tale-bearing to someone else or clear himself in any other way from the blame. Any informant who withdraws his assertion prevailed upon by the insinuations of the accused shall be condemned to death.

[Thus ends Chapter 8, 'Detection of What Is Embezzled by Government Servants out of State Revenue', in Book II, 'The Duties of Government Superintendents', of the Arthashastra of Kautilya. End of twenty-ninth chapter from the beginning.]

Chapter 9

EXAMINATION OF THE CONDUCT OF GOVERNMENT SERVANTS

THOSE who are possessed of ministerial qualifications shall, in accordance with their individual capacity, be appointed as superintendents of government departments. While engaged in work, they shall be daily examined; for men are naturally fickle-minded and like horses at work exhibit constant change in their temper. Hence the agency and tools which they make use of, the place and time of the work they are engaged in, as well as the precise form of the work, the outlay, and the results shall always be ascertained.

Without dissension and without any concert among themselves, they shall carry on their work as ordered.

When in concert, they eat up (the revenue). When in disunion, they mar the work. Without bringing to the knowledge of their master (*bhartri*, the king), they shall undertake nothing except remedial measures against imminent dangers.

A fine of twice the amount of their daily pay and of the expenditure (incurred by them) shall be fixed for any inadvertence on their part. Whoever of the superintendents makes as much as, or more than, the amount of fixed revenue shall be honoured with promotion and rewards.

(My) teacher holds that that officer who spends too much and brings in little revenue eats it up; while he who proves the revenue (i.e., brings in more than he spends) as well as the officer who brings inasmuch as he spends does not eat up the revenue.

But Kautilya holds that cases of embezzlement or no embezzlement can be ascertained through spies alone.

Whoever lessens the revenue eats the king's wealth. If owing to inadvertence he causes diminution in revenue, he shall be compelled to make good the loss.

Whoever doubles the revenue eats into the vitality of the country. If he brings in double the amount to the king, he shall, if the offence is small, be warned not to repeat the same; but if the offence be grave he should proportionally be punished.

Whoever spends the revenue (without bringing in any profit) eats up the labour of workmen. Such an officer shall be punished in proportion to the value of the work done, the number of days taken, the amount of capital spent, and the amount of daily wages paid.

Hence the chief officer of each department (*adhikarana*) shall thoroughly scrutinize the real amount of the work done, the receipts realized from, and the expenditure incurred in that departmental work both in detail and in the aggregate.

He shall also check (*pratishedhayet*) prodigal, spendthrift and niggardly persons.

Whoever unjustly eats up the property left by his father and grandfather is a prodigal person (*mulahara*).

Whoever eats all that he earns is a spendthrift (*tadatvika*). Whoever hordes money, entailing hardship both on himself and his servants is niggardly.

Whoever of these three kinds of persons has the support of a strong party shall not be disturbed; but he who has no such support shall be caught hold of (*paryadatavyah*).

Whoever is niggardly in spite of his immense property, hordes, deposits, or sends out—hordes in his own house, deposits with citizens or country people or sends out to foreign countries;—a spy shall find out the advisers, friends, servants, relations, partisans, as well as the income and expenditure of such a niggardly person. Whoever in a foreign country carries out the work of such a niggardly person shall be prevailed upon to give out the secret. When the secret is known, the niggardly person shall be murdered apparently under the orders of (his) avowed enemy.

Hence the superintendents of all the departments shall carry on their respective works in company with accountants, writers, coin examiners, the treasurers, and military officers (*uttaradhyaksha*).

Those who attend upon military officers and are noted for their honesty and good conduct shall be spies to watch the conduct of accountants and other clerks.

Each department shall be officered by several temporary heads.

Just as it is impossible not to taste the honey or the poison that finds itself at the tip of the tongue, so it is impossible for a government servant not to eat up, at least, a bit of the king's revenue. Just as fish moving underwater cannot possibly be found out either as drinking or not drinking water, so government servants employed in the government work cannot be found out (while) taking money (for themselves).

It is possible to mark the movements of birds flying high up in the sky; but not so is it possible to ascertain the movement of government servants of hidden purpose.

Government servants shall not only be confiscated of their ill-earned hordes, but also be transferred from one work to another, so that they cannot either misappropriate government money or vomit what they have eaten up.

Those who increase the king's revenue instead of eating it up and are loyally devoted to him shall be made permanent in service.

[Thus ends Chapter 9, 'Examination of the Conduct of Government Servants', in Book II, 'The Duties of Government Superintendents', of the Arthashastra of Kautilya. End of thirtieth chapter from the beginning.]

Chapter 10

THE PROCEDURE OF FORMING ROYAL WRITS

(TEACHERS) say that (the word) *sasana*, command, (is applicable only to) royal writs (*sasana*).

Writs are of great importance to kings inasmuch as treaties and ultimate leading to war depend upon writs.

Hence one who is possessed of ministerial qualifications, acquainted with all kinds of customs, smart in composition, good in legible writing, and sharp in reading shall be appointed as a writer (*lekhaka*).

Such a writer, having attentively listened to the king's order and having well thought out the matter under consideration, shall reduce the order in writing.

As to a writ addressed to a lord (*isvara*), it shall contain a polite mention of his country, his possessions, his family and his name, and as to that addressed to a common man (*anisvara*), it shall make a polite mention of his country and name.

Having paid sufficient attention to the caste, family, social rank, age, learning (*sruta*), occupation, property, character (*sila*), blood-relationship (*yaunanubandha*) of the addressee, as well as to the place and time (of writing), the writer shall form a writ befitting the position of the person addressed.

Arrangement of subject matter (*arthakrama*), relevancy (*sambandha*), completeness, sweetness, dignity, and lucidity are the necessary qualities of a writ.

The act of mentioning facts in the order of their importance is arrangement.

When subsequent facts are not contradictory to facts just or previously mentioned, and so on till the completion of the letter, it is termed relevancy.

Avoidance of redundancy or deficiency in words or letters; impressive description of subject matter by citing reasons, examples, and illustrations; and the use of appropriate and suitably strong words (*asrantapada*) is completeness.

The description in exquisite style of a good purport with a pleasing effect is sweetness.

The use of words other than colloquial (*agramya*) is dignity.

The use of well-known words is lucidity.

The alphabetical letters beginning with *Akara* are sixty-three.

The combination of letters is a word (*pada*). The word is of four kinds—nouns, verbs, prefixes of verbs, and particles (*nipata*).

A noun is that which signifies an essence (*satva*).

A verb is that which has no definite gender and signifies an action.

'*Pra*' and other words are the prefixes of verbs.

'*Cha*' and other indeclinable words are particles.

A group of words conveying a complete sense is a sentence (*vakya*).

Combination of words (*varga*) consisting of not more than three words and not less than one word shall be so formed as to harmonize with the meaning of immediately following words.

The word, '*iti*', is used to indicate the completion of a writ; and also to indicate an oral message as in the phrase '*vachikamasyeti*', an oral message along with this (writ).

Calumniation (*ninda*), commendation, inquiry, narration request, refusal, censure, prohibition, command, conciliation, promise of help, threat, and persuasion are the thirteen purposes for which writs are issued.

Calumniation (*ninda*) consists in speaking ill of one's family, body and acts.

Commendation (*prasamsa*) consists in praising one's family, person and acts.

To inquire 'how is this?' is inquiry.

To point out the way as 'thus', is narration (*akhyana*).

To entreat as '*give*', is request.

To say that 'I do not give', is refusal.

To say that 'it is not worthy of thee', is censure (*upalambhah*).

To say as 'do not do so', is prohibition (*pratishedha*).

To say that 'this should be done', is command (*chodana*).

To say 'what I am, thou art that; whichever article is mine is thine also, is conciliation (*santvam*).

To hold out help in trouble is promise of help (*abhyavapattih*).

Pointing out the evil consequences that may occur in future is threat (*abhibartsanam*).

Persuasion is of three kinds: that made for the purpose of money, that made in case of one's failure to fulfil a promise, and that made on occasion of any trouble.

Also writs of information, of command, and of gift; likewise writs of remission, of licence, of guidance, of reply, and of general proclamation are other varieties.

Thus says (the messenger); so says (the king); if there is any truth in this (statement of the messenger), then the thing (agreed to) should at once be surrendered; (the messenger) has informed the king of all the deeds of the enemy. (*Parakara*);—this is the writ of information which is held to be of various forms.

Wherever, and especially regarding government servants, the king's order either for punishment or for rewards is issued, it is called writ of command (*ajnalekha*).

Where the bestowal of honour for deserving merit is contemplated either as help to alleviate affliction (*adhi*) or as gift (*paridana*), there are issued writs of gift (*upagrahalekha*).

Whatever favour (*anugraha*) to special castes, cities, villages, or countries of various description is announced in obedience to the king's order, it is called writ of remission (*pariharalekha*) by those who know it.

Likewise licence or permission (*nisrishti*) shall be enjoined either in word or deed; accordingly it is styled verbal order or writ of licence.

Various kinds of providential visitations or well-ascertained evils of human make are believed to be the cause for issuing writs of guidance (*pravrittilekha*) to attempt remedies against them.

When having read a letter and discussed as to the form of reply thereto, a reply in accordance with the king's order is made, it is called a writ of reply (*pratilekha*).

When the king directs his viceroys (*isvara*) and other officers to protect and give material help to travellers either on roads or in the interior of the country, it is termed writ of general proclamation (*sarvatraga lekha*).

Negotiation, bribery, causing dissension, and open attack are forms of stratagem (*upaya*).

Negotiation is of five kinds:

Praising the qualities (of an enemy), narrating the mutual relationship, pointing out mutual benefit, showing vast future prospects, and identity of interests.

When the family, person, occupation, conduct, learning, properties, etc., (of an enemy) are commended with due attention to their worth, it is termed praising the qualities (*gunasankirthana*).

When the fact of having agnates, blood relations, teachers (*maukha*), priestly heirarchy (*srauva*), family, and friends in common is pointed out, it is known as narration of mutual relationship (*sambandhopakhyana*).

When both parties, the party of a king and that of his enemy are shown to be helpful to each other, it is known as pointing out mutual benefit (*parasparopakarasamdarsanam*).

Inducement such as 'This being done thus, such result will accrue to both of us', is showing vast future prospects (*Ayatipradarsanam*).

To say, 'what I am, that thou art; thou mayest utilize in thy works whatever is mine', is identity of interests (*atmopanidhanam*).

Offering money is bribery (*upapradana*).

Causing fears and suspicion as well as threatening is known as sowing dissension.

Killing, harassing and plundering is attack (*danda*).

Clumsiness, contradiction, repetition, bad grammar, and misarrangement are the faults of a writ.

Black and ugly leaf, (*kalapatrakamacharu*) and uneven and uncoloured (*viraga*) writing cause clumsiness (*akanti*).

Subsequent portion disagreeing with previous portion of a letter, causes contradiction (*vyaghata*).

Stating for a second time what has already been said above is repetition.

Wrong use of words in gender, number, time and case is bad grammar (*apasabda*).

Division of paragraphs (*varga*) in unsuitable places, omission of necessary division of paragraphs, and violation of any other necessary qualities of a writ constitute misarrangement (*samplava*).

Having followed all sciences and having fully observed forms of writing in vogue, these rules of writing royal writs have been laid down by Kautilya in the interest of kings.

[Thus ends Chapter 10, 'The Procedure of Forming Royal Writs', in Book II, 'The Duties of Government Superintendents', of the Arthashastra of Kautilya. End of thirty-first chapter from the beginning.]

Chapter 11

EXAMINATION OF GEMS THAT ARE TO BE ENTERED INTO THE TREASURY

THE superintendent of the treasury shall, in the presence of qualified persons, admit into the treasury whatever he ought to, gems (*ratna*) and articles of superior or inferior value.

Tamraparnika, that which is produced in the *Tamraparni*; *Pandyakavataka*, that which is obtained in *Pandyakavata*; *Pasikya*, that which is produced in the *Pasa*; *Kauleya*, that which is produced in the *Kula*; *Chaurneya*, that which is produced in the *Churna*; *Mahendra*, that which is obtained near the mountain of *Mahendra*; *Kardamika*, that which is produced in the *Kardama*; *Srautasiya*, that which is produced in the *Srotasi*; *Hradiya*, that which is produced in (a deep pool of water known as) *Hrada*; and *Haimavata*, that which is obtained in the vicinity of the Himalayas are the several varieties of pearls.

Oyster shells, conch shells and other miscellaneous things are the wombs of pearls.

That which is like *masura* (*ervum hirsutam*), that which consists of three joints (*triputaka*), that which is like a tortoise (*kurmaka*), that which is semicircular, that which consists of several coatings, that which is double (*yamaka*), that which is scratched, that which is of rough surface, that which is possessed of spots (*siktakam*), that which is like the water pot used by an ascetic, that which is of dark-brown or blue colour, and that which is badly perforated are inauspicious.

That which is big, circular, without bottom (*nistalam*), brilliant, white, heavy, soft to the touch, and properly perforated is the best.

Sirshaka, *upasirshaka*, *prakandaka*, *avaghataka* and *taralapratibandha* are several varieties of pearl necklaces.

One thousand and eight strings of pearls form the necklace *Indrachchhanda*.

Half of the above is *Vijayachchhanda*.

Sixty-four strings make up *Ardhahara*.

Fifty-four strings make up *Rasmikalapa*.

Thirty-two strings make up *Guchchha*.

Twenty-seven strings make up *Nakshatramala*.

Twenty-four strings make up *Ardhaguchchha*.

Twenty strings make up *Manavaka*.

Half of the above is *Ardhamanavaka*.

The same necklaces with a gem at the centre are called by the same names with the word '*Manavaka*' suffixed to their respective names.

When all the strings making up a necklace are of *sirshaka* pattern, it is called pure necklace (*suddhahara*); likewise with strings of other pattern. That which contains a gem in the centre is (also) called *Ardhamanavaka*.

That which contains three slab-like gems (*triphalaka*) or five slab-like gems (*panchaphalaka*) in the centre is termed *Phalakahara*.

An only string of pearls is called pure *Ekavali*; the same with a gem in the centre is called *Yashti*; the same variegated with gold globules is termed *Ratnavali*.

A string made of pearls and gold globules alternately put is called *Apavartaka*.

Strings of pearls with a gold wire between two strings is called *Sopanaka*.

The same with a gem in the centre is called *Manisopanaka*.

The above will explain the formation of head strings, bracelets, anklets, waist bands, and other varieties.

Kauta, that which is obtained in the *Kuta*; *Mauleyaka*, that which is found in the *Muleya*; and *Parasamudraka*, that which is found beyond the ocean are several varieties of gems.

That which possesses such pleasant colour as that of the red lotus flower, or that of the flower of *Parijata* (*Erithrina indica*), or that of the rising sun is the *Saugandhika* gem.

That which is of the colour of blue lotus flower, or of *sirisha* (*Acacia sirisa*), or of water, or of fresh bamboo, or of the colour of the feathers of a parrot is the *Vaidurya* gem *Pushyaraga*, *Gomutraka*, and *Gomedika* are other varieties of the same.

That which is characterized with blue lines, that which is of the colour of the flower of *Kalaya* (a kind of *Phraseolus*), or which is intensely blue, which possesses the colour of *Jambu* fruit (rose apple), or which is as blue as the clouds is the *Indranila* gem; *Nandaka* (pleasing gem), *Sravanmadhya* (that which appears to pour water from its centre), *Sitavrishti* (that which appears to pour cold shower), and *Suryakanta* (sunstone) are other forms of gems.

Gems are hexagonal, quadrangular or circular, possessed of dazzling glow, pure, smooth, heavy, brilliant, transparent (*antargataprabha*) and illuminating; such are the qualities of gems.

Faint colour, sandy layer, spots, holes, bad perforation, and scratches are the defects of gems.

Vimalaka (pure), *Sasyaka* (plant-like), *Anjanamulaka* (deep-dark), *Pittaka* (like the bile of a cow), *Sulabhaka* (easily procurable), *Lohitaka* (red), *Amritamsuka* (of white rays), *Jyotirasaka* (glowing), *Maileyaka*, *Ahichchhatraka* (procured in the country of *Ahichchhatra*), *Kurpa*, *Putikurpa*, and *Sugandhikurpa*, *Kshirapaka*, *Suktichurnaka* (like the powder of an oyster shell), *Silapravalaka* (like coral), *Pulaka*, *Sukrapulaka* are varieties of inferior gems.

The rest are metalic beads (*kachamani*).

Sabharashtraka, that which is found in the country of *Sabharashtra*; *Madhyamarashtraka*, that which is found in the Central Province; *Kasmaka*, that which is found in the country of *Kasmaka*; *Srikatanaka*, that which is found in the vicinity of the mountain, *Vedotkata*; *Manimantaka*, that which is found near the mountain *Maniman* or *Manimanta*; and *Indravanaka* are diamonds.

Mines, streams and other miscellaneous places are their sources.

The colour of a diamond may be like that of a cat's eye, that of the flower of *Sirisha* (*Acacia sirisa*), the urine of a cow, the bile of a cow, like alum (*Sphatika*), the flower of *Malati*, or like that of any of the gems (described above).

That which is big, heavy, hard (*praharasaham*, tolerant of hitting), regular (*samakona*), capable of scratching on the surface of vessels (*bhajanalekhi*), refractive of light (*kubrami*), and brilliant is the best.

That which is devoid of angles, uneven (*nirasrikam*), and bent on one side (*parsvapavrittam*) is inauspicious.

Alakandaka, and *Vaivarnaka* are the two varieties of coral which are possessed of ruby-like colour, which are very hard, and which are free from the contamination of other substances inside.

Satana is red and smells like the earth; *Gosirshaka* is dark red and smells like fish; *Harichandana* is of the colour of the feathers of a parrot and smells like tamarind or mango fruit; likewise *Tarnasa*; *Grameruka* is red or dark red and smells like the urine of a goat; *Daivasabheya* is red and smells like a lotus flower; likewise *Aupaka* (*Japaka*); *Jongaka* and *Taurupa* are red or dark red and soft; *Maleyaka* is reddish white; *Kuchandana* is as black as *Agaru* (resin of the aloe) or red or dark red and very rough; *Kala-parvataka* is of pleasant appearance; *Kosakaraparvataka* (that which is the product of that mountain which is of the shape of a bud) is black or variegated black; *Sitodakiya* is black and soft, and smells like a lotus flower; *Nagaparvataka* (that which is the product of Naga mountain) is rough and is possessed of the colour of *Saivala* (*Vallisneria*); and *Sakala* is brown.

Light, soft, moist (*asyana*, not dry), as greasy as ghee, of pleasant smell, adhesive to the skin, of mild smell, retentive of colour and smell, tolerant of heat, absorptive of heat, and comfortable to the skin—these are the characteristics of sandal (*chandana*).

(As to) *Agaru* (*Agallochum*, resin of aloe):

Jongaka is black or variegated black and is possessed of variegated spots; *Dongaka* is black; and *Parasamudraka* is of variegated colour and smells like cascus or like *Navamalika* (*jasminum*).

(*Agaru* is) heavy, soft, greasy, smells far and long, burns slowly, gives out continuous smoke while burning, is of uniform smell, absorbs heat, and is so adhesive to the skin as not to be removable by rubbing;—these are the characteristics of *Agaru*.

(As to) *Tailaparnika*:

Asokagramika, the product of *Asokagrama*, is of the colour of meat and smells like a lotus flower; *Jongaka* is reddish yellow and smells like a blue lotus flower or like the urine of a cow; *Grameruka* is greasy and smells like a cow's urine; *Sauvarnakudyaka*, product of the country of *Suvarnakudya*, is reddish yellow and smells like *Matulunga* (the fruit of citron tree or sweet lime); *Purnadvipaka*, the product of the island, *Purnadviipa*, smells like a lotus flower or like butter; *Bhadrasriya* and *Paralauhityaka* are of the colour of nutmeg; *Antarvatya* is of the colour of cascus—the last two smell like *Kushtha* (*Costus Speciosus*); *Kaleyaka* which is a product of *Svarnabhumi*, gold-producing land, is yellow and greasy; and *Auttaraparvataka* (a product of, the northern mountain) is reddish yellow.

The above (fragrant substances) are commodities of superior value (*Sara*).

The smell of the *Tailaparnika* substances is lasting, no matter whether they are made into a paste or boiled or burnt; also it is neither changed nor affected even when mixed with other substances; and these substances resemble sandal and *Agallochum* in their qualities.

Kantanavaka, *Praiyaka*, and *Auttaraparvataka* are the varieties of skins.

Kantanavaka is of the colour of the neck of the peacock; *Praiyaka* is variegated with blue, yellow, and white spots; these two are eight *angulas* (inches) long.

Also *Bisi* and *Mahabisi* are the products of *Dvadasagrama*, twelve villages.

That which is of indistinct colour, hairy, and variegated (with spots) is (called) *Bisi*.

That which is rough and almost white is *Mahabisi* (great *Bisi*); These two are twelve *angulas* long.

Syamika, *Kalika*, *Kadali*, *Chandrottara* and *Sakula* are (other kinds of skins) procured from *Aroha* (*Arohaja*).

Syamika is brown and contains variegated spots; *Kalika* is brown or of the colour of a pigeon; these two are eight *angulas* long. *Kadali* is rough and two feet long; when *Kadali* bears variegated moonlike spots, it is called *Chandrottarakadali* and is one-third of its length; *Sakula* is variegated with large round spots similar to those that manifest themselves in a kind of leprosy (*kushtha*), or is furnished with tendrils and spotted like a deer's skin.

Samura, *Chinasi* and *Samuli* are (skins procured from *Bahlava*, ([*Bahlaveya*]).

Samura is thirty-six *angulas* long and black; *Chinasi* is reddish black or blackish white; *Samuli* is of the colour of wheat.

Satina, *Nalatula*, and *Vrittapuchchha* are the skins of aquatic animals (*Audra*).

Satina is black; *Nalatula* is of the colour of the fibre of *Nala*, a kind of grass; and *Vrittapuchchha* (that which possesses a round tail) is brown.

The above are the varieties of skins.

Of skins, that which is soft, smooth and hairy is the best.

Blankets made of sheep's wool may be white, purely red, or as red as a lotus flower. They may be made of worsted threads by sewing (*khachita*); or may be woven of woollen threads of various colour (*vanachitra*); or may be made of different pieces (*khandasanghatya*); or may be woven of uniform woollen threads (*tantuvichchhinna*).

Woollen blankets are (of ten kinds):

Kambala, *Kauchapaka*, *Kulamitika*, *Saumitika*, *Turagastarana*, *Varnaka*, *Talichchhaka*, *Varavana*, *Paristoma* and *Samantabhadraka*.

Of these, that which is slippery (*pichchhila*) as a wet surface, possessed of fine hair, and soft, is the best.

That (blanket) which is made up of eight pieces and black in colour is called *Bhingisi* used as rainproof; likewise is *Apasaraka*; both are the products of Nepal.

Samputika, *Chaturasrika*, *Lambara*, *Katavanaka*, *Pravaraka*, and *Sattalika* are (blankets made of) the wool of wild animals.

That which is manufactured in the country, *Vanga* (*vangaka*) is a white and soft fabric (*dukula*); that of *Pandya* manufacture (*Paundraka*) is black and as soft as the surface of a gem; and that which is the product of the country *Suvarnakudya*, is as red as the sun, as soft as the surface of the gem, woven while the threads are very wet, and of uniform (*chaturasra*) or mixed texture (*vyamisravana*).

Single, half, double, treble and quadruple garments are varieties of the same.

The above will explain other kinds of fabrics such as *Kasika*, Benares products, and *Kshauma* which is manufactured in *Pandya* (*Paundraka*).

Magadhika (product of the Magadha country), *Paundraka*, and *Sauvarnakudyaka* are fibrous garments.

Nagavriksha (a species of a tree), *Likucha* (*Artocarpus lakucha*), and *Vakula* (*Mimusops elengi*), and *Vata* (*Ficus indica*) are the sources (of their fibres).

That of *Nagavriksha* is yellow (*pita*); that of *Likucha* is of the colour of wheat; that of *Vakula* is white; and the rest is of the colour of butter.

Of these, that which is produced in the country of *Suvarnakudya* is the best.

The above will explain the fabrics known as *Kauseya*, silk cloth, and *Chinapatta*, fabrics of China manufacture.

Of cotton fabrics, those of *Madhura*, of *Aparanta*, western parts, of Kalinga, of Kasi, of Vanga, of *Vatsa*, and of *Mahisha* are the best.

As to other kinds of gems (which are not treated of here), the superintendent shall ascertain their size, their value, species, form, utility, their treatment, the repair of old ones, any adulteration that is not easily detected, their wear and tear due to lapse of time and place, as well as remedies against those which are inauspicious (*himsra*).

[Thus ends Chapter 11, 'Examination of Gems That Are to Be entered into the Treasury', in Book II, 'The Duties of Government Superintendents', of the Arthashastra of Kautilya. End of thirty-second chapter from the beginning.]

Chapter 12

CONDUCTING MINING OPERATIONS AND MANUFACTURE

POSSESSED of the knowledge of the science dealing with copper and other minerals (*Sulbadhatusastra*), experienced in the art of distillation and condensation of mercury (*rasapaka*) and of testing gems, aided by experts in mineralogy and equipped with mining labourers and necessary instruments, the superintendent of mines shall examine mines which, on account of their containing mineral excrement (*kitta*), crucibles, charcoal, and ashes, may appear to have been once exploited or which may be newly discovered on plains or mountain slopes possessing mineral ores, the richness of which can be ascertained by weight, depth of colour, piercing smell, and taste.

Liquids which ooze out from pits, eaves, slopes, or deep excavations of well-known mountains; which have the colour of the fruit of rose apple (*jambu*), of mango, and of *fan palm*; which are as yellow as ripe turmeric, sulphurate of arsenic (*haritala*), honeycomb and vermilion; which are as resplendent as the petals of a lotus, or the feathers of a parrot or a peacock; which are adjacent to (any mass of) water or shrubs of similar colour; and which are greasy (*chikkana*), transparent (*visada*), and very heavy are ores of gold (*kanchanika*). Likewise liquids which, when dropped on water, spread like oil to which dirt and filth adhere, and which amalgamate themselves more than cent per cent (*satadupari veddharah*) with copper or silver.

Of similar appearance as the above (*tatpratirupakam*), but of piercing smell and taste is bitumen.

Those ores which are obtained from plains or slopes of mountains; which are either yellow or as red as copper or reddish yellow; which are disjoined and marked with blue lines; which have the colour of black beans (*masha*, *Phraseolus radiatus*), green beans (*mudga*, *Phraseolus mungo*), and sesamum; which are marked with spots like a drop of curd and resplendent as turmeric, yellow myrobalan, petals of a lotus, acquatic plant, the liver or the spleen; which possess a sandy layer within them and are marked with figures of a circle or a *svastika*; which contain globular masses (*sagulika*); and which, when roasted, do not split, but emit much foam and smoke are the ores of gold (*suvarnadhatavah*), and are used to form amalgams with copper or silver (*prativaparthaste stamrarupyavedharah*).

Those ores which have the colour of a conch shell, camphor, alum, butter, a pigeon, turtle-dove, *Vimalaka* (a kind of precious stone), or the neck of a peacock; which are as resplendent as opal (*sasyaka*), agate (*gomedaka*), cane sugar (*guda*), and granulated sugar (*matsyandika*) which has the colour of the flower of *kovidara* (*Bauhinia variegata*), of lotus, of *patali* (*Bignonia suaveolens*), of *kalaya* (a kind of *Phraseolus*), of *kshauma* (flax), and of *atasi* (*Dinuin usitatissimum*); which may be in combination with lead or iron (*anjana*); which smell like raw meat, are disjoined grey or blackish white, and are marked with lines or spots; and which, when roasted, do not split, but emit much foam and smoke are silver ores.

The heavier the ores, the greater will be the quantity of metal in them (*satvavriddhih*).

The impurities of ores, whether superficial or inseparably combined with them can be got rid of and the metal melted when the ores are (chemically) treated with *Tikshna* urine (*mutra*) and alkalies (*kshara*), and are mixed or smeared over with the mixture of (the powder of) *Rajavriksha* (*Clitoria ternatea*), *Vata* (*Ficus indica*), and *Pelu* (*Carnea arborea*), together with cow's bile and the urine and dung of a buffalo, an ass and an elephant.

(Metals) are rendered soft when they are treated with (the powder of) *kandali* (mushroom), and *vajrakanda* (*Antiquorum*) together with the ashes of barley, black beans, *palasa* (*Butea frondosa*), and *pelu* (*Carnea arborea*), or with the milk of both the cow and the sheep. Whatever metal is split into a hundred thousand parts is rendered soft when it is thrice soaked in the mixture made up of honey (*madhu*), *madhuka* (*Bassia latifolia*), sheep's milk, sesamum oil, clarified butter, jaggery, *kinva* (ferment) and mushroom.

Permanent softness (*mridustambhana*) is also attained when the metal is treated with the powder of cow's teeth and horn.

Those ores which are obtained from plains or slopes of mountains; and which are heavy, greasy, soft, tawny, green, dark, bluish yellow (*harita*), pale red, or red are ores of copper.

Those ores which have the colour of *kakamechaka* (*Solanum indica*), pigeon, or cow's bile, and which are marked with white lines and smell like raw meat are the ores of lead.

Those ores which are as variegated in colour as saline soil or which have the colour of a burnt lump of earth are the ores of tin.

Those ores which are of orange colour (*kurumba*), or pale-red (*pandurohita*), or of the colour of the flower of *sinduvara* (*Vitex trifolia*) are the ores of *tikshna*. Those ores which are of the colour of the leaf of *kanda* (*Artemisia indica*) or of the leaf of birch are the ores of *vaikrintaka*.

Pure, smooth, effulgent, sounding (when struck), very hard (*satativrah*), and of little colour (*tanuraga*) are precious stones.

The yield of mines may be put to such uses as are in vogue. Commerce in commodities manufactured from mineral products shall be centralized and punishment for manufacturers, sellers, and purchasers of such commodities outside the prescribed locality shall also be laid down.

A mine labourer who steals mineral products except precious stones shall be punished with a fine of eight times their value.

Any person who steals mineral products or carries on mining operations without licence shall be bound (with chains) and caused to work (as a prisoner).

Mines which yield such minerals as are made use of in preparing vessels (*bhanda*) as well as those mines which require large outlay to work out may be leased out for a fixed number of the shares of the output or for a fixed rent (*bhagena prakrayena va*) Such mines as can be worked out without much outlay shall be directly exploited (by government agency).

The superintendent of metals (*lohadhyakshah*) shall carry on the manufacture of copper, lead, tin, *vaikrintaka* (mercury [?]), *arakuta* (brass), *vritta*(?); *kamsa* (bronze or bell metal), *tala* (sulphurate of arsenic), and *lodhra* (?), and also of commodities (*bhanda*) from them.

The superintendent of mint (*lakshnadhyakshah*), shall carry on the manufacture of silver coins (*rupyarupa*) made up of four parts of copper and one-sixteenth part (*masha*) of anyone of the metals, *tikshna*, *trapu*, *sisa*, and *anjana*. There shall be a *pana*, half a *pana*, a quarter and one-eighth.

Copper coins (*tamrarupa*) made up of four parts of an alloy (*padajivam*), shall be a *mashaka*, half a *mashaka*, *kakani* and half a *kakani*.

The examiner of coins (*rupadarsaka*) shall regulate currency both as a medium of exchange (*vyavaharikim*) and as legal tender admissible into the treasury (*kosapravesyam*): The premia levied on coins paid into the treasury shall be 8 per cent, known as *rupika*, 5 per cent known as *vyaji*, one-eighth *pana* per cent as *parikshika* (testing charge), besides (*cha*) a fine of 25 *pana* to be imposed on offenders other than the manufacturer, the seller, the purchaser and the examiner.

The superintendent of ocean mines (*khanyadhyakshah*) shall attend to the collection of conch shells, diamonds, precious stones, pearls, corals, and salt (*kshara*) and also regulate the commerce in the above commodities.

Soon after crystalization of salt is over, the superintendent of salt shall in time collect both the money rent (*prakraya*) and the quantity of the shares of salt due to the government; and by the sale of salt (thus collected as shares) he shall realize not only its value (*mulyam*), but also the premium of 5 per cent (*vyajim*), both in cash (*rupa*).

Imported salt (*agantulavanam*) shall pay one-sixth portion (*shadbhaga*) to the king. The sale of this portion (*bhagavibhaga*) shall fetch the premia of 5 per cent (*vyaji*), of 8 per cent (*rupika*) in cash (*rupa*). The purchasers shall pay not only the toll (*sulka*), but also the compensation (*vaidharana*) equivalent to the loss entailed on the king's commerce. In default of the above payment, he shall be compelled to pay a fine of 600 *pana*s.

Adulteration of salt shall be punished with the highest amercement; likewise persons other than hermits (*vanaprastha*) manufacturing salt without licence.

Men learned in the Vedas, persons engaged in penance, as well as labourers may take with them salt for food; salt and alkalies for purposes other than this shall be subject to the payment of toll.

Thus, besides collecting from mines the ten kinds of revenue such as (1) value of the output (*mulya*), (2) the share of the output (*vibhaga*), (3) the premium of 5 per cent (*vyaji*), (4) the testing charge of coins (*parigha*), (5) fine previously announced (*atyaya*), (6) toll (*sulka*), (7) compensation for loss entailed on the king's commerce (*vaidharana*), (8) fines to be determined in proportion to the gravity of crimes (*danda*), (9) coinage (*rupa*), (10) the premium of 8 per cent (*rupika*) the government shall keep as a state monopoly both mining and commerce (in minerals).

Thus taxes (*mukhasangraha*) on all commodities intended for sale shall be prescribed once for all.

[Thus ends Chapter 12, 'Conducting Mining Operations and Manufacture', in Book II', 'The Duties of Government Superintendents', of the Arthashastra of Kautilya. End of thirty-third chapter from the beginning.]

Chapter 13

SUPERINTENDENT OF GOLD IN THE GOLDSMITH'S OFFICE

IN order to manufacture gold and silver jewellry, each being kept apart, the superintendent of gold shall have a goldsmith office (*akshasala*) consisting of four rooms and one door.

In the centre of the high road a trained, skilful goldsmith of high birth and of reliable character shall be appointed to hold his shop.

Jambunada, that which is the product of the river, *Jambu*; *Satakumbha*, that which is extracted from the mountain of *Satakumba*; *Hataka*, that which is extracted from the mines known as *Hataka*; *Vainava*, that which is the product of the mountain *Venu*; and *Sringasuktija*, that which is extracted from *sringasukti* (?) are the varieties of gold.

(Gold may be obtained) either pure or amalgamated with mercury or silver or alloyed with other impurities as mine gold (*akarodgata*).

That which is of the colour of the petals of a lotus, ductile, glossy, incapable of making any continuous sound (*anadi*), and glittering is the best; that which is reddish yellow (*raktapita*) is of middle quality; and that which is red is of low quality.

Impure gold is of whitish colour. It shall be fused with lead of four times the quantity of the impurity. When gold is rendered brittle owing to its contamination with lead, it shall be heated with dry cow dung (*sushkapatala*). When it splits into pieces owing to hardness, it shall be drenched (after heating) into oil mixed with cow dung (*tailagomaye*).

Mine gold which is brittle owing to its contamination with lead shall be heated wound round with cloth (*pakapatrani kritva*); and hammered on a wooden anvil. Or it may be drenched in the mixture made of mushroom and *vajrakhanda* (*Antiquorum*).

Tutthodgata, that which is extracted from the mountain, *Tuttha*; *gaudika*, that which is the product of the country known as *Gauda*; *kambuka*, that which is extracted from the mountain, *Kambu*; and *chakravalika*, that which is extracted from the mountain *Chakravala* are the varieties of silver.

Silver which is white, glossy and ductile is the best; and that which is of the reverse quality is bad.

Impure silver shall be heated with lead of one-fourth the quantity of the impurity.

That which becomes full of globules, white, glowing, and of the colour of curd is pure.

When the streak of pure gold (made on touchstone) is of the colour of turmeric, it is termed suvarna. When from one to sixteen *kakanis* of gold in a *suvarna* (of sixteen *mashakas*) are replaced by from one to sixteen *kakani*s of copper, so that the copper is inseparably alloyed with the whole mass of the remaining quantity of the gold, the sixteen varieties (carats) of the standard of the purity of gold (*shodasavarnakah*) will be obtained.

Having first made a streak with suvarna on a touchstone, then (by the side of the streak) a streak with a piece of the gold (to be compared with it) shall be made.

Whenever a uniform streak made on the even surface of a touchstone can be wiped off or swept away or when the streak is due to the sprinkling of any glittering powder (*gairika*) by the nail on touchstone, then an attempt for deception can be inferred.

If, with the edge of the palm dipped in a solution, of vermilion (*jatihingulaka*) or of sulphate of iron (*pushpakasisa*) in cow's urine, gold (suvarna) is touched, it becomes white.

A touchstone with soft and shining splendour is the best. The touchstone of the Kalinga country with the colour of green beans is also the best. A touchstone of even or uniform colour is good in sale or purchase (of gold). That which possesses the colour of an elephant, tinged with green colour and capable of reflecting light (*pratiragi*) is good in selling gold. That which is hard, durable, and of uneven colour and not reflecting light, is good for purchasers (*krayahitah*). That which is grey, greasy, of uniform colour, soft and glossy is the best.

That (gold) which, when heated, keeps the same colour (*tapo bahirantascha samah*), is as glittering as tender sprouts, or of the colour of the flower of *karandaka* (?) is the best.

That which is black or blue (in gold) is the impurity (*apraptaka*).

We shall deal with the balance and weights under the 'Superintendent of Weights and Measures' (Chapter 19, Book II). In accordance with the instructions given thereunder silver and gold (*rupyasuvarnam*) may be given in exchange.

No person who is not an employee shall enter the goldsmiths' office. Any person who so enters shall be beheaded (*uchchhedyah*).

Any workman who enters the office with gold or silver shall have to forfeit the same.

Goldsmiths who are engaged to prepare various kinds of ornaments such as *kanchana* (pure gold), *prishita* (hollow ornaments), *tvashtri* (setting gems in gold) and *tapaniya*; as well as blowers and sweepers shall enter into or exit from the office after their person and dress are thoroughly examined. All of their instruments together with their unfinished work shall be left where they have been at work. That amount of gold which they have received and the ornamental work which they were doing shall be put in the centre of the office. (Finished articles) shall be examined both morning and evening and be locked up with the seal of both the manufacturer and the superintendent (*karayatri*, the owner getting the articles prepared).

Kshepana, *guna*, and *kshudra* ate three kinds of ornamental work.

Setting jewels (*kacha*, glass bead) in gold is termed *kshepana*.

Thread making or string making is called *guna*. Solid work (*ghana*), hollow work (*sushira*), and the manufacture of globules furnished with a rounded orifice is what is termed *kshudra*, low or ordinary work.

For setting jewels in gold, five parts of *kanchana* (pure gold) and ten parts of gold alloyed with four parts of copper or silver shall be the required quantity (*mana*). Here the pure gold shall be preserved from the impure gold.

For setting jewels in hollow ornaments (*prishitakacha karmanah*), three parts of gold to hold the jewel and four parts for the bottom (shall be the required quantity).

For the work of *tvashtri*, copper and gold shall be mixed in equal quantities.

For silver article either solid or hollow, silver may be mixed with half of the amount of gold; or by making use of the powder or solution of vermilion, gold equal to one-fourth the amount of silver of the ornament may be painted (*vasayet*) on it.

Pure and glittering gold is *tapaniya*. This combined with an equal quantity of lead and heated with rock salt (*saindhav'ika*) to melting point under dry cow dung becomes the basis of gold alloys of blue, red, white, yellow (*harita*), parrot and pigeon colours.

The colouring ingredient of gold is one *kakani* of *tikshna* which is of the colour of the neck of a peacock, tinged with white, and which is dazzling and full of copper (*pitapurnitam*).

Pure or impure silver (*tara*) may be heated four times with *asthituttha* (copper sulphate mixed with powdered bone), again four times with an equal quantity of lead, again four times with dry copper sulphate (*sushkatuttha*) again three times in skull (*kapala*), and lastly twice in cow dung. Thus the silver acted upon seventeen times by *tuttha* (*shodasatutthatikrantam*) and lastly heated to white light with rock salt may be made to alloy with *suvarna* to the extent of from one *kakani* to two *mashas*. Then the *suvarna* attains white colour and is called *svetatara*.

When three parts of *tapaniya* (pure gold) are melted with thirty-two parts of *svetatara*, the compound becomes reddish white (*svetalohitakam*). When three parts of *tapaniya* are combined with thirty-two parts of copper, the compound becomes yellow (*pita*, red!). Also when three parts of the colouring ingredient (*ragatribhaga*, i.e., *tikshna* referred to above) are heated with *tapaniya*, the compound becomes yellowish red (*pita*).

When two parts of *svetatara* and one part of *tapaniya* are heated, the whole mass becomes as green as *mudga* (*Phraseolus mungo*). When *tapaniya* is drenched in a solution of half the quantity of black iron (*kalayasa*), it becomes black.

When *tapaniya* is twice drenched in (the above) solution mixed with mercury (*rasa*), it acquires the colour of the feathers of a parrot.

Before these varieties of gold are put to use, their test streak shall be taken on touchstone. The process of assaying *tikshna* and copper shall be well understood. Hence the various counterweights (*avaneyimana*) used in weighing diamonds, rubies, pearls, corals, and coins, (*rupa*), as well as the proportional amount of gold and silver necessary for various kinds of ornaments can be well understood.

Uniform in colour, equal in the colour of test streak to the standard gold, devoid of hollow bulbs, ductile (*sthira*), very smooth, free from alloys, pleasing when worn as an ornament, not dazzling though glittering, sweet in its uniformity of mass, and pleasing the mind and eyes—these are the qualities of *tapaniya*, pure gold.

[Thus ends Chapter 13, 'The Superintendent of Gold in the Goldsmiths' Office', in Book II, 'The Duties of Government Superintendents', of the Arthashastra of Kautilya. End of thirty-fourth chapter from the beginning.]

Chapter 14

THE DUTIES OF THE STATE GOLDSMITH IN THE HIGH ROAD

THE state goldsmith shall employ artisans to manufacture gold and silver coins (*rupyasuvarna*) from the bullion of citizens and country people.

The artisans employed in the office shall do their work as ordered and in time. When, under the excuse that time and nature of the work has not been prescribed, they spoil the work, they shall not only forfeit their wages, but also pay a fine of twice the amount of their wages. When they postpone work, they shall forfeit one-fourth the amount of their wages and pay a fine of twice the amount of the forfeited wages.

(The goldsmith of the mint) shall return (to the owners coins or ornaments) of the same weight, and of the same quality (*varna*) as that of the bullion (*nikshepa*) which they received (at the mint). With the exception of those (coins) which have been worn out or which have undergone diminution (*kshinaparisirna*), they shall receive the same coins (back into the mint) even after the lapse of a number of years.

The state goldsmith shall gather from the artisans employed in the mint information concerning pure gold, metallic mass (*pudgala*), coins (*lakshana*), and rate of exchange (*prayoga*).

In getting a *suvarna* coin (of 16 *masha*s) manufactured from gold or from silver, one *kakani* (one-fourth *masha*) weight of the metal more shall be given to the mint towards the loss in manufacture.

The colouring ingredient (*ragaprakshepa*) shall be two *kakani*s of *tikshna* (copper sulphate ?), one-sixth of which will be lost during the manufacture.

When the quality (*varna*) of a coin less than the standard of a *masha* is lowered, the artisans (concerned) shall be punished with the first amercement. When its weight is less than the standard weight, they shall be punished with the middlemost amercement. Deception in balance or weights shall be punished with the highest amercement. Deception in the exchange of manufactured coins (*kritabhandopadhau*) shall also be punished with the highest amercement.

Whoever causes (gold or silver articles) to be manufactured in any place other than the mint or without being noticed by the state goldsmith shall be fined 12 *panas*, while the artisan who does that work shall, if found out, be punished with twice the above fine. If he is not found out, measures such as are described in Book IV shall be taken to detect him. When thus detected, he shall be fined 200 *panas* or shall have his fingers cut off.

Weighing balance and counterweights shall be purchased from the superintendent in charge of them. Otherwise a fine of 12 *panas* shall be imposed.

Compact work (*ghana*), compact and hollow work (*ghanasushira*), soldering (*samyuhya*), amalgamation (*avalepya*), enclosing (*samghatya*), and gilding (*vasitakam*) are the various kinds of artisan work (*karukasma*).

False balances (*tulavishama*), removal (*apasarana*), dropping (*visravana*), folding (*petaka*), and confounding (*pinka*) are the several means employed by goldsmiths to deceive the public.

False balances are—that of bending arms (*sannamini*); that of high helm or pivot (*utkarnika*); that of broken head (*bhinnamastaka*); that of hollow neck (*upakanthi*); that of bad strings (*kusikya*); that of bad cups or pans (*sakatukakshya*); that which is crooked or shaking (*parivellya*); and that which is combined with a magnet (*ayaskanta*).

When, by what is called *Triputaka* which consists of two parts of silver and one part of copper, an equal portion of pure alluvial gold is replaced, that deceitful act is termed copper-removal (*triputakavasaritam*); when, by copper, an equal portion of gold is replaced, that act is termed copper-removal (*sulbavasaritam*); when by *vellakaan* equal portion of gold is replaced, it is termed *vellaka*-removal; and when pure alluvial gold is replaced by that gold half of which is mixed with copper, it is termed gold removal (*hemavasaritam*).

A crucible with a base metallic piece hidden in it; metallic excrement; pincers; a pair of tongs; metallic pieces (*jongani*); and borax (*sauvarchikalavanam*)—these are the several things which are made use of by goldsmiths in stealing gold.

When, intentionally causing the crucible (containing the bullion) to burst, a few sand-like particles of the metal are picked up along with other particles of a base metal previously put therein, and the whole is wrought into a mass for the intended coin or ornament), this act is termed dropping (*visravana*); or when examining the folded or inlaid leaves of an ornament (*achitakapatraparikshayam*) deception is perpetrated by substituting silver for gold, or when particles of a base metal are substituted for those of gold, it is termed dropping (*visravana*) likewise.

Folding (*petaka*) either firm (*gadha*) or loose (*abhyuddharya*) is practised in soldering, in preparing amalgams, and in enclosing (a piece of base metal with two pieces of a superior metal).

When a lead piece (*sisarupa*–lead coin) is firmly covered over with gold leaf by means of wax (*ashtaka*), that act is termed *gadhapetaka*, firm folding; and when the same is loosely folded, it is termed loose folding.

In amalgams, a single or double layer (of a superior metal) is made to cover a piece (of base metal). Copper or silver may also be placed between two leaves (of a superior metal). A copper piece (*sulbarupya*) may be covered over with gold leaf, the surface and the edges being smoothened; similarly a piece of any base metal may be covered over with double leaf of copper or silver, the surface and the edges being smoothened.

The two forms of folding may be detected by heating, by testing on touchstone (*nikasha*) or by observing absence of sound when it is rubbed (*nissabdollekhana*).

(They) find out loose folding in the acid juice of *badaramla* (*Flacourtia cataphracta* or jujube fruit) or in salt water—so much for folding (*petaka*).

In a compact and hollow piece (*ghana-sushire rupe*), small particles of gold-like mud (*suvarnamrinvalukah*) or bit of vermilion (*hingulakalkah*) are so heated as to make them firmly adhere to the piece inside. Even in a compact piece (*dridhavastuke rupe*), the wax-like mud of Gandhara mixed with the particles of gold-like sand is so heated as to adhere to the piece. These two kinds of impurities are got rid of by hammering the pieces when red hot.

In an ornament or a coin (*sapari-bhande va rupe*) salt mixed with hard sand (*katusarkara*) is so heated in flame as to make it firmly adhere to (the ornament or coin). This (salt and sand) can be got rid of by boiling (*kvathana*).

In some pieces, mica may be firmly fixed inside by wax and covered over with a double leaf (of gold or silver). When such a piece with mica or glass inside is suspended in water (*udake*), one of its sides dips more than the other; or when pierced by a pin, the pin goes very easily in the layers of mica in the interior (*patalantareshu*).

Spurious stones and counterfeit gold and silver may be substituted for real ones in compact and hollow pieces (*ghanasushira*). They are detected by hammering the pieces when red hot—so much for confounding (*pinka*).

Hence (the state goldsmith) shall have a thorough knowledge of the species, characteristics, colour, weight and formation (*pudgala-lakshana*) of diamonds, precious stones (*mani*), pearls, corals and coins (*rupa*).

There are four ways of deception perpetrated when examining new pieces or repairing old ones: they are hammering, cutting, scratching and rubbing.

When, under the excuse of detecting the deception known as folding (*petaka*) in hollow pieces or in threads or in cups (made of gold or silver), the articles in question are hammered, that act is termed hammering.

When a lead piece (covered over with gold or silver leaf) is substituted for a real one and its interior is cut off, it is termed cutting (*avachchhedanam*).

When compact pieces are scratched by *tikshna* (copper sulphate?), that act is termed scratching (*ullekhana*).

When, by a piece of cloth painted with the powder of sulphurate of arsenic (*haritala*), red arsenic (*manassila*), or vermilion or with the powder of *kuruvinda* (black salt?), gold or silver articles are rubbed, that act is termed rubbing.

By these acts, gold and silver articles (*bhandani*) undergo diminution; but no other kind of injury is done to them.

In all those pieces which are hammered, cut, scratched, or rubbed the loss can be inferred by comparing them with intact pieces of similar description. In amalgamated pieces (*avalepya*) which are cut off, the loss can be ascertained by cutting off an equal portion of a similar piece. Those pieces the appearance of which has changed shall be often heated and drenched in water.

(The state goldsmith) shall infer deception (*kacham vidyat*) when [the artisan preparing articles pays undue attention to] throwing away, counterweight, fire, anvil (*gandika*), working instruments (*bhandika*), the seat (*adhikarani*), the assaying balance, folds of dress (*chellachollakam*), his head, his thigh, flies, eagerness to look at his own body, the waterpot and the firepot.

Regarding silver, bad smell like that of rotten meat, hardness due to any alloy (*mala*), projection (*prastina*), and bad colour may be considered as indicating adulteration.

Thus articles (of gold and silver) new or old, or of bad or unusual colour are to be examined and adequate fines as described above shall be imposed.

[Thus ends Chapter 14, 'The Duties of the State Goldsmith in the High Road', in Book II, 'The Duties of Government Superintendents', of the Arthashastra of Kautilya. End of thirty-fifth chapter from the beginning.]

Chapter 15

THE SUPERINTENDENT OF STOREHOUSE

THE superintendent of storehouse (*Koshthagara*) shall supervise the accounts of agricultural produce (*sita*); taxes coming under *Rashtra*, country parts; commerce (*krayima*); barter (*parivartana*); begging for grains (*pramityaka*); grains borrowed with promise to repay (*apamityaka*); manufacture of rice, oils, etc., (*simhanika*); accidental revenue (*anyajata*); statements to check expenditure (*vyayapratyaya*); and recovery of past arrears (*upasthanam*).

Whatever in the shape of agricultural produce is brought in by the superintendent of agriculture, (of crown lands) is termed *sita*.

The taxes that are fixed (*pindakara*), taxes that are paid in the form of one-sixth of produce (*shadbhaga*), provision paid (by the people) for the army (*senabhakta*), taxes that are levied for religious purposes (*bali*), taxes or subsidies that are paid by vassal kings and others (*kara*), taxes that are specially collected on the occasion of the birth of a prince (*utsanga*), taxes that are collected when there is some margin left for such collection (*parsva*), compensation levied in the shape of grains for any damage done by cattle to crops (*parihinaka*), presentation made to the king, (*aupayanika*), and taxes that are levied on lands below tanks, lakes, etc., built by the king (*Kaushtheyaka*)—all these come under the head '*Rashtra*'.

Sale proceeds of grains, grains purchased and the collection of interest in kind or grain debts (*prayogapratyadana*) are termed commerce.

Profitable exchange of grains for grains is termed barter (*parivarthana*).

Grains collected by begging is termed *pramityaka*. Grains borrowed with promise to repay the same is termed *apamityaka*.

Pounding (rice, etc.), dividing (pulses, etc.), frying (corns and beans), manufacture of beverages (*suktakarma*), manufacture of flour by employing those persons who live upon such works, extracting oil by employing shepherds and oil makers, and manufacture of sugar from the juice of sugar cane are termed *simhanika*. Whatever is lost and forgotten (by others) and the like form accidental revenue (*anyajata*).

Investment, the relic of a wrecked undertaking, and savings from an estimated outlay are the means to check expenditure (*vyayapratyaya*).

That amount or quantity of compensation which is claimed for making use of a different balance or for any error in taking a handful is termed *vyaji*.

Collection of arrears is termed '*upasthana*', 'recovery of past arrears'.

Of grains, oils, sugar and salt, all that concerns grains will be treated of in connection with the duties of the 'Superintendent of Agriculture'.

Clarified butter, oil, serum of flesh and pith or sap (of plants, etc.), are termed oils (*sneha*).

Decoction (*phanita*), jaggery, granulated sugar, and sugar candy are termed *kshara*.

Saindhava, that which is the product of the country of Sindhu; Samudra, that which is produced from seawater; *Bida*; *Yavakshara*, nitre, *Sauvarchala*, that which is the product of the country of Suvarchala; and *udbhedaja*, that which is extracted from saline soil are termed *lavana*, salt.

The honey of the bee as well as the juice extracted from grapes are called *madhu*.

Mixture made by combining anyone of the substances, such as the juice of sugar cane, jaggery, honey, the juice of grapes, the essence of the fruits of *jambu* (*Euginia jambolana*) and of *jaka* tree—with the essence of *meshasringa* (a kind of plant) and long pepper, with or without the addition of the essence of *chirbhita* (a kind of gourd), cucumber, sugar cane, mango fruit and the fruit of myrobalan, the mixture being prepared so as to last for a month, or six months, or a year, constitute the group of astringents (*suktavarga*).

The fruits of those trees which bear acid fruits, those of *karamarda* (*Carissa carandas*), those of *vidalamalaka* (*myrobalan*), those of *matulanga* (citron tree), those of *kola* (small jujuba), those of *badara* (*Flacourtia cataphracta*), those of *sauvira* (big jujuba), and those of *parushaka* (*Grewia asiatica*) and the like come under the group of acid fruits.

Curds, acid prepared from grains and the like are acids in liquid form.

Long pepper, black pepper, ginger, cumin seed, *kiratatikta* (*Agathotes chirayta*), white mustard, coriander, *choraka* (a plant), *damanaka* (*Artemisia indica*), *maruvaka* (*Vangueria spinosa*), *sigru* (*Hyperanthera moringa*), and the like together with their roots (*kanda*) come under the group of pungent substances (*tiktavarga*).

Dried fish, bulbous roots (*kandamula*), fruits and vegetables form the group of edibles (*sakavarga*).

Of the store, thus collected, half shall be kept in reserve to ward off the calamities of the people and only the other half shall be used. Old collection shall be replaced by new supply.

The superintendent shall also personally supervise the increase or diminution sustained in grains when they are pounded (*kshunna*), or frayed (*ghrishta*), or reduced to flour (*pishta*), or fried (*bhrashta*), or dried after soaking in water.

The essential part (*sara*, i.e., that which is fit for food) of *kodrava* (*Paspalam scrobiculatum*) and of *vrihi* (rice) is one half; that of *sali* (a kind of rice) is (half) less by one-eighth part; that of *varaka* (*Phraseolus trilobus*) is (half) less by one-third part; that of *priyangu* (panic seed or millet) is one-half ; that of *chamasi* (barley), of *mudga* (*Phraseolus mungo*) and of *masha* (*Phraseolus radiatus*) is (half) less by one-eighth part; that of *saibya* (*simbi*) is one-half; that of *masura* (*Ervum hirsutum*) is (half) less by one-third part (than the raw material or grains from which it is prepared).

Raw flour and *kulmasha* (boiled and forced rice) will be as much as one-and-a-half of the original quantity of the grains.

Barley gruel as well as its flour baked will be twice the original quantity.

Kodrava (*Paspalam scrobiculatum*), *varaka* (*Phraseolus trilobus*), *udaraka* (*Panicum*), and *priyangu* (millet) will increase three times the original quantity when cooked. *Vrihi* (rice) will increase four times when cooked. *Sali* (a kind of rice) will increase five times when cooked. Grains will increase twice the original quantity when moistened; and two-and-a-half times when soaked to sprouting condition.

Grains fried will increase by one-fifth the original quantity; leguminous seeds (*kalaya*), when fried, will increase twice the original; likewise rice when fried.

Oil extracted from *atasi* (linseed) will be one-sixth (of the quantity of the seed); that extracted from the seeds of *nimba* (*Azadirachta indica*), *kusamra* (?), and *kapittha* (*Feronia elephantum*) will be one-fifth; and that extracted from *tila* (seasumum), *kusumba* (a sort of kidney bean), *madhuka* (*Bassia latifolia*), and *ingudi* (*Terminalia catappa*) will be one-fourth.

Five *palas* of *karpasa* (cotton) and of *kshauma* (flax) will yield one *pala* of threads.

Rice prepared in such a way that five *dronas* of *sali* yield ten *adhakas* of rice will be fit to be the food of young elephants; eleven *adhakas* from five *dronas* for elephants of bad temper (*vyala*); ten *adhakas* from the same quantity for elephants trained for riding; nine *adhakas* from the same quantity for elephants used in war; eight *adhaka*s from the same for infantry; eleven *adhaka*s from the same for chiefs of the army; six *adhaka*s from the same for queens and princes and five *adhaka*s from the same quantity for kings.

One *prastha* of rice, pure and unsplit, one-fourth *prastha* of *supa*, and clarified butter or oil equal to one-fourth part of (*supa*) will suffice to form one meal of an Arya. One-sixth *prastha* of *supa* for a man; and half the above quantity of oil will form one meal for low castes (*avara*). The same rations less by one-fourth the above quantities will form one meal for a woman; and half the above rations for children. For dressing twenty *pala*s of flesh, half a *kutumba* of oil, one *pala* of salt, one *pala* of sugar (*kshara*), two *dharana*s of pungent substances (*katuka*, spices), and half a *prastha* of curd (will be necessary).

For dressing greater quantities of flesh, the same ingredients can be proportionally increased. For cooking *saka*s (dried fish and vegetables), the above substances are to be added one-and-a-half times as much. For dressing dried fish, the above ingredients are to be added twice as much.

Measures of rations for elephants and horses will be described in connection with the 'Duties of Their Respective Superintendents'. For bullocks, one *drona* of *masha* (*Phraseolus radiatus*) or one *drona* of barley cooked with other things, as prescribed for horses, is the requisite quantity of food, besides the special and additional provision of one *tula* of oilcakes (*ghanapinyaka*) or ten *adhaka*s of bran (*kanakuttana-kundaka*).

Twice the above quantity for buffaloes and camels.

Half a *drona* for asses, red spotted deer and deer with white stripes. One *adhaka* for an antelope and big red deer. Half an *adhaka* or one *adhaka* of grain together with bran for a goat, a ram and a boar. One *prastha* of cooked rice for dogs. Half a *prastha* for a *hamsa* (goose), a *krauncha* (heron) and a peacock. From the above, the quantity of rations enough for one meal for other beasts, cattle, birds and rogue elephants (*vyala*) may be inferred.

Charcoal and chaff may be given over for iron smelting and lime kiln (*bhittilepya*).

Bran and flour (*kanika*) may be given to slaves, labourers and cooks. The surplus of the above may be given to those who prepare cooked rice, and rice cakes.

The weighing balance, weights, measures, millstone (*rochani*), pestle, mortar, wooden contrivances for pounding rice, etc., (*kuttakayantra*), contrivances for splitting seeds into pieces (*rochakayantra*), winnowing fans, sieves (*chalani*) grain baskets (*kandoli*), boxes, and brooms are the necessary instruments.

Sweepers; preservers; those who weigh things (*dharaka*); those who measure grains, etc.; those who supervise the work of measuring grains (*mapaka*); those who supervise the supply of commodities to the storehouse (*dapaka*); those who supply commodities (*dayaka*); those who are employed to receive compensation for any real or supposed error in measuring grains, etc. (*salakaipratigrahaka*); slaves; and labourers—all these are called *vishti*.

Grains are heaped up on the floor; jaggery (*kshara*) is bound round in grass-rope (*muta*); oils are kept in earthenware or wooden vessels; and salt is heaped up on the surface of the ground.

[Thus ends Chapter 15, 'The Superintendent of Storehouse', in Book II, 'The Duties of Government Superintendents', of the Arthashastra of Kautilya. End of the thirty-sixth chapter from the beginning.]

Chapter 16

THE SUPERINTENDENT OF COMMERCE

THE superintendent of commerce shall ascertain demand or absence of demand for, and rise or fall in the price of, various kinds of merchandise which may be the products either of land or of water and which may have been brought in either by land or by water path. He shall also ascertain the time suitable for their distribution, centralization, purchase and sale.

That merchandise which is widely distributed shall be centralized and its price enhanced. When the enhanced rate becomes popular, another rate shall be declared.

That merchandise of the king which is of local manufacture shall be centralized; imported merchandise shall be distributed in several markets for sale. Both kinds of merchandise shall be favourably sold to the people.

He shall avoid such large profits as will harm the people.

There shall be no restriction to the time of sale of those commodities for which there is frequent demand; nor shall they be subject to the evils of centralization (*sankuladosha*).

Or pedlars may sell the merchandise of the king at a fixed price in many markets and pay necessary compensation (*vaidharana*) proportional to the loss entailed upon it (*chhedanurupam*).

The amount of *vyaji* due on commodities sold by cubical measure is one-sixteenth of the quantity (*shodasabhago manavyaji*); that on commodities sold by weighing balance is one-twentieth of the quantity; and that on commodities sold in numbers is one-eleventh of the whole.

The superintendent shall show favour to those who import foreign merchandise: mariners (*navika*) and merchants who import foreign merchandise shall be favoured with remission of the trade taxes, so that they may derive some profit (*ayatikshamam pariharam dadyat*).

Foreigners importing merchandise shall be exempted from being sued for debts unless they are (local) associations and partners (*anabhiyogascharthesshvagantunamanyatassabhyopakari bhyah*).

Those who sell the merchandise of the king shall invariably put their sale proceeds in a wooden box kept in a fixed place and provided with a single aperture on the top. During the eighth part of the day, they shall submit to the superintendent the sale report, saying, 'This much has been sold and this much remains.' They shall also hand over the weights and measures. Such are the rules applicable to local traffic.

As regards the sale of the king's merchandise in foreign countries:

Having ascertained the value of local produce as compared with that of foreign produce that can be obtained in barter, the superintendent will find out (by calculation) whether there is any margin left for profit after meeting the payments (to the foreign king) such as the toll (*sulka*), road cess (*vartani*), conveyance cess (*ativahika*), tax payable at military stations (*gulmadeya*), ferry charges (*taradeya*), subsistence to the merchant and his followers (*bhakta*), and the portion of merchandise payable to the foreign king (*bhaga*).

If no profit can be realized by selling the local produce in foreign countries, he has to consider whether any local produce can be profitably bartered for any foreign produce. Then he may send one quarter of his valuable merchandise through safe roads to different markets on land. In view of large profits, he (the deputed merchant) may make friendship with the forest guards, boundary guards, and officers in charge of cities and of country parts (of the foreign king). He shall take care to secure his treasure (*sara*) and life from danger. If he cannot reach the intended market, he may sell the merchandise (at any market) free from all dues (*sarvadeyavisuddham*).

Or he may take his merchandise to other countries through rivers (*nadipatha*).

He shall also gather information as to conveyance-charges (*yanabhagaka*), subsistence on the way (*pathyadana*), value of foreign merchandise that can be obtained in barter for local merchandise, occasions of pilgrimages (*yatrakala*), means that can be employed to ward off dangers (of the journey), and the history of commercial towns (*panyapattanacharitra*).

Having gathered information as to the transaction in commercial towns along the banks of rivers, he shall transport his merchandise to profitable markets and avoid unprofitable ones.

[Thus ends Chapter 16, 'The Superintendent of Commerce', in Book II, 'The Duties of Government Superintendents', of Arthashastra of Kautilya. End of thirty-seventh chapter from the beginning.]

Chapter 17

THE SUPERINTENDENT OF FOREST PRODUCE

THE superintendent of forest produce shall collect timber and other products of forests by employing those who guard productive forests. He shall not only start productive works in forests, but also fix adequate fines and compensations to be levied from those who cause any damage to productive forests except in calamities.

The following are forest products.

Saka (teak), *tinisa* (*Dalbergia ougeinensis*), *dhanvana* (?), *arjuna* (*Terminalia arjuna*), *madhuka* (*Bassia latifolia*), *tilaka* (*Barleria cristata*), *tala* (palmyra), *simsupa* (*Dalbergia sissu*), *arimeda* (*Fetid mimosa*), *rajadana* (*Mimosops kauki*), *sirisha* (*Mimosa sirisha*), *khadira* (*Mimosa catechu*), *sarala* (*Pinus longifolia*), *talasarja* (*sal* tree or *Shorea robesta*), *asvakarna* (*Vatica robesta*), *somavalka* (a kind of white *khadira*), *kasamra* (?), *priyaka* (yellow *sal* tree), *dhava* (*Mimosa hexandra*), etc., are the trees of strong timber (*saradaruvarga*).

Utaja, chimiya, chava, venu, vamsa, satina, kantaka, bhalluka, etc., form the group of bamboo.

Vetra (cane), *sokavalli, vasi* (*Justicia ganderussa*?), *syamalata* (*Ichnocarpus*), *nagalata* (betel), etc., form the group of creepers. *Malati* (*Jasminum grandiflorum*), *durva* (panic grass), *arka* (*Calotropis gigantea*), *sana* (hemp), *gavedhuka* (*Coix barbata*), *atasi* (*Linum usitatis simum*), etc., form the group of fibrous plants (*valkavarga*).

Munja (*Saccharum munja*), *balbaja* (*Eleusine indica*), etc., are plants which yield rope-making material (*rajjubhanda*).

Tali (*Corypha taliera*), *tala* (palmyra or *Borassus flabelliformis*), and *bhurja* (birch) yield leaves (*patram*).

Kimsuka (*Butea frondosa*), *kusumbha* (*Carthamus tinctorius*), and *kumkuma* (*Crocus sativus*) yield flowers.

Bulbous roots and fruits are the group of medicines.

Kalakuta, Vatsanabha, Halahala, Meshasringa, Musta, (*Cyperus rotundus*), *kushtha, mahavisha, vellitaka, gaurardra, balaka, markata, haimavata, kalingaka, daradaka, kolasaraka, ushtraka*, etc., are poisons.

Likewise snakes and worms kept in pots are the group of poisons.

Skins are those of *godha* (alligator), *seraka* (?), *dvipi* (leopard), *simsumara* (porpoise), *simha* (lion), *vyaghra* (tiger), *hasti*, (elephant), *mahisha* (buffalo), *chamara* (*Bos grunniens*), *gomriga* (*Bos gavaeus*), and *gavaya* (the *gayal*).

Bones, bile (*pitta*), *snayu* (?), teeth, horn, hoofs and tails of the above animals as well as of other beasts, cattle, birds and snakes (*vyala*). *Kalayasa* (iron), *tamra* (copper), *vritta* (?), *kamsya* (bronze), *sisa* (lead), *trapu* (tin), *vaikrintaka* (mercury ?) and *arakuata* (brass) are metals.

Utensils (*bhanda*), are those made of cane, bark (*vidala*), and clay (*mrittika*).

Charcoal, bran and ashes are other things.

Menageries of beasts, cattle, and birds.

Collection of firewood and fodder.

The superintendent of forest produce shall carry on either inside or outside (the capital city) the manufacture of all kinds of articles which are necessary for life or for the defence of forts.

[Thus ends Chapter 17, 'The Superintendent of Forest Produce', in Book II, 'The Duties of Government Superintendents', of the Arthashastra of Kautilya. End of thirty-eighth chapter from the beginning.]

Chapter 18

THE SUPERINTENDENT OF ARMOURY

THE superintendent of the armoury shall employ experienced workmen of tried ability to manufacture in a given time and for fixed wages wheels, weapons, mail armour and other accessory instruments for use in battles, in the construction or defence of forts, or in destroying the cities or strongholds of enemies.

All these weapons and instruments shall be kept in places suitably prepared for them. They shall not only be frequently dusted and transferred from one place to another, but also be exposed to the sun. Such weapons as are likely to be affected by heat and vapour (*ushmopasneha*) and to be eaten by worms shall be kept in safe localities. They shall also be examined now and then with reference to the class to which they belong, their forms, their characteristics, their size, their source, their value and their total quantity.

Sarvatobhadra, *jamadagnya*, *bahumukha*, *visvasaghati*, *samghati*, *yanaka*, *parjanyaka*, *ardhabahu*, and *urdhvabahu* are immoveable machines (*sthirayantram*).

Panchalika, *devadanda*, *sukarika*, *musala*, *yashti*, *hastivaraka*, *talavrinta*, *mudgara*, *gada*, *spriktala*, *kuddala*, *asphatima*, *audhghatima*, *sataghni*, *trisula*, and *chakra* are moveable machines.

Sakti, *prasa*, *kunta*, *hataka*, *bhindivala*, *sula*, *tomara*, *varahakarna*, *kanaya*, *karpana*, *trasika*, and the like are weapons with edges like a ploughshare (*halamukhani*).

Bows made of *tala* (palmyra), of *chapa* (a kind of bamboo), of *daru* (a kind of wood), and *sringa* (bone or horn) are respectively called *karmuka*, *kodanda*, *druna*, and *dhanus*.

Bowstrings are made of *murva* (*Sansviera roxburghiana*), *arka* (*Catotropis gigantea*), *sana* (hemp), *gavedhu* (*Coix barbata*), *venu* (bamboo bark), and *snayu* (sinew).

Venu, *sara*, *salaka*, *dandasana*, and *naracha* are different kinds of arrows. The edges of arrows shall be so made of iron, bone or wood as to cut, rend or pierce.

Nistrimsa, *mandalagra*, and *asiyashti* are swords. The handles of swords are made of the horn of rhinoceros or buffalo, of the tusk of elephants, of wood, or of the root of bamboo.

Parasu, *kuthara*, *pattasa*, *khanitra*, *kuddala*, *chakra*, and *kandachchhedana* are razor-like weapons.

Yantrapashana, *goshpanapashana*, *mushtipashana*, *rochani* (mill-stone) and stones are other weapons (*ayudhani*).

Lohajalika, *patta*, *kavacha* and *sutraka* are varieties of armour made of iron or of skins with hoofs and horns of porpoise, rhinoceros, bison, elephant or cow.

Likewise *sirastrana* (cover for the head), *kanthatrana* (cover for the neck) *kurpasa* (cover for the trunk), *kanchuka* (a coat extending as far as the knee joints), *varavana* (a coat extending as far as the heels), *patta* (a coat without cover for the arms), and *nagodarika* (gloves) are varieties of armour.

Veti, *charma*, *hastikarna*, *talamula*, *dharmanika*, *kavata*, *kitika*, *apratihata*, and *valahakanta* are instruments used in self-defence (*avaranani*).

Ornaments for elephants, chariots and horses as well as goads and hooks to lead them in battlefields constitute accessory things (*upakaranani*).

(Besides the above) such other delusive and destructive contrivances (as are treated of in Book XIV) together with any other new inventions of expert workmen (shall also be kept in stock.)

The superintendent of armoury shall precisely ascertain the demand and supply of weapons, their application, their wear and tear, as well as their decay and loss.

[Thus ends Chapter 18, 'The Superintendent of the Armoury', in Book II, 'The Duties of Government Superintendents', of the Arthashastra of Kautilya. End of chapter thirty-ninth from the beginning.]

Chapter 19

THE SUPERINTENDENT OF WEIGHTS AND MEASURES

THE superintendent of weights and measures shall have the same manufactured.

10 seeds of *masha* (*Phraseolus radiatus*) or 5 seeds of *gunja* (*Cabrus precatorius*)	= 1 suvarna-masha.
16 *mashas*	= 1 *suvarna* or *karsha*.
4 *karshas*	= 1 *pala*.
88 white mustard seeds	= 1 silver *masha*.
16 silver *mashas* or 20 *saibya* seeds	= 1 dharana.
20 grains of rice	= 1 dharana of a diamond.

Ardhamasha (half a *masha*), one *masha*, two *mashas*, four *mashas*, eight *mashas*, one *suvarna*, two *suvarnas*, four *suvarnas*, eight *suvarnas*, ten *suvarnas*, twenty *suvarnas*, thirty *suvarnas*, forty *suvarnas* and one hundred *suvarnas* are different units of weights. Similar series of weights shall also be made in *dharanas*. Weights (*pratimanani*) shall be made of iron or of stones available in the countries of Magadha and Mekala; or of such things as will neither contract when wetted, nor expand under the influence of heat.

Beginning with a lever of six *angula*s in length and of one *pala* in the weight of its metallic mass, there shall be made ten (different) balances with levers successively increasing by one *pala* in the weight of their metallic masses, and by eight *angula*s in their length. A scale-pan shall be attached to each of them on one or both sides.

A balance called *samavritta*, with its lever 72-*angula*s long and weighing 53 *pala*s in its metallic mass shall also be made. A scalepan of 5 *pala*s in the weight of its metallic mass being attached to its edge, the horizontal position of the lever (*samakarana*) when weighing a *karsha* shall be marked (on that part of the lever where, held by a thread, it stands horizontal). To the left of that mark, symbols such as 1 *pala*, 12, 15 and 20 *pala*s shall be marked. After that, each place of tens up to 100 shall be marked. In the place of *Aksha*s, the sign of *Nandi* shall be marked.

Likewise a balance called *parimani* of twice as much metallic mass as that of *samavritta* and of 96 *angula*s in length shall be made. On its lever, marks such as 20, 50 and 100 above its initial weight of 100 shall be carved.

20 *tula*s	=	1 *bhara*.
10 *dharana*s	=	1 pala.
100 such *pala*s	=	1 ayamani (measure of royal income).

Public balance (*vyavaharika*), servants' balance (*bhajini*), and harem balance (*antahpurabhajini*) successively decrease by five *pala*s (compared with *ayamani*). A *pala* in each of the above successively falls short of the same in *ayamani* by half a *dharana*. The metallic mass of the levers of each of the above successively decreases in weight by two ordinary *pala*s and in length by six *angula*s.

Excepting flesh, metals, salt, and precious stones, an excess of five *pala*s (*prayama*) of all other commodities (shall be given to the king) when they are weighed in the two first-named balances.

A wooden balance with a lever 8 hands long, with measuring marks and counterpoise weights shall be erected on a pedestal like that of a peacock.

Twenty-five *pala*s of firewood will cook one *prastha* of rice.

This is the unit (for the calculation) of any greater or less quantity (of firewood). Thus weighing balance and weights are commented upon.

Then,

200 *palas* in the grains of *masha*	=	1 *drona* which is an *ayamana*, a measure of royal income.
187½ *palas* in the grains of *masha*	=	1 public *drona*.
175 *palas* in the grains of *masha*	=	1 *bhajaniya*, servants' measure.
162½ *palas* in the grains of *masha*	=	1 *antahpurabhajaniya*, harem measure.

Adhaka, *prastha* and *kudumba* are each ¼ of the one previously mentioned.

16 *dronas*	=	1 *vari*.
20 *dronas*	=	1 *kumbha*.
10 *kumbhas*	=	1 *vaha*.

Cubic measures shall be so made of dry and strong wood that when filled with grains, the conically heaped-up portion of the grains standing on the mouth of the measure is equal to one-fourth of the quantity of the grains (so measured); or the measures may also be so made that a quantity equal to the heaped-up portion can be contained within (the measure).

But liquids shall always be measured level to the mouth of the measure.

With regard to wine, flowers, fruits, bran, charcoal and slaked lime, twice the quantity of the heaped-up portion (i.e., one-fourth of the measure) shall be given in excess.

1¼ *panas* are the price of	a *drona*.
¾ pana is the price of	an *adhaka*.
6 *mashas* are the price of	a *prastha*.
1 *masha* is the price of	a *kudumba*.

The price of similar liquid measures is double the above.

20 *panas* is the price	of a set of counterweights.
6¼ *panas* is the price	of a *tula* (balance).

The superintendent shall charge 4 *mashas* for stamping weights or measures. A fine of 27¼ *panas* shall be imposed for using unstamped weights or measures.

Traders shall every day pay one *kakani* to the superintendent towards the charge of stamping the weights and measures.

Those who trade in clarified butter, shall give (to purchasers) 1/32 part more as *taptavyaji* (i.e., compensation for decrease in the quantity of ghee owing to its liquid condition). Those who trade in oil shall give 1/64 part more as *taptavyaji*.

(While selling liquids, traders) shall give 1/50 part more as *manasrava* (i.e., compensation for diminution in the quantity owing to its overflow or adhesion to the measuring can).

Half, one-fourth and one-eighth parts of the measure, *kumbha*, shall also be manufactured.

84 *kudumbas* of clarified butter are held to be equal to a *waraka* of the same;

64 *kudumbas* of clarified butter are held to be equal to make one *waraka* of oil (*taila*); and ¼ of a *waraka* is called *ghatika*, either of ghee or of oil.

[Thus ends Chapter 19, 'The Superintendent of Weights and Measures', in Book II, 'The Duties of Government Superintendents', of the Arthashastra of Kautilya. End of the fortieth chapter from the beginning.

Chapter 20

MEASUREMENT OF SPACE AND TIME

THE superintendent of lineal measure shall possess the knowledge of measuring space and time.

8 atoms (*paramanavah*) are equal to	1 particle thrown off by the wheel of a chariot.
8 particles are equal to	1 *liksha*.
8 *likshas* are equal to	the middle of a *yuka* (louse) or a *yuka* of medium size.
8 *yukas* are equal to	1 *yava* (barley) of middle size.
8 *yavas* are equal to	1 *angula* (¾ of an English inch) or the middlemost joint of the middle finger of a man of medium size may be taken to be equal to an *angula*.
4 *angulas* are equal to	1 *dhanurgraha*.
8 *angulas* are equal to	1 *dhanurmushti*.
12 *angulas* are equal to	1 *vitasti*, or 1 *chhayapaurusha*.
14 *angulas* are equal to	1 *sama*, *sala*, *pariraya*, or *pada*.
2 *vitastis* are equal to	1 aratni or 1 prajapatya hasta
2 *vitastis* plus 1 *dhanurmusti* are equal to	1 hasta used in measuring balances and cubic measures, and pasturelands.
2 *vitastis* plus 1 *dhanurmusti* are equal to	1 *kishku* or 1 *kamsa*.
42 *angulas* are equal to	1 *kishku* according to sawyers and blacksmiths and used in measuring the grounds for the encampment of the army, for forts and palaces.
54 *angulas* are equal to	1 *hasta* used in measuring timber forests.
84 *angulas* are equal to	1 *vyama*, used in measuring ropes and the depth of digging, in terms of a man's height.
4 *aratnis* are equal to	1 *danda*, 1 *dhanus*, 1 *nalika* and 1 *paurusha*.
108 *angulas* are equal to	1 *garhapatya dhanus* (i.e., a measure used by carpenters called *grihapati*). This measure is used in measuring roads and fort walls.

The same (108 *angulas*) are equal to	1 *paurusha*, a measure used in building sacrificial altars.
6 *kamsas* or 192 *angulas* are equal to	1 *danda*, used in measuring such lands as are gifted to Brahmans.
10 *dandas* are equal to	1 *rajju*.
2 *rajjus* are equal to	1 *paridesa* (square measure).
3 *rajjus* are equal to	1 *nivartana* (square measure).
The same (3 *rajjus*) plus 2 *dandas* on one side only are equal to	1 *bahu* (arm).
1,000 dhanus are equal to	1 *goruta* (sound of a cow).
4 *gorutas* are equal to	1 yojana.

Thus are the lineal and square measures dealt with.

Then with regard to the measures of time:

(The divisions of time are) a *truti*, *lava*, *nimesha*, *kashtha*, *kala*, *nalika*, *muhurta*, forenoon, afternoon, day, night, *paksha*, month, *ritu* (season), *ayana* (solstice); *samvatsara* (year), and *yuga*.

2 *trutis* are equal to	1 *lava*.
2 *lavas* are equal to	1 *nimesha*.
5 *nimeshas* are equal to	1 *kashtha*.
30 *kashthas* are equal to	1 *kala*.
40 *kalas* are equal to	1 *nalika*, or the time during which one *adhaka* of water passes out of a pot through an aperture of the same diameter as that of a wire of 4 *angulas* in length and made of 4 *mashas* of gold.
2 *nalikas* are equal to	1 *muhurta*.
15 *muhurtas* are equal	1 day or 1 night.

Such a day and night happen in the months of *Chaitra* and *Asvayuja*. Then after the period of six months it increases or diminishes by three *muhurta*s.

When the length of shadow is eight *paurusha*s (96 *angula*s), it is 1/18th part of the day.

When it is 6 *paurusha*s (72 *angula*s), it is 1/14th part of the day; when 4 *paurusha*s, 1/8th part; when 2 *paurusha*s, 1/6th part; when 1 paurusha, 1/4th part; when it is 8 *angula*s, 3/10th part (*trayodasabhagah*); when 4 *angula*s, 3/8th part; and when no shadow is cast, it is to be considered midday.

Likewise when the day declines, the same process in reverse order shall be observed.

It is in the month of *Ashadha* that no shadow is cast in midday. After *Ashadha*, during the six months from *Sravana* upwards, the length of shadow successively increases by two *angula*s and during the next six months from *Magha* upwards, it successively decreases by two *angula*s.

Fifteen days and nights together make up one *paksha*. That *paksha* during which the moon waxes is white (*sukla*) and that *paksha* during which the moon wanes is *bahula*.

Two pakshas make one month (*masa*). Thirty days and nights together make one work-a-month (*prakarmamasah*). The same (30 days and nights) with an additional half a day makes one solar month (*saura*).

The same (30) less by half a day makes one lunar month (*chandramasa*).

Twenty-seven (days and nights) make a sidereal month (*nakshatramasa*).

Once in thirty-two months there comes one *malamasa,* profane month, i.e., an extra month added to lunar year to harmonize it with the solar.

Once in thirty-five months there comes a *malamasa* for *asvavahas*.

Once in forty months there comes a *malamasa* for *hastivahas*.

Two months make one *ritu* (season).

Sravana and *Proshthapada* make the rainy season (*varsha*).

Asvayuja and *Kartika* make the autumn (*sarad*).

Margasirsha and *Pausha* make the winter (*hemanta*).

Magha and *Phalguna* make the dewy season (*sisira*).

Chaitra and *Vaisakha* make the spring (*vasanta*).
Jyeshthamuliya and *Ashadha* make the summer (*grishma*).

Seasons from sisira and upwards are the summer solstice (*uttarayana*), and (those) from *varsha* and upwards are the winter solstice (*dakshinayana*). Two solstices (*ayanas*) make one year (*samvatsara*). Five years make one yuga.

The sun carries off (*harati*) 1/60th of a whole day every day and thus makes one complete day in every two months (*ritau*). Likewise the moon (falls behind by 1/60th of a whole day every day and falls behind one day in every two months). Thus in the middle of every third year, they (the sun and the moon) make one *adhimasa*, additional month, first in the summer season and second at the end of five years.

[Thus ends Chapter 20, 'Measurement of Space and Time', in Book II, 'The Duties of Government Superintendents', of the Arthashastra of Kautilya. End of the forty-first chapter from the beginning.]

Chapter 21

THE SUPERINTENDENT OF TOLLS

THE superintendent of tolls shall erect near the large gate of the city both the toll house and its flag facing either the north or the south. When merchants with their merchandise arrive at the toll-gate, four or five collectors shall take down who the merchants are, whence they come, what amount of merchandise they have brought and where for the first time the seal mark (*abhijnanamudra*) has been made (on the merchandise).

Those whose merchandise has not been stamped with seal mark shall pay twice the amount of toll. For counterfeit seal they shall pay eight times the toll. If the seal mark is effaced or torn, (the merchants in question) shall be compelled to stand in *ghatikasthana*. When one kind of seal is used for another or when one kind of merchandise has been otherwise named (*namakrite*), the merchants shall pay a fine of 1¼ *pana*s for each load (*sapadapanikam vahanam dapayet*).

The merchandise being placed near the flag of the toll house, the merchants shall declare its quantity and price, cry out thrice, 'Who will purchase this quantity of merchandise for this amount of price', and hand over the same to those who demand it (for that price). When purchasers happen to bid for it, the enhanced amount of the price together with the toll on the merchandise shall be paid into the king's treasury. When under the fear of having to pay a heavy toll, the quantity or the price of merchandise is lowered, the excess shall be taken by the king or the merchants shall be made to pay eight times the toll. The same punishment shall be imposed when the price of the merchandise packed in bags is lowered by showing an inferior sort as its sample or when valuable merchandise is covered over with a layer of an inferior one.

When under the fear of bidders (enhancing the price), the price of any merchandise is increased beyond its proper value, the king shall receive the enhanced amount or twice the amount of toll on it. The same punishment or eight times the amount of toll shall be imposed on the superintendent of tolls if he conceals (merchandise).

Hence commodities shall be sold only after they are precisely weighed, measured or numbered.

With regard to inferior commodities as well as those which are to be let off free of toll, the amount of toll due shall be determined after careful consideration.

Those merchants who pass beyond the flag of the toll house without paying the toll shall be fined eight times the amount of the toll due from them.

Those who pass by to and from (the city) shall ascertain (whether or not toll has been paid on any merchandise going along the road.)

Commodities intended for marriages, or taken by a bride from her parents' house to her husband's (*anvayanam*), or intended for presentation, or taken for the purpose of sacrificial performance, confinement of women, worship of gods, ceremony of tonsure, investiture of sacred thread, gift of cows (*godana*, made before marriage), any religious rite, consecration ceremony (*diksha*), and other special ceremonials shall be let off free of toll.

Those who utter a lie shall be punished as thieves.

Those who smuggle a part of merchandise on which toll has not been paid with that on which toll has been paid as well as those who, with a view to smuggle with one pass a second portion of merchandise, put it along with the stamped merchandise after breaking open the bag shall forfeit the smuggled quantity and pay as much fine as is equal to the quantity so smuggled.

He who, falsely swearing by cow dung, smuggles merchandise, shall be punished with the highest amercement.

When a person imports such forbidden articles as weapons (*sastra*), mail armour, metals, chariots, precious stones, grains and cattle, he shall not only be punished as laid down elsewhere, but also be made to forfeit his merchandise. When any of such commodities has been brought in for sale, they shall be sold, free of toll far outside (the fort).

The officer in charge of boundaries (*antapala*) shall receive a *pana* and a quarter as road cess (*vartani*) on each load of merchandise (*panyavahanasya*).

He shall levy a *pana* on a single-hoofed animal, half a *pana* on each head of cattle, and a quarter on a minor quadruped.

He shall also receive a *masha* on a head load of merchandise.

He shall also make good whatever has been lost by merchants (in the part of the country under his charge).

After carefully examining foreign commodities as to their superior or inferior quality and stamping them with his seal, he shall send the same to the superintendent of tolls.

Or he may send to the king a spy in the guise of a trader with information as to the quantity and quality of the merchandise. (Having received this information,) the king shall in turn send it to the superintendent of tolls in view of exhibiting the king's omniscient power. The superintendent shall tell the merchants (in question) that such and such a merchant has brought such and such amount of superior or inferior merchandise, which none can possibly hide, and that that information is due to the omniscient power of the king.

For hiding inferior commodities, eight times the amount of toll shall be imposed; and for hiding or concealing superior commodities, they shall be wholly confiscated.

Whatever causes harm or is useless to the country shall be shut out; and whatever is of immense good as well as seeds not easily available shall be let in free of toll.

[Thus ends Chapter 21, 'The Superintendent of Tolls', in Book II, 'The Duties of Government Superintendents', of the Arthashastra of Kautilya. End of the forty-second chapter from the beginning.]

Chapter 22

REGULATION OF TOLL DUES

MERCHANDISE, external (*bahyam*, i.e., arriving from country parts), internal (*abhyantaram*, i.e., manufactured inside forts), or foreign (*atithyani*, *i.e.*, imported from foreign countries) shall all be liable to the payment of toll alike when exported (*nishkramya*) and imported (*pravesyam*).

Imported commodities shall pay 1/5th of their value as toll.

Of flower, fruit, vegetables (*saka*), roots (*mula*), bulbous roots (*kanda*), *pallikya* (?), seeds, dried fish, and dried meat, the superintendent shall receive 1/6th as toll.

As regards conch-shells, diamonds, precious stones, pearls, corals and necklaces, experts acquainted with the time, cost and finish of the production of such articles shall fix the amount of toll.

Of fibrous garments (*kshauma*), cotton cloths (*dukula*), silk (*krimitana*), mail armour (*kankata*), sulphurate of arsenic (*haritala*), red arsenic (*manassila*), vermilion (*hingulaka*), metals (*loha*), and colouring ingredients (*varnadhatu*); of sandal, brown sandal (*agaru*), pungents (*katuka*), ferments (*kinva*), dress (*avarana*), and the like; of wine, ivory, skins, raw materials used in making fibrous or cotton garments, carpets, curtains (*pravarana*), and products yielded by worms (*krimijata*); and of wool and other products yielded by goats and sheep, he shall receive 1/10th or 1/15th as toll.

Of cloths (*vastra*), quadrupeds, bipeds, threads, cotton, scents, medicines, wood, bamboo, fibres (*valkala*), skins, and clay pots; of grains, oils, sugar (*kshara*), salt, liquor (*madya*) cooked rice and the like, he shall receive 1/20th or 1/25th as toll.

Gate dues (*dvaradeya*) shall be 1/5th of toll dues; this tax may be remitted if circumstances necessitate such favour. Commodities shall never be sold where they are grown or manufactured.

When minerals and other commodities are purchased from mines, a fine of 600 *panas* shall be imposed.

When flower or fruits are purchased from flower or fruit gardens, a fine of 54 *panas* shall be imposed.

When vegetables, roots, bulbous roots are purchased from vegetable gardens, a fine 51¾ *panas* shall be imposed.

When any kind of grass or grain is purchased from field, a fine of 53 *panas* shall be imposed.

(Permanent) fines of 1 *pana* and 1½ *panas* shall be levied on agricultural produce (*sitatyayah*).

Hence in accordance with the customs of countries or of communities, the rate of toll shall be fixed on commodities, either old or new; and fines shall be fixed in proportion to the gravity of offences.

[Thus ends Chapter 22, 'Regulation of Toll Dues', in Book II, 'The Duties of Government Superintendents', of the Arthashastra of Kautilya. End of the forty-third chapter from the beginning.]

Chapter 23

SUPERINTENDENT OF WEAVING

THE superintendent of weaving shall employ qualified persons to manufacture threads (*sutra*), coats (*varma*), cloths (*vastra*), and ropes.

Widows, cripple women, girls, mendicant or ascetic women (*pravrajita*), women compelled to work in default of paying fines (*dandapratikarini*), mothers of prostitutes, old women-servants of the king, and prostitutes (*devadasi*) who have ceased to attend temples on service shall be employed to cut wool, fibre, cotton, panicle (*tula*), hemp and flax.

Wages shall be fixed according as the threads spun are fine, coarse (*sthula*, i.e., big) or of middle quality and in proportion to a greater or less quantity manufactured, and in consideration of the quantity of thread spun, those (who turn out a greater quantity) shall be presented with oil and dried cakes of myrobalan fruits (*tailamalakodvartanaih*).

They may also be made to work on holidays (*tithishu*) by payment of special rewards (*prativapadanamanaih*).

Wages shall be cut short, if making allowance for the quality of raw material, the quantity of the threads spun out is found to fall short.

Weaving may also be done by those artisans who are qualified to turn out a given amount of work in a given time and for a fixed amount of wages.

The superintendent shall closely associate with the workmen.

Those who manufacture fibrous cloths, raiments, silkcloths, woollen cloths and cotton fabrics shall be rewarded by presentations such as scents, garlands of flowers, or any other prizes of encouragement.

Various kinds of garments, blankets and curtains shall be manufactured.

Those who are acquainted with the work shall manufacture mail armour.

Those women who do not stir out of their houses (*anishkasinyah*), those whose husbands are gone abroad, and those who are cripple or girls may, when obliged to work for subsistence, be provided with work (spinning out threads) in due courtesy through the medium of maidservants (of the weaving establishment.)

Those women who can present themselves at the weaving house shall at dawn be enabled to exchange their spinnings for wages (*bhandavetanavinimayam*). Only so much light as is enough to examine the threads shall be kept. If the superintendent looks at the face of such women or talks about any other work, he shall be punished with the first amercement. Delay in paying the wages shall be punished with the middlemost amercement. Likewise when wages are paid for work that is not completed.

She who, having received wages, does not turn out the work shall have her thumb cut off.

Those who misappropriate, steal or run away with (the raw material supplied to them) shall be similarly punished.

Weavers, when guilty, shall be fined out of their wages in proportion to their offences.

The superintendent shall closely associate with those who manufacture ropes and mail armour and shall carry on the manufacture of straps (*varatra*) and other commodities.

He shall carry on the manufacture of ropes from threads and fibres and of straps from cane and bamboo bark, with which beasts for draught are trained or tethered.

[Thus ends Chapter 23, 'The Superintendent of Weaving', in Book II, 'The Duties of Government Superintendents', of the Arthashastra of Kautilya. End of the forty-fourth chapter from the beginning.]

Chapter 24

THE SUPERINTENDENT OF AGRICULTURE

POSSESSED of the knowledge of the science of agriculture dealing with the plantation of bushes and trees (*krishitantragulmavrikshshayurvedajnah*), or assisted by those who are trained in such sciences, the superintendent of agriculture shall in time collect the seeds of all kinds of grains, flowers, fruits, vegetables, bulbous roots, roots, *pallikya* (?), fibre-producing plants and cotton.

He shall employ slaves, labourers and prisoners (*dandapratikartri*) to sow the seeds on crown lands which have been often and satisfactorily ploughed.

The work of the above men shall not suffer on account of any want in ploughs (*karshanayantra*) and other necessary instruments or of bullocks. Nor shall there be any delay in procuring to them the assistance of blacksmiths, carpenters, borers (*medaka*), rope makers, as well as those who catch snakes, and similar persons.

Any loss due to the above persons shall be punished with a fine equal to the loss.

The quantity of rain that falls in the country of *jangala* is 16 *dronas*; half as much more in moist countries (*anupanam*); as to the countries which are fit for agriculture (*desavapanam*);—13½ *drona*s in the country of *asmaka*s; 23 *drona*s in *avanti*; and an immense quantity in western countries (*aparantanam*), the borders of the Himalayas, and the countries where water channels are made use of in agriculture (*kulyavapanam*).

When one-third of the requisite quantity of rain falls both during the commencement and closing months of the rainy season and two-thirds in the middle, the rainfall is (considered) very even (*sushumarupam*).

A forecast of such rainfall can be made by observing the position, motion and pregnancy (*garbhdhana*) of Jupiter (Brihaspati), the rise and set and motion of Venus, and the natural or unnatural aspect of Sun.

From Sun, the sprouting of seeds can be inferred; from (the position of) Jupiter, the formation of grains (*stambakarita*) can be inferred; and from the movements of Venus, rainfall can be inferred.

Three are the clouds that continuously rain for seven days; eighty are they that pour minute drops; and sixty are they that appear with the sunshine—this is termed rainfall. Where rain, free from wind and unmingled with sunshine, falls so as to render three turns of ploughing possible, there the reaping of good harvest is certain.

Hence, i.e., according as the rainfall is more or less, the superintendent shall sow the seeds which require either more or less water.

Sali (a kind of rice), *vrihi* (rice), *kodrava* (*Paspalum scrobiculatum*), *tila* (sesamum), *priyangu* (panic seeds), *daraka* (?), and *varaka* (*Phraseolus trilobus*) are to be sown at the commencement (*purvavapah*) of the rainy season.

Mudga (*Phraseolus mungo*), *masha* (*Phraseolus radiatus*) and *saibya* (?) are to be sown in the middle of the season.

Kusumbha (safflower), *masura* (*Ervum hirsutum*), *kuluttha* (*Dolichos uniflorus*), *yava* (barley), *godhuma* (wheat), *kalaya* (leguminus seeds), *atasi* (linseed) and *sarshapa* (mustard) are to be sown last.

Or seeds may be sown according to the changes of the season.

Fields that are left unsown (*vapatiriktam*, i.e., owing to the inadequacy of hands) may be brought under cultivation by employing those who cultivate for half the share in the produce (*ardhasitika*); or those who live by their own physical exertion (*svaviryopajivinah*) may cultivate such fields for ¼th or ⅕th of the produce grown; or they may pay (to the king) as much as they can without entailing any hardship upon themselves (*anavasitam bhagam*), with the exception of their own private lands that are difficult to cultivate.

Thosewhocultivateirrigatingbymanuallabour(*hastapravartimam*) shall pay ⅕th of the produce as water-rate (*udakabhagam*); by carrying water on shoulders (*skandhapravartimam*) ¼th of the produce; by water lifts (*srotoyantrapravartimam*), ⅓ rd of the produce; and by raising water from rivers, lakes, tanks, and wells (*nadisarastatakakupodghatam*), ⅓rd or ¼th of the produce.

The superintendent shall grow wet crops (*kedara*), winter crops (*haimana*), or summer crops (*graishmika*) according to the supply of workmen and water.

Rice crops and the like are the best (*jyashtha*, i.e., to grow); vegetables (*shanda*) are of intermediate nature; and sugarcane crops (*ikshu*) are the worst (*pratyavarah*, i.e., very difficult to grow), for they are subject to various evils and require much care and expenditure to reap.

Lands that are beaten by foam (*phenaghatah*, i.e., banks of rivers, etc.), are suitable for growing *valliphala* (pumpkin, gourd and the like); lands that are frequently overflown by water (*parivahanta*) for long pepper, grapes (*mridvika*), and sugar cane; the vicinity of wells for vegetables and roots; low grounds (*hariniparyantah*) for green crops; and marginal furrows between any two rows of crops are suitable for the plantation of fragrant plants, medicinal herbs, cascus roots (*usinara*), *hira* (?), *beraka* (?), and *pindaluka* (lac) and the like.

Such medicinal herbs as grow in marshy grounds are to be grown not only in grounds suitable for them, but also in pots (*sthalyam*).

The seeds of grains are to be exposed to mist and heat (*tusharapayanamushnam cha*) for seven nights; the seeds of *kosi* are treated similarly for three nights; the seeds of sugar cane and the like (*kandabijanam*) are plastered at the cut end with the mixture of honey, clarified butter, the fat of hogs, and cow dung; the seeds of bulbous roots (*kanda*) with honey and clarified butter; cotton seeds (*asthibija*) with cow dung; and water pits at the root of trees are to be burnt and manured with the bones and dung of cows on proper occasions.

The sprouts of seeds, when grown, are to be manured with a fresh haul of minute fishes and irrigated with the milk of *snuhi* (*Euphorbia antiquorum*).

Where there is the smoke caused by burning the essence of cotton seeds and the slough of a snake, snakes will not stay.

Always while sowing seeds, a handful of seeds bathed in water with a piece of gold shall be sown first and the following mantra recited:–

> "Prajapataya Kashyapa devaya namah. Sada sita medhyatam
> devi bijeshu cha dhaneshu cha.
> Chandavata he."
>
> "Salutation to God Prajapati Kasyapa.
> Agriculture may always flourish and
> the Goddess (may reside) in seeds and wealth."

Provisions shall be supplied to watchmen, slaves and labourers in proportion to the amount of work done by them.

They shall be paid a *pana* and a quarter per mensem. Artisans shall be provided with wages and provision in proportion to the amount of work done by them.

Those that are learned in the Vedas and those that are engaged in making penance may take from the fields ripe flowers and fruits for the purpose of worshipping their gods, and rice and barley for the purpose of performing *agrayana*, a sacrificial performance at the commencement of harvest season, also those who live by gleaning grains in fields may gather grains where grains had been accumulated and removed from.

Grains and other crops shall be collected as often as they are harvested. No wise man shall leave anything in the fields, nor even chaff. Crops, when reaped, shall be heaped up in high piles or in the form of turrets. The piles of crops shall not be kept close, nor shall their tops be small or low. The threshing floors of different fields shall be situated close to each other. Workmen in the fields shall always have water but no fire.

[Thus ends Chapter 24, 'The Superintendent of Agriculture', in Book II, 'The Duties of Government Superintendents', of the Arthashastra of Kautilya. End of the forty-fifth chapter from the beginning.]

Chapter 25

THE SUPERINTENDENT OF LIQUOR

BY employing such men as are acquainted with the manufacture of liquor and ferments (*kinva*), the superintendent of liquor shall carry on liquor traffic not only in forts and country parts, but also in camps.

In accordance with the requirements of demand and supply (*krayavikrayavasena*) he may either centralize or decentralize the sale of liquor.

A fine of 600 *panas* shall be imposed on all offenders other than those who are manufacturers, purchasers or sellers in liquor traffic.

Liquor shall not be taken out of villages, nor shall liquor shops be close to each other.

Lest workmen spoil the work in hand, and Aryas violate their decency and virtuous character, and lest firebrands commit indiscreet acts, liquor shall be sold to persons of well-known character in such small quantities as one-fourth or half a *kudumba*, one *kudumba*, half a *prastha*, or one *prastha*. Those who are well known and of pure character may take liquor out of shop.

Or all may be compelled to drink liquor within the shops and not allowed to stir out at once in view of detecting articles such as sealed deposits, unsealed deposits, commodities given for repair, stolen articles, and the like which the customer's may have acquired by foul means. When they are found to possess gold and other articles not their own, the superintendent shall contrive to cause them to be arrested outside the shop. Likewise those who are too extravagant or spend beyond their income shall be arrested.

No fresh liquor other than bad liquor shall be sold below its price. Bad liquor may be sold elsewhere or given to slaves or workmen in lieu of wages; or it may form the drink of beasts for draught or the subsistence of hogs.

Liquor shops shall contain many rooms provided with beds and seats kept apart. The drinking room shall contain scents, garlands of flowers, water, and other comfortable things suitable to the varying seasons.

Spies stationed in the shops shall ascertain whether the expenditure incurred by customers in the shop is ordinary or extraordinary and also whether there are any strangers. They shall also ascertain the value of the dress, ornaments and gold of the customers lying there under intoxication.

When customers under intoxication lose any of their things, the merchants of the shop shall not only make good the loss but also pay an equivalent fine.

Merchants seated in half-closed rooms shall observe the appearance of local and foreign customers who, in real or false guise of Aryas lie down in intoxication along with their beautiful mistresses.

Of various kinds of liquor such as *medaka*, *prasanna*, *asava*, *arista*, *maireya* and *madhu*:

Medaka is manufactured with one *drona* of water, half an *adaka* of rice, and three *prasthas* of *kinva* (ferment).

Twelve *adakas* of flour (*pishta*), five *prasthas* of *kinva* (ferment), with the addition of spices (*jatisambhara*) together with the bark and fruits of *putraka* (a species of tree) constitute *prasanna*.

One hundred *palas* of *kapittha* (*Feronia elephantum*) 500 *palas* of *phanita* (sugar), and one *prastha* of honey (*madhu*) form *asava*.

With an increase of one quarter of the above ingredients, a superior kind of *asava* is manufactured; and when the same ingredients are lessened to the extent of one quarter each, it becomes of an inferior quality.

The preparation of various kinds of *arishta* for various diseases are to be learnt from physicians.

A sour gruel or decoction of the bark of *meshasringi* (a kind of poison) mixed with jaggery (*guda*) and with the powder of long pepper and black pepper or with the powder of *triphala* (*Terminalia chebula, Terminalia bellerica and Phyllanthus emblica*) forms *Maireya.*

To all kinds of liquor mixed with jaggery, the powder of *triphala* is always added.

The juice of grapes is termed *madhu.* Its own native place (*svadesa*) is the commentary on such of its various forms as *kapisayana* and *harahuraka.*

One *drona* of either boiled or unboiled paste of *masha* (*Phraseolus radiatus*), three parts more of rice, and one *karsha* of *morata* (*Alangium hexapetalum*) and the like form *kinva* (ferment).

In the manufacture of *medaka* and *prasanna,* five *karsha*s of the powder of each of *patha* (*Clypea hermandifolio*), *lodhra* (*Symplocos racemosa*), *tejovati* (*Piper chaba*), *elavaluka* (*Solanum melongena*) honey, the juice of grapes (*madhurasa*), *priyangu* (panic seeds), *daruharidra* (a species of turmeric) black pepper and long pepper are added as *sambhara,* requisite spices.

The decoction of *madhuka* (*Bassia latifolia*) mixed with granulated sugar (*katasarkara*), when added to *prasanna,* gives it a pleasing colour.

The requisite quantity of spices to be added to *asava* is one *karsha* of the powder of each of *chocha* (bark of cinnamon), *chitraka* (*Plumbago zeylanica*), *vilanga,* and *gajapippali* (*Scindapsus officinalis*), and two *karsha*s of the powder of each of *kramuka* (betel nut), *madhuka* (*Bassia latifolia*), *musta* (*Cyprus rotundus*) and *lodhra* (*Symlocos racemosa*).

The addition of one-tenth of the above ingredients (i.e., *chocha, kramuka,* etc.), is (termed) *bijabandha.*

The same ingredients as are added to *prasanna* are also added to white liquor (*svetasura*).

The liquor that is manufactured from mango fruits (*sahakarasura*) may contain a greater proportion of mango essence (*rasottara*), or of spices (*bijottara*). It is called *mahasura* when it contains *sambhara* (spices as described above).

When a handful (*antarnakho mushtih,* i.e., so much as can be held in the hand, the fingers being so bent that the nails cannot be seen) of the powder of granulated sugar dissolved in the decoction of *morata* (*Alangium hexapetalum*), *palasa* (*Butea frondosa*), *dattura* (*Dattura fastuosa*), *karanja* (*Robinia mitis*), *meshasringa* (a kind of poison) and the bark of milky trees (*kshiravriksha*) mixed with one-half of the paste formed by combining the powders of *lodhra* (*Symplocos racemosa*), *chitraka* (*Plumbago zeylanica*), *vilanga*, *patha* (*clypea hermandifolia*), *musta* (*cyprus rotundus*), *kalaya* (leguminous seeds), *daruharidra* (*Amonum xanthorrhizon*), *indivara* (blue lotus), *satapushpa* (*Anethum sowa*), *apamarga* (*Achyranthes aspera*) *saptaparna* (*Echites scholaris*), and *nimba* (*Nimba melia*) is added to (even) a *kumbha* of liquor payable by the king, it renders it very pleasant. Five *pala*s of *phanita* (sugar) are added to the above in order to increase its flavour.

On special occasions (*krityeshu*), people (*kutumbinah*, i.e., families) shall be allowed to manufacture white liquor (*svetasura*), *arishta* for use in diseases, and other kinds of liquor.

On the occasions of festivals, fairs (*samaja*), and pilgrimage, right of manufacture of liquor for four days (*chaturahassaurikah*) shall be allowed.

The superintendent shall collect the daily fines (*daivasikamatyayam*, i.e., licence fees) from those who on these occasions are permitted to manufacture liquor.

Women and children shall collect '*sura*', and '*kinva*', 'ferment'.

Those who deal with liquor other than that of the king shall pay five percent as toll.

With regard to *sura*, *medaka*, *arishta*, wine, *phalamla* (acid drinks prepared from fruits), and *amlasidhu* (spirit distilled from molasses):

Having ascertained the day's sale of the above kinds of liquor, the difference of royal and public measures (*manavyaji*), and the excessive amount of sale proceeds realized thereby, the superintendent shall fix the amount of compensation (*vaidharana*) due to the king (from local or foreign merchants for entailing loss on the king's liquor traffic) and shall always adopt the best course.

[Thus ends Chapter 25, 'The Superintendent of Liquor', in Book II, 'The Duties of Government superintendents', of the Arthashastra of Kautilya. End of the forty-sixth chapter from the beginning.]

Chapter 26

THE SUPERINTENDENT OF SLAUGHTERHOUSE

WHEN a person entraps, kills or molests deer, bison, birds and fish which are declared to be under state protection or which live in forests under state protection (*abhayaranya*), he shall be punished with the highest amercement.

Householders trespassing in forest preserves shall be punished with the middlemost amercement.

When a person entraps, kills or molests either fish or birds that do not prey upon other animals, he shall be fined 26¾ *panas*; and when he does the same to deer and other beasts, he shall be fined twice as much.

Of beasts of prey that have been captured, the superintendent shall take one-sixth; of fish and birds (of similar nature), he shall take one-tenth or more than one-tenth; and of deer and other beasts (*mrigapasu*), one-tenth or more than one-tenth as toll.

One-sixth of live animals such as birds and beasts shall be let off in forests under state protection.

Elephants, horses or animals having the form of a man, bull or an ass living in oceans as well as fish in tanks, lakes, channels and rivers; and such game birds as *krauncha* (a kind of heron), *utkrosaka* (osprey), *datyuha* (a sort of cuckoo), *hamsa* (flamingo), *chakravaka* (a brahmany duck), *jivanjivaka* (a kind of pheasant), *bhringaraja* (*Lanius malabaricus*), *chakora* (partridge), *mattakokila* (cuckoo), peacock, parrot, and maina (*madanasarika*) as well as other auspicious animals, whether birds or beasts, shall be protected from all kinds of molestations.

Those who violate the above rule shall be punished with the first amercement.

(Butchers) shall sell fresh and boneless flesh of beasts (*mrigapasu*) just killed.

If they sell bony flesh, they shall give an equivalent compensation (*pratipakam*).

If there is any diminution in weight owing to the use of a false balance, they shall give eight times the diminution.

Cattle such as a calf, a bull, or a milch cow shall not be slaughtered.

He who slaughters or tortures them to death shall be fined 50 *panas*.

The flesh of animals which have been killed outside the slaughterhouse (*parisunam*), headless, legless and boneless flesh, rotten flesh, and the flesh of animals which have suddenly died shall not be sold. Otherwise a fine of 12 *panas* shall be imposed.

Cattle, wild beasts, elephants (*vyala*), and fish living in forests under state protection shall, if they become of vicious nature, be entrapped and killed outside the forest preserve.

[Thus ends Chapter 26, 'The Superintendent of Slaughterhouse', in Book II, 'The Duties of Government Superintendents', of the Arthashastra of Kautilya. End of the forty-seventh chapter from the beginning.]

Chapter 27

THE SUPERINTENDENT OF PROSTITUTES

THE superintendent of prostitutes shall employ (at the king's court) on a salary of 1,000 *panas* (per annum) a prostitute (*ganika*), whether born or not born of a prostitute's family, and noted for her beauty, youth, and accomplishments.

A rival prostitute (*pratiganika*) on half the above salary (*kutumbardhena*) shall also be appointed.

Whenever such a prostitute goes abroad or dies, her daughter or sister shall act for her and receive her property and salary. Or her mother may substitute another prostitute. In the absence of any of these, the king himself shall take the property.

With a view to adding to the splendour of prostitutes holding the royal umbrella, golden pitcher and fan, and attending upon the king seated on his royal litter, throne or chariot, prostitutes shall be classified as of first, middle and highest rank according to their beauty and splendid jewellery; likewise their salary shall be fixed by thousands.

She who has lost her beauty shall be appointed as a nurse (*matrika*).

A prostitute shall pay 24,000 *panas* as ransom to regain her liberty; and a prostitute's son 12,000 *panas*.

From the age of eight years, a prostitute shall hold musical performance before the king.

Those prostitutes, female slaves, and old women who are incapable of rendering any service in the form of enjoyment (*bhagnabhogah*) shall work in the storehouse or kitchen of the king.

A prostitute who, putting herself under the protection of a private person, ceases to attend the king's court shall pay a *pana* and a quarter per mensem (to the government).

The superintendent shall determine the earnings, inheritance, income (*aya*), expenditure and future earnings (*ayati*) of every prostitute.

He shall also check their extravagant expenditure.

When a prostitute puts her jewellery in the hands of any person but her mother, she shall be fined 4¼ *panas*.

If she sells or mortgages her property (*svapateyam*), she shall be fined 50¼ *panas*.

A prostitute shall be fined 24 *panas* for defamation; twice as much for causing hurt; and 50¼ *panas* as well as 1½ *panas* for cutting off the ear (of any person).

When a man has connection with a prostitute against her will or with a prostitute girl (*kumari*), he shall be punished with the highest amercement. But when he has connection with a willing prostitute, (under age), he shall be punished with the first amercement.

When a man keeps under confinement, or abducts, a prostitute against her will, or disfigures her by causing hurt, he shall be fined 1,000 *panas* or more rising up to twice the amount of her ransom (*nishkraya*) according to the circumstances of the crime and the position and the status of the prostitute (*sthanaviseshena*).

When a man causes hurt to a prostitute appointed at the court (*praptadhikaram*), he shall be fined thrice the amount of her ransom.

When a man causes hurt to a prostitute's mother, to her young daughter, or to a *rupadasi*, he shall be punished with the highest amercement.

In all cases of offences, punishment for offences committed for the first time shall be the first amercement; twice as much for offences committed for a second time; thrice as much for the third time; and for offences committed for the fourth time, the king may impose any punishment he likes.

When a prostitute does not yield her person to anyone under the orders of the king, she shall receive 1,000 lashes with a whip or pay a fine of 5,000 *pana*s.

When having received the requisite amount of fees, a prostitute dislikes to yield her person, she shall be fined twice the amount of the fees.

When, in her own house, a prostitute deprives her paramour of his enjoyment, she shall be fined eight times the amount of the fees unless the paramour happens to be unassociable on account of disease and personal defects.

When a prostitute murders her paramour, she shall be burnt alive or thrown into water.

When a paramour steals the jewellery or money of, or deceives to pay the fees due to, a prostitute, he shall be fined eight times that amount.

Every prostitute shall supply information to the superintendent as to the amount of her daily fees (*bhoga*), her future income (*ayati*), and the paramour (under her influence).

The same rules shall apply to an actor, dancer, singer, player on musical instruments, a buffoon (*vagjivana*), a mimic player (*kusilava*), rope dancer (*plavaka*), a juggler (*saubhika*), a wandering bard or herald (*charana*), pimps and unchaste women.

When persons of the above description come from foreign countries to hold their performances, they shall pay 5 *pana*s as license fee (*prekshavetana*).

Every prostitute (*rupajiva*) shall pay every month twice the amount of a day's earning (*bhogadvigunam*) to the government.

Those who teach prostitutes, female slaves and actresses arts such as singing, playing on musical instruments, reading, dancing, acting, writing, painting, playing on the instruments like *vina*, pipe, and drum, reading the thoughts of others, manufacture of scents and garlands, shampooing, and the art of attracting and captivating the mind of others shall be endowed with maintenance from the state.

They (the teachers) shall train the sons of prostitutes to be chief actors (*rangopajivi*) on the stage.

The wives of actors and others of similar profession who have been taught various languages and the use of signals (*sanja*) shall, along with their relatives, be made use of in detecting the wicked and murdering or deluding foreign spies.

[Thus ends Chapter 27, 'The Superintendent of Prostitutes', in Book II, 'The Duties of Government Superintendents', of the Arthashastra of Kautilya. End of the forty-eighth chapter from the beginning.]

Chapter 28

THE SUPERINTENDENT OF SHIPS

THE superintendent of ships shall examine the accounts relating to navigation not only on oceans and mouths of rivers, but also on lakes, natural or artificial, and rivers in the vicinity of *sthaniya* and other fortified cities.

Villages on seashores or on the banks of rivers and lakes shall pay a fixed amount of tax (*kliptam*).

Fishermen shall give ⅙th of their haul as fees for fishing licence (*naukahatakam*).

Merchants shall pay the customary toll levied in port towns.

Passengers arriving on board the king's ship shall pay the requisite amount of sailing fees (*yatravetanam*).

Those (who make use of the king's boats in) fishing out conch shells and pearls shall pay the requisite amount of hire (*Naukahatakam*), or they may make use of their own boats.

The duties of the superintendent of mines will explain those of the superintendent of conch shells and pearls.

The superintendent of ships shall strictly observe the customs prevalent in commercial towns as well as the orders of the superintendent of towns (*pattana*, port town).

Whenever a weatherbeaten ship arrives at a port town, he shall show fatherly kindness to it.

Vessels carrying on merchandise spoiled by water may either be exempted from toll or may have their toll reduced to half and let to sail when the time for setting sail approaches. Ships that touch at harbours on their way may be requested the payment of toll.

Pirate ships (*himsrika*), vessels which are bound for the country of an enemy, as well as those which have violated the customs and rules in force in port towns shall be destroyed.

In those large rivers which cannot be forded even during the winter and summer seasons, there shall be launched large boats (*mahanavah*) provided with a captain (*sasaka*), a steersman (*niyamaka*), and servants to hold the sickle and the ropes and to pour out water.

Small boats shall be launched in those small rivers which overflow during the rainy season.

Fording or crossing the rivers (without permission) shall be prohibited lest traitors may cross them (and escape).

When a person fords or crosses a river outside the proper place and in unusual times, he shall be punished with the first amercement.

When a man fords or crosses a river at the usual place and time without permission, he shall be fined 26¾ *pana*s.

Fishermen, carriers of firewood, grass, flowers, and fruits, gardeners, vegetable dealers, herdsmen, persons pursuing suspected criminals, messengers following other messengers going in advance, servants engaged to carry things, provisions and orders to the army, those who use their own ferries, as well as those who supply villages of marshy districts with seeds, necessaries of life, commodities and other accessary things shall be exempted (to cross rivers at any time and place).

Brahmans, ascetics (*pravrajita*), children, the aged, the afflicted, royal messengers, and pregnant women shall be provided by the superintendent with free passes to cross rivers.

Foreign merchants who have often been visiting the country as well as those who are well known to local merchants shall be allowed to land in port towns.

Any person who is abducting the wife or daughter of another, one who is carrying off the wealth of another, a suspected person, one who seems to be of perturbed appearance, one who has no baggage, one who attempts to conceal or evade the cognisance of the valuable load in one's hand, one who has just put on a different garb, one who has removed or renounced one's usual garb, one who has just turned out an ascetic, one who pretends to be suffering from disease, one who seems to be alarmed, one who is stealthily carrying valuable things, or going on a secret mission, or carrying weapons or explosives (*agniyoga*), one who holds poison in one's hand, and one who has come from a long distance without a pass shall all be arrested.

A minor quadruped as well as a man carrying some load shall pay one *masha*.

A head load, a load carried on shoulders (*kayabharah*), a cow, and a horse shall each pay 2 *masha*s.

A camel and a buffalo shall each pay 4 *masha*s.

A small cart (*laghuyana*)5 *mashas*; and a cart (of medium size) drawn by bulls (*golingam*) shall pay 6 *masha*s and a big cart (*sakata*) 7 *masha*s.

A head load of merchandise ¼ *mash*a; this explains other kinds of loads. In big rivers, ferry-fees are double the above. Villages near marshy places shall give (to the ferry men) the prescribed amount of foodstuff and wages.

In boundaries, ferry men shall receive the toll, carriage cess, and road cess. They shall also confiscate the property of the person travelling without a pass. The superintendent of boats shall make good the loss caused by the loss of the boat due to the heavy load, sailing in improper time or place, want of ferry-men, or lack of repair. Boats should be launched between the months of *Ashadha*, the first seven days being omitted, and *Kartika*; the evidence of a ferry man should be given and the daily income should be remitted.

[Thus ends Chapter 28, 'The Superintendent of Ships', in Book II, 'The Duties of Government Superintendents', of the Arthashastra of Kautilya. End of the forty-ninth chapter from the beginning.]

Chapter 29

THE SUPERINTENDENT OF COWS

THE superintendent of cows shall supervise (1) herds maintained for wages (*vetanopagrahikam*), (2) herds surrendered for a fixed amount of dairy produce (*karapratikara*), (3) useless and abandoned herds (*bhagnotsrishtakam*), (4) herds maintained for a share in dairy produce (*bhaganupravishtam*), (5) classes of herds (*vrajaparyagram*), (6) cattle that strayed (*nashtam*), (7) cattle that are irrecoverably lost (*vinashtam*), and (8) the amassed quantity of milk and clarified butter.

(1) When a cowherd, a buffalo herdsman, a milker, a churner, and a hunter (*lubdhaka*) fed by wages graze milch cows (*dhenu*) in hundreds (*satam satam*)—for if they graze the herds for the profit of milk and ghee, they will starve the calves to death—that system of rearing the cattle is termed 'herds maintained for wages'.

(2) When a single person rears a hundred heads (*rupasatam*) made up of equal numbers of each of aged cows, milch cows, pregnant cows, heifers, and calves (*vatsatari*) and gives (to the owner) 8 *varaka*s of clarified butter per annum, as well as the branded skin (of dead cows if any), that system is called 'herds surrendered for a fixed amount of dairy produce'.

(3) When those who rear a hundred heads made up of equal numbers of each of afflicted cattle, crippled cattle, cattle that cannot be milked by anyone but the accustomed person, cattle that are not easily milked, and cattle that kill their own calves give in return (to the owner) a share in dairy produce, it is termed 'useless and abandoned herd'.

(4) When under the fear of cattle-lifting enemies (*parachakratavibhayat*), cattle are kept under the care of the superintendent, giving him 1/10th of the dairy produce for his protection, it is termed 'herds maintained for a share in dairy produce'.

(5) When the superintendent classifies cattle as calves, steers, tameable ones, draught oxen, bulls that are to be trained to yoke,

bulls kept for crossing cows, cattle that are fit only for the supply of flesh, buffaloes and draught buffaloes; female calves, female steer, heifer, pregnant cows, milch cattle, barren cattle—either cows or buffaloes; calves that are a month or two old as well as those which are still younger; and when, as he ought to, he brands them all inclusive of their calves of one or two months old along with those stray cattle which have remained unclaimed in the herds for a month or two; and when he registers the branded marks, natural marks, colour and the distance from one horn to another of each of the cattle, that system is known as 'class of herds'.

(6) When an animal is carried off by thieves or finds itself into the herds of others or strays unknown, it is called 'lost'.

(7) When an animal is entangled in a quagmire or precipice or dies of disease or of old age, or drowned in water: or when it is killed by the fall of a tree or of river bank, or is beaten to death with a staff or stone, or is struck by lightening (*isana*), or is devoured by a tiger or bitten by a cobra, or is carried off by a crocodile, or is involved in the midst of a forest fire, it is termed as 'irrecoverably lost'.

Cowherds shall endeavour to keep them away from such dangers.

Whoever hurts or causes another to hurt, or steals or causes another to steal a cow, should be slain.

When a person substitutes an animal (*rupa*) bearing the royal brand mark for a private one, he shall be punished with the first amercement.

When a person recovers a local cattle from thieves, he shall receive the promised reward (*panitam rupam*); and when a man rescues a foreign cattle (from thieves), he shall receive half its value.

Cowherds shall apply remedies to calves or aged cows or cows suffering from diseases.

They shall graze the herds in forests which are severally allotted as pasture grounds for various seasons and from which thieves, tigers and other molesting beasts are driven away by hunters aided by their hounds.

With a view to scaring out snakes and tigers and as a definite means of knowing the whereabouts of herds, sounding bells shall be attached to (the neck of) timid cattle.

Cowherds shall allow their cattle to enter into such rivers or lakes as are of equal depth all round, broad, and free from mire and crocodiles, and shall protect them from dangers under such circumstances.

Whenever an animal is caught hold of by a thief, a tiger, a snake or a crocodile, or when it is too infirm owing to age or disease, they shall make a report of it; otherwise they shall be compelled to make good the loss.

When an animal dies a natural death, they shall surrender the skin with the brand mark, if it is a cow or a buffalo; the skin together with the ear (*karnalakshanam*) if it is a goat or sheep; the tail with the skin containing the brand mark, if it is an ass or a camel; the skin, if it is a young one; besides the above, (they shall also restore) the fat (*vasti*), bile, marrow (*snayu*), teeth, hoofs, horns and bones.

They (the cowherds) may sell either fresh flesh or dried flesh. They shall give buttermilk as drink to dogs and hogs, and reserve a little (buttermilk) in a bronze vessel to prepare their own dish: they may also make use of coagulated milk or cheese (*kilata*) to render their oilcakes relishing (*ghanapinyaka-kledartha*).

He who sells his cow (from among the herds) shall pay (to the king) ¼th *rupa* (value of the cow).

During the rainy, autumnal, and the first part of winter (*hemanta*) seasons, they shall milk the cattle both the times (morning and evening); and during the latter part of winter and the whole of the spring and summer seasons, they shall milk only once (i.e., only in the morning). The cowherd who milks a cow a second time during these seasons shall have his thumb cut off.

If he allows the time of milking to lapse, he shall forfeit the profit thereof (i.e., the milk).

The same rule shall hold good in case of negligence of the opportune moment for putting a string through the nose of a bull and other animals, and for taming or training them to the yoke.

One *drona* of a cow's milk will, when churned, yield one *prastha* of butter; the same quantity of a buffalo's milk will yield 1/7th *prastha* more; and the same quantity of milk of goats and sheep will produce ½ *prastha* more.

In all kinds of milk, the exact quantity of butter shall be ascertained by churning; for increase in the supply of milk and butter depends on the nature of the soil and the quantity and quality of fodder and water.

When a person causes a bull attached to a herd to fight with another bull, he shall be punished with the first amercement; when a bull is injured (under such circumstances), he shall be punished with the highest amercement.

Cattle shall be grouped in herds of ten each of similar colour, while they are being grazed.

According to the protective strength of the cowherds the capacity of the cattle to go far and wide to graze, cowherds shall take their cattle either far or near.

Once in six months, sheep and other animals shall be shorn of their wool.

The same rules shall apply to herds of horses, asses, camels and hogs.

For bulls which are provided with nose rings, and which equal horses in speed and in carrying loads, half a *bhara* of meadow grass (*yavasa*), twice the above quantity of ordinary grass (*trina*), one *tula* (100 *pala*s) of oil cakes, 10 *adhaka*s of bran, 5 *pala*s of salt (*mukhalavanam*), one *kudumba* of oil for rubbing over the nose (*nasya*), 1 *prastha* of drink (*pana*), one *tula* of flesh, 1 *adhaka* of *curis*, 1 *drona* of barley or of cooked *masha* (*Phraseolus radiatus*), 1 *drona* of milk; or half an *adhaka* of *sura* (liquor), 1 *prastha* of oil or ghee (*sneha*) 10 *pala*s of sugar or jaggery, 1 *pala* of the fruit of *sringibera* (ginger) may be substituted for milk (*pratipana*).

The same commodities less by one quarter each will form the diet for mules, cows, and asses; twice the quantity of the above things for buffaloes and camels.

Draught oxen and cows, supplying milk (*payah*), shall be provided with subsistence in proportion to the duration of time the oxen are kept at work, and the quantity of milk which the cows supply.

All cattle shall be supplied with abundance of fodder and water.

Thus the manner of rearing herds of cattle has been dealt with.

A herd of 100 heads of asses and mules shall contain five male animals; that of goats and sheep ten; and a herd of ten heads of either cows or buffaloes shall contain four male animals.

[Thus ends Chapter 29, 'The Superintendent of Cows', in Book II, 'The Duties of Government Superintendents', of the Arthashastra of Kautilya. End of the fiftieth chapter from the beginning.]

Chapter 30

THE SUPERINTENDENT OF HORSES

THE superintendent of horses shall register the breed, age, colour, marks, group or classes, and the native place of horses, and classify as (1) those that are kept in sale house for sale (*panyagarikam*), (2) those that are recently purchased (*krayopagatam*), (3) those that have been captured in wars (*ahavalabdham*), (4) those that are of local breed (*ajatam*), (5) those that are sent thither for help (*sahayyakagatam*), (6) those that are mortgaged (*panasthitam*), and (7) those that are temporarily kept in stables (*yavatkalikam*).

He shall make a report (to the king) of such animals as are inauspicious, crippled or diseased.

Every horseman shall know how to make an economic use of whatever he has received from the king's treasury and storehouse.

The superintendent shall have a stable constructed as spacious as required by the number of horses to be kept therein twice as broad as the length of a horse, with four doors facing the four quarters, with its central floor suited for the rolling of horses, with projected front provided with wooden seats at the entrance, and containing monkeys, peacocks, red spotted deer (*prishata*), mangoose, partridges (*chakora*), parrots and maina birds (*sarika*); the room for every horse shall be four times as broad or long as the length of a horse, with its central floor paved with smoothened wooden planks, with separate compartments for fodder (*khadanakoshthakam*), with passages for the removal of urine and dung, and with a door facing either the north or the east. The distinction of quarters (*digvibhaga*) may be made as a matter of fact or relatively to the situation of the building.

Steeds, stallions and colts shall be separately kept.

A steed that has just given birth to a colt shall be provided for the first three days with a drink of 1 *prastha* of clarified butter; afterwards it shall be fed with a *prastha* of flour (*saktu*) and made to drink oil mixed with medicine for ten nights; after that time, it shall have cooked grains, meadow grass, and other things suited to the season of the day.

A colt, ten days old, shall be given a *kudumba* of flour mixed with ¼th *kudumba* of clarified butter, and 1 *prastha* of milk till it becomes six months old; then the above rations shall be increased half as much during each succeeding month, with the addition of 1 *prastha* of barley till it becomes three years old, then one *drona* of barley till it grows four years old; at the age of four or five, it attains its full development and becomes serviceable.

The face (*mukha*) of the best horse measures 32 *angulas*; its length is 5 times its face; its shank is 20 *angulas*; and its height is 4 times its shank.

Horses of medium and lower sizes fall short of the above measurement by two and three *angulas*, respectively.

The circumference (*parinaha*) of the best horse measures 100 *angulas*, and horses of medium and lower sizes fall short of the above measurement by five parts (*panchabhagavaram*).

For the best horse (the diet shall be) 2 *dronas* of anyone of the grains, rice (*sali, vrihi*) barley, panic seeds (*priyangu*) soaked or cooked, cooked *mudga* (Phraseolus munga) or *masha* (*Phraseolus radiatus*); one *prastha* of oil, 5 *palas* of salt, 50 *palas* of flesh, 1 *adhaka* of broth (*rasa*) or 2 *adhakas* of curd, 5 *palas* of sugar (*kshara*), to make their diet relishing, 1 *prastha* of *sura*, liquor, or 2 *prasthas* of milk.

The same quantity of drink shall be specially given to those horses which are tired of long journey or of carrying loads.

One *prastha* of oil for giving enema (*anuvasana*), 1 *kudumba* of oil for rubbing over the nose, 1,000 *palas* of meadow grass, twice as much of ordinary grass (*trina*); and hay-stalk or grass shall be spread over an area of 6 *aratnis*.

The same quantity of rations less by one-quarter for horses of medium and lower size.

A draught horse or stallion of medium size shall be given the same quantity as the best horse; and similar horses of lower size shall receive the same quantity as a horse of medium size.

Steeds and *parasamas* shall have one quarter less of rations. Half of the rations given to steeds shall be given to colts.

Thus is the distribution of ration dealt with.

Those who cook the food of horses, grooms, and veterinary surgeons shall have a share in the rations (*pratisvadabhajah*).

Stallions which are incapacitated owing to old age, disease or hardships of war, and, being therefore rendered unfit for use in war live only to consume food shall in the interests of citizens and country people be allowed to cross steeds.

The breed of Kambhoja, Sindhu, Aratta and Vanayu countries are the best; those of Bahlika, Papeya, Sauvira and Taitala, are of middle quality; and the rest ordinary (*avarah*).

These three sorts may be trained either for war or for riding according as they are furious (*tikshna*), mild (*bhadra*) or stupid or slow (*manda*).

The regular training of a horse is its preparation for war (*sannahyam karma*).

Circular movement (*valgana*), slow movement (*nichairgata*), jumping (*langhana*), gallop (*dhorana*) and response to signals (*naroshtra*) are the several forms of riding (*aupavahya*).

Aupavenuka, *vardhamanaka*, *yamaka*, *alidhapluta*, *vrithatta* and *trivachali* are the varieties of circular movement (*valgana*).

The same kind of movements with the head and ear kept erect are called slow movements.

These are performed in sixteen ways:

Prakirnaka, *prakirnottara*, *nishanna*, *parsvanuvritta*, *urmimarga*, *sarabhakridita*, *sarabhapluta*, *tritala*, *bahyanuvritta*, *panchapani*, *simhayata*, *svadhuta*, *klishta*, *slaghita*, *brimhita*, *pushpabhikirna*.

Jumping like a monkey (*kapipluta*), jumping like a frog (*bhekapluta*), sudden jump (*ekapluta*), jumping with one leg (*ekapadapluta*), leaping like a cuckoo (*kokilasamchari*), dashing with its breast almost touching the ground (*urasya*), and leaping like a crane (*bakasamchari*) are the several forms of jumping.

Flying like a vulture (*kanka*), dashing like a water duck (*varikanaka*), running like a peacock (*mayura*), halting the speed of a peacock (*ardhmayura*), dashing like a mangoose (*nakula*), at half the speed of a mangoose (*ardhanakula*), running like a hog (*varaha*) and at half the speed of a hog (*ardhavaraha*) are the several forms of gallop.

Movement following a signal is termed *naroshtra*. Six, nine, and twelve *yojanas* (a day) are the distances (to be traversed) by carriage horses.

Five, eight, and ten *yojana*s are the distances (to be traversed) by riding horses (*prishthavahya*).

Trotting according to its strength (*vikrama*), trotting with good breathing (*bhadrasvasa*), and pacing with a load on its back are the three kinds of trot.

Trotting according to strength (*vikrama*), trot combined with circular movement (*valgita*), ordinary trot (*upakantha*), middlemost speed (*upajava*), and ordinary speed are also the several kinds of trot (*dhara*).

Qualified teachers shall give instructions as to the manufacture of proper ropes with which to tether the horses.

Charioteers shall see to the manufacture of necessary war accoutrements of horses.

Veterinary surgeons shall apply requisite remedies against undue growth or diminution in the body of horses and also change the diet of horses according to changes in seasons.

Those who move the horses (*sutragrahaka*), those whose business is to tether them in stables, those who supply meadow grass, those who cook the grains for the horses, those who keep watch in the stables, those who groom them and those who apply remedies against poison shall satisfactorily discharge their specified duties and shall, in default of it, forfeit their daily wages.

Those who take out for the purpose of riding such horses as are kept inside (the stables) either for the purpose of waving lights (*nirajana*) or for medical treatment shall be fined 12 *pana*s.

When, owing to defects in medicine or carelessness in the treatment, the disease (from which a horse is suffering) becomes intense, a fine of twice the cost of the treatment shall be imposed; and when, owing to defects in medicine, or not administering it, the result becomes quite the reverse, a fine equal to the value of the animal (*patramulya*) shall be imposed.

The same rule shall apply to the treatment of cows, buffaloes, goats and sheep.

Horses shall be washed, bedaubed with sandal powder, and garlanded twice a day. On new moon days sacrifice to *Bhuta*s, and on full moon days the chanting of auspicious hymns shall be performed. Not only on the ninth day of the month of *Asvayuja*, but also both at the commencement and close of journeys (*yatra*) as well as in the time of disease shall a priest wave lights invoking blessings on the horses.

[Thus ends Chapter 30, 'The Superintendent of Horses', in Book II, 'The Duties of Government Superintendents', of the Arthashastra of Kautilya. End of the fifty-first chapter from the beginning.]

Chapter 31

THE SUPERINTENDENT OF ELEPHANTS

THE superintendent of elephants shall take proper steps to protect elephant forests and supervise the operations with regard to the standing or lying in stables of elephants, male, female or young, when they are tired after training, and examine the proportional quantity of rations and grass, the extent of training given to them, their accoutrements and ornaments, as well as the work of elephant doctors, of trainers of elephants in warlike feats, and of grooms, such as drivers, binders and others.

There shall be constructed an elephant stable twice as broad and twice as high as the length (*ayama*) of an elephant, with separate apartments for female elephants, with projected entrance (*sapragrivam*), with posts called *kumari*, and with its door facing either the east or the north.

The space in front of the smooth posts (to which elephants are tied) shall form a square, one side of which is equal to the length of an elephant and shall be paved with smooth wooden planks and provided with holes for the removal of urine and dung.

The space where an elephant lies down shall be as broad as the length of an elephant and provided with a flat form raised to half the height of an elephant for leaning on.

Elephants serviceable in war or for riding shall be kept inside the fort; and those that are still being tamed or are of bad temper shall be kept outside.

The first and the seventh of the eight divisions of the day are the two bathing times of elephants; the time subsequent to those two periods is for their food; forenoon is the time for their exercise; afternoon is the time for drink; two (out of eight) parts of the night are the time for sleep; one-third of the night is spent in taking wakeful rest.

The summer is the season to capture elephants.

That which is 20 years old shall be captured.

Young elephants (*bikka*), infatuated elephants (*mugdha*), elephants without tusks, diseased elephants, elephants which suckle their young ones (*dhenuka*), and female elephants (*hastini*) shall not be captured.

(That which is) seven *aratnis* in height, nine *aratnis* in length, ten *aratni*s in circumference and is (as can be inferred from such measurement), 40 years old, is the best.

That which is 30 years old is of middle class; and that which is 25 years old is of the lowest class. The diet (for the last two classes) shall be lessened by one quarter according to the class.

The rations for an elephant (of seven *aratni*s in height) shall be 1 *drona* of rice, ½ *adhaka* of oil, 3 *prastha*s of *ghi*, 10 *pala*s of salt, 50 *pala*s of flesh, 1 *adhaka* of broth (*rasa*) or twice the quantity (i.e., 2 *adhaka*s) of curd; in order to render the dish tasteful, 10 *pala*s of sugar (*kshara*), 1 *adhaka* of liquor, or twice the quantity of milk (*payah*);1 *prastha* of oil for smearing over the body, ⅛ *prastha* (of the same) for the head and for keeping a light in the stables; 2 *bharas* of meadow grass, 2¼ *bharas* of ordinary grass (*sashpa*), and 2½ *bhara*s of dry grass and any quantity of stalks of various pulses (*kadankara*).

An elephant in rut (*atyarala*) and of 8 *aratni*s in height shall have equal rations with that of 7 *aratni*s in height.

The rest of 6 or 5 *aratni*s in height shall be provided with rations proportional to their size.

A young elephant (*bikka*) captured for the mere purpose of sporting with it shall be fed with milk and meadow grass.

That which is blood-red (*samjatalohita*), that which is fleshed, that which has its sides evenly grown (*samaliptapaksha*), that which has its girths full or equal (*samakakshya*), that whose flesh is evenly spread, that which is of even surface on its back (*samatalpatala*) and that which is of uneven surface (*jatadronika*) are the several kinds of physical splendour of elephants.

Suitably to the seasons as well as to their physical spendour, elephants of sharp or slow sense (*bhadra* and *mandra*) as well as elephants possessed of the characteristics of other beasts shall be trained and taught suitable work.

[Thus ends Chapter 31, 'The Superintendent of Elephants', in Book II, 'The Duties of Government Superintendents', of the Arthashastra of Kautilya. End of the fifty-second chapter from the beginning.]

Chapter 32

TRAINING OF ELEPHANTS

ELEPHANTS are classified into four kinds in accordance with the training they are given: that which is tameable (*damya*), that which is trained for war (*sannahya*), that which is trained for riding (*aupavahya*) and rogue elephants (*vyala*).

Those which are tameable fall under five groups: that which suffers a man to sit on its withers (*skandhagata*), that which allows itself to be tethered to a post (*stambhagata*), that which can be taken to water (*varigata*), that which lies in pits (*apapatagata*) and that which is attached to its herd (*yuthagata*).

All these elephants shall be treated with as much care as a young elephant (*bikka*).

Military training is of seven kinds: drill (*upasthana*), turning (*samvartana*), advancing (*samyana*), trampling down and killing (*vadhavadha*), fighting with other elephants (*hastiyuddha*), assailing forts and cities (*nagarayanam*) and warfare.

Binding the elephants with girths (*kakshyakarma*), putting on collars (*graiveyakakarma*), and making them work in company with their herds (*yuthakarma*) are the first steps (*upavichara*) of the above training.

Elephants trained for riding fall under seven groups: that which suffers a man to mount over it when in company with another elephant (*kunjaropavahya*), that which suffers riding when led by a warlike elephant (*sannahyopavahya*), that which is taught trotting (*dhorana*), that which is taught various kinds of movements (*adhanagatika*), that which can be made to move by using a staff (*yashtyupavahya*), that which can be made to move by using an iron hook (*totropavahya*), that which can be made to move without whips (*suddhopavahya*), and that which is of help in hunting.

Autumnal work (*saradakarma*), mean or rough work (*hinakarma*), and training to respond to signals are the first steps for the above training.

Rogue elephants can be trained only in one way. The only means to keep them under control is punishment. It has a suspicious aversion to work, is obstinate, of perverse nature, unsteady, wilful, or of infatuated temper under the influence of rut.

Rogue elephants whose training proves a failure may be purely roguish (*suddha*), clever in roguery (*suvrata*), perverse (*vishama*), or possessed of all kinds of vice.

The form of fetters and other necessary means to keep them under control shall be ascertained from the doctor of elephants.

Tetherposts (*alana*), collars, girths, bridles, leg chains, frontal fetters are the several kinds of binding instruments.

A hook, a bamboo staff and machines (*yantra*) are instruments.

Necklaces such as *vaijayanti* and *kshurapramala*, and litter and housings are the ornaments of elephants.

Mail armour (*varma*), clubs (*totra*), arrow bags and machines are war accoutrements.

Elephant doctors, trainers, expert riders, as well as those who groom them, those who prepare their food, those who procure grass for them, those who tether them to posts, those who sweep elephant stables, and those who keep watch in the stables at night are some of the persons that have to attend to the needs of elephants.

Elephant doctors, watchmen, sweepers, cooks and others shall receive (from the storehouse,) 1 *prastha* of cooked rice, a handful of oil, land 2 *pala*s of sugar and of salt. Excepting the doctors, others shall also receive 10 *pala*s of flesh.

Elephant doctors shall apply necessary medicines to elephants which, while making a journey, happen to suffer from disease, overwork, rut or old age.

Accumulation of dirt in stables, failure to supply grass, causing an elephant to lie down on hard and unprepared ground, striking on vital parts of its body, permission to a stranger to ride over it, untimely riding, leading it to water through impassable places, and allowing it to enter into thick forests are offences punishable with fines. Such fines shall be deducted from the rations and wages due to the offenders.

During the period of *Chaturmasya* (the months of July, August, September and October) and at the time when two seasons meet, waving of lights shall be performed thrice. Also on new moon and full moon days, commanders shall perform sacrifices to *Bhuta*s for the safety of elephants.

Leaving as much as is equal to twice the circumference of the tusk near its root, the rest of the tusks shall be cut off once in two-and-a-half years in the case of elephants born in countries irrigated by rivers (*nadija*), and once in five years in the case of mountain elephants.

[Thus ends Chapter 32, 'The Training of Elephants', in Book II, 'The Duties of Government Superintendents', of the Arthashastra of Kautilya. End of the fifty-third chapter from the beginning.]

Chapter 33

THE SUPERINTENDENT OF CHARIOTS; THE SUPERINTENDENT OF INFANTRY AND THE DUTY OF THE COMMANDER-IN-CHIEF

THE functions of the superintendent of horses will explain those of the superintendent of chariots.

The superintendent of chariots shall attend to the construction of chariots.

The best chariot shall measure 10 *purushas* in height (i.e., 120 *angulas*), and 12 *purushas* in width. After this model, seven more chariots with width decreasing by one *purusha* successively down to a chariot of six *purushas* in width shall be constructed. He shall also construct chariots of gods (*devaratha*), festal chariots (*pushyaratha*), battle chariots (*sangramika*), travelling chariots (*pariyanika*), chariots used in assailing an enemy's strongholds (*parapurabhiyanika*), and training chariots.

He shall also examine the efficiency in the training of troops in shooting arrows, in hurling clubs and cudgels, in wearing mail armour, in equipment, in charioteering, in fighting seated on a chariot, and in controlling chariot horses.

He shall also attend to the accounts of provision and wages paid to those who are either permanently or temporarily employed (to prepare chariots and other things). Also he shall take steps to maintain the employed contented and happy by adequate reward (*yogyarakshanushthanam*), and ascertain the distance of roads.

The same rules shall apply to the superintendent of infantry.

The latter shall know the exact strength or weakness of hereditary troops (*maula*), hired troops (*bhrita*), the corporate body of troops (*sreni*), as well as that of the army of friendly or unfriendly kings and of wild tribes.

He shall be thoroughly familiar with the nature of fighting in low grounds, of open battle, of fraudulent attack, of fighting under the cover of entrenchment (*khanakayuddha*), or from heights (*akasayuddha*), and of fighting during the day and night, besides the drill necessary for such warfare.

He shall also know the fitness or unfitness of troops on emergent occasions.

With an eye to the position which the entire army (*chaturangabala*) trained in the skilful handling of all kinds of weapons and in leading elephants, horses, and chariots have occupied and to the emergent call for which they ought to be ready, the commander-in-chief shall be so capable as to order either advance or retreat (*ayogamayogam cha*).

He shall also know what kind of ground is more advantageous to his own army, what time is more favourable, what the strength of the enemy is, how to sow dissension in an enemy's army of united mind, how to collect his own scattered forces, how to scatter the compact body of an enemy's army, how to assail a fortress, and when to make a general advance.

Being ever mindful of the discipline which his army has to maintain not merely in camping and marching, but in the thick of battle, he shall designate the regiments (*vyuha*) by the names of trumpets, boards, banners or flags.

[Thus ends Chapter 33, 'The Superintendent of Chariots, the Superintendent of Infantry, and the Duties of the Commander-in-Chief ', in Book II, 'The Duties of Government Superintendents', of the Arthashastra of Kautilya. End of the fifty-fourth chapter from the beginning.]

Chapter 34

THE SUPERINTENDENT OF PASSPORTS AND THE SUPERINTENDENT OF PASTURELANDS

THE superintendent of passports shall issue passes at the rate of a *masha* per pass. Whoever is provided with a pass shall be at liberty to enter into, or go out of, the country. Whoever, being a native of the country enters into or goes out of the country without a pass shall be fined 12 *pana*s. He shall be punished with the first amercement for producing a false pass. A foreigner guilty of the same offence shall be punished with the highest amercement.

The superintendent of pasturelands shall examine passes.

Pasture grounds shall be opened between any two dangerous places.

Valleys shall be cleared from the fear of thieves, elephants, and other beasts.

In barren tracts of the country, there shall be constructed not only tanks, buildings for shelter, and wells but also flower gardens and fruit gardens.

Hunters with their hounds shall reconnoitre forests. At the approach of thieves or enemies, they shall so hide themselves by ascending trees or mountains as to escape from the thieves, and blow conch shells or beat drums. As to the movements of enemies or wild tribes, they may send information by flying the pigeons of royal household with passes (*mudra*) or causing fire and smoke at successive distances.

It shall be his duty to protect timber and elephant forests, to keep roads in good repair, to arrest thieves, to secure the safety of mercantile traffic, to protect cows, and to conduct the transaction of the people.

[Thus ends Chapter 34, 'The Superintendent of Passports and the Superintendent of Pasturelands', in Book II, 'The Duties of Government Superintendents', of the Arthashastra of Kautilya. End of the fifty-fifth chapter from the beginning.]

Chapter 35

THE DUTY OF REVENUE COLLECTORS; SPIES IN THE GUISE OF HOUSEHOLDERS, MERCHANTS AND ASCETICS

HAVING divided the kingdom (*janapada*) into four districts, and having also subdivided the villages (*grama*) as of first, middle and lowest rank, he shall bring them under one or another of the following heads:

Villages that are exempted from taxation (*pariharaka*); those that supply soldiers (*ayudhiya*); those that pay their taxes in the form of grains, cattle, gold (*hiranya*) or raw material (*kupya*); and those that supply free labour (*vishti*) and dairy produce in lieu of taxes (*karapratikara*).

It is the duty of *gopa*, village accountant, to attend to the accounts of five or ten villages as ordered by the collector general.

By setting up boundaries to villages, by numbering plots of grounds as cultivated, uncultivated, plains, wetlands, gardens, vegetable gardens, fences (*vata*), forests, altars, temples of gods, irrigation works, cremation grounds, feeding houses (*sattra*), places where water is freely supplied to travellers (*prapa*), places of pilgrimage, pasture grounds and roads, and thereby fixing the boundaries of various villages, of fields, of forests, and of roads, he shall register gifts, sales, charities, and remission of taxes regarding fields.

Also having numbered the houses as tax-paying or non-tax-paying, he shall not only register the total number of the inhabitants of all the four castes in each village, but also keep an account of the exact number of cultivators, cowherds, merchants, artisans, labourers, slaves, and biped and quadruped animals, fixing at the same time the amount of gold, free labour, toll, and fines that can be collected from it (each house).

He shall also keep an account of the number of young and old men that reside in each house, their history (*charitra*), occupation (*ajiva*), income (*aya*) and expenditure (*vyaya*).

Likewise *sthanika*, district officer, shall attend to the accounts of one quarter of the kingdom.

In those places which are under the jurisdiction of *gopa* and *sthanika*, commissioners (*prodeshtarah*) specially deputed by the collector general shall not only inspect the work done and the means employed by the village and district officers, but also collect the special religious tax known as *bali* (*balipragraham kuryuh*).

Spies under the disguise of householders (*grihapatika*, cultivators) who shall be deputed by the collector general for espionage shall ascertain the validity of the accounts (of the village and district officers) regarding the fields, houses and families of each village—the area and output of produce regarding fields, right of ownership and remission of taxes with regard to houses, and the caste and profession regarding families.

They shall also ascertain the total number of men and beasts (*janghagra*) as well as the amount of income and expenditure of each family.

They shall also find out the causes of emigration and immigration of persons of migratory habit, the arrival and departure of men and women of condemnable (*anarthya*) character, as well as the movements of (foreign) spies.

Likewise spies under the guise of merchants shall ascertain the quantity and price of the royal merchandise such as minerals, or products of gardens, forests and fields or manufactured articles.

As regards foreign merchandise of superior or inferior quality arriving thither by land or by water, they shall ascertain the amount of toll, road cess, conveyance cess, military cess, ferry fare, and one-sixth portion (paid or payable by the merchants), the charges incurred by them for their own subsistence, and for the accommodation of their merchandise in warehouse (*panyagara*).

Similarly spies under the guise of ascetics shall, as ordered by the collector general, gather information as to the proceedings, honest or dishonest, of cultivators, cowherds, merchants, and heads of government departments.

In places where altars are situated or where four roads meet, in ancient ruins, in the vicinity of tanks, rivers, bathing places, in places of pilgrimage and hermitage, and in desert tracts, mountains and thick-grown forests, spies under the guise of old and notorious thieves with their student bands shall ascertain the causes of arrival and departure, and halt of thieves, enemies and persons of undue bravery.

The collector general shall thus energetically attend to the affairs of the kingdom. Also his subordinates constituting his various establishments of espionage shall along with their colleagues and followers attend to their duties likewise.

[Thus ends Chapter 35, 'The Duty of Revenue Collectors; Spies in the Guise of Householders, Merchants and Ascetics', in Book II, 'The Duties of Government Superintendents', of the Arthashastra of Kautilya. End of the fifty-sixth chapter from the beginning.]

Chapter 36

THE DUTY OF A CITY SUPERINTENDENT

LIKE the collector general, the officer in charge of the capital city (*Nagaraka*) shall look to the affairs of the capital.

A *gopa* shall keep the accounts of ten households, twenty households, or forty households. He shall not only know the caste, *gotra*, the name and occupation of both men and women in those households but also ascertain their income and expenditure.

Likewise, the officer known as *sthanika* shall attend to the accounts of the four quarters of the capital.

Managers of charitable institutions shall send information (to *gopa* or *sthanika*) as to any heretics (*pashanda*) and travellers arriving to reside therein. They shall allow ascetics and men learned in the Vedas to reside in such places only when those persons are known to be of reliable character.

Artisans and other handicraftsmen may, on their own responsibility, allow others of their own profession to reside where they carry on their own work (i.e., in their own houses).

Similarly merchants may on their own responsibility allow other merchants to reside where they themselves carry on their mercantile work (i.e., their own houses or shops).

They (the merchants) shall make a report of those who sell any merchandise in forbidden place or time, as well as of those who are in possession of any merchandise other than their own.

Vintners, sellers of cooked flesh and cooked rice as well as prostitutes may allow any other person to reside with them only when that person is well known to them.

They (vintners, etc.) shall make a report of spendthrifts and foolhardy persons who engage themselves in risky undertakings.

Any physician who undertakes to treat in secret a patient suffering from ulcer or excess of unwholesome food or drink, as well as the master of the house (wherein such treatment is attempted) shall be innocent only when they (the physician and the master of the house) make a report of the same to either *gopa* or *sthanika*; otherwise both of them shall be equally guilty with the sufferer.

Masters of houses shall make a report of strangers arriving at, or departing from, their houses; otherwise they shall be guilty of the offence (theft, etc.) committed during that night. Even during safe nights (i.e., nights when no theft, etc., seems to have been committed), they shall be fined 3 *panas* (for not making such a report).

Wayfarers going along a high road or by a footpath shall catch hold of any person whom they find to be suffering from a wound or ulcer, or possessed of destructive instruments, or tired of carrying a heavy load, or timidly avoiding the presence of others, or indulging in too much sleep, or fatigued from a long journey, or who appears to be a stranger to the place in localities such as inside or outside the capital, temples of gods, places of pilgrimage, or burial grounds.

(Spies) shall also make a search for suspicious persons in the interior of deserted houses, in the workshops or houses of vintners and sellers of cooked rice and flesh, in gambling houses, and in the abode of heretics.

Kindling of fire shall be prohibited during the two middlemost parts of daytime divided into four equal parts during the summer. A fine of ⅛th of a *pana* shall be imposed for kindling fire at such a time.

Masters of houses may carry on cooking operations outside their houses.

(If a houseowner is not found to have ready with him) five water pots (*pancha ghatinam*), a *kumbha*, a *drona*, a ladder, an axe, a winnowing basket, a hook (such as is used to drive an elephant), pincers (*kachagrahini*), and a leather bag (*driti*), he shall be fined ¼th of a *pana*.

They shall also remove thatched roofs. Those who work by fire (blacksmiths) shall all together live in a single locality.

Each houseowner shall ever be present (at night) at the door of his own house.

Vessels filled with water shall be kept in thousands in a row without confusion not only in big streets and at places where four roads meet but also in front of the royal buildings (*rajaprigraheshu*).

Any houseowner who does not run to give his help in extinguishing the fire of whatever is burning shall be fined 12 *panas*; and a renter (*avakrayi*, i.e., one who has occupied a house for rent) not running to extinguish fire shall be fined 6 *panas*.

Whoever carelessly sets fire (to a house) shall be fined 54 *panas*; but he who intentionally sets fire (to a house) shall be thrown into fire.

Whoever throws dirt in the street shall be punished with a fine of ⅛th of a *pana*; whoever causes mire or water to collect in the street shall be fined ¼th of a *pana*; whoever commits the above offences in the king's road (*rajamarga*) shall be punished with double the above fines.

Whoever excretes faeces in places of pilgrimage, reservoirs of water, temples, and royal buildings shall be punished with fines rising from one *pana* and upwards in the order of the offences; but when such excretions are due to the use of medicine or to disease no punishment shall be imposed.

Whoever throws inside the city the carcass of animals such as a cat, dog, mangoose, and a snake shall be fined 3 *panas*; of animals such as an ass, a camel, a mule, and cattle shall be fined 6 *panas*; and of human corpse shall be punished with a fine of 50 *panas*.

When a dead body is taken out of a city through a gate other than the usual or prescribed one or through a path other than the prescribed path, the first amercement shall be imposed; and those who guard the gates (through which the dead body is taken out) shall be fined 200 *panas*.

When a dead body is interred or cremated beyond the burial or cremation grounds, a fine of 12 *panas* shall be imposed.

The interval between six *nalikas* (2⅖ hours) after the fall of night and 6 *nalikas* before dawn shall be the period when a trumpet shall be sounded prohibiting the movement of people.

The trumpet having been sounded, whoever moves in the vicinity of royal buildings during the first or the last *yama* (3 hours?) of the period shall be punished with a fine of one *pana* and a quarter; and during the middlemost *yamas*, with double the above fine; and whoever moves outside (the royal buildings or the fort) shall be punished with four times the above fine.

Whoever is arrested in suspicious places or as the perpetrator of a criminal act shall be examined.

Whoever moves in the vicinity of royal buildings or ascends the defensive fortifications of the capital shall be punished with the middlemost amercement.

Those who go out at night in order to attend to the work of midwifery or medical treatment, or to carry off a dead body to the cremation or burial grounds, or those who go out with a lamp in hand at night, as well as those who go out to visit the officer in charge of the city, or to find out the cause of a trumpet sound (*turyapreksha*), or to extinguish the outbreak of fire or under the authority of a pass shall not be arrested.

During the nights of free movement (*chararatrishu*) those who move out under disguise, those who stir out though forbidden (*pravarjitah*), as well as those who move with clubs and other weapons in hand shall be punished in proportion to the gravity of their guilt.

Those watchmen who stop whomever they ought not to stop, or do not stop whomever they ought to stop shall be punished with twice the amount of fine levied for untimely movement.

When a watchman has carnal connection with a slave woman, he shall be punished with the first amercement; with a free woman, the middlemost amercement; with a woman arrested for untimely movement, the highest amercement; and with a woman of high birth (*kulastri*), he shall be put to death.

When the officer in charge of the city (*nagaraka*) does not make a report (to the king) of whatever nocturnal nuisance of animate or inanimate nature (*chetanâchetana*) has occurred, or when he shows carelessness (in the discharge of his duty), he shall be punished in proportion to the gravity of his crime.

He shall make a daily inspection of reservoirs of water, of roads, of the hidden passage for going out of the city, of forts, fort walls, and other defensive works. He shall also keep in his safe custody of whatever things he comes across as lost, forgotten or left behind by others.

On the days to which the birth star of the king is assigned, as well as on full moon days, such prisoners as are young, old, diseased, or helpless (*anatha*) shall be let out from the jail (*bandhanâgâra*); or those who are of charitable disposition or who have made any agreement with the prisoners may liberate them by paying an adequate ransom.

Once in a day or once in five nights, jails may be emptied of prisoners in consideration of the work they have done, or of whipping inflicted upon them, or of an adequate ransom paid by them in gold.

Whenever a new country is conquered, when an heir apparent is installed on the throne, or when a prince is born to the king, prisoners are usually set free.

[Thus ends Chapter 36, 'The Duty of a City Superintendent', in Book II, 'The Duties of Government Superintendents', of the Arthashastra of Kautilya. End of the fifty-seventh chapter from the beginning. With this ends Book II 'The Duties of Government Superintendents', of the Arthashastra of Kautilya.]

Book III

Concerning Law

Chapter 1

DETERMINATION OF FORMS OF AGREEMENT; DETERMINATION OF LEGAL DISPUTES

IN the cities of Sangrahana, Dronamukha and Sthaniya, and at places where districts meet, three members acquainted with Sacred Law (*dharmasthas*) and three ministers of the king (*amatyas*) shall carry on the administration of justice.

Valid and Invalid Transactions

They shall hold as void agreements (*vyavahara*) entered into in seclusion, inside the houses, in the dead of night, in forests, in secret, or with fraud.

The proposer and the accessory shall be punished with the first amercement (a fine ranging from 48 to 96 *panas* is called first amercement; from 200 to 500 *panas*, the middlemost; and from 500 to 1,000 *panas* the highest amercement [see Chapter 17, Book III]); the witnesses (*srotri,* voluntary hearers) shall each be punished with half of the above fine; and accepters shall suffer the loss they may have sustained.

But agreements entered into within the hearing of others, as well as those not otherwise condemnable shall be valid.

Those agreements which relate to the division of inheritance, sealed or unsealed deposits, or marriage; or those in which are concerned women who are either afflicted with disease or who do not stir out; as well as those entered into by persons who are not known to be of unsound mind shall be valid though they might be entered into inside houses.

Transactions relating to robbery, duel, marriage, or the execution of the king's order, as well as agreements entered into by persons who usually do their business during the first part of the night shall be valid though they might be done at night.

With regard to those persons who live most part of their life in forests, whether as merchants, cowherds, hermits, hunters or spies, their agreements though entered into in forests shall be valid.

If fraudulent agreements, only such shall be valid as are entered into by spies.

Agreements entered into by members of any association among themselves shall be valid though entered into in private.

Such agreements (i.e., those entered into in seclusion, etc.) except as detailed above shall be void.

So also agreements entered into by dependent or unauthorized persons, such as a father's mother, a son, a father having a son, an outcast brother, the youngest brother of a family of undivided interests, a wife having her husband or son, a slave, a hired labourer, any person who is too young or too old to carry on business, a convict (*abhisasta*), a cripple, or an afflicted person, shall not be valid. But it would be otherwise if he were authorized.

Even agreements entered into by an authorized person shall be void if he was at the time (of making the agreements) under provocation, anxiety or intoxication, or if he was a lunatic or a haunted person.

In all these cases, the proposer, his accessory and witnesses shall each be punished as specified above.

But such agreements as are entered into in person by anyone with others of his own community in suitable place and time are valid provided the circumstances, the nature, the description and the qualities of the case are credible.

Such agreements with the exception of orders (*adesa*, probably a bill of exchange) and hypothecations may be binding though entered into by a third person. Thus the determination of the forms of agreement.

The Trial

The year, the season, the month, the fortnight (*paksha*), the date, the nature and place of the deed, the amount of the debt as well as the country, the residence, the caste, the *gotra*, the name and occupation of both the plaintiff and the defendant both of whom must be fit to sue and defend (*kritasamarthavasthayoh*), having been registered first, the statements of the parties shall be taken down in such order as is required by the case. These statements shall then be thoroughly scrutinized.

The Offence of *Parokta*

Leaving out the question at issue, either of the parties takes resort to another; his previous statement is not consistent with his subsequent one; he insists on the necessity of considering the opinion of a third person, though it is not worthy of any such consideration; having commenced to answer the question at issue, he breaks off at once, even though he is ordered to continue; he introduces questions other than those specified by himself; he withdraws his own statement; he does not accept what his own witnesses have deposed to; and he holds secret conversation with his witnesses where he ought not to do so.

These constitute the offence of *Parokta*.

Punishment for Parokta

Fine for *parokta* is five times the amount (*paroktadandah panchabandha*).

Fine for self-assertion (*svayamvadi*—asserting without evidence) is ten times the amount (*dasabandha*.)

Payments for Witnesses

Fees for witnesses (*purushabhritih*) shall cover ⅛th of the amount (*astanga*). Provision proportional to the amount sued for may also be made for the expenses incurred by witnesses in their journey. The defeated party shall pay these two kinds of costs.

Countersuits

In cases other than duel, robbery, as well as disputes among merchants or trade guilds, the defendant shall file no counter-case against the plaintiff. Nor can there be a counter-case for the defendant.

Adjournments

The plaintiff shall ('rejoin') reply soon after the defendant has answered the questions at issue. Else he shall be guilty of *parokta*, for the plaintiff knows the determining factors of the case. But the defendant does not do so. The defendant may be allowed three or seven nights to prepare his defence. If he is not ready with his defence within that time, he shall be punished with a fine ranging from 3 to 12 *panas*. If he does not answer even after three fortnights, he shall be fined for *parokta*, and the plaintiff shall recover out of the defendant's property the amount of the case. But if the plaintiff sues for a mere return of gratitude (*pratyupakarana*), no (decree shall be passed).

The same punishment shall be meted out to such of the defendants as fail in their defence.

If the plaintiff fails to prove his case, he shall (also) be guilty of *parokta*. If he fails to substantiate his case against a dead or diseased defendant, he shall pay a fine and perform the (funeral) ceremonies of the defendant, as determined by the witnesses. If he proves his case, he may be permitted to take possession of the property hypothecated to him.

But if he is not a Brahman, he may, on his failure to prove his case, be caused to perform such ceremonials as drive out demons (*rakshoghna rakshitakam*.)

• In virtue of his power to uphold the observance of the respective duties of the four castes and of the four divisions of religious life, and in virtue of his power to guard against the violation of the *dharmas*, the king is the fountain of justice (*dharmapravartaka*.)

• Sacred law (*dharma*), evidence (*vyavahara*), history (*charitra*) and edicts of kings (*rajasasana*) are the four legs of law. Of these four in order, the later is superior to the one previously named.

• *Dharma* is eternal truth holding its sway over the world; *vyavahara*, evidence, is in witnesses; *charitra*, history, is to be found in the tradition (*sangraha*) of the people; and the order of kings is what is called *sasana*.

• As the duty of a king consists in protecting his subjects with justice, its observance leads him to heaven. He who does not protect his people or upsets the social order wields his royal sceptre (*danda*) in vain.

• It is power and power (*danda*) alone which, only when exercised by the king with impartiality and in proportion to guilt either over his son or his enemy, maintains both this world and the next.

• The king who administers justice in accordance with sacred law (*dharma*), evidence (*vyavahara*), history (*samstha*) and edicts of kings

(*Nyaya*) which is the fourth will be able to conquer the whole world bounded by the four quarters (*chaturantam mahim*).

• Whenever there is disagreement between history and sacred law or between evidence and sacred law, the matter shall be settled in accordance with sacred law.

• But whenever sacred law (*sastra*) is in conflict with rational law (*dharmanyaya*, i.e., king's law), reason shall be held authoritative; for there the original text (on which the sacred law has been based) is not available.

• Self-assertion (*svayamvada*) on the part of either of the parties has often been found faulty. Examination (*anuyoga*), honesty (*arjava*), evidence (*hetu*) and asseveration by oath (*sapatha*)—these alone can enable a man to win his cause.

• Whenever by means of the deposition of witnesses, the statements of either of the parties are found contradictory, and whenever the cause of either of the parties is found through the king's spies to be false, the decree shall be passed against that party.

[Thus ends Chapter 1, 'Determination of Forms of Agreement; Determination of Legal Disputes', in Book III, 'Concerning Law', of the Arthashastra of Kautilya. End of the fifty-eighth chapter from the beginning.]

Chapter 2

CONCERNING MARRIAGE: THE DUTY OF MARRIAGE, THE PROPERTY OF A WOMAN, AND COMPENSATIONS FOR REMARRIAGE

MARRIAGE precedes the other calls of life (*vyavahara*.) The giving in marriage of a maiden well adorned is called *brahma* marriage. The joint performance of sacred duties (by a man and a woman) is known as *prajapatya* marriage.

(The giving in marriage of a maiden) for a couple of cows is called *arsha*. (The giving in marriage of a maiden) to an officiating priest in a sacrifice is called *daiva*. The voluntary union of a maiden with her lover is called *gandharva*. Giving a maiden after receiving plenty of wealth (*sulka*) is termed *asura*. The abduction of a maiden is called *Rakshasa* marriage. The abduction of a maiden while she is asleep and in intoxication is called *paisacha* marraige.

Of these, the first four are ancestral customs of old and are valid on their being approved of by the father. The rest are to be sanctioned by both the father and the mother; for it is they that receive the money (*sulka*) paid by the bridegroom for their daughter. In case of the absence by death of either the father or the mother, the survivor will receive the *sulka*. If both of them are dead, the maiden herself shall receive it. Any kind of marriage is approvable, provided it pleases all those (that are concerned in it.)

Property of Women

Means of subsistence (*vritti*) or jewellery (*abadhya*) constitutes what is called the property of a woman. Means of subsistence valued at above two thousand shall be endowed (on her name). There is no limit to jewellery. It is no guilt for the wife to make use of this property in maintaining her son, her daughter-in-law or herself whenever her absent husband has made no provision for her maintenance. In calamities, disease and famine, in warding off dangers and in charitable acts, the husband too may make use of this property. Neither shall there be any complaint against the enjoyment of this property by mutual consent by a couple who have brought forth a twin. Nor shall there be any complaint if this property has been enjoyed for three years by those who are wedded in accordance with the customs of the first four kinds of marriage. But the enjoyment of this property in the cases of *gandharva* and *asura* marriages shall be liable to be restored together with interest on it. In the case of such marriages as are called *rakshasa* and *paisacha*, the use of this property shall be dealt with as theft. Thus the duty of marriage is dealt with.

On the death of her husband a woman, desirous to lead a pious life, shall at once receive not only her endowment and jewellery (*sthapyabharanam*) but also the balance of *sulka* due to her. If both of these two things are not actually in her possession, though nominally given to her, she shall at once receive both of them together with interest (on their value.) If she is desirous of a second marriage (*kutumbakama*), she shall be given on the occasion of her remarriage (*nivesakale*) whatever either her father-in-law or her husband or both had given to her. The time at which women can remarry shall be explained in connection with the subject of long sojourn of husbands.

If a widow marries any man other than of her father-in-law's selection (*svasurapratilo-myenanivishta*), she shall forfeit whatever had been given to her by her father-in-law and her husband.

The kinsmen (*gnatis*) of a woman shall return to her whatever property of her own she had placed in their custody. Whoever justly takes a woman under his protection shall equally protect her property. No woman shall succeed in her attempt to establish her title to the property of her husband.

If she lives a pious life, she may enjoy it (*dharmakama bhunjita*). No woman with a son or sons shall be at liberty to make free use of her own property (*stridhana*); for that property of hers her sons shall receive.

If a woman attempts to take possession of her own property under the plea of maintaining her sons, she shall be made to endow it in their name. If a woman has many male children, she shall conserve her own property in the same condition as she had received from her husband. Even that property which has been given her with full powers of enjoyment and disposal she shall endow in the name of her sons.

A barren widow who is faithful to the bed of her dead husband may, under the protection of her teacher, enjoy her property as long as she lives: for it is to ward off calamities that women are endowed with property. On her death, her property shall pass into the hands of her kinsmen (*dayada*). If the husband is alive and the wife is dead, her sons and daughters shall divide her property among themselves. If there are no sons, her daughters shall have it. In their absence her husband shall take that amount of money (*sulka*) which he had given her, and her relatives shall retake whatever in the shape of gift or dowry they had presented her. Thus the determination of the property of a woman is dealt with.

Remarriage of Males

If a woman either brings forth no (live) children, or has no male issue, or is barren, her husband shall wait for eight years (before marrying another). If she bears only a dead child, he has to wait for ten years. If she brings forth only females, he has to wait for twelve years. Then if he is desirous to have sons, he may marry another. In case of violating this rule, he shall be made to pay her not only *sulka*, her property (*stridhana*) and an adequate monetary compensation (*adhivedanikamartham*), but also a fine of 24 *panas* to the government. Having given the necessary amount of *sulka* and property (*stridhana*) even to those women who have not received such things on the occasion of their marriage with him, and also having given his wives the proportionate compensation and an adequate subsistence (*vritti*), he may marry any number of women; for women are created for the sake of sons. If many or all of them are at the same time in menses, he shall lie with that woman among them, whom he married earlier or who has a living son. In case of his concealing the fact of her being in menses or neglecting to lie with any of them after her menses, he shall pay a fine of 96 *panas*. Of women who either have sons or are pious or barren, or bring forth only a dead child or are beyond the age of menstruation, none shall be associated with against her liking. If a man has no inclination, he may not lie with his wife who is either afflicted with leprosy or is a lunatic. But if a woman is desirous of having sons, she may lie with men suffering from such disease.

If a husband either is of bad character or is long gone abroad or has become a traitor to his king or is likely to endanger the life of his wife or has fallen from his caste or has lost virility, he may be abandoned by his wife.

[Thus ends Chapter 2, 'The Duty of Marriage, the Property of a Woman, and Compensation for Remarriage', in Book III, 'Concerning Law', of the Arthashastra of Kautilya. End of the fifty-ninth chapter from the beginning.]

Chapter 3

THE DUTY OF A WIFE; MAINTENANCE OF A WOMAN; CRUELTY TO WOMEN; ENMITY BETWEEN HUSBAND AND WIFE; A WIFE'S TRANSGRESSION; HER KINDNESS TO ANOTHER; AND FORBIDDEN TRANSACTIONS

WOMEN, when twelve years old, attain their majority (*praptavyavahara*) and men when sixteen years old. If after attaining their majority, they prove disobedient to lawful authority (*asusrushayam*), women shall be fined 15 *pana*s and men, twice the amount.

Maintenance of a Woman

A woman who has a right to claim maintenance for an unlimited period of time shall be given as much food and clothing (*grasacchadana*) as is necessary for her or more than is necessary in proportion to the income of the maintainer (*yatha-purushaparivapam va*). If the period (for which such things are to be given to her) is limited, a certain amount of money fixed in proportion to the income of the maintainer shall be given to her; so also if she has not been given her *sulka*, property, and compensation (due to her for allowing her husband to remarry). If after parting with her husband, she places herself under the protection of anyone belonging to her father-in-law's family (*svasrakula*), or if she begins to live independently, her husband shall not be sued for (for her maintenance). Thus the determination of maintenance is dealt with.

Cruelty to Women

Women of refractive nature shall be taught manners by using such general expressions as 'Thou, half naked; thou, fully naked; thou, cripple; thou, fatherless; thou, motherless (*nagne vinagne nyange pitrke matrke vinagne ityanirdesena vinayagrahanam*). Or three beats either with a bamboo bark or with a rope or with the palm of the hand may be given on her hips. Violation of the above rules shall be liable to half the punishment levied for defamation and criminal hurt. The same kind of punishment shall be meted out to a woman who, moved with jealousy or hatred, shows cruelty to her husband. Punishments for engaging in sports at the door of, or outside her husband's house, shall be as dealt with elsewhere. Thus cruelty to women is dealt with.

Enmity Between Husband and Wife

A woman, who hates her husband, who has passed the period of seven turns of her menses, and who loves another shall immediately return to her husband both the endowment and jewellery she has received from him, and allow him to lie down with another woman. A man, hating his wife, shall allow her to take shelter in the house of a mendicant woman, or of her lawful guardians or of her kinsmen. If a man falsely accuses his wife of adultery with one of her or his kinsmen or with a spy—an accusation which can only be proved by eyewitnesses (*drishtilinge*)—or falsely accuses her of her intention to deprive him of her company, he shall pay a fine of 12 *panas*. A woman, hating her husband, cannot dissolve her marriage with him against his will. Nor can a man dissolve his marriage with his wife against her will. But from mutual enmity, divorce may be obtained (*parasparam dveshanmokshah*). If a man, apprehending danger from his wife desires divorce (*mokshamichhet*), he shall return to her whatever she was given (on the occasion of her marriage). If a woman, under the apprehension of danger from her husband, desires divorce, she shall forfeit her claim to her property; marriages contracted in accordance with the customs of the first four kinds of marriages cannot be dissolved.

Transgression

If a woman engages herself in amorous sports, or drinking in the face of an order to the contrary, she shall be fined 3 *panas*. She shall pay a fine of 6 *panas* for going out at daytime to sports or to see a woman or spectacles. She shall pay a fine of 12 *pana*s if she goes out to see another man or for sports. For the same offences committed at night, the fines shall be doubled. If a woman abducts another woman while the latter is asleep or under intoxication (*suptamatta-pravrajane*), or if she drags her husband as far as the door of the house, she shall be fined 12 *pana*s. If a woman leaves her house at night, she shall pay double the above fine. If a man and a woman make signs to each other with a view to sensual enjoyment, or carry on secret conversation (for the same purpose), the woman shall pay a fine of 24 *pana*s, and the man, double the amount. A woman, holding out her hair, the tie of her dress round her loins, her teeth or her nails, shall pay the first amercement, and a man, doing the same, twice the first amercement.

For holding conversation in suspicious places, whips may be substituted for fines. In the centre of the village, an outcaste person (*chandala*) may whip such women five times on each of the sides of their body. She may get rid of being whipped by paying a *pana* for each whip (*panikam va praharam mokshayet*). Thus transgression is dealt with.

Forbidden Transactions

With regard to a man and a woman who, though forbidden to carry on any mutual transaction, help each other, the woman shall be fined 12, 24 and 54 *pana*s respectively according as the help consists of (i) small things, (ii) heavy things and (iii) gold or gold coin (*hiranyasuvarnayoh*); and the man, at double the above rates. With regard to similar transaction between a man and a woman who cannot mix with each other (*agamvayoh*), half of the above punishment shall be levied. Similar punishment shall be meted out for any forbidden transaction with any men. Thus forbidden transactions are dealt with.

Treason, transgression and wandering at will shall deprive a woman of her claim not only to (i) *stridhana*, some form of subsistence of above 2,000 *pana*s and jewellery, (ii) and *ahita*, compensation she may have obtained for allowing her husband to marry another woman, but also (iii) to *sulka*, money which her parents may have received from her husband.

[Thus ends Chapter 3, 'The Duty of a Wife; Maintenance of a Woman; Enmity Between Husband and Wife; a Wife's Transgression; Her Kindness to Another; and Forbidden Transactions' in Book III, 'Concerning Law', of the Arthashastra of Kautilya. End of the sixtieth chapter from the beginning.]

Chapter 4

VAGRANCY, ELOPEMENT, AND SHORT AND LONG SOJOURNMENTS

IF under any other excuse than danger, a woman gets out of her husband's house, she shall be fined 6 *pana*s. If she gets out against the order (of her husband) to the contrary, she shall be fined 12 *pana*s. If she goes beyond her neighbouring house (*prativesagrihatigatayah*), she shall be fined 6 *pana*s. If she allows into her house her neighbour, takes into her house the alms of any mendicant, or the merchandise of any merchant, she shall be fined 12 *pana*s. If she deals as above though expressly forbidden, she shall be punished with the first amercement. If she goes out beyond the surrounding houses (*parigrihatigatayam*), she shall be fined 24 *pana*s. If under any other excuse than danger, she takes into her house the wife of another man, she shall be fined 100 *pana*s. But she will not be guilty if the entrance is effected without her knowledge or against her orders to the contrary.

My teacher says: With a view to avoiding danger, it is no offence for women to go to any male person who is a kinsman of her husband, or is a rich and prosperous gentleman (*sukhavastha*), or is the headman of the village or is one of her guardians (*anvadhikula*), or who belongs to the family of a mendicant woman, or to anyone of her own kinsmen.

But Kautilya questions: How is it possible for good women (*sadhvijana*) to know at least this fact that the family of her own kinsmen consisting of a number of males is good? It is no offence for women to go to the houses of kinsmen under the circumstances of death, disease, calamities, and confinement of women. Whoever prevents her going under such circumstances, shall be fined 12 *panas*. If a woman conceals herself under such circumstances, she shall forfeit her endowment. If her kinsmen conceal her (with a view to exempt her from giving her aid under such circumstances), they shall lose the balance of *sulka*, money due to them from her husband for giving her in marriage. Thus vagrancy is dealt with.

Elopement or Criminal Rendezvous

If leaving her husband's house, a woman goes to another village, she shall not only pay a fine of 12 *panas* but also forfeit her endowment and jewels (*sthapyabharanalopascha*). If under any other excuse than receiving her subsistence or pilgrimage (*bharmadanatirthagamanabhyamanyatra*), a woman goes to any other place even in company with an associable man, she shall not only pay a fine of 24 *panas* but also lose all kinds of social privileges (*sarvadharmalopascha*). But the man who allows such a woman to accompany him in his journey shall be punished with the first amercement. If both of them (man, and woman) have similar ideals in life (*tulyasreyasoh*) and are of sinful life (*papiyasoh*), each of them shall be punished with the middlemost amercement. If he whom a woman accompanies in her journey is her near relative, he shall not be punished. If a relative allows a woman to accompany him, though he is forbidden, he shall be punished with half the above fine (middlemost amercement). If on a road, or in the middle of a forest, or in any other concealed places a woman falls into the company of any other man, or if, with a view to enjoyment, she accompanies a suspicious or forbidden man, she shall be guilty of elopement (*sangrahanam vidyat*). It is no offence for women to fall into the company of actors, players, singers, fishermen, hunters, herdsmen, vintners, or persons of any other kind who usually travel with their women. If a man takes a woman with him on his journey, though forbidden to do so, or if a woman accompanies a man though she is forbidden to do so, half of the above fines shall be meted out to them. Thus elopement is dealt with.

Remarriage of Women

Wives who belong to Sudra, Vaisya, Kshatriya or Brahman caste, and who have not given birth to children, should wait as long as a year for their husbands who have gone abroad for a short time; but if they are such as have given birth to children, they should wait for their absent husbands for more than a year. If they are provided with maintenance, they should wait for twice the period of time just mentioned. If they are not so provided with, their well-to-do *jnatis* should maintain them either for four or for eight years. Then the *jnatis* should leave them to marry after taking what had been presented to them on the occasion of their marriages. If the husband is a Brahman, studying abroad, his wife who has no issue should wait for him for ten years; but if she has given birth to children, she should wait for twelve years. If the husband is of Kshatriya caste, his wife should wait for him till her death; but even if she bears children to a *savarna* husband, (i.e., a second husband belonging to the same *gotra* as that of the former husband) with a view to avoiding the extinction of her race, she shall not be liable to contempt thereof (*savarnatascha prajata na pavadam labheta*). If the wife of an absent husband lacks maintenance and is deserted by well-to-do *jnatis*, she may remarry one whom she likes and who is in a position to maintain her and relieve her misery.

A young wife (*kumari*) who is wedded in accordance with the customs of the first four kinds of marriage (*dharmavivahat*), and whose husband has gone abroad and is heard of shall wait for him for the period of seven menses (*saptatirthanyakanksheta*), provided she has not publicly announced his name; but she shall wait for him a year in case of her having announced the name of her absent husband who is heard of. In the case of a husband who is gone abroad but who is not heard of, his wife shall wait for the period of five menses, but if the absent husband is not heard of, his wife shall wait for him for the period of ten menses. In the case of a husband who is gone abroad and is not heard of, his wife shall, if she has received only a part of *sulka* from him, wait for him for the period of three menses; but if he is heard of, she shall wait for him for the period of seven menses. A young wife who has received the whole amount of *sulka* shall wait for the period of five menses for her absent husband who is not heard of; but if he is heard of, she shall wait for him for the period of ten menses. Then with the permission of judges (*dharma-sthairvisrishta*), she may marry one whom she likes; for neglect of intercourse with wife after her monthly ablution is, in the opinion of Kautilya, a violation of one's duty (*tirthoparodho hi dharmavadha iti Kautilyah*).

In the case of husbands who have long gone abroad (*dirgrhapravasinah*), who have become ascetics, or who have been dead, their wives, having no issue, shall wait for them for the period of seven menses; but if they have given birth to children, they shall wait for a year. Then (each of these women) may marry the brother of her husband. If there are a number of brothers to her lost husband, she shall marry such one of them as is next in age to her former husband, or as is virtuous and is capable of protecting her, or one who is the youngest and unmarried. If there are no brothers to her lost husband, she may marry one who belongs to the same *gotra* as her husband's or relative. But if there are many such persons as can be selected in marriage, she shall choose one who is a nearer relation of her lost husband.

If a woman violates the above rule by remarrying one who is not a kinsman (*dayada*) of her husband, then the woman and the man who remarry each other, those that have given her in remarriage and those who have given their consent to it shall all be liable to the punishment for elopement.

[Thus ends Chapter 4, 'Vagrancy; Elopement and Short and Long Sojournments', in Book III, 'Concerning Law', of the Arthashastra of Kautilya. End of the sixty-first chapter from the beginning.]

Chapter 5

DIVISION OF INHERITANCE

SONS whose fathers and mothers or ancestors are alive cannot be independent (*anisvarah*). After their time, division of ancestral property among descendants from the same ancestor shall take place, calculating per *sterpes* (according to fathers).

Self-acquired property of any of the sons with the exception of that kind of property which is earned by means of parental property is not divisible. Sons or grandsons till the fourth generation from the first parent shall also have prescribed shares (*amsabhajah*) in that property which is acquired by means of their undivided ancestral property; for the line (*pindah*) as far as the fourth generation is uninterrupted (*avichchhinnah*). But those whose line or genealogy from the first ancestor is interrupted (*vichchhinnapindah*, i.e., those who are subsequent to the fourth generation), shall have equal divisions. Those who have been living together shall redivide their property whether they had already divided their ancestral property before or they had received no such property at all. Of sons, he who brings the ancestral property to a prosperous condition shall also have a share of the profit.

If a man has no male issue, his own brothers, or persons who have been living with him, (*saha jivino va*), shall take possession of his movable property (*dravyam*); and his daughters, (born of marriages other than the first four), shall have his immovable property (*riktham*). If one has sons, they shall have the property; if one has (only) daughters born of such marriage as is contracted in accordance with the customs of any of the first four kinds of marriage, they shall have the property; if there are neither sons nor such daughters, the dead man's father, if living, shall have it; if he too is not alive, the dead man's brothers and the sons of his brothers shall have it; if there are many fatherless brothers, all of them shall divide it; and each of the many sons of such brothers shall have one share due to his father (*piturekamamsam*); if the brothers (*sodarya*) are the sons of many fathers, they shall divide it calculating from their fathers.

Among a dead man's father, brother, and brother's sons, the succeeding ones shall depend on the preceding ones if living (for their shares); likewise the youngest or the eldest claiming his own share.

A father, distributing his property while he is alive, shall make no distinction in dividing it among his sons. Nor shall a father deprive without sufficient reason any of the sons of his share. Father being dead, the elder sons shall show favour to the younger ones, if the latter are not of bad character.

Time of Dividing Inheritance

Division of inheritance shall be made when all the inheritors have attained their majority. If it is made before, the minors shall have their shares, free of all debts.

These shares of the minors shall be placed in the safe custody of the relatives of their mothers, or of aged gentlemen of the village, till they attain their majority. The same rule shall hold good in the case of those who have gone abroad. Unmarried brothers shall also be paid as much marriage cost as is equal to that incurred in the marriages of married brothers (*sannivishtasamamasannivishtebhyo naivesanikam dadyuh*). Daughters too (unmarried) shall be paid adequate dowry (*pradanikam*), payable to them on the occasion of their marriages.

Both assets and liabilities shall be equally divided.

My teacher says that poor people (*nishkinchanah*) shall equally distribute among themselves even the mud vessels (*udapatram*).

In the opinion of Kautilya, it is unnecessary to say so (*chhalam*); for as a rule, division is to be made of all that is in existence, but of nothing that is not in existence. Having declared before witnesses the amount of property common to all (*samanya*) as well as the property constituting additional shares (*amsa*) of the brothers (in priority of their birth), division of inheritance shall be carried on. Whatever is badly and unequally divided or is involved in deception, concealment or secret acquisition, shall be redivided.

Property for which no claimant is found (*adayadakam*) shall go to the king, except the property of a woman, of a dead man for whom no funeral rites have been performed, or of a niggardly man with the exception of that of a Brahman learned in the Vedas. That (the property of the learned) shall be made over to those who are well versed in the three Vedas.

Persons fallen from caste, persons born of outcaste men, and eunuchs shall have no share; likewise idiots, lunatics, the blind and lepers. If the idiots, etc., have wives with property, their issues who are not equally idiots, etc., shall share inheritance. All these persons excepting those that are fallen from caste (*patitavarjah*) shall be entitled to only food and clothing.

If these persons have been married (before they became fallen, etc.) and if their line is likely to become extinct, their relatives may beget sons for them and give proportional shares of inheritance to those sons.

[Thus ends Chapter 5, 'Division of Inheritance' in Book III, 'Concerning Law', of the Arthashastra of Kautilya. End of the sixty two chapter from the beginning.]

Chapter 6

SPECIAL SHARES IN INHERITANCE

GOATS shall be the special shares of the eldest of sons, born of the same mother, among, Brahmans; horses among Kshatriyas; cows among Vaisyas; and sheep among Sudras. The blind of the same animals shall be the special shares to the middlemost sons; species of variegated colour of the same animals shall be the special shares to the youngest of sons. In the absence of quadruped, the eldest shall take an additional share of the whole property excepting precious stones; for by this act alone, he will be bound in his duty to his ancestors.

The above method is in accordance with the rules observed among the followers of Usanas.

The father being dead, his carriage and jewellery shall be the special share to the eldest; his bed, seat, and bronze plate in which he used to take his meals (*bhuktakamsyam*), to the middlemost; and black grains, iron, domestic utensils, cows and cart to the youngest. The rest of the property, or the above things too may be equally divided among themselves. Sisters shall have no claim to inheritance; they shall have the bronze plate and jewellery of their mother after her death. An impotent eldest son shall have only one-third of the special share usually given to the eldest; if the eldest son follows a condemnable occupation or if he has given up the observance of religious duties, he shall have only one-fourth of the special share; if he is unrestrained in his actions he shall have nothing.

The same rule shall hold good with the middlemost and youngest sons; of these two, one who is endowed with manliness (*manushopetah*), shall have half the special share usually given to the eldest.

With regard to sons of many wives:

Of sons of two wives of whom only one woman has gone through all the necessary religious ceremonials, or both of whom have not, as maidens, observed necessary religious rites, or one of whom has brought forth twins, it is by birth that primogenitureship is decided.

Shares in inheritance for such sons as *Suta*, *Magadha*, *Vratya* and *Rathakara* shall depend on the abundance of paternal property; the rest, i.e., sons other than *Suta*, etc., of inferior birth, shall be dependent on the eldest for their subsistence. Dependent sons shall have equal divisions.

Of sons begotten by a Brahman in the four castes, the son of a Brahman woman shall take four shares; the son of a Kshatriya woman three shares; the son of a Vaisya woman two shares, and the son of a Sudra woman one share.

The same rule shall hold good in the case of Kshatriya and Vaisya fathers begetting sons in three or two castes in order.

An *anantara* son of a Brahman, i.e., a son begotten by a Brahman on a woman of next lower caste, shall, if endowed with manly or superior qualities (*manushopetah*), take an equal share (with other sons of inferior qualities); similarly *anantara* sons of Kshatriya or Vaisya fathers shall, if endowed with manly or superior qualities, take half or equal shares (with others). An only son to two mothers of different castes shall take possession of the whole property and maintain the relatives of his father. A *palrasava* son begotten by a Brahman on a Sudra woman, shall take one-third share; a *sapinda* (an agnate) or a *kulya* (the nearest cognate) of the Brahman shall take the remaining two shares, being thereby obliged to offer funeral libation; in the absence of agnates or cognates, the deceased father's teacher or student shall take the two shares.

Or on the wife of such a Brahman shall a *sagotra*, relative bearing the same family name, or a (*matribandha*) relative of his mother, beget a natural son (*kshetraja*), and this son may take that wealth.

[Thus ends Chapter 6, 'Special Shares in Inheritance' in Book III, 'Concerning Law', of the Arthashastra of Kautilya. End of the 63rd chapter from the beginning.]

Chapter 7

DISTINCTION BETWEEN SONS

MY preceptor says that the seed sown in the field of another shall belong to the owner of that field. Others hold that the mother being only the receptacle for the seed (*mata bhastra*), the child must belong to him from whose seed it is born. Kautilya says that it must belong to both the living parents.

The son begotten by a man on his wife who has gone through all the required ceremonials is called *aurasa*, natural son; equal to him is the son of an appointed daughter (*putrikaputra*); the son begotten on a wife by another man, appointed for the purpose, and of the same *gotra* as that of the husband; or of a different *gotra*, is called *kshetraja*; on the death of the begetter, the *kshetraja* son will be the son to both the fathers, follow the *gotras* of both, offer funeral libations to both, and take possession of the immovable property (*riktha*) of both of them; of the same status as the *kshetraja* is he who is secretly begotten in the house of relatives and is called *gudhaja*, secretly born; the son cast off by his natural parents is called *apaviddha* and will belong to that man who performs necessary religious ceremonials to him; the son born of a maiden (before wedlock) is called *kanina*; the son born of a woman married while carrying is called *sahodha*; the son of a remarried woman (*punarbhatayah.*) is called *paunarbhava*. A natural son can claim relationship both with his father and his father's relatives; but a son born to another man can have relationship only with his adopter. Of the same status as the latter is he who is given in adoption with water by both the father and mother and is called *datta*. The son who, either of his own accord or following the intention of his relatives, offers himself to be the son of another, is called *upagata*. He who is appointed as a son is called *kritaka*; and he who is purchased is called *krita*.

On the birth of a natural son, *asavarna* sons shall have one-third of inheritance while *asavarna* sons shall have only food and clothing.

Sons begotten by Brahmans or Kshatriyas on women of next lower caste (*anantaraputrah*) are called *savarnas*; but on women of castes lower by two grades are called *asavarnas*. (Of such *asavarna* sons), the son begotten by a Brahman on a Vaisya woman is called *ambashtha*; on a Sudra woman is called nishada or parasava. The son begotten by a Kshatriya on a Sudra woman is known as ugra; the son begotten by a Vaisya on a Sudra woman is no other than a Sudra. Sons begotten by men of impure life of any of the four castes on women of lower castes next to their own are called *vratyas*.

The above kinds of sons are called *anuloma*, sons begotten by men of higher on women of lower castes.

Sons begotten by a Sudra on women of higher castes are *ayogava*, *kshatta*, and *chandala*; by a Vaisya, *magadha*, and *vaidehaka*; and by a *Kshatriya*, *suta*. But men of the names, *suta* and *magadha*, celebrated in the Puranas, are quite different and of greater merit than either Brahmans or Kshatriyas. The above kinds of sons are *pratiloma*, sons begotten by men of lower on women of higher castes, and originate on account of kings violating all *dharmas*.

The son begotten by an *ugra* on a *nishada* woman is called *kukkuta* and the same is called *pulkasa*, if begotten in the inverse order. The son begotten by an *ambhashtha* on a *vaidehaka* woman is named *vaina*; the same in the reverse order is called *kusilava*. An *ugra* begets on a *kshatta* woman as *vapaka*. These and other sons are of mixed castes (*Antaralas*).

A *vainya* becomes a *rathakara*, chariot maker, by profession. Members of this caste shall marry among themselves.

Both in customs and avocations they shall follow their ancestors. They may either become Sudras or embrace any other lower castes excepting *chandalas*.

The king who guides his subjects in accordance with the above rules will attain heaven; otherwise he will fall into the hell.

Offsprings of mixed castes (*antaralas*) shall have equal divisions of inheritance.

Partition of inheritance shall be made in accordance with the customs prevalent in the country, caste, guild (*sangha*), or the village of the inheritors.

[Thus ends Chapter 7 'Distinction Between Sons' in Book III, 'Concerning Law', of the Arthashastra of Kautilya. End of the sixty-fouth chapter from the beginning.]

Chapter 8

BUILDINGS

DISPUTES concerning *Vastu* are dependent for settlement on the evidences to be furnished by people living in the neighbourhood.

Houses, fields, gardens, building of any kind (*setubandhah*), lakes and tanks are each called *Vastu*.

The fastening of the roof of a house to the transverse beam by means of iron bolts is called *setu* (*karna-kilaya-sabandho' nugriham setuh*). In conformity with the stability of the *setu*, houses shall be constructed. Not encroaching upon what belongs to others, new houses may be constructed.

Foundation (*pade bandhah*) shall be 2 *aratni*s by 3 *pada*s. Except in the case of temporary structures for the confinement of women for ten days, all permanent houses shall be provided with a dunghill (*avaskara*), water course (*bhrama*), and a well (*udapanum*). Violation of this rule shall be punished with the first amercement.

The same rule shall hold good regarding the necessity of constructing closets, pits and water courses on festive occasions.

From each house a water course of sufficient slope and 3 *pada*s or 11 *aratni*s long shall be so constructed that water shall either flow from it in a continuous line or fall from it (into the drain).

Violation of this rule shall be punished with a fine of 54 *pana*s.

Beginning with a *pada* or an *aratni*, an apartment measuring 3 *pada*s by 4 *pada*s shall be made for locating the fire for worship (*agnishtham*), or a water butt, (*udanjaram*), or a corn mill (*rochanim*), or a mortar (*kuttinin*).

Violation of this rule shall be punished with a fine of 24 *panas*.

Between any two houses or between the extended portions of any two houses, the intervening space shall be 4 *padas*, or 3 *padas*. The roofs of adjoining houses may either be 4 *angulas* apart, or one of them may cover the other. The front door (*anidvaram*) shall measure a *kishku*; there shall be no impediment inside the house for opening one or the other of the folds of the door. The upper story shall be provided with a small but high window. [If a neighbouring house is obstructed by it, the window should be closed.] The owners of houses may construct their houses in any other way they collectively like, but they shall avoid whatever is injurious. With a view to warding off the evil consequences of rain, the top of the roof (*vanalatyaschordhvam*) shall be covered over with a broad mat, not blowable by the wind. Neither shall the roof be such as will easily bend or break. Violation of this rule shall be punished with the first amercement. The same punishment shall be meted out for causing annoyance by constructing doors or windows facing those of others houses except when these houses are separated by the king's road or the high road.

If a pit, steps, water course, ladder, dunghill, or, any other parts of a house offer or cause annoyance to outsiders, or in any way obstruct the enjoyment of others (*bhoganigrahe cha*), or cause water to collect and thereby injure the wall of a neighbouring house, the owner shall be punished with a fine of 12 *panas*. If the annoyance is due to feces and urine, the fine shall be double the above. The water-course or gutter shall offer free passage for water; otherwise the fine shall be 12 *panas*.

The same fine (12 *panas*) shall be meted out not only to a tenant who, though asked to evacuate, resides in the house, but also to the owner who forces out a renter who has paid his rent (for his house), unless the renter is involved in such acts as defamation, theft, robbery, abduction, or enjoyment with a false title. He who voluntarily evacuates a house shall pay the balance of the annual rent.

If anyone of a party does not take part in the construction of a building which is intended for the common use of all the members of that party or if anyone obstructs another member of a party in making use of any part of such a building, he shall be fined 12 *panas*. Similarly if anyone mars another's enjoyment of such a building, he shall be fined double the above.

With the exception of private rooms and parlours, (*angana*) all other open parts of houses as well as apartments where fire is ever kindled for worship or a mortar is situated shall be thrown open for common use.

[Thus ends Chapter 8, 'Buildings', in Book III, 'Concerning Law', of the Arthashastra of Kautilya. End of the sixty-fifth chapter from the beginning.]

Chapter 9

SALE OF BUILDINGS, BOUNDARY DISPUTES, DETERMINATION OF BOUNDARIES, AND MISCELLANEOUS HINDRANCES

RICH persons among kinsmen or neighbours shall in succession go for the purchase of land and other holdings. Neighbours of good family, forty in number and different from the purchasers above mentioned, shall congregate in front of the building for sale and announce it as such. Accurate description of the exact boundaries of fields, gardens, buildings of any kind, lakes or tanks shall be declared before the elders of the village or of the neighbourhood. If, on crying aloud thrice 'Who will purchase this at such and such a price'? no opposition is offered, the purchaser may proceed to purchase the holding in question. If at this time the value of the property is increased by bidding even among persons of the same community, the increased amount together with the toll on the value shall be handed over into the king's treasury. The bidder (*vikrayapratikroshta*) shall pay the toll. Bidding for a property in the absence of its owner shall be punished with a fine of 24 *panas*. If the owner does not come forward even on the expiration of seven nights, the bidder may take possession of the property. Sale of building, etc. (*vastu*) to other than the bidder shall be punished with a fine of 200 *panas*; if the property is other than buildings, etc. (*vastu*), the fine for the above offence shall be 24 *panas*. Thus the sale of buildings is dealt with.

Boundary Disputes

In all disputes regarding the boundary between any two villages, neighbours or elders of five or ten villages (*panchagrami dasagrami va*) shall investigate the case on the evidence to be furnished from natural or artificial boundary marks.

Elders among cultivators and herdsmen, or outsiders who have had the experience of former possession in the place, or one or many persons (not) personally acquainted with the boundary marks under dispute shall first describe the boundary marks, and then, wearing unusual dress (*viparitaveshah*), shall lead the people (to the place). If the boundary marks just described are not found, a fine of 1,000 *panas* shall be imposed (on the misleading or guilty person). If, however, they arrive at the exact spot, the party that has either encroached upon the boundary or has destroyed the boundary marks shall be similarly punished.

The king shall beneficially distribute among others those holdings which have no boundary marks or which have ceased to be enjoyed by any person.

Disputes About Fields

Disputes concerning fields shall be decided by the elders of the neighbourbood or of the village. If they are divided in their opinions, decision shall be sought for from a number of pure and respectable people, or, the disputants may equally divide the disputed holding among themselves. If both of these methods fail, the holding (*vastu*) under dispute shall be taken possession of by the king. The same rule shall hold good in the case of a holding for which no claimant is forthcoming; or it may beneficially be distributed among the people. Occupation of a holding (*vastu*) by force shall be punished as theft.

If a holding is taken possession of by another on some reasonable grounds, he shall be made to pay to the owner some rent, the amount of which is to be fixed after mature considerations of what is necessary for the subsistence of the cultivator of the holding by him.

Encroachment upon boundaries shall be punished with the first amercement. Destruction of boundaries shall be punished with a fine of 24 *panas*. The same rules shall hold good in disputes concerning hermitage in forests, pasturelands, high roads, cremation grounds, temples, sacrificial places, and places of pilgrimage. Thus the determination of boundaries is dealt with.

Miscellaneous Hindrances

All kinds of disputes shall depend for their settlement on the evidence to be furnished by neighbours. Of pasturelands, fields (*kedara*), flower gardens, a threshing floor (*khala*), houses, and stables of horses (*vahanakoshtha*), hindrance to anyone coming first in order shall be removed in preference to the one or more coming later in the series. With the exception of people in forests of Brahmans and of *soma* plants, temples, and places of sacrifice and pilgrimage, any person causing, while making use of a by-path to go to tanks, rivers, or fields, damage to the seeds sown in the fields of others, shall pay as much compensation to the sufferers as is equivalent to the damage.

If the owner of anyone of the following, viz., wet-fields, parks, or any kinds of buildings, causes damage to the rest owned by others, the fine shall be double the value of the damage.

The water of a lower tank shall not submerge the field irrigated by a higher tank.

The natural flow of water from a higher to a lower tank shall not be stopped unless the lower tank has ceased to be useful for three consecutive years. Violation of this rule shall be punished with the first amercement. The same punishment shall be meted out for emptying a tank of its water (*tatakavamanam cha*). Buildings of any kind (*setubandha*), neglected for five consecutive years shall be forfeited, except in calamities.

Remission of Taxes

In the case of construction of new works, such as tanks, lakes, etc., taxes (on the lands below such tanks) shall be remitted for five years (*panchavarshikah pariharah*). For repairing neglected or ruined works of similar nature, taxes shall be remitted for four years. For improving or extending waterworks, taxes shall be remitted for three years. In the case of acquiring such newly started works by mortgage or purchase, taxes on the lands below such works shall be remitted for two years. If uncultivated tracts are acquired (for cultivation) by mortgage, purchase or in any other way, remission of taxes shall be for two years. Out of crops grown by irrigation by means of wind power or bullocks (*vatapravartimanandinibandhayatana*) or below tanks, in fields, parks, flower gardens, or in any other way, so much of the produce as would not entail hardship on the cultivators may be given to the government. Persons who cultivate the lands below tanks, etc., of others at a stipulated price (*prakraya*), or for annual rent (*avakraya*), or for certain number of shares of the crops grown (*bhaga*) or persons who are permitted to enjoy such lands free of rent of any kind, shall keep the tanks, etc., in good repair; otherwise they shall be punished with a fine of double the loss.

Persons, letting out the water of tanks, etc., at any other place than their sluice gate (*apare*), shall pay a fine of 6 *panas*; and persons who recklessly obstruct the flow of water from the sluice gate of tanks shall also pay the same fine.

[Thus ends Chapter 9, 'Sale of Buildings, Boundary Disputes, Determination of Boundaries, and Miscellaneous Hindrances' in Book III, 'Concerning Law' of the Arthashastra of Kautilya. End of the sixty-sixth chapter from the beginning.]

Chapter 10

DESTRUCTION OF PASTURELANDS, FIELDS AND ROADS, AND NONPERFORMANCE OF AGREEMENTS

PERSONS who obstruct, or make any kind of mischief with the flow of water intended for cultivation shall be punished with the first amercement. Construction in the sites belonging to others, of any buildings with a view to attracting pilgrims thereto, of abodes of worship (*chaitya*), or of temples of gods; as also the sale or mortgage, or causing the sale or mortgage, of any long- continued charitable building (*purvanuvrittam dharmasetum*) shall be punished with the middlemost amercement. Those who are witnesses to such transactions shall be punished with the highest amercement excepting in the case of neglected or ruined buildings. In the absence of claimants to dilapidated religious buildings, villagers (*gramah*), or charitable people (*punyasilava*) may repair them.

Blocking the Roads

Forms of roads and paths have been dealt with in connection with the construction of forts (Chapter 3, Book II).

Obstruction to roads for inferior beasts or men shall be punished with a fine of 12 *panas*; to roads for superior beasts 24 *panas*; to roads for elephants or to those leading to fields, 54 *panas*; to those leading to any buildings or forests (*setuvanapatham*), 600 *panas*; to those for burial grounds or villages, 200 *panas*; to those for *dronamukha*, a fortress, 500 *panas*; and those leading to *sthaniya*, country parts, or pasture grounds, 1,000 *panas*. The same fines shall be meted out in case of ploughing the several roads too deep (*atikarshane chaisham*); and one-fourth of the same fines for ploughing merely on their surface.

If a cultivator or a neighbour makes encroachment upon a field during the time of sowing seeds, he shall be fined 12 *panas*, unless the encroachment is due to evils, calamities or intolerable occurrences arising otherwise from the field (*anyatra doshopanipatavishahyebhyah*).

Settling in Villages

Taxpayers shall sell or mortgage their fields to taxpayers alone; Brahmans shall sell or mortgage their *brahmadaya* or gifted lands only to those who are endowed with such lands; otherwise they shall be punished with the first amercement. The same punishment shall be meted out to a taxpayer who settles in a village not inhabited by taxpayers. If a taxpayer takes the place of another taxpayer, he shall enjoy all the holdings but the house of the latter. Even the house may be given to the new settler. If a person cultivates an inalienable land of another person who does not cultivate it, such a person shall restore the same after five years' enjoyment on taking a certain amount of compensation equivalent to the improvement he made on the lands. Persons who are not taxpayers and who sojourn abroad shall retain the right of ownership (*bhogam*) of their lands.

The Headman of the Village

When the headman of a village has to travel on account of any business of the whole village, the villagers shall by turns accompany him.

Those who cannot do this shall pay 1½ *panas* for every *yojana*. If the headman of a village sends out of the village any person except a thief, or an adulterer, he shall be punished with a fine of 24 *panas*, and the villagers with the first amercement (for doing the same).

Re-entrance into a village for a person previously sent out of it (*nirastasya*) is explained by 'settlement of persons in villages' (treated of above).

At a distance of 800 *angulas* around every village, an enclosure with timber posts shall be constructed.

Trespassing Cattle

Pasturelands, plains and forests may be availed of for grazing cattle.

For camels or buffaloes allowed to stray after grazing in pasture grounds, the fine shall be one-fourth of a *pana*; for cows, horses or asses, one-eighth of a *pana*; for inferior quadrupeds one-sixteenth of a *pana*; and for cattle found lying thereon after grazing, fines shall be double the above; for cattle ever found to live in the vicinity of pasture grounds, the fines shall be four times the above.

Bulls, let out in the name of the village deity (*gramadevavrishah*), cows which have not passed ten days inside the enclosure after calving, or bulls or bullocks kept for crossing cows shall not be punished. If crops are eaten away by animals, the owner or owners of them shall, if proven guilty, be made to pay twice as much as the loss. Persons driving their cattle through a field without intimating the owner shall be fined 12 *pana*s. Any person who allows his cattle to stray shall be fined 24 *pana*s; cowherds doing the same with the cattle under their care shall be fined half the above. The same punishment shall be meted out for letting cattle graze in flower gardens. For breaking the fence of fields, the punishment shall be double the above. If cattle are allowed to stray and eat the grains stored in houses, a threshing floor, or a courtyard, the owners of the cattle shall pay adequate compensation. If beasts maintained in reserve forests are found grazing in a field, they shall be brought to the notice of the forest officers and the beasts shall be driven out without being hurt or killed. Stray cattle shall be driven out by the use of ropes or whips. Persons hurting them in any way shall be liable to the punishment for assault or violence. Persons who invite (cattle to graze in the fields of others) or who are caught while committing such offences shall by all means be put down. Thus the destruction of pasturelands, fields, and roads is dealt with.

Non-performance of Agreement

The fine levied on a cultivator, who arriving at a village for work does not work, shall be taken by the village itself. He shall refund not only double the amount of the wages he received promising to work, but also double the value of food and drink with which he has been provided. If the work is one of sacrificial performance (*prahavaneshu*), then also he shall pay double the amount of the wages. Any person who does not cooperate in the work of preparation for a public show, shall, together with his family, forfeit his right to enjoy the show (*preksha*). If a man who has not cooperated in preparing for a public play or spectacle is found hearing or witnessing it under hiding, or if anyone refuses to give his aid in a work beneficial to all, he shall be compelled to pay double the value of the aid due from him. The order of any person attempting to do a work beneficial to all shall be obeyed. Disobedience in such a case shall be punished with a fine of 12 *panas*. If others unitedly beat or hurt such a person so ordering, each of them shall pay double the amount of the fine usually levied for such offence. If among the above offenders one is a Brahman or a person superior to a Brahman, he shall first be punished. If a Brahman does not take part in the combined performance of any sacrifice of his village, he shall not be violated but may be persuaded to pay a share.

The above rules shall also apply to non-performance of agreements among countries (*desa*), castes, families, and assemblies.

Those who, with their united efforts, construct on roads buildings of any kind (*setubandha*) beneficial to the whole country and who not only adorn their villages but also keep watch on them shall be shown favourable concessions by the king.

[Thus ends Chapter 10 'Destruction of Pasturelands, Fields and Roads, and Nonperformance of Agreements', in Book III, 'Concerning Law', of the Arthashastra of Kautilya. End of the sixty-seventh chapter from the beginning.]

Chapter 11

RECOVERY OF DEBTS

AN interest of a *pana* and a quarter per cent per month is just. Five *panas* per cent per month is commercial interest (*vyavahariki*). Ten *panas* per month prevails among forests. Twenty *panas* per cent per month prevails among sea traders (*samudranam*). Persons exceeding, or causing to exceed, the above rate of interest shall be punished with the first amercement; and hearers of such transactions shall each pay half of the above fine.

The nature of the transactions between creditors and debtors, on which the welfare of the kingdom depends, shall always be scrutinized. Interest in grains in seasons of good harvest shall not exceed more than half when valued in money. Interest on stocks (*prakshepa*) shall be one half of the profit and be regularly paid as each year expires. If it is allowed to accumulate owing either to the intention or to the absence abroad (of the receiver or payer), the amount payable shall be equal to twice the share or principal (*mulyadvigunah*). A person claiming interest when it is not due, or representing as principal the total amount of his original principal and the interest thereon, shall pay a fine of four times the amount under dispute (*bandhachaturgunah*).

A creditor who sues for four times the amount lent by him shall pay a fine of four times the unjust amount.

Of this fine, the creditor shall pay ¾ths and the debtor ¼th. Interest on debts due from persons who are engaged in sacrifices taking a long time (*dirghasatra*), or who are suffering from disease, or who are detained in the houses of their teachers (for learning), or who are either minors or too poor, shall not accumulate.

A creditor refusing to receive the payment of his debt shall pay a fine of 12 *panas*. If the refusal is due to some (reasonable) cause, the amount free from interest (for subsequent time) shall be kept in the safe custody of others. Debts neglected for ten years, except in the case of minors, aged persons, diseased persons, persons involved in calamities, or persons who are sojourning abroad or have fled the country and except in the case of disturbances in the kingdom (*rajyavibhrama*), shall not be received back.

Sons of a deceased debtor shall pay the principal with interest (*kusi dam*). (In the absence of sons), kinsmen claiming the share of the dead man, or sureties, such as joint partners of the debt (*sahagrahinah pratibhuvo va*) shall pay the same. No other kind of surety is valid (*na pratibhavyamanyat*); a minor, as surety, is inefficient (*balapratibhavyam asaram,* i.e., surety of a minor is not strong).

A debt, the payment of which is not limited by time or place or both (*asamkhyatadesakalam*), shall be paid by the sons, grandsons or any other heirs of the dead debtor. Any debt, the payment of which is not limited by time or place or both and for which life, marriage, or land is pledged, shall be borne by sons or grandsons.

Regarding Many Debts Against One

Excepting the case of a debtor going abroad, no debtor shall simultaneously be sued for more than one debt by one or two creditors. Even in the case of a debtor going abroad, he shall pay his debts in the order in which he borrowed them or shall first pay his debts due to the king or a learned Brahman.

Debts contracted from each other by either a husband or a wife, either a son or a father, or by anyone among brothers of undivided interests shall be irrecoverable.

Cultivators or government servants shall not be caught hold of for debts while they are engaged in their duties (or at work).

A wife, though she has (not) heard of the debt (*pratisravani*), shall not be caught hold of for the debt contracted by her husband, excepting in the case of herdsmen and joint cultivators (*gopalakardhasitikebhyah*). But a husband may be caught for the debt contracted by his wife. If it is admitted that a man fled the country without providing for the debt contracted by his wife, the highest amercement shall be meted out; if not admitted, witnesses shall be depended upon.

Witnesses

It is obligatory to produce three witnesses who are reliable, honest and respected. At least two witnesses acceptable to the parties are necessary; never one witness in the case of debts.

Wife's brothers, co-partners, prisoners (*abaddha*), creditors, debtors, enemies, maintained persons, or persons once punished by the government shall not be taken as witnesses. Likewise persons legally unfit to carry on transactions, the king, persons learned in the Vedas, persons depending for their maintenance on villages (*gramabhritaka*), lepers, persons suffering from bodily erruptions, outcast persons, persons of mean avocation, the blind, the deaf, the dumb, egotistic persons, females, or government servants shall not be taken as witnesses excepting in the case of transactions in one's own community. In dispute concerning assault, theft or abduction, persons other than wife's brothers, enemies and co-partners, can be witnesses. In secret dealings, a single woman or a single man who has stealthily heard or seen them can be a witness, with the exception of the king or an ascetic. On the side of prosecution, masters against servants, priests or teachers against their disciples, and parents against their sons can be witnesses (*nigrahanasakshyam kuryuh*); persons other than these may also be witnesses in criminal cases. If the above persons (masters and servants, etc.) sue each other (*parasparabhiyoge*), they shall be punished with the highest amercement. Creditors guilty of *parokta* shall pay a fine of ten times the amount (*dasabandha*) but if incapable to pay so much, they shall at least pay five times the amount sued for (*panchabandham*). Thus the section on witnesses is dealt with.

Taking Oaths

Witness shall be taken before Brahmans, vessels of water and fire. A Brahman witness shall be told, 'Tell the truth;' a Kshatriya or a Vaisya witness shall be told thus: 'If thou utterest falsehood, thou do not attain the fruit of thy sacrificial and charitable deeds; but having broken the array of thy enemies in war, thou, do go a beggar with a skull in thy hand'.

A Sudra witness thus: 'Whatever thy merits are, in thy former birth or after thy death, shall they go to the king and whatever sins the king may have committed, shall they go to thee, if thou utterest falsehood; fines also shall be levied on thee, for facts as they have been heard or seen will certainly be subsequently revealed'.

If in the course of seven nights, witnesses are found to have unanimously made a false consert among themselves, a fine of 12 *panas* shall be levied. If they are thus found in the course of three fortnights, they shall pay the amount sued for (*abhiyogam dadyuh*).

If witnesses differ, judgment may be given in accordance with the statements of a majority of pure and respectable witnesses; or the mean of their statements may be followed; or the amount under dispute may be taken by the king. If witnesses give testimony for a less amount, the plaintiff shall pay a fine proportional to the increased amount; if they attest to a greater amount, the excess shall go to the king. In cases where the plaintiff proves himself stupid, or where bad hearing (on the part of witnesses at the time of the transaction) or bad writing is the cause of difficulty, or where the debtor is dead, the evidence of witnesses alone shall be depended on (*sakshipratyayameva syat*).

'Only,' say the followers of Usanas, 'in those cases where witnesses prove themselves to have been stupid or senseless and where the investigation of the place, time or nature of the transaction is of no avail, the three amercements shall be levied.'

'False witnesses,' say the followers of Manu, 'shall be fined ten times the amount which, no matter whether it is true or false, they cause to be lost.'

'If,' say the followers of Brihaspati, 'owing to their having been stupid, they render a case suspicious, they shall be tortured to death.'

'No,' says Kautilya, 'it is the truth that witnesses have to hear (when they are called to attest to any transaction); if they have not minded it, they shall be fined 24 *pana*s; if they have attested to a false case (without scrutinizing), they shall be fined half of the above fine.'

Parties shall themselves produce witnesses who are not far removed either by time or place; witnesses who are very far removed either by time or place; witnesses who are very far, or who will not stir out, shall be made to present themselves by the order of the judges.

[Thus ends Chapter 11, 'Recovery of Debts', in Book III, 'Concerning Law', of the Arthashastra of Kautilya. End of the sixty-eighth chapter from the beginning.]

Chapter 12

CONCERNING DEPOSITS

THE rules concerning debts shall also apply to deposits. Whenever forts or country parts are destroyed by enemies or wild tribes; whenever villages, merchants, or herds of cattle are subjected to the inroads of invaders; whenever the kingdom itself is destroyed; whenever extensive fires or floods bring about entire destruction of villages, or partly destroy immovable properties, movable properties having been rescued before;

whenever the spread of fire or rush of floods is so sudden that even movable properties could not be removed; or whenever a ship laden with commodities is either sunk or plundered (by pirates)—deposits lost in any of the above ways shall not be reclaimed. The depositary who has made use of the deposit for his own comfort shall not only pay a compensation (*bhogavetanam*) to be fixed after considering the circumstances of the place and time but also a fine of 12 *panas*. Not only shall any loss in the value of the deposit, due to its use, be made good, but a fine of 24 *panas* also be paid. Deposits damaged or lost in any way shall also be made good. When the depositary is either dead or involved in calamities, the deposit shall not be sued for. If the deposit is either mortgaged or sold or lost, the depositary shall not only restore four times its value, but pay a fine of five times the stipulated value (*pancbabandho dandah*). If the deposit is exchanged for a similar one (by the depositary), or lost in any other way, its value shall be paid.

Pledges

The same rules shall hold good in the case of pledges whenever they are lost, used up, sold, mortgaged or misappropriated.

A pledge, if productive, (i.e., a usufructory mortgage), shall never be lost to the debtor (*nadhissopakarassidet*), nor shall any interest on the debt be charged; but if unproductive (i.e., hypothecation), it may be lost, and interest on the debt shall accumulate. The pledgee who does not re-convey the pledge when the debtor is ready for it shall be fined 12 *panas*.

In the absence of the creditor or mediator (*prayojahasannidhana*), the amount of the debt may be kept in the custody of the elders of the village and the debtor may have the pledged property redeemed; or with its value fixed at the time and with no interest chargeable for the future, the pledge may be left where it is. When there is any rise in the value of the pledge or when it is apprehended that it may be depriciated or lost in the near future, the pledgee may, with permission from the judges (*dharmasthas*), or on the evidence furnished by the officer in charge of pledges (*adhipalapratyayo va*), sell the pledge either in the presence of the debtor or under the presidency of experts who can see whether such apprehension is justified.

An immovable property, pledged and enjoyable with or without labour (*prayasabhogyhah phalabhogyova*), shall not be caused to deteriorate in value while yielding interest on the money lent, and profit on the expenses incurred in maintaining it.

The pledgee who enjoys the pledge without permission shall not only pay the net profit he derived from it, but also forfeit the debt. The rules regarding deposits shall hold good in other matters connected with pledges.

Property Entrusted to Another for Delivery to a Third Person

The same rules shall apply to orders (*adesa*), and property entrusted for delivery to a third person (*anvadhi*).

If, through a merchant, a messenger is entrusted with a property for delivery to a third person (*anvadhihasta*) and such messenger does not reach the destined place, or is robbed of the property by thieves, the merchant shall not be responsible for it; nor shall a kinsman of the messenger who dies on his way be responsible for the property.

For the rest, the rules regarding deposits shall also hold good here.

Borrowed or Hired Properties

Properties either borrowed (*yachitakam*) or hired (*avakritakam*) shall be returned as intact as they were when received. If owing to distance in time or place, or owing to some inherent defects of the properties or to some unforeseen accidents, properties either borrowed or hired are lost or destroyed, they need not be made good. The rules regarding deposits shall also apply here.

Retail Sale

Retail dealers, selling the merchandise of others at prices prevailing at particular localities and times shall hand over to the wholesale dealers as much of the sale proceeds and profit as is realized by them. The rules regarding pledges shall also apply here. If owing to distance in time or place there occurs any fall in the value of the merchandise, the retail dealers shall pay the value and profit at that rate which obtained when they received the merchandise.

Servants selling commodities at prices prescribed by their masters shall realize no profit. They shall only return the actual sale proceeds. If prices fall, they shall pay only as much of the sale proceeds as is realized at the low rate.

But such merchants as belong to trade guilds (*samvyavaharikeshu*) or are trustworthy and are not condemned by the king need not restore even the value of that merchandise which is lost or destroyed owing to its inherent defects or to some unforeseen accidents. But of such merchandise as is distanced by time or place, they shall restore as much value and profit as remains after making allowance for the wear and tear of the merchandise.

For the rest the rules regarding deposits shall apply here. It explains retail sale.

Sealed Deposits

The rules laid down concerning unsealed deposits (*upanidhis*) shall apply to sealed deposits also. A man handing over a sealed deposit to other than the real depositor shall be punished. In the case of a depositary's denial of having received a deposit, the antecedent circumstances (*purvapadanam*) of the deposit and (the character and social position of) the depositor are the only evidences. Artisans (*karavah*) are naturally of impure character. It is not an approved custom with them to deposit for some reliable reason.

When a depositary denies having received a sealed deposit which was not, however, deposited for any reasonable cause, the depositor may obtain secret permission (from the judges) to produce such witnesses as he might have stationed under a wall (*gudhabhitti*) while depositing.

In the midst of a forest or in the middle of a voyage an old or afflicted merchant might with confidence put in the custody of a depositary some valuable article with certain secret mark, and go on his way. On his sending this information to his son or brother, the latter may ask for the sealed deposit. If the depositary does not quietly return it, he shall not only forfeit his credit, but be liable to the punishment for theft besides being made to restore the deposit.

A reliable man, bent on leaving this world and becoming an ascetic, may place a certain sealed deposit with some secret mark in the custody of a man, and, returning after a number of years, ask for it. If the depositary dishonestly denies it, he shall not only be made to restore it, but be liable to the punishment for theft.

A childish man with a sealed deposit with some secret mark may, while going through a street at night, feel frightened at his being captured by the police for untimely walking, and, placing the deposit in the custody of a man, go on his way. But subsequently put into the jail, he may ask for it. If the depositary dishonestly denies, he shall not only be made to restore it, but be liable to the punishment for theft.

By recognizing the sealed deposit in the custody of a man, anyone of the depositor's family may probably ask not only for the deposit, but also for information as to the whereabouts of the depositor. If the custodian denies either, he shall be treated as before.

In all these cases, it is of first importance to inquire how the property under dispute came in one's possession, what are the circumstances connected with the various transactions concerning the property and what is the status of the plantiff in society as to wealth (*arthasamarthyam*).

The above rules shall also apply to all kinds of transaction between any two persons (*mithassamavayah*).

Hence before witnesses and with no secrecy whatever, shall all kinds of agreements be entered into; either with one's own or different people, shall the circumstances of the time and place be minutely considered first.

[Thus ends Chapter 12 'Concerning Deposits', in Book III, 'Concernig Law', of the Arthashastra of Kautilya. End of the sixty-ninth chapter from the beginning.]

Chapter 13

RULES REGARDING SLAVES AND LABOURERS

THE selling or mortgaging by kinsmen of the life of a Sudra who is not a born slave, and has not attained majority, but is an Arya in birth shall be punished with a fine of 12 *panas*; of a Vaisya, 24 *panas*;

of a Kshatriya, 36 *panas*; and of a Brahman, 48 *panas*. If persons other than kinsmen do the same, they shall be liable to the three amercements and capital punishment respectively; purchasers and abettors shall likewise be punished. It is no crime for *Mlecchas* to sell or mortgage the life of their own offspring. But never shall an Arya be subjected to slavery.

But if in order to tide over family troubles, to find money for fines or court decrees, or to recover the (confiscated) household implements, the life of an Arya is mortgaged, they (his kinsmen) shall as soon as possible redeem him (from bondage); and more so if he is a youth or an adult capable of giving help.

Any person who has once voluntarily enslaved himself shall, if guilty of an offence (*nishpatitah*), be a slave for life. Similarly, any person whose life has been twice mortgaged by others shall, if guilty of an offence, be a slave for life. Both of these two sorts of men shall, if they are once found desirous to run away to foreign countries, be slaves for life.

Deceiving a slave of his money or depriving him of the privileges he can exercise as an Arya (*Aryabhava*), shall be punished with half the fine (levied for enslaving the life of an Arya).

A man who happens to have taken in mortgage the life of a convict, or of a dead or an afflicted man, shall be entitled to receive back (from the mortgager) the value he paid for the slave.

Employing a slave to carry the dead or to sweep ordure, urine, or the leavings of food; keeping a slave naked; or hurting or abusing him; or violating (the chastity of) a female slave shall cause the forfeiture of the value paid for him or her. Violation (of the chastity) of nurses, female cooks, or female servants of the class of joint cultivators or of any other description shall at once earn their liberty for them. Violence towards an attendant of high birth shall entitle him to run away. When a master has connection with a nurse or pledged female slave against her will, he shall be punished with the first amercement; a stranger doing the same shall be punished with the middlemost amercement. When a man commits or helps another to commit rape with a girl or a female slave pledged to him, he shall not only forfeit the purchase value, but also pay a certain amount of money (*sulka*) to her and a fine of twice the amount (of *sulka* to the government).

The offspring of a man who has sold off himself as a slave shall be an Arya. A slave shall be entitled to enjoy not only whatever he has earned without prejudice to his master's work, but also the inheritance he has received from his father.

On paying the value (for which one is enslaved), a slave shall regain his *Aryahood*. The same rule shall apply either to born or pledged slaves.

The ransom necessary for a slave to regain his freedom is equal to what he has been sold for. Any person who has been enslaved for fines or court decrees (*dandapranitah*) shall earn the amount by work. An Arya, made captive in war shall for his freedom pay a certain amount proportional to the dangerous work done at the time of his capture, or half the amount.

If a slave who is less than eight years old and has no relatives, no matter whether he is born a slave in his master's house, or fell to his master's share of inheritance, or has been purchased or obtained by his master in any other way, is employed in mean avocations against his will or is sold or mortgaged in a foreign land; or if a pregnant female slave is sold or pledged without any provision for her confinement, his or her master shall be punished with the first amercement. The purchaser and abettors shall likewise be punished.

Failure to set a slave at liberty on the receipt of a required amount of ransom shall be punished with a fine of 12 *panas*; putting a slave under confinement for no reason (*samrodhaschakaranat*) shall likewise be punished.

The property of a slave shall pass into the hands of his kinsmen; in the absence of any kinsmen, his master shall take it.

When a child is begotten on a female slave by her master, both the child and its mother shall at once be recognized as free. If for the sake of subsistence, the mother has to remain in her bondage, her brother and sister shall be liberated.

Selling or mortgaging the life of a male or a female slave once liberated shall be punished with a fine of 12 *panas* with the exception of those who enslave themselves. Thus the rules regarding slaves.

Power of Masters Over Their Hired Servants

Neighbours shall know the nature of agreement between a master and his servant. The servant shall get the promised wages. As to wages not previously settled the amount shall be fixed in proportion to the work done and the time spent in doing it (*karmakalanurupam,* i.e., at the rate prevailing at the time.) Wages being previously unsettled, a cultivator shall obtain one-tenth of the crops grown, a herdsman one-tenth of the butter clarified, a trader one-tenth of the sale proceeds. Wages previously settled shall be paid and received as agreed upon.

Artisans, musicians, physicians, buffoons, cooks, and other workmen, serving of their own accord, shall obtain as much wages as similar persons employed elsewhere usually get or as much as experts (*kusalah*) shall fix.

Disputes regarding wages shall be decided on the strength of evidences furnished by witnesses. In the absence of witnesses, the master who has provided his servant with work shall be examined. Failure to pay wages shall be punished with a fine of ten times the amount of wages (*dasabandhah*), or 6 *pana*s; misappropriation of wages shall be punished with a fine of 12 *pana*s or of five times the amount of the wages (*panchabandho va*).

Any person who, while he is being carried away by floods, or is caught in a fire, or is in danger from elephants or tigers, is rescued on his promise to offer to his rescuer not only the whole of his property, but also his sons, wife and himself as slaves, shall pay only as much as will be fixed by experts. This rule shall apply to all cases where help of any kind is rendered to the afflicted.

A public woman shall surrender her person as agreed upon; but insistence on the observance of any agreement which is ill-considered and improper shall not succeed.

[Thus ends Chapter 13, 'Rules Regarding Slaves' in Book III, 'Concerning Law', of the Arthashastra of Kautilya. End of the seventieth chapter from the beginning.]

Chapter 14

RULES REGARDING LABOURERS; AND COOPERATIVE UNDERTAKING

A servant neglecting or unreasonably putting off work for which he has received wages shall be fined 12 *pana*s and be caught-hold of till the work is done. He who is incapable to turn out work, or is engaged to do a mean job, or is suffering from disease, or is involved in calamities, shall be shown some concession or allowed to get the work done by a substitute. The loss incurred by his master or employer owing to such delay shall be made good by extra work.

An employer may be at liberty to get the work done by (another) provided there is no such adverse condition that the former shall not employ another servant to execute the work, nor shall the latter go elsewhere for work.

An employer not taking work from his labourer or an employee not doing his employer's work shall be fined 12 *pana*s. An employee who has received wages to do a certain work which is however, not brought to termination shall not, of his own accord, go elsewhere for work.

My preceptor holds that not taking work on the part of an employer from his employee when the latter is ready, shall be regarded as work done by the labourer.

But Kautilya objects to it; for wages are to be paid for work done, but not for work that is not done. If an employer, having caused his labourer to do a part of work, will not cause him to do the rest for which the latter may certainly be ready, then also the unfinished portion of the work has to be regarded as finished. But owing to consideration of changes that have occurred in time and place or owing to bad workmanship of the labourer, the employer may not be pleased with what has already been turned out by the labourer. Also the workman may, if unrestrained, do more than agreed upon and thereby cause loss to the employer.

The same rules shall apply to guilds of workmen (*sanghabhritah.*)

Guilds of workmen shall have a grace of seven nights over and above the period agreed upon for fulfilling their engagement. Beyond that time they shall find substitutes and get the work completed. Without taking permission from their employer, they shall neither leave out anything undone nor carry away anything with them from the place of work. They shall be fined 24 *panas* for taking away anything and 12 *panas* for leaving out anything undone. Thus the rules regarding labourers.

Guilds of workmen (*sanghabhritah*, workmen employed by companies) as well as those who carry on any cooperative work (*sambhuya samutthatarah*) shall divide their earnings (*vetanam*, i.e., wages) either equally or as agreed upon among themselves.

Cultivators or merchants shall, either at the end or in the middle of their cultivation or manufacture, pay to their labourers as much of the latter's share as is proportional to the work done. If the labourers, giving up work in the middle, supply substitutes, they shall be paid their wages in full.

But when commodities are being manufactured, wages shall be paid out according to the amount of work turned out; for such payment does not affect the favourable or unfavourable results on the way (i.e., in the sale of merchandise by peddlars).

A healthy person who deserts his company after work has been begun shall be fined 12 *panas*; for none shall, of his own accord, leave his company. Any person who is found to have neglected his share of work by stealth shall be shown mercy (*abhayam*) for the first time and given a proportional quantity of work anew with promise of proportional share of earnings as well. In case of negligence for a second time or of going elsewhere, he shall be thrown out of the company (*pravasanam*). If he is guilty of a glaring offence (*mahaparadhe*), he shall be treated as the condemned.

Cooperation in Sacrificial Acts

Priests cooperating in a sacrifice shall divide their earnings either equally or as agreed upon excepting what is especially due to each or any of them. If a priest employed in such sacrifices as *agnishtoma*, etc., dies after the ceremony of consecration, (his claimant) shall get one-fifth of the promised or prescribed present (*dakshina*); after the ceremony consecrating the purchase of *soma*, one-fourth of the present; after the ceremony called *madhyamopasad*; or *Pravargyodvasana*, one-Third of the present; and after the ceremony called *maya*, have of the share. If in the sacrifice called *sutya*, the same thing happens after the ceremony called *pratassavana*, three-fourths, of the share shall be paid; after the ceremony called *madhyandina*, the present shall be paid in full; for by that time the payment of presents shall be over. In every sacrifice except the one called *brihaspatisavana*, it is usual to pay presents. The same rule shall apply to the presents payable in *aharganas*, sacrifices so called.

The surviving priests carrying the balance of the present or any other relatives of a dead priest shall perform the funeral ceremony of the dead for ten days and nights.

If the sacrificer himself (he who has instituted the sacrifice) dies, the remaining priests shall complete the sacrifice and carry away the presents. If a sacrificer sends out any priest before completing the sacrifice, he shall be punished with the first amercement. If a sacrificer sending out a priest happens to be a person who has not kept the sacrificial fire, or to be a preceptor or one who has already performed sacrifices, then the fines shall be 100, 1,000, and 1,000 *panas*, respectively.

As it is certain that sacrificial merits fall in value when performed in company with a drunkard, the husband of a Sudra woman, a murderer of a Brahman, or one who has violated the chastify of the wife of his preceptor, a receiver of condemnable gifts, or is a thief, or one whose performance of sacrificial acts is condemnable, it is no offence to send out such a priest.

[Thus ends Chapter 14, 'Rules Regarding Labourers, and Cooperative Undertaking' in Book III, 'Concerning Law', of the Arthashastra of Kautilya. End of the seventy-first chapter from the beginning.]

Chapter 15

RESCISSION OF PURCHASE AND SALE

A merchant refusing to give his merchandise that he has sold shall be punished with a fine of 12 *panas*, unless the merchandise is naturally bad, or is dangerous, or is intolerable.

That which has inherent defects is termed naturally bad; whatever is liable to be confiscated by the king, or is subject to destruction by thieves, fire or floods is termed as being dangerous; and whatever is devoid of all good qualities, or is manufactured by the deceased is called intolerable.

Time for rescission of a sale is one night for merchants; three nights for cultivators; five nights for herdsmen; and with regard to the sale or barter of precious things and articles of mixed qualities (*vivrittivikraye*), seven nights.

Merchandise which is likely to perish sooner may, if there is no loss to others, be shown the favour of early disposal by prohibiting the sale elsewhere of similar merchandise which is not likely to perish so soon. Violation of this rule shall be punished with a fine of 24 *panas* or one-tenth of the value of the merchandise sold against this rule.

A person who attempts to return an article purchased by him shall if the article is other than what is naturally bad, or is dangerous, or is intolerable, be punished with a fine of 12 *panas*. The same rescission rules that apply to a seller shall apply to the purchaser also.

Marriage Contracts

As regards marriages among the three higher castes, rejection of a bride before the rite of *panigrahana*, clasping of hands, is valid; likewise among the Sudras, observing religious rites. Even in the case of a couple that has gone through the rite of *panigrahana*, rejection of a bride whose guilt of having lain with another man has been afterwards detected is valid. But never so in the case of brides and bridegrooms of pure character and high family. Any person who has given a girl in marriage without announcing her guilt of having lain with another shall not only be punished with a fine of 96 *panas*, but also be made to return the *sulka* and *stridhana*. Any person receiving a girl in marriage without announcing the blemishes of the bridegroom shall not only pay double the above fine, but also forfeit the *sulka* and *stridhana* (he paid for the bride).

Sale of Bipeds, etc.

Sale of bipeds and quadrupeds as strong, healthy and clean though they are either unclean or actually suffering from leprosy and other diseases, shall be punished with a fine of 12 *panas*. The time of rescission of sale is three fortnights for quadrupeds and one year for men; for it is possible to know by that time their good or bad condition.

An assembly convened for the purpose shall, in the matter of rescending sales or gifts, decide in such a way that neither the giver nor the receiver shall be injured thereby.

[Thus ends Chapter 15, 'Rescission of Purchase and Sale', in Book III, 'Concerning Law', of the Arthashastra of Kautilya. End of the seventy-second chapter from the beginning.]

Chapter 16

RESUMPTION OF GIFTS, SALE WITHOUT OWNERSHIP, AND OWNERSHIP

RULES concerning recovery of debts shall also apply to resumption of gifts. Invalid gifts shall be kept in the safe custody of some persons. Any person who has given as gift not only his whole property, his sons and his wife, but also his own life shall bring the same for the consideration of rescissors. Gifts or charitable subscriptions to the wicked or for unworthy purposes, monetary help to such persons as are malevolent or cruel, and promise of sexual enjoyment to the unworthy shall be so settled by rescissors that neither the giver nor the receiver shall be injured thereby.

Those who receive any kind of aid from timid persons, threatening them with legal punishment, defamation, or loss of money, shall be liable to the punishment for theft; and the persons who yield such aids shall likewise be punished.

Cooperation in hurting a person, and showing a haughty attitude towards the king shall be punished with the highest amercement. No son, or heir claiming a dead man's property shall, against his own will, pay the value of the bail borne by the dead man (*pratibhavyadanda*), the balance of any dowry (*sulkasesha*), or the stakes of gambling; nor shall he fulfil the promise of gifts made by the dead man under the influence of liquor or love. Thus resumption of gifts is dealt with.

Sale Without Ownership

As regards sale without ownership, on the detection of a lost property in the possession of another person, the owner shall cause the offender to be arrested through the judges of a court. If time or place does not permit this action, the owner himself shall catch hold of the offender and bring him before the judges. The judge shall put the question—how the offender came by the property. If he narrates how he got it, but cannot produce the person who sold it to him, he shall be left off, and shall forfeit the property. But the seller, if produced, shall not only pay the value of the property, but also be liable to the punishment for theft.

If a person with a stolen property in his possession runs away or hides himself till the property is wholly consumed, he shall not only pay the value, but also be liable to the punishment for theft.

After proving his claim to a lost property (*svakaranam kritva*), its owner shall be entitled to take possession of it. On his failure to prove his title to it, he shall be fined five times the value of the property, (*panchabandhadandah*), and the property shall be taken by the king.

If the owner takes possession of a lost article without obtaining permission from the court, he shall be punished with the first amercement.

Stolen or lost articles shall, on being detected, be kept in the toll gate. If no claimant is forthcoming within three fortnights, such articles shall be taken by the king.

He who proved his title to a lost or stolen biped shall pay 5 *panas* towards ransom (before taking possession of it). Likewise the ransom for a single-hoofed animal shall be 4 *panas*; for a cow or a buffalo, 2 *panas*, for minor quadrupeds one-fourth of a *pana*; and for articles such as precious stones, superior or inferior raw materials, 5 per cent of their value.

Whatever of the property of his own subjects the king brings back from the forests and countries of enemies, shall be handed over to its owner. Whatever of the property of citizens robbed by thieves the king cannot recover, shall be made good from his own pocket. If the king is unable to recover such things, he shall either allow any self-elected person (*svayamgraha*) to fetch them, or pay an equivalent ransom to the sufferer. An adventurer may enjoy whatever the king graciously gives him out of the booty he has plundered from an enemy's country, excepting the life of an Arya and the property belonging to gods, Brahmans or ascetics. Thus sale without ownership is dealt with.

Ownership

As to the title of an owner to his property, the owners who have quitted their country where their property lies shall continue to have their title to it. When the owners other than minors, the aged, those that are afflicted with decease or calamities, those that are sojourning abroad, or those that have deserted their country during national disturbances, neglect for ten years their property which is under the enjoyment of others, they shall forfeit their title to it.

Buildings left for twenty years in the enjoyment of others shall not be reclaimed. But the mere occupation of the buildings of others during the absence of the king by kinsmen, priests or heretics shall not give them the right of possession. The same shall obtain with regard to open deposits, pledges, treasure trove (*nidhi*), boundary or any property belonging to kings or priests (*srotriya*s).

Ascetics and heretics shall, without disturbing each other, reside in a large area. A newcomer shall, however, be provided with the space occupied by an old resident. If not willing to do so, the old occupier shall be sent out.

The property of hermits (*vanaprastha*), ascetics (*yati*) or bachelors learning the Vedas (*brahmachari*) shall on their death be taken by their preceptors, disciples, their brethren (*dharmabhratri*) or classmates in succession.

Whenever hermits, etc., have to pay any fines, they may, in the name of the king, perform penance, oblation to gods, fireworship, or the ritual called *mahakachchhavardhana* for as many nights as the number of *panas* of their fines. Those heretics (*pashandah*) who have neither gold nor gold coin shall similarly observe their fasts except in the case of defamation, theft, assault and abduction of women. Under these circumstances, they shall be compelled to undergo punishment.

The king shall, under penalty of fines, forbid the wilful or improper proceedings of ascetics; for vice overwhelming righteousness will in the long run destroy the ruler himself.

[Thus ends Chapter 16, 'Resumption of Gifts, Sale Without Ownership, and Ownership', in Book III, 'Concerning Law', of the Arthashastra of Kautilya. End of the seventy-third chapter from the beginning.]

Chapter 17

ROBBERY

SUDDEN and direct seizure (of person or property) is termed *sahasa*; fraudulent or indirect seizure (*niranvaye'pavyayane cha*) is theft.

The school of Manu holds that the fine for direct seizure of precious stones and superior or inferior raw materials shall be equal to their value. It is equal to twice the value of the articles according to the followers of Usanas.

But Kautilya holds that it shall be proportional to the gravity of the crime.

In the case of such articles of small value as flowers, fruits, vegetables, roots, turnips, cooked rice, skins, bamboo, and pots (earthenware) the fine shall range from 12 to 24 *panas*; for articles of great value such as iron (*kalayasa*), wood, roping materials and herds of minor quadrupeds, the fine shall range from 24 to 48 *panas*; and for such articles of still greater value as copper, brass, bronze, glass, ivory and vessels, etc., it shall range from 48 to 96 *panas*. This fine is termed the first amercement.

For the seizure of big quadrupeds, men, fields, houses, gold, gold-coins, fine fabrics, etc., the fine shall range from 200 to 500 *panas*, which is termed the middlemost amercement.

My preceptor holds that keeping or causing to keep by force either men or women in prison, or releasing them by force from imprisonment, shall be punished with fines ranging from 500 to 1,000 *panas*. This fine is termed the highest amercement.

He who causes another to commit *sahasa* after the plans prepared by himself shall be fined twice the value (of the person or property seized). An abettor who employs a hireling to comit *sahasa* by promising 'I shall pay thee as much gold as thou makest use of', shall be fined four times the value.

The school of *Brihaspati* are of opinion that if with the promise 'I will pay thee this amount of gold', an abettor causes another to commit *sahasa*, the former shall be compelled to pay the promised amount of gold and a fine. But Kautilya holds that if an abettor extenuates his crime by pleading anger, intoxication or loss of sense (*moham*), he shall be punished as described above.

In all kinds of fines below 100 *panas*, the king shall take in addition to the fine 8 per cent more as *rupa* and in fines above 100 *panas*, 5 per cent more; these two kinds of exaction are just inasmuch as the people are full of sins on the one hand, and kings are naturally misguided on the other.

[Thus ends Chapter 17, 'Robbery', in Book III, 'Concerning Law', of the Arthashastra of Kautilya. End of the seventy-fourth chapter from the beginning.]

Chapter 18

DEFAMATION

CALUMNY, contemptuous talk or intimidation constitutes defamation.

Among abusive expressions relating to the body, habits, learning, occupation, or nationalities, that of calling a deformed man by his right name such as 'the blind', 'the lame', etc., shall be punished with a fine of 3 *panas*; and by false name 6 *panas*. If the blind, the lame, etc., are insulted with such ironical expressions as 'a man of beautiful eyes', 'a man of beautiful teeth', etc., the fine shall be 12 *panas*. Likewise when a person is taunted for leprosy, lunacy, impotency and the like. Abusive expressions in general, no matter whether true, false or reverse with reference to the abused, shall be punished with fines ranging above 12 *panas*, in the case of persons of equal rank.

If persons abused happen to be of superior rank, the amount of the fines shall be doubled; if of lower rank, it shall be halved. For calumniating the wives of others, the amount of the fines shall be doubled.

If abuse is due to carelessness, intoxication, or loss of sense, etc., the fines shall be halved.

As to the reality of leprosy and lunacy, physicians or neighbours shall be authorities.

As to the reality of impotency, women, the scum of urine, or the low specific gravity of faeces in water (the sinking of faeces in water) shall furnish the necessary evidence.

Speaking Ill of Habits

If among Brahmans, Kshatriyas, Vaisyas, Sudras, and outcastes (*antavasayins*), anyone of a lower caste abuses the habits of one of a higher caste, the fines imposed shall increase from 3 *panas* upwards (commencing from the lowest caste). If anyone of a higher caste abuses one of a lower caste, fines imposed shall decrease from 2 *panas*.

Contemptuous expressions such as 'a bad Brahman' shall also be punished as above.

The same rules shall apply to calumnies regarding learning (*sruta*), the profession of buffoons (*vagjivana*), artisans, or musicians, and relating to nationalities such as *Prajjunaka*, *Gandhara*, etc.

Intimidation

If a person intimidates another by using such expressions as 'I shall render thee thus', the bravado shall be punished with half as much fine as will be levied on him who actually does so.

If a person, being unable to carry his threat into effect, pleads provocation, intoxication or loss of sense as his excuse, he shall be fined 12 *panas*.

If a person capable to do harm and under the influence of enmity intimidates another, he shall be compelled to give lifelong security for the well-being of the intimidated.

Defamation of one's own nation or village shall be punished with the first amercement; that of one's own caste or assembly with the middlemost; and that of gods or temples (*chaitya*) with the highest amercement.

[Thus ends Chapter 18, 'Defamtion', in Book III, 'Concerning Law', of the Arthashastra of Kautilya. End of the seventy-fifth chapter from the beginning.]

Chapter 19

ASSAULT

TOUCHING, striking or hurting constitutes assault.

When a person touches with hand, mud, ashes or dust the body of another person below the navel, he shall be punished with a fine of 3 *panas*; with same but unclean things, with the leg, or spittle, 6 *panas*; with saliva (*chhardi*), urine, faeces, etc., 12 *panas*. If the same offence is committed above the navel, the fines shall be doubled; and on the head, quadrupled.

If the same offence is committed on persons of superior rank, the fines shall be twice as much; and on persons of lower rank, half of the above fines. If the same offence is committed on the women of others, the fines shall be doubled.

If the offence is due to carelessness, intoxication or loss of sense, the fines shall be halved.

For catching hold of a man by his legs, clothes, hands or hair, fines ranging above 6 *panas* shall be imposed. Squeezing, rounding with arms, thrusting, dragging or sitting over the body of another person shall be punished with the first amercement.

Running away, after making a person fall, shall be punished with half of the above fines.

That limb of a Sudra with which he strikes a Brahman shall be cut off.

Striking

For striking compensation is to be paid and half of the fines levied for touching. This rule shall also apply to *chandala*s and other profane persons (committing the same offence). Striking with the hand. shall be punished with fines below 3 *pana*s, with the leg twice as much as the above fine; and striking with an instrument so as to cause swellings shall be punished with the first amercement; and striking so as to endanger life shall be punished with the middlemost amercement.

Hurting

Causing a bloodless wound with a stick, mud, a stone, an iron bar or a rope shall be punished with a fine of 24 *pana*s. Causing the blood to gush out excepting bad or diseased blood shall be punished with double the fine.

Beating a person almost to death, though without causing blood, breaking the hands, legs or teeth, tearing off the ear or the nose, or breaking open the flesh of a person, except in ulcers or boils, shall be punished with the first amercement. Causing hurt in the thigh or the neck, wounding the eye, or hurting so as to impede eating, speaking, or any other bodily movements shall not only be punished with the middlemost amercement, but also be made liable to the payment (to the sufferer) of such compensation as is necessary to cure him.

If time or place does not permit the immediate arrest of an offender, he shall be dealt with as described in Book IV, treating of the measures to suppress the wicked.

Each one of a confederacy of persons who have inflicted hurt on another person shall be punished with double the usual fine.

My preceptor holds that quarrels or assaults of a remote date shall not be complained of. But Kautilya holds that there shall be no acquittal for an offender.

My preceptor thinks that he who is the first to complain of a quarrel wins inasmuch as it is pain that drives one to law.

But Kautilya objects to it; for whether a complaint is lodged first or last, it is the evidence of witnesses that must be depended upon. In the absence of witnesses, the nature of the hurt and other circumstances connected with the quarrel in question shall be evidences. Sentence of punishment shall be passed the very day that a defendant accused of assault fails to answer the charge made against him.

Robbery in Quarrels

A person stealing anything under the tumult of a quarrel shall be fined 10 *panas*. Destruction of articles of small value shall be punished with a fine equal to the value of the articles besides the payment (to the sufferer) of an adequate compensation. Destruction of big things with a compensation equal to the value of the articles and a fine equal to twice the value. In the case of destruction of such things as clothes, gold, gold coins, and vessels or merchandise, the first amercement together with the value of the articles shall be levied.

Causing damage to a wall of another man's house by knocking shall be fined 3 *panas*; breaking open or demolishing the same shall be fined 6 *panas*, besides the restoration of the wall.

Throwing harmful things inside the house of a man shall be fined 12 *panas*; and throwing such things as endanger the lives of the inmates shall be punished with the first amercement.

For causing pain with sticks, etc., to minor quadrupeds one or two *panas* shall be levied; and for causing blood to the same, the fine shall be doubled. In the case of large quadrupeds, not only double the above fines but also an adequate compensation necessary to cure the beasts shall be levied.

For cutting off the tender sprouts of fruit trees, flower trees or shady trees in the parks near a city, a fine of 6 *panas* shall be imposed; for cutting off the minor branches of the same trees, 12 *panas*; and for cutting off the big branches, 24 *panas* shall be levied. Cutting off the trunks of the same shall be punished with the first amercement; and felling the same shall be punished with the middlemost amercement.

In the case of plants which bear flowers, fruits, or provide shade, half of the above fines shall be levied.

The same fines shall be levied in the case of trees that have grown in places of pilgrimage, forests of hermits, or cremation or burial grounds. which mark boundaries, or which are worshipped or observed (*chaityeshvalakshiteshu cha,*) or trees which are grown in the king's forests, double the above fines shall be levied.

[Thus ends Chapter 19, 'Assault', in Book III, 'Concerning Law', of the Arthashastra of Kautilya. End of the seventy-sixth chapter from the beginning.]

Chapter 20

GAMBLING AND BETTING AND MISCELLANEOUS OFFENCES

WITH a view to finding out spies or thieves, the superintendent of gambling shall, under the penalty of a fine of 12 *pana*s if played elsewhere, centralize gambling.

My preceptor is of the opinion that in complaints regarding gambling, the winner shall be punished with the first amercement and the vanquished with the middlemost amercement; for though not skilful enough to win as ardently desired by him, the vanquished fellow does not tolerate his defeat.

But Kautilya objects to it: for if the punishment for the vanquished were to be doubled, none would complain to the king. Yet gamblers are naturally false players.

The superintendents of gambling shall, therefore, be honest and supply dice at the rate of a *kakani* of hire per pair. Substitution by tricks of hand of dice other than thus supplied shall be punished with a fine of 12 *pana*s. A false player shall not only be punished with the first amercement and fines leviable for theft and deceipt but also be made to forfeit the stakes he has won.

The superintendent shall take not only 5 per cent of the stakes won by every winner, and the hire payable for supplying dice and other accessories of dice play, but also the fee chargeable for supplying water and accommodation, besides the charge for licence.

He can at the same time carry on the transactions of sale or mortgage of things. If he does not forbid tricks of hand and other deceitful practices, be shall be punished with twice the amount of the fine (levied from the deceitful gamblers.)

The same rules shall apply to betting and challenging except those in learning and art.

Miscellaneous Offences

As regards miscellaneous offences:

When a person does not return in required place or time the property he has borrowed or hired, or placed in his custody as a deposit, sits under the shade for more than one-and-a-quarter of an hour (*ayama*) as prescribed, evades under the excuse of being a Brahman the payment due while passing military stations or crossing rivers, and bawls out or invites others to fight against his neighbours, he shall be punished with a fine of 12 *pana*s.

When a person does not hand over the property entrusted to him for delivery to a third person, drags with his hand the wife of his brother, has connection with a public woman kept by another, sells merchandise that is under ill repute, breaks open the sealed door of a house, or causes hurt to any of the forty householders or neighbours, a fine of 48 *pana*s shall be imposed.

When a person misappropriates the revenue he collects as the agent of a household, violates by force the chastity of a widow of independent living, when an outcast (*chandala*) person touches an Arya woman, when a person does not run to render help to another in danger, or runs without a cause, and when a person entertains, in dinner dedicated to gods or ancestors Buddhists (*sakya*,) *ajivaka*s, Sudras and exiled persons, (*pravrajita*) a fine of 100 *pana*s shall be imposed.

When an unauthorized person examines (an offender) on oath, executes government work though not a government servant, renders minor quadrupeds impotent, or causes abortion to a female slave by medicine, he shall be punished with the first amercement.

When between father and son, husband and wife, brother and sister, maternal uncle and nephew, or teacher and student, one abandons the other while neither of them is an apostate; and when a person abandons in the centre of a village another person whom he brought there for his own help, the first amercement shall be levied.

When a person abandons his companion in the midst of a forest, he shall be punished with the middlemost amercement.

When a person threatens and abandons his companion in the midst of a forest, he shall be punished with the highest amercement.

Whenever persons who have started together on some journey abandon one another as above, half of the above fine shall be levied.

When a person keeps or causes to keep another person in illegal confinement, releases a prisoner from prison, keeps or causes another to keep a minor in confinement, he shall be punished with a fine of 1,000 *panas*.

The rates of fines shall vary in accordance with the rank of persons concerned and the gravity of the crimes.

Such persons as a pilgrim, an ascetic engaged in penance, a diseased person, anyone suffering from hunger, thirst, or fatigue from journey, a villager from country parts, anyone that has suffered much from punishment and a moneyless pauper shall be shown mercy.

Such transactions as pertain to gods, Brahman*s*, ascetics, women, minors, aged persons, diseased persons and helpless creatures shall, though not be complained of, be settled by the judges themselves; and in such transactions as the above, excuses due to time, place or possession shall not be pleaded.

Such persons as are noted for their learning, intelligence, bravery, high birth or magnificent works shall be honoured.

Judges shall thus settle disputes free from all kinds of circumvention, with mind unchanged in all moods or circumstances, pleasing and affable to all.

[Thus ends Chapter 20, 'Gambling and Betting and Miscellaneous offences', in Book III, 'Concerning Law', of the Arthashastra of Kautilya. End of the seventy-seventh chapter from the beginning. With this, ends Book III, 'Concerning Law' of the Arthashastra of Kautilya.]

Book IV

The Removal of Thorns

Chapter 1

PROTECTION OF ARTISANS

THREE commissioners (*pradeshtarah*) or three ministers shall deal with measures to suppress disturbance to peace (*kantakasodhanam kuryuh*).

Those who can be expected to relieve misery, who can give instructions to artisans, who can be trusted with deposits, who can plan artistic work after their own design, and who can be relied upon by guilds of artisans, may receive the deposits of the guilds. The guilds (*sreni*) shall receive their deposits back in time of distress.

Artisans shall, in accordance with their agreement as to time, place and form of work, fulfil their engagements. Those who postpone their engagements under the excuse that no agreement as to time, place and form of work has been entered into shall, except in troubles and calamities, not only forfeit one-fourth of their wages, but also be punished with a fine equal to twice the amount of their wages. They shall also make good whatever is thus lost or damaged. Those who carry on their work contrary to orders shall not only forfeit their wages, but also pay a fine equal to twice the amount of their wages.

Weavers

Weavers shall increase the threads (supplied to them for weaving cloths) in the proportion of 10 to 11 (*dasaikadasikam*). They shall otherwise not only pay either a fine equal to twice the loss in threads or the value of the whole yarn but also forfeit their wages.

In weaving linen or silk cloths (*kshaumakauseyanam*), the increase shall be 1 to 1½. In weaving fibrous or woollen garments or blankets (*patronakambaladukulanam*), the increase shall be 1 to 2.

In case of loss in length, the value of the loss shall be deducted from the wages and a fine equal to twice the loss shall be imposed. Loss in weight (*tulahine*) shall be punished with a fine equal to four times the loss. Substitution of other kind of yarn, shall be punished with a fine equal to twice the value of the original.

The same rules shall apply to the weaving of broad cloths (*dvipatavanam*).

The loss in weight in woollen threads due to threshing or falling of hair is 5 *pala*s.

Washermen

Washermen shall wash clothes either on wooden planks or on stones of smooth surface. Washing elsewhere shall not only be punished with a fine of 6 *pana*s, but also be subject for the payment of a compensation equal to the damage.

Washermen wearing clothes other than such as are stamped with the mark of a cudgel shall be fined 3 *pana*s. For selling, mortgaging, or letting out for hire the clothes of others, a fine of 12 *pana*s shall be imposed.

In case of substitution of other clothes, they shall not only be punished with a fine equal to twice the value of the clothes, but also be made to restore the true ones.

For keeping for more than a night clothes which are to be made as white as a jasmin flower, or which are to attain the natural colour of their threads on washing on the surface of stones, or which are to be made whiter merely by removing their dirt by washing, proportional fines shall be imposed. For keeping for more than five nights such clothes as are to be given thin colouring, for more than six nights such as are to be made blue, for more than seven nights such as are to be made either as white as flowers or as beautiful and shiny as lac, saffron, or blood and such clothes as require much skill and care in making brilliant, wages shall be forfeited.

Trustworthy persons shall be judges in disputes regarding colour and experts shall determine the necessary wages.

For washing the best garments, the wages shall be one *pana*; for those of middle quality, half a *pana*; and for those of inferior quality one-fourth of a *pana*.

For rough washing on big stones, the wages shall be one-eighth of a pana. In the first wash of red-coloured clothes, there is a loss of one-fourth part (of the colour); in the second wash, one-fifth part. This explains subsequent losses. The rules pertaining to washermen are also applicable to weavers.

Goldsmiths who, without giving information (to the government), purchase from unclean hands silver or golden articles without changing the form of the articles shall be fined 12 *panas*; if they do the same changing the form of the articles (i.e., melting), they shall be fined 24 *panas*; if they purchase the same from the hands of a thief, they shall be fined 48 *panas*; if they purchase an article for less than its value after melting it in secret, they shall be liable to the punishment for theft; likewise for deception with manufactured articles. When a goldsmith steals from a *suvarna* gold equal to the weight of a *masha* (one-sixteenth of a *suvarna*), he shall be punished 200 *panas*; when he steals from a silver *dharana* silver equal to the value of a *masha*, he shall be fined 12 *panas*. This explains the proportional enhancement of punishments. When a goldsmith removes the whole amount of the gold (*karsha*) from a *suvarna* by *apasarana* method or by any other deceitful combination (*yoga*), he shall be punished with a fine of 500 *panas*. In case of contaminating them (gold and silver) in any way, the offence shall be regarded as loss of their intrinsic colour.

One *masha* shall be the fee for the manufacture of a silver *dharana*; for the manufacture of a *suvarna*, one-eighth of the same; or fees may be increased to twice the above according to the skill of the manufacturer. This explains the proportional increase of fees.

Fees for the manufacture of articles from copper, brass, *vaikrinataka*, and *arakuta* shall be 5 per cent. In the manufacture of articles from copper (?), one-tenth of the copper will be lost. For the loss of a *pala* in weight, a fine of twice the loss shall be imposed. This explains the proportional increase of punishments. In the manufacture of articles from lead and tin, one-twentieth of the mass will be lost. One *kakani* shall be the fee for manufacturing an article of a *pala* in weight of the above. In the manufacture of articles from iron, one-fifth of the mass will be lost; two *kakani*s shall be the fee for manufacturing an article of a *pala* in weight from iron. This explains the proportional increase of fees.

When the examiner of coins declares an unacceptable current coin to be worthy of being entered into the treasury or rejects an acceptable current coin, he shall be fined 12 *pana*s. When the examiner of coins misappropriates a *masha* from a current coin of a *pana*, the tax, (*vyaji*) of 5 per cent on the coin having been duly paid, he shall be fined 12 *pana*s. This explains the proportional increase of fines. When a person causes a counterfeit coin to be manufactured, or accepts it, or exchanges it, he shall be fined 1,000 *pana*s; he who enters a counterfeit coin into the treasury shall be put to death.

Scavengers

Of whatever precious things sweepers come across while sweeping, one-third shall be taken by them and two-thirds by the king. But precious stones shall be wholly surrendered to the king. Seizure of precious stones shall be punished with the highest amercement.

A discoverer of mines, precious stones or treasure troves shall, on supplying the information to the king, receive one-sixth of it as his share; but if the discoverer happens to be a peon (*bhritaka*), his share shall be only one-twelfth of it.

Treasure troves valued beyond 100,000 *pana*s shall wholly be taken by the king. But if they are of less value, the discover shall receive one-sixth of it as his share.

Such treasure troves as a man of pure and honest life can prove to be his ancestral property shall wholly be taken by the man himself. Taking possession of a treasure trove without establishing such claim shall be punished with a fine of 500 *pana*s. Taking possession of the same in secret shall be punished with a fine of 1,000 *pana*s.

Medical Practice

Physicians undertaking medical treatment without intimating (to the government) the dangerous nature of the disease shall, if the patient dies, be punished with the first amercement. If the death of a patient under treatment is due to carelessness in the treatment, the physician shall be punished with the middlemost amercement.

Growth of disease due to negligence or indifference (*karmavadha*) of a physician shall be regarded as assault or violence.

Musicians

Bands of musicians (*kusilavah*) shall, during the rainy season, stay in a particular place. They shall strictly avoid giving too much indulgence or causing too much loss (*atipatam*) to anyone. Violation of the above rule shall be punished with a fine of 12 *panas*. They may hold their performances to their liking in accordance with the procedure of their country, caste, family, profession, or population.

The same rules shall apply to dancers, dumb players and other mendicants.

For offences, mendicants shall receive as many lashes with an iron rod as the number of *panas* imposed on them.

Wages for the works of other kinds of artisans shall be similarly determined.

Thus traders, artisans, musicians, beggers, buffoons and other idlers who are thieves in effect though not in name shall be restrained from oppression on the country.

[Thus ends Chapter 1, 'Protection of Artisans', in Book IV, 'The Removal of Thorns', of the Arthashastra of Kautilya. End of the seventy-eighth chapter from the beginning.]

Chapter 2

PROTECTION OF MERCHANTS

THE superintendent of commerce shall allow the sale or mortgage of any old commodition (*purana bhandanam*) only when the seller or mortgagor of such articles proves his ownership of the same. With a view to prevent deception, he shall also supervise weights and measures.

Difference of half a *pala* in such measures as are called *parimani* and *drona* is no offence. But difference of a *pala* in them shall be punished with a fine of 12 *panas*.

Fines for greater differences shall be proportionally increased.

Difference of a *karsha* in the balance called *tula* is no offence. Difference of two *karsha*s shall be punished with a fine of 6 *pana*s. Fines for greater differences shall be proportionally increased.

Difference of half a *karsha* in the measure called *adhaka* is no offence; but difference of a *karsha* shall be punished with a fine of 3 *pana*s.

For greater differences, fines shall be proportionally increased.

Fines for differences in weight in other kinds of balances shall be inferred on the basis of the above rule.

When a merchant purchases by a false balance a greater quantity of a commodity and sells under the same nominal weight a less quantity by the same or another false balance, he shall be punished with double the above fines.

Deception on the part of a seller to the extent of one-eighth part of the articles valued at a *pana* and sold by number shall be punished with a fine of 96 *pana*s.

The sale or mortgage of articles such as timber, iron, brilliant stones, ropes, skins, earthenware, threads, fibrous garments and woollen clothes as superior though they are really inferior shall be punished with a fine of eight times the value of the articles thus sold.

When a trader sells or mortgages inferior as superior commodities, articles of some other locality, as the produce of a particular locality, adulterated things or deceitful mixtures, or when he dexterously substitutes other articles for those just sold (*samutparivartimam*), he shall not only be punished with a fine of 54 *pana*s but also be compelled to make good the loss.

By making the fine two *pana*s for the loss of the value of a *pana*, and 200 *pana*s for that of 100, fines can be determined for any of such false sales.

Those who conspire to lower the quality of the works of artisans, to hinder their income, or to obstruct their sale or purchase shall be fined 1,000 *pana*s.

Merchants who conspire either to prevent the sale of merchandise or to sell or purchase commodities at higher prices shall be fined 1,000 *pana*s.

Middlemen who cause to a merchant or a purchaser the loss of one-eighth of a *pana* by substituting with tricks of hand false weights or measures or other kinds of inferior articles shall be punished with a fine of 200 *panas*.

Fines for greater losses shall be proportionally increased commencing from 200 panas.

Adulteration of grains, oils, alkalis, salts, scents, and medicinal articles with similar articles of no quality shall be punished with a fine of 12 *panas*.

It is the duty of the trader to calculate the daily earnings of middlemen and to fix that amount on which they are authorized to live; for whatever income falls between sellers and purchasers (i.e., brokerage) is different from profit.

Hence authorized persons alone shall collect grains and other merchandise. Collection of such things without permission shall be confiscated by the superintendent of commerce.

Hence shall merchants be favourably disposed towards the people in selling grains and other commodities.

The superintendent of commerce shall fix a profit of 5 per cent over and above the fixed price of local commodities, and 10 per cent on foreign produce. Merchants who enchance the price or realize profit even to the extent of half a *pana* more than the above in the sale or purchase of commodities shall be punished with a fine of from 5 *panas* in case of realizing 100 *panas* up to 200 *panas*.

Fines for greater enhancement shall be proportionally increased.

In case of failure to sell collected merchandise wholesale at a fixed rate, the rate shall be altered.

In case of obstruction to traffic, the superintendent shall show necessary concessions.

Whenever there is an excessive supply of merchandise, the superintendent shall centralize its sale and prohibit the sale of similar merchandise elsewhere before the centralized supply is disposed of.

Favourably disposed towards the people, shall merchants sell this centralized supply for daily wages.

The superintendent shall, on consideration of the outlay, the quantity manufactured, the amount of toll, the interest on outlay, hire, and other kinds of accessory expenses, fix the price of such merchandise with due regard to its having been manufactured long ago or imported from a distant country (*desakalantaritanam panyanam.*)

[Thus ends Chapter 2, 'Protection of Merchants', in Book IV 'The Removal of Thorns', of the Arthashastra of Kautilya. End of the seventy-ninth chapter from the beginning.]

Chapter 3

REMEDIES AGAINST NATIONAL CALAMITIES

THERE are eight kinds of providential visitations: They are fire, floods, pestilential diseases, famine, rats, tigers (*vyalah*), serpents and demons. From these shall the king protect his kingdom.

Fire

During the summer, villages shall carry on cooking operations outside. Or they shall provide themselves with the ten remedial instruments (*dasamuli*).

Precautionary measures against fire have been dealt with in connection with the description not only of the duties of superintendents of villages but also of the king's harem and retinue.

Not only on ordinary days, but also on full moon days shall offerings, oblations and prayers be made to fire.

Floods

Villagers living on the banks of rivers shall, during the rainy reason, remove themselves to upcountries. They shall provide themselves with wooden planks, bamboos and boats. They shall, by means of bottle gourds, canoes, trunks of trees, or boats rescue persons that are being carried off by floods. Persons neglecting rescue with the exception of those who have no boats, etc., shall be fined 12 *panas*. On new and full moon days shall rivers be worshipped. Experts in sacred magic and mysticism (*mayayogavidah*), and persons learned in the Vedas, shall perform, incantations against rain.

During drought shall Indra (*sachinatha*), the Gange, mountains, and *Mahakachchha* be worshipped.

Pestilences

Such remedial measures as will be treated of in Book XIV shall be taken against pestilences. Physicians with their medicines, and ascetics and prophets with their auspicious and purificatory ceremonials, shall also overcome pestilences. The same remedial measures shall be taken against epidemics (*maraka,* i.e., killer). Besides the above measures, oblations to gods, the ceremonial called *Mahakachchhavardhana*, milking the cows on cremation or burial grounds, burning the trunk of a corpse, and spending nights in devotion to gods shall also be observed.

With regard to cattle diseases (*pasuvyadhimarake*), not only the ceremony of waving lights in cowsheds (*nirajanam*) shall be half-done, but also the worship of family-gods be carried out.

Famines

During famine, the king shall show favour to his people by providing them with seeds and provision (*bijabhaktopagraham*).

He may either do such works as are usually resorted to in calamities; he may show favour by distributing either his own collection of provisions or the hoarded income of the rich among the people; or seek for help from his friends among kings.

Or the policy of thinning the rich by exacting excessive revenue (*karsanam*), or causing them to vomit their accumulated wealth (*vamanam*) may be resorted to.

Or the king with his subjects may emigrate to another kingdom with abundant harvest.

Or he may remove himself with his subjects to seashores or to the banks of rivers or lakes. He may cause his subjects to grow grains, vegetables, roots and fruits wherever water is available. He may, by hunting and fishing on a large scale, provide the people with wild beasts, birds, elephants, tigers or fish.

Rats

To ward off the danger from rats, cats and mongooses may be let loose. Destruction of rats that have been caught shall be punished with a fine of 12 *panas*. The same punishment shall be meted out to those who, with the exception of wild tribes, do not hold their dogs in check.

With a view to destroying rats, grains mixed with the milk of the milk-hedge plants (*snuhi*: *Euphorbia antiquorum*), or grains mixed with such ingredients as are treated of in Book XIV may be left on the ground. Asceties and prophets may perform auspicious ceremonials. On new and full moon days rats may be worshipped.

Similar measures may also be taken against the danger from locusts, birds and insects.

Snakes

When there is fear from snakes, experts in applying remedies against snake poison shall resort to incantations and medicines; or they may destroy snakes in a body; or those who are learned in the Atharvaveda may perform auspicious rites. On new and full moon days, (snakes) may be worshipped. This explains the measures to be taken against the dangers from water animals.

Tigers

In order to destroy tigers, either the carcasses of cattle mixed with the juice of *madana* plant, or the carcasses of calves filled with the juice of *madana* and *kodrava* plants may be thrown in suitable places.

Or hunters or keepers of hounds may catch tigers by entrapping them in nets. Or persons under the protection of armour may kill tigers with arms.

Negligence to rescue a person under the clutches of a tiger shall be punished with a fine of 12 *panas*. Similar sum of money shall be given as a reward to him who kills a tiger.

On new and full moon days mountains may be worshipped. Similar measures may be taken against the inroad of beasts, birds or crocodiles.

Demons

Persons acquainted with the rituals of the Atharvaveda, and experts in sacred magic and mysticism shall perform such ceremonials as ward off the danger from demons.

On full moon days the worship of *chaityas* may be performed by placing on a verandah offerings such as an umbrella, the picture of an arm, a flag and some goat's flesh.

In all kinds of dangers from demons, the incantation 'we offer thee cooked rice' shall be performed.

The king shall always protect the afflicted among his people as a father his sons.

Such ascetics as are experts in magical arts, and being endowed with supernatural powers, can ward off providential visitations, shall therefore be honoured by the king and made to live in his kingdom.

[Thus ends Chapter 3, 'Remedies Against National Calamities', in Book IV, 'The Removal of Thorns', of the Arthashastra of Kautilya. End of the eightieth chapter from the beginning.]

Chapter 4

SUPPRESSION OF THE WICKED LIVING BY FOUL MEANS

MEASURES necessary for the protection of countries have been briefly dealt with in connection with the description of the duties of the collector general.

We are now going to treat of in detail such measures as can remove the disturbing elements of peace.

The collector general shall employ spies disguized as persons endowed with supernatural power, persons engaged in penance, ascetics, world trotters (*chakra-chara*), bards, buffoons, mystics (*prachchhandaka*), astrologers, prophets foretelling the future, persons capable of reading good or bad time, physicians, lunatics, the dumb, the deaf, idiots, the blind, traders, painters, carpenters, musicians, dancers, vintners, and manufacturers of cakes, flesh and cooked rice, and send them abroad into the country for espionage.

The spies shall ascertain the fair or foul dealings of villagers, or of the superintendents of villages and report the same.

If any person is found to be of foul life (*gudhajivi*), a spy who is acquainted with similar avocation shall be let loose upon him.

On acquiring friendship with the suspected person who may be either a judge or a commissioner, the spy may request him that the misfortune in which a friend of the spy is involved may be warded off and that a certain amount of money may be accepted. If the judge accedes to the request, he shall be proclaimed as the receiver of bribes and banished. The same rule shall also apply to commissioners.

A spy may tell the congregation of villages (*gramakutam*) or its superintendent that a wealthy man of wicked character is involved in some trouble and that this opportunity may be availed of to squeeze money from him. If either the one or the other complies with the spy, banishment shall be ordered under the proclamation of 'extortion'.

Under the pretence of having been charged with criminal offence, a spy may, with promise of large sums of money, begin to deal with false witnesses. If they agree with him, they shall be proclaimed as false witnesses and banished.

Manufacturers of counterfeit coins shall also be treated similarly.

Whoever is believed to secure for others the love of women by means of magical charms, drugs or ceremonials performed on cremation grounds may be approached by a spy with the request that the wife, daughter or daughter-in-law of someone, whom the spy pretends to love may be made to return the love and that a certain amount of money may be accepted. If he consents to it, he shall be proclaimed as one engaged in witchcraft (*samvadanakaraka*) and banished.

Similar steps may be taken against persons engaged in such witchcraft as is hurtful to others.

Whoever is suspected of administering poison (*rasa,* i.e., mercury) to others by reason of his talking of it or selling or purchasing mercury, or using it in preparing medicines, may be approached with the tale that a certain enemy of the spy may be killed and that a certain amount of money may be received as reward. If he does so, he shall be proclaimed as a poisoner (*rasada*), and banished.

Similar steps may be taken against those who deal with medicines prepared from *madana* plant.

Whoever is suspected of manufacturing counterfeit coins in that he often purchases various kinds of metals, alkalis, charcoal, bellows, pincers, crucibles, stove and hammers, has his hands and clothes dirty with ashes and smoke, or possesses such other accessory instruments as are necessary for this illegal manufacture, may be requested by a spy to take the latter as an apprentice, and being gradually betrayed by the spy, such person, on proclamation of his guilt as the manufacturer of false coins, shall be banished.

Similar steps may be taken against those who lower the quality of gold by mixing it with an alloy, or deal with counterfeit gold (*suvarna*, i.e., coin ?).

There are thirteen kinds of criminals who, secretly attempting to live by foul means, destroy the peace of the country. They shall either be banished or made to pay an adequate compensation according as their guilt is light or serious.

[Thus ends Chapter 4, 'Suppression of the Wicked Living by Foul Means', in Book IV 'The Removal, Thorns', of the Arthashastra of Kautilya. End of the eighty-first chapter from the beginning.]

Chapter 5

DETECTION OF YOUTHS OF CRIMINAL TENDENCY BY ASCETIC SPIES

ON availing themselves of the opening made by ordinary spies sent in advance, special spies pretending to be endowed with supernatural powers may, under the pretence of knowing such incantations as cause rapid speed in running away, or render persons invisible, or cause hard-fastened doors to open, induce highway robbers to robbery; and may under the pretence of knowing such incantations as secure the love of women, entice adulterers to take part in criminal actions planned for the purpose of proving their criminal intentions.

On taking these enthusiasts thus induced to a village, where persons under the guise of women and men are previously stationed and which is different from the one intended to be reached, the youths may be told that it is difficult to reach in time the village aimed at and that the power of incantation may be seen then and there alone.

Having opened the doors seemingly with the power of incantation, the youths may be asked to get in. Having, in the midst of wakeful watchmen under concert, rendered the youths invisible with incantation, they may be asked to go into the interior. Having caused the watchmen seemingly sleepy, the youths may, as ordered, move the beds of the watchmen with no hesitation. Persons under the guise of others wives may, seemingly under the influence of incantation, please the youths.

Soon after the youths have actually experienced the powers of incantation, they may be taught the recitation and other accessory procedure of that art. They may afterwards be asked to test the power of their new learning in plundering such houses as contain articles or money with marks of identification, and simultaneously caught hold of in the very act. They may either be arrested while selling, purchasing or mortgaging articles with marks of identification, or caught hold of while under intoxication brought about by medicinal drinks (*yogasuramatta*).

From these youths thus arrested may be gathered information regarding the past life of them and of their accomplices.

Spies under the disguise of old and notorious thieves may similarly associate with robbers and, instituting similar measures, cause the latter to be arrested.

The collector general shall exhibit these arrested robbers and announce to the public that their arrest is due to the instructions obtained from the king who has learnt the divine art of catching robbers: 'I shall similarly catch hold of other robbers again and again, and you, people, ought to prevent anyone of your own kinsmen from his wicked deeds'.

Whoever is known, through the information of spies, to have been a robber of yoking ropes, whips and other (agricultural) implements may be arrested and told that his arrest is due to the omniscient power of the king. Spies under the disguise of old and notorious robbers, herdsmen, hunters or keepers of hounds may mix themselves with criminal tribes living in forests, and conspire with them to attack villages or caravanserais which, according to previous plan, contain plenty of counterfeit gold and other articles. During the tumult, they may be killed by armed men concealed for the purpose. Or on their securing plenty of stolen treasure, the robbers may either be made to eat such food as is mixed with the intoxicating juice of *madana* plant, or caught hold of either while sleeping with fatigue caused by incessant movements or while under intoxication due to the drinking of medicinal beverage on the occasions of religious festivals.

The collector general shall exhibit in public these and other arrested criminals and proclaim the omniscient power of the king among the people at large.

[Thus ends Chapter 5, 'Detection of Youths of Criminal Tendency by Ascetic Spies', in Book IV, 'The Removal of Thorns', of the Arthashastra of Kautilya. End of the eighty-second chapter from the beginning.]

Chapter 6

SEIZURE OF CRIMINALS ON SUSPICION OR IN THE VERY ACT

IN addition to the measures taken by spies under the guise of prophets, such steps as are suggested by suspicious movements or possession of stolen articles may also be taken.

Suspicion

Persons whose family subsists on slender means of inheritance; who have little or no comfort; who frequently change their residence, caste and the names not only of themselves but also of their family (*gotra*); who conceal their own avocations and calls; who have betaken themselves to such luxurious modes of life as eating flesh and condiments, drinking liquor, wearing scents, garlands, fine dress, and jewels; who have been squandering away their money; who constantly move with profligate women, gamblers, or vintners; who frequently leave their residence; whose commercial transaction, journey or destination is difficult to understand; who travel alone in such solitary places as forests and mountainous tracts; who hold secret meetings in lonely places near to, or far from, their residence; who hurry on to get their fresh wounds or boils cured; who always hide themselves in the interior of their houses; who are excessively attached to women; who are always inquisitive to gather information as to the women and property of others; who associate themselves with men of condemnable learning and work; who loiter in the dark behind walls or under shades; who purchase rare or suspicious articles in suspicious times or places; who are known for their inimical dealings; whose caste and avocation are very low; who keep false appearances or put on different caste signs; who change their ancestral customs under false excuses; whose notoriety is already marked; who, though in charge of villages, are terribly afraid of appearing before the prime minister and conceal themselves or go elsewhere; who pant in fear while sitting alone; who show undue agitation or palpitation of heart; whose face is pale and dry while the voice is indistinct and stammering; who always move in company with armed men; or who keep threatening appearance—these and other persons may be suspected to be either murderers or robbers or offenders guilty of misappropriation of treasure trove or deposits or to be any other kind of knaves subsisting by foul means secretly employed.

Thus the seizure of criminals on suspicion is dealt with.

Seizure of stolen articles

As regards the seizure of criminals in the very act, information regarding such articles as are either lost or stolen shall, if the articles are not found out, be supplied to those who trade in similar articles. Traders who conceal the articles as to the loss of which they have already received information shall be condemned as abettors. If they are found not to be aware of the loss, they may be acquitted on restoring the articles.

No person shall, without giving information to the superintendent of commerce, mortgage or purchase for himself any old or second-hand article.

On receiving information regarding the sale or mortgage of old articles, the superintendent shall ask the owner how he came by it. He may reply, 'It has been inherited; it has been received from a third person; it is purchased by himself; or it has been made to order; or it is a secret pledge.' He may definitely state the time and place when and where it came into being. Or he may adduce evidence as to the price and commission (*kshanamulyam*) for which it was purchased. If his statement regarding the antecedent circumstances of the article is found to be true, he shall be let off.

If the article in question is found to be the one lost by another person whose deposition regarding the antecedent circumstances of the article in no way differs from the previous story, the article shall be considered to belong to that person who is found to have long been enjoying it and whose life is very pure. For while even quadrupeds and bipeds are found to bear such common evidences of identification as colour, gait and form, can there be any difficulty in identifying such articles as, in the form of raw materials, jewels, or vessels, are the product of a single source, definite materials, a particular manufacturer for a definite purpose?

The possessor of an article in question may plead that the article is either borrowed or hired, a pledge or a sealed deposit, or one obtained from a particular person for retail sale.

If he proves his allegation by producing the referee, he shall be let off; or the referee may deny having had any concern in the matter.

With regard to the reasons which a person, seized with an article lost by another, assigns as to his having taken the article as a gift from a third person, he shall corroborate them by producing as witnesses not only those who gave and caused to give the article to him, but also those who, being mediators, custodians, bearers, or witnesses, arranged for the transfer of the article.

When a person is found possessed of an article which he alleges to have been thrown out, lost, or forgotten by a third person, he shall prove his innocence by adducing evidence as to the time, place and circumstances of finding the article. Otherwise he shall restore the article, besides paying a fine equal to its value; or he may be punished as a thief.

Thus the seizure of criminals in the very act is dealt with.

Circumstancial Evidence

As regards the seizure of criminals on the clue of circumstancial evidence:

In cases of housebreaking and theft the circumstances, such as entrance and exit effected through other than doors; breaking the door by means of special contrivances breaking the windows with or without lattice work, or pulling off the roof in houses consisting of upstairs, ascending and descending upstairs; breaking the wall; tunnelling; such contrivances as are necessary to carry off the treasure secretly hoarded, information about which can only be gathered from internal sources; these and other accessory circumstances of wear and tear cognizable in the interior shall tend to indicate the concern of internal hands in the crime, and those of reverse nature, external agencies. The blending of these two kinds of circumstances shall indicate both internal and external agencies.

Regarding crimes suspected to be the work of internal agencies: Any person of miserable appearance, present on the occasion, associated with rogues or thieves, and possessed of such instruments as are necessary for theft; a woman who is born of a poor family, or has placed her affections elsewhere; servants of similar condemnable character; any person addicted to too much sleep or who is suffering from want of sleep; any person who shows signs of fatigue, or whose face is pale and dry with voice stammering and indistinct and who may be watching the movements of others or bewailing too much; any person whose body bears the signs of scaling heights; any person whose body appears to have been scratched or wounded with dress torn off; anyone whose legs and hands bear the signs of rubbing and scratching; anyone whose hair and nails are either full of dirt or freshly broken; anyone who has just bathed and daubed his body with sandal; anyone who has smeared his body with oil and has just washed his hands and legs;

anyone whose footprints can be identified with those made near the house during ingress or egress; anyone whose broken fragments of garlands, sandal or dress can be identified with those thrown out in or near the house during entrance or exit; any person the smell of whose sweat or drink can be ascertained from the fragments of his dress thrown out in or near the house—these and other persons shall be examined.

A citizen or a person of adulterous habits may also be suspected.

A commissioner (*pradeshta*) with his retinue of *gopa*s and *sthanika*s shall take steps to find out external thieves; and the officer in charge of a city (*nagaraka*) shall, under the circumstances sketched above, try to detect internal thieves inside fortified towns.

[Thus ends Chapter 6, 'Seizure of Criminals on Suspicion or in the Very Act', in Book IV, 'The Removal of Thorns', of the Arthashastra of Kautilya. End of the eighty-third chapter from the beginning.]

Chapter 7

EXAMINATION OF SUDDEN DEATH

IN cases of sudden death, the corpse shall be smeared over with oil and examined.

Any person whose corpse is tainted with mucus and urine, with organs inflated with wind, with hands and legs swollen, with eyes open, and with neck marked with ligatures may be regarded as having been killed by suffocation and suppression of breathing.

Any person with contracted arms and thighs may be regarded as having been killed by hanging.

Any dead person with swollen hands, legs and belly, with sunken eyes and inflated navel may be regarded as having been killed by hanging.

Any dead person with stiffened rectum and eyes, with tongue bitten between the teeth, and with belly swollen, may be considered as having been killed by drowning.

Any dead person, wetted with blood and with limb wounded and broken, may be regarded as having been killed with sticks or ropes.

Any dead person with fractures and broken limbs may be regarded as having been thrown down.

Any dead person with dark-coloured hands, legs, teeth and nails, with loose skin, hairs fallen, flesh reduced, and with face bedaubed with foam and saliva, may be regarded as having been poisoned.

Any dead person of similar description with marks of a bleeding bite, may be considered as baving been bitten by serpents and other poisonous creatures.

Any dead person, with body spread and dress thrown out after excessive vomitting and purging may be considered as having been killed by the administration of the juice of the *madana* plant.

Death due to anyone of the above causes is, sometimes under the fear of punishment, made to appear as having been brought about by voluntary hanging, by causing marks of ligature round the neck.

In death due to poison, the undigested portion of meat may be examined in milk. Or the same extracted from the belly and thrown on fire may, if it makes '*chitchita*' sound and assumes the rainbow colour, be declared as poisoned.

Or when the belly (*hridayam*) remains unburnt, although the rest of the body is reduced to ashes, the dead man's servants may be examined as to any violent and cruel treatments they may have received at the hands of the dead. Similarly such of the dead man's relatives as a person of miserable life, a woman with affections placed elsewhere or a relative defending some woman that has been deprived of her inheritance by the dead man may also be examined.

The same kind of examination shall be conducted concerning the hanging of the body of an already dead man.

Causes such as past evils or harm done to others by a dead man, shall be inquired into regarding any death due to voluntary hanging.

All kinds of sudden death centre round one or the other of the following causes:

Offence to women or kinsmen, claiming inheritance, professional competition, hatred against rivals, commerce, guilds and anyone of the legal disputes, is the cause of anger; and anger is the cause of death.

When, owing to false resemblance, one's own hirelings, or thieves for money, or the enemies of a third person murder one, the relatives of the deceased shall be inquired as follows:

Who called the deceased; who was with him; who accompanied him on his journey; and who took him to the scene of death?

Those who happened to be at the locality of murder shall be severally asked as follows:

By whom the deceased was brought there; whether they (the witnesses) saw any armed person lurking in the place and showing signs of troubled appearance?

Any clue afforded by them shall be followed in further inquiry.

• After examining the personal property such as travelling requisites, dress, jewels or other things which the deceased had on his body while murdered, such persons as supplied or had something to do with those things shall be examined as to the associates, residence, causes of journey, profession and other calls of the deceased.

• If a man or woman under the infatuation of love, anger or other sinful passions commits or causes to commit suicide by means of ropes, arms or poison, he or she shall be dragged by means of a rope along the public road by the hands of a *chandala*.

• For such murderers as the above, neither cremation rites nor any obsequies usually performed by relatives shall be observed.

• Any relative who performs funeral rites to such wretches, shall either himself be deprived of his own funerals or be abandoned by his kith and kin.

• Whoever associates himself with such persons as perform forbidden rites, shall with his other associates, if any, forfeit within a year the privileges of conducting or superintending a sacrifice, of teaching, and of giving or receiving gifts.

[Thus ends Chapter 7, 'Examination of Sudden Death', in Book IV, 'The Removal of Thorns', of the Arthasasatra of Kautilya. End of the 84th chapter from the beginning.]

Chapter 8

TRIAL AND TORTURE TO ELICIT CONFESSION

WHETHER an accused is a stranger or a relative to a complainant, his defence witness shall, in the presence of the complainant, be asked as to the defendant's country, caste, family, name, occupation, property, friends and residence. The answers obtained shall be compared with the defendant's own statements regarding the same. Then the defendant shall be asked as to not only the nature of the work he did during the day previous to the theft but also the place where he spent the night till he was caught hold of. If his answers for these questions are attested to by reliable referees or witnesses, he shall be acquitted. Otherwise he shall be subjected to torture (*anyatha karmapraptah*).

Three days after the commission of a crime, no suspected person (*sankitakah*) shall be arrested inasmuch as there is no room for questions unless there is strong evidence to bring home the charge.

Persons who charge an innocent man with theft, or conceal a thief, shall themselves be liable to the punishment for theft.

When a person accused of theft proves in his defence the complainant's enmity or hatred towards himself he shall be acquitted.

Any person who keeps an innocent man in confinement (*parivasayatah suddham*) shall be punished with the first amercement.

Guilt against a suspected person shall be established by the production of such evidences as the instruments made use of by the accused, his accomplices or abettors, the stolen article, and any middlemen involved in selling or purchasing the stolen article. The validity of the above evidences shall also be tested with reference to both the scene of the theft and the circumstances connected with the possession and distribution of the stolen article.

When there are no such evidences and when the accused is wailing much, he shall be regarded as innocent. For owing to one's accidental presence on the scene of theft, or to one's accidental resemblance to the real thief in respect to his appearance, his dress, his weapons, or possession of articles similar to those stolen, or owing to one's presence near the stolen articles, as in the case of Mandavya who under the fear of torture admitted himself to be the thief, one, though innocent, is often seized as a thief. Hence the production of conclusive evidences shall be insisted upon (*tasmatsamaptakaranam niyamayet,* i.e., hence punishment shall be meted out only when the charge is quite established against the accused).

Ignoramuses, youngsters, the aged, the afflicted, persons under intoxication, lunatics, persons suffering from hunger, thirst, or fatigue from journey, persons who have just taken more than enough of meal, persons who have confessed of their own accord (*atmakasitam*), and persons who are very weak—none of these shall be subjected to torture.

Among the spies such as harlots, suppliers of water and other drinks to travellers, storytellers, hotel-keepers providing travellers with board and lodging, anyone who happens to be acquainted with the work similar to that of the suspected may be let off to watch his movements, as described in connection with misappropriation of sealed deposits.

Those whose guilt is believed to be true shall be subjected to torture (*aptadosham karma karayet*). But not women who are carrying or who have not passed a month after delivery.

Torture of women shall be half of the prescribed standard. Or women with no exception may be subjected to the trial of cross-examination (*vakyanuyogo va*).

Those of Brahman caste and learned in the Vedas as well as asceties shall only be subjected to espionage.

Those who violate or cause to violate the above rules shall be punished with the first amercement. The same punishment shall be imposed in case of causing death to anyone by torture.

There are in vogue four kinds of torture (*karma*):

Six punishments (*shatdandah*), seven kinds of whipping (*kasa*), two kinds of suspension from above (*upari nibandhau*), and water tube (*udakanalika cha*).

As to persons who have committed grave offences, the form of torture will be nine kinds of blows with a cane: twelve beats on each of the thighs; twenty-eight beats with a stick of the tree (*naktamala*); thirth-two beats on each palm of the hands and on each sole of the feet; two on the knuckles, the hands being joined so as to appear like a scorpion; two kinds of suspensions, face downwards (*ullambane chale*); burning one of the joints of a finger after the accused has been made to drink rice gruel; heating his body for a day after be has been made to drink oil; causing him to lie on coarse green grass for a night in winter. These are the 18 kinds of torture.

The instruments of the accused such as ropes, clubs, arrows, spades, knives, etc., shall be paraded on the back of an ass.

Each day a fresh kind of the torture may be employed.

Regarding those criminals who rob in accordance with the threat previously made by them, who have made use of the stolen articles in part, who have been caught hold of in the very act or with the stolen articles, who have attempted to seize the king's treasury, or who have committed culpable crime, may, in accordance with the order of the king, be subjected once or many times to one or all of the above kinds of torture.

Whatever may be the nature of the crime, no Brahman offender shall be tortured. The face of a Brahman convict shall be branded so as to leave a mark indicating his crime—the sign of a dog in theft, that of a headless body in murder; that of the female part (*bhaga*) in rape with the wife of a teacher, and that of the flag of vintners for drinking liquor.

After having thus branded to a wound and proclaimed his crime in public, the king shall either banish a Brahman offender or send him to the mines for life.

[Thus ends Chapter 8, 'Trial and Torture to Elicit Confession', in Book IV, 'The Removal of Thorns', of the Arthashastra of Kautilya. End of the eighty-fifth chapter from the beginning.]

Chapter 9

PROTECTION OF ALL KINDS OF GOVERNMENT DEPARTMENTS

COMMISSIONERS appointed by the collector general shall first check (the proceedings of) superintendents and their subordinates.

Those who seize valuable articles or precious stones from either mines or any great manufactories shall be beheaded. Those who seize ordinary articles or necessaries of life from manufactories of articles of small value shall be punished with the first amercement. Those who seize from manufactories or from the king's granary articles of one-sixteenth to one-fourth a *pana* in value shall be fined 12 *panas*; articles of one-fourth to half of a *pana* in value, 24 *panas*; articles half to three-fourths *pana* in value, 36 *panas*; and articles of three-fourths to 1 *pana* in value, 48 *panas*.

Those who seize articles of 1 to 2 *panas* in value shall be punished with the first amercement; articles of 2 to 4 *panas* in value with the middlemost; and articles of 4 to 8 *panas* in value with the highest amercement. Those who seize articles of 8 to 10 *panas* in value shall be condemned to death.

When anyone seizes from courtyards, shops or arsenals commodities such as raw materials, manufactured articles, etc., of half the above value, he shall also be punished as above. When any person seizes articles of one-fourth of the above value from government treasury, granaries, or offices of superintendents, he shall be punished with twice the above fines.

It has already been laid down in connection with the king's harem that those who intimidate thieves (with a view to giving them a signal to run away) shall be tortured to death.

When any person other than a government servant steals during the day from fields, yards prepared for threshing out grains, houses, or shops, commodities such as raw materials, manufactured articles, or necessaries of life, of one-sixteenth to one-fourth of a *pana* in value, he shall be fined 3 *panas* or paraded through the streets, his body being smeared over with cow dung, and an earthenware pan with blazing light tied round his loins (*saravamekhalaya*). When any person steals articles of one-fourth to half of a *pana* in value, he shall be fined 6 *panas*, or his head may be shaved, or he may be exiled (*mundanam pravrajanam va*). When a person steals articles of half to one-third of a *pana* in value, he shall be fined 9 *panas*, or he may be paraded through streets, his body being bedaubed with cow dung or ashes or with an earthenware pan with blazing light tied round his waist. When a person steals articles of one-third to a *pana* in value, be shall be fined 12 *panas*, or his head may be shaved, or he may be banished. When a person steals commodities of 1 to 2 *panas* in value, he shall be fined 24 *panas*, or his head may be shaved with a piece of brick, or he may be exiled. When a person steals articles of 2 to 4 *panas* in value, he shall be punished with a fine of 36 *panas*; articles of 4 to 5 *panas* in value, 48 *panas*; articles of 5 to 10 *panas* in value, with the first amercement; articles of 10 to 20 *panas* in value, with a fine of 200 *panas*; articles of 20 to 30 *panas* in value, with a fine of 500 *panas*; articles of 30 to 40 *panas* in value, with a fine of 1,000 *panas*; and articles of 40 to 50 *panas* in value, he shall be condemned to death.

When a person seizes by force, whether during the early part of the day or night, articles of half the above values, he shall be punished with double the above fines.

When any person with weapons in hand seizes by force, whether during the day or night, articles of one-fourth of the above values, he shall be punished with the same fines.

When a master of a household (*kutumbadhyaksha*,) a superintendent, or an independent officer (*mukhyaswami*) issues or makes use of unauthorized orders or seals, he shall be punished with the first, middlemost, or highest amercement, or he may be condemned to death, or punished in any other way in proportion to the gravity of his crime.

When a judge threatens, browbeats, sends out, or unjustly silences anyone of the disputants in his court, he shall first of all be punished with the first amercement. If he defames or abuses anyone of them, the punishment shall be doubled. If he does not ask what ought to be asked, or asks what ought not to be asked, or leaves out what he himself has asked, or teaches, reminds, or provides anyone with previous statement, he shall be punished with the middlemost amercement.

When a judge does not inquire into necessary circumstances, inquires into unnecessary circumstances, (*desa*), makes unnecessary delay in discharging his duty, postpones work with spite, causes parties to leave the court by tiring them with delay, evades or causes to evade statements that lead to the settlement of a case, helps witnesses giving them clues, or resumes cases already settled or disposed of, he shall be punished with the highest amercement. If he repeats the offence, he shall both be punished with double the above fine and dismissed.

When a clerk does not take down what has been deposed by parties, but enters what has not been deposed, evades what has been badly said (*duruktam*), or renders either diverse or ambiguous in meaning such depositions as are satisfactorily given out, he shall be punished either with the first amercement or in proportion to his guilt.

When a judge or commissioner imposes an unjust fine in gold, he shall be fined either double the amount of the fine, or eight times that amount of imposition which is either more or less than the prescribed limit.

When a judge or commissioner imposes an unjust corporeal punishment, he shall himself be either condemned to the same punishment or made to pay twice the amount of ransom leviable for that kind of injustice.

When a judge falsifies whatever is a true amount or declares as true whatever amount is false, he shall be fined eight times that amount.

When an officer lets out or causes to let out offenders from lock-up (*charaka*), obstructs or causes to obstruct prisoners in such of their daily avocations as sleeping, sitting, eating or execreting, he shall be punished with fines ranging from 3 *pana*s and upwards.

When any person lets out or causes to let out debtors from lock-up, he shall not only be punished with the middlemost amercement, but also be compelled to pay the debt the offender has to pay.

When a person lets out or causes to let out prisoners from jails (*bandhanagara*), he shall be condemned to death and the whole of his property confiscated.

When the superintendeat of jails puts any person in lock-up without declaring the grounds of provocation (*samkrudhakamanakhyaya*), he shall be fined 24 *pana*s; when he subjects any person to unjust torture, 48 *pana*s; when he transfers a prisoner to another place, or deprives a prisoner of food and water, 96 *pana*s; when be troubles or receives bribes from a prisoner, he shall be punished, with the middlemost amercement; when he beats a prisoner to death, he shall be fined 1,000 *pana*s. When a person commits rape with a captive, slave, or hired woman in lock-up, he shall be punished with the first amercement; when he commits rape with the wife of a thief, or of any other man who is dead in an epidemic (*damara*), he shall be punished with the middlemost amercement; and when he commits rape with an Arya woman in lock-up, he shall be punished with the highest amercement.

When an offender kept in lock-up commits rape with an Arya woman in the same lock-up, he shall be condemned to death in the very place.

When an officer commits rape with an Arya woman who has been arrested for untimely movement at night (*akshanagrihitayam*), he shall also be hanged at the very spot; when a similar offence is committed with a woman under slavery, the offender shall be punished with the first amercement.

(An officer) who causes a prisoner to escape from a lock-up without breaking it open shall be punished with the middlemost amercement. (An officer) who causes a prisoner to escape from a lock-up after breaking it open shall be condemned to death. When he lets out a prisoner from the jail, he shall be put to death and his property confiscated.

Thus shall the king, with adequate punishments, test first the conduct of government servants, and then shall, through those officers of approved character, examine the conduct of his people both in towns and villages.

[Thus ends Chapter 9, 'Protection of All Kinds of Government Departments', in Book IV, 'The Removal of Thorns', of the Arthashastra of Kautilya. End of the eighty-sixth chapter from the beginning.]

Chapter 10

FINES IN LIEU OF MUTILATION OF LIMBS

WHEN government servants (*arthachara*) commit for the first time such offences as violation of sacred institutions (*tirthaghata*), or pickpocketing (*granthibheda*), they shall have their index finger cut off or shall pay a fine of 54 *panas*; when for a second time they commit the same, they shall have their (......) cut off or pay a fine of 100 *panas*; when for a third time, they shall have their right hand cut off or pay a fine of 400 *panas*; and when for a fourth time, they shall in any way be put to death.

When a person steals or destroys cocks, mangoose, cats, dogs or pigs, of less than 54 *panas* in value, he shall have the edge of his nose cut off or pay a fine of 54 *panas*. If these animals belong to either *chandalas* or wild tribes half of the above fine shall be imposed.

When any person steals wild beasts, cattle, birds, elephants, tigers, fish, or any other animals confined in traps, fences, or pits, he shall not only pay a fine equal to the value of the stolen animals, but also restore the animals.

For stealing beasts or raw materials from forests, a fine of 100 *panas* shall be imposed. For stealing or destroying dolls, beasts or birds from infirmaries, twice the above fine shall be levied.

When a person steals articles of small value, belonging to artisans, musicians or ascetics he shall pay a fine of 100 *panas*; and when he steals big articles or any agricultural implements, he shall pay double the above fine.

When any person enters into a fort without permission, or carries off treasure through a hole or passage in the wall of the fort, he shall either be beheaded or be made to pay a fine of 200 *panas*.

When a person steals a cart, a boat or a minor quadruped, he shall have one of his legs cut off or pay a fine of 300 *panas*.

When a gambler substitutes false dice to be hired for a *kakani* or any other accessory things of dice play, or commits fraud by tricks of hand, he shall have his hand cut off or pay a fine of 400 *panas*.

When any person abets a thief or an adulterer, he as well as the woman who voluntarily yields herself for adultery shall have their ears and nose cut off or pay each a fine of 500 *panas*, while the thief or the adulterer shall pay double the above fine.

When any person steals a big animal, abducts a male or female slave, or sells the articles belonging to a dead body (*pretabhandam*), he shall have both of his legs cut off or pay a fine of 600 *panas*.

When a man contemptuously rushes against the hands or legs of any person of a higher caste, or of a teacher, or mounts the horse, elephant, coach, etc., of the king, he shall have one of his legs and one of his hands cut off or pay a fine of 700 *panas*.

When a Sudra calls himself a Brahman, or when any person steals the property of gods, conspires against the king, or destroys both the eyes of another, he shall either have his eyes destroyed by the application of poisonous ointment, or pay a fine of 800 *panas*.

When a person causes a thief or an adulterer to be let off or adds or omits anything while writing down the king's order, abducts a girl or a slave possessed of gold, carries off any deceitful transaction, or sells rotten flesh, he shall either have his two legs and one hand cut off or pay a fine of 900 *panas*.

Any person who sells human flesh shall be condemned to death.

When a person steals images of gods or of animals, abducts men, or takes possession of fields, houses, gold, gold-coins, precious stones, or crops of others, he shall either be beheaded or compelled to pay the highest amercement.

Taking into consideration the (social position of) persons, the nature of the offence, the cause, whether grave or slight (that led to the perpetration of the offence), the antecedent and present circumstances, the time and the place; and without failing to notice equitable distinctions among offenders, whether belonging to royal family or to the common people, shall the commissioner determine the propriety of imposing the first, middlemost or highest amercements.

[Thus ends Chapter 10, 'Fines in Lieu of Mutilation of Limbs', in Book IV, 'The Removal of Thorns', of the Arthashastra of Kautilya. End of the eighty-seventh chapter from the beginning.]

Chapter 11

DEATH WITH OR WITHOUT TORTURE

WHEN a man murders another in a quarrel, he shall be tortured to death. When a person wounded in a fight dies within seven nights, he who caused the wound shall be put to instantaneous death (*suddhavadhah*). If the wounded man dies within a fortnight, the offender shall be punished with the highest amercement. If the wounded man dies within a month, the offender shall be compelled to pay not only a fine of 500 *panas*, but also an adequate compensation (to the bereaved).

When a man hurts another with a weapon, he shall pay the highest amercement; when he does so under intoxication, his hand shall be cut off; and when he causes instantaneous death, be shall be put to death.

When a person causes abortion in pregnancy by striking, or with medicine, or by annoyance, the highest, middlemost, and first amercements shall be imposed respectively.

Those who cause violent death either to men or women, or those who are in the habit of often going to meet prostitutes (*abhisaraka*), those who inflict unjust punishment upon others, those who spread false or contemptuous rumours, who assault or obstruct travellers on their way, who commit housebreaking, or who steal or cause hurt to royal elephants, horses, or carriages shall be hanged.

Whoever burns or carries away the corpses of the above offenders shall meet with similar punishment or pay the highest amercement.

When a person supplies murderers or thieves with food, dress, any requisites, fire, information, any plan, or assistance in any way, he shall be punished with the highest amercement. When he does so under ignorance, he shall be censured.

Sons or wives of murderers or of thieves shall, if they are found not in concert, be acquitted; but they shall be seized if found to have been in concert.

Any person who aims at the kingdom, who forces entrance into the king's harem, who instigates wild tribes or enemies (against the king), or who creates disaffection in forts, country parts, or in the army shall be burnt alive from head to foot.

If a Brahman does similar acts, he shall be drowned.

Any person who murders his father, mother, son, brother, teacher, or an ascetic, shall be put to death by burning both his head and skin; if he insults any of the above persons, his tongue shall be cut off; if he bites any limb of these persons, be shall be deprived of the corresponding limb.

When a man wantonly murders another, or steals a herd of cattle, he shall be beheaded.

A herd of cattle shall be considered to consist of not more than ten heads.

When a person breaks the dam of a tank full of water, he shall be drowned in the very tank; of a tank without water, he shall be punished with the highest amercement; and of a tank which is in ruins owing to neglect, he shall be punished with the middlemost amercement.

Any man who poisons another and any woman who murders a man shall be drowned.

Any woman who murders her husband, preceptor, or offspring, sets fire to another's property, poisons a man or cuts off any of the bodily joints of another shall be torn off by bulls, no matter whether or not she is big with a child, or has not passed a month after giving birth to a child.

Any person who sets fire to pasturelands, fields, yards prepared for threshing out grains, houses, forests, of timber or of elephants, shall be thrown into fire.

Any person who insults the king, betrays the king's council, makes evil attempts (against the king), or disregards the sanctity of the kitchens of Brahmans shall have his tongue cut off.

When a man other than a soldier steals weapons or armour, he shall be shot down by arrows; if he is a soldier, he shall pay the highest amercement.

He who castrates a man shall have his generative organ cut off.

He who hurts the tongue or nose of another shall have his fingers cut off.

Such painful punishments (*klesadanda*) as the above have been laid down in the *Sastras* of great sages; but it has been declared as just to put to simple death those offenders who have not been cruel.

[Thus ends Chapter 11, 'Death with or Without Torture', in Book IV, 'The Removal of Thorns', of the Arthashastra of Kautilya. End of the eighty-eighth chapter from the beginning.]

Chapter 12

SEXUAL INTERCOURSE WITH IMMATURE GIRLS

HE who defiles a maiden of equal caste before she has reached her maturity shall have his hand cut off or pay a fine of 400 *pana*s; if the maiden dies in consequence, the offender shall be put to death.

He who defiles a maiden who has attained maturity shall have his middle finger cut off or pay a fine of 200 *pana*s, besides giving an adequate compensation to her father.

No man shall have sexual intercourse with any woman against her will.

He who defiles a willing maiden shall pay a fine of 54 *pana*s, while the maiden herself shall pay a fine of half the amount.

When a man impersonates another man who has already paid the nuptial fee to a woman (*parasulkopadhayam*), he shall have his hand cut off or pay a fine of 400 *pana*s, besides making good the nuptial fee.

No man who has connection with a maiden that has passed seven menses and has not yet succeeded in marrying her, though she has been betrothed to him, shall either be guilty or pay any compensation to her father; for her father has lost his authority over her in consequence of having deprived her so long of the result of her menses.

It is no offence for a man of equal caste and rank to have connection with a maiden who has been unmarried three years after her first menses. Nor is it an offence for a man, even of different caste, to have connection with a maiden who has spent more than three years after her first menses and has no jewellery on her person; for taking possession of paternal property (under such circumstances) shall be regarded as theft.

Any person who, while pretending to secure a bride to a particular person, ultimately obtains her for a third person shall be fined 200 *pana*s.

If a person substitutes in marriage another maiden for the one he has before shown, he shall, if the substitute is of the same rank, be fined 100 *panas*, and 200 *panas* if she is of lower rank. The substituted maiden shall be fined 54 *panas*, while the offender shall also be compelled to return both the nuptial fee and the amount of expenditure (incurred by the bridegroom).

When a man refuses to live in marriage a particular maiden as agreed upon, he shall pay double the above fine.

When a man substitutes in marriage a maiden of different blood or is found to have bestowed false praises (on her quality), he shall not only pay a fine of 200 *panas* and return the nuptial fee, but also make good the expenditure.

No man shall have sexual intercourse with any woman against her will.

When a woman, being desirous of intercourse, yields herself to a man of the same caste and rank, she shall be fined 12 *panas*, while any other woman who is an abettor in the case shall be fined twice as much. Any woman who abets a man in having intercourse with a maiden against her will shall not only pay a fine of 100 *panas*, but also please the maiden providing her with an adequate nuptial fee.

A woman who, of her own accord, yields herself to a man shall be a slave to the king.

For committing intercourse with a woman outside a village, or for spreading false report regarding such things, double the usual fines shall be imposed.

He who carries off a maiden by force shall be fined 200 *panas*; if the maiden thus carried off has golden ornaments on her person, the highest amercement shall be imposed. If a number of persons abduct a maiden, each of them shall be punished as above.

When a man has connection with a harlot's daughter, he shall not only pay a fine of 54 *panas*, but also give her mother sixteen times her daily income.

When a man defiles the daughter of his own male or female slave, he shall not only pay a fine of 24 *panas*, but also provide the maiden with an adequate nuptial fee (*sulka*) and jewellery (*abaddhya*).

When a man has connection with a woman who has been held in slavery on account of certain ransom due from her, he shall not only pay a fine of 12 *panas*, but also provide the woman with dress and maintenance.

Abettors in all the above cases shall each have the same punishment as the principal offender.

A relative, or a servant of an absentee husband, may take the latter's wife of loose character under his own protection (*samgrihniyat*, i.e., may marry her). Being under such protection, she shall wait for the return of her husband. If her husband, on his return, entertains no objection, both the protector and the woman shall be acquitted. If he raises any objection, the woman shall have her ears and nose cut off, while her keeper shall be put to death as an adulterer.

When a man falsely accuses another of having committed theft while in reality the latter is guilty of adultery, the complainant shall be fined 500 *panas*.

He who lets off an adulterer by receiving gold shall pay a fine of eight times the value of the gold (he received).

(Adultery may be proved by circumstances such as) hand-to-hand fight, abduction, any marks made on the body of the culprits, opinion of experts on consideration of the circumstances, or the statements of women involved in it.

When a man rescues a woman from enemies, forests or floods, or saves the life of a woman who has been abandoned in forests, forsaken in famine, or thrown out as if dead, he may enjoy her as agreed upon during the rescue.

A woman of high caste, with children and having no desire for sexual enjoyment, may be let off after receiving an adequate amount of ransom.

• Those women who have been rescued from the hands of thieves, from floods, in famine, or in national calamities, or who, having been abandoned, missed, or thrown out as if dead in forests, have been taken home may be enjoyed by the rescuer as agreed upon.

• But no such women as have been cast out under royal edict, or by their own kinsmen; nor such as belong to high caste, or do not like to be rescued, nor even those who have children, shall be rescued either for ransom or for their person.

[Thus ends Chapter 12, 'Sexual Intercourse with Immature Girls', in Book IV, 'The Removal of Thorns', of the Arthashastra of Kautilya. End of the eighty-ninth chapter from the beginning.]

Chapter 13

PUNISHMENT FOR VIOLATING JUSTICE

HE who causes a Brahman to partake of whatever food or drink is prohibited shall be punished with the highest amercement. He who causes a Kshatriya to do the same shall be punished with the middlemost amercement; a Vaisya, with the first amercement; and a Sudra, with a fine of 54 *panas*.

Those who voluntarily partake of whatever is condemned either as food or drink shall be outcast.

He who forces his entrance into another's house during the day shall be punished with the first amercement; and during the night with the middlemost. Any person who with weapon in hand enters into another's house either during the day or night shall be punished with the highest amercement.

When beggars or peddlers and lunatics or mad persons attempt to enter into a house by force, or when neighbours force their entrance into a house in danger, they shall not be punished provided no such entrance is specially prohibited.

He who mounts the roof of his own house after midnight shall be punished with the first amercement; and of another's house, with the middlemost amercement.

Those who break the fences of villages, gardens or fields shall also be punished with the middlemost amercement.

Having made the value, etc., of their merchandise known (to the headman of the village), traders shall halt in some part of a village. When any part of their merchandise which has not been truly sent out of the village during the night has been stolen or lost, the headman of the village shall make good the loss.

Whatever of their merchandise is stolen or lost in the intervening places between any two villages shall the superintendent of pasturelands make good. If there are no pasturelands (in such places), the officer called *Chorarajjuka* shall make good the loss. If the loss of merchandise occurs in such parts of the country as are not provided even with such security (a *Chorarajjuka*), the people in the boundaries of the place shall contribute to make up the loss. If there are no people in the boundaries, the people of five or ten villages of the neighbourhood shall make up the loss.

Harm due to the construction of unstable houses, carts with no support or with a beam or weapon hung above or with damaged support or with no covering, and harm due to causing a cart to fall in pits, or a tank, or from a dam, shall be treated as assault.

Cutting of trees, stealing the rope with which a tameable animal is tied, employing untamed quadrupeds, throwing sticks, mud, stones, rods, or arrows on chariots or elephants, raising or waiving the arm against chariots or elephants, shall also be treated as assault.

(The charioteer) who cries out (to a passer-by) 'get out' shall not be punished for collision (*samghattane*).

A man who is hurt to death by an elephant under provocation (caused by himself) shall supply not only a *kumbha* of liquor (less by a *drona*), garlands, and scents but also as much cloth as is necessary to wash the tusks; for death caused by an elephant is as meritorious as the sacred bath taken at the end of a horse sacrifice. Hence this offer (of liquor, etc.), is known as 'washing the legs'.

When an indifferent passer-by is killed by an elephant the driver shall be punished with the highest amercement.

When the owner of a horned or tusked animal does not rescue a man from being destroyed by his animal, he shall be punished with the first amercement. If he heedlessly keeps quite from rescuing though entreated, he shall be punished with twice the first amercement.

When a person causes or allows horned or tusked animals to destroy each other, he shall not only pay a fine equal to the value of the destroyed animal or animals, but also make good the loss (to the sufferer).

When a man rides over an animal which is left off in the name of gods, or over a bull, an ox, or over a female calf, he shall be fined

500 *panas*. He who drives away the above animals shall be punished with the highest amercement.

When a person carries off such inferior quadrupeds as are productive of wool or milk, or are useful for loading or riding, he shall not only pay a fine equal to their value but also restore them.

The same punishment shall be imposed in the case of driving away inferior quadrupeds for purposes other than ceremonials performed in honour of gods or ancestors.

When an animal which has its nose string cut off or which is not well tamed to yoke causes hurt; or when an animal, either coming furiously against a man or receding backwards with the cart to which it is tied, causes hurt or when an animal causes hurt in confusion brought about by the thronging of people and other animals; the owner of the animal shall not be punished; but for hurt caused to men under circumstances other than the above, fines shall be imposed as laid down before, while the loss of any animal life due to such causes shall be made good. If the driver of a cart or carriage causing hurt is a minor, the master inside the cart or carriage shall be punished. In the absence of the master, any person who is seated inside, or the driver himself if he has attained his majority shall be punished. Carts or carriages occupied by a minor or with no person shall be taken possession of by the king.

Whatever a man attempts to do to others by witchcraft shall be (practically) applied to the doer himself. Witchcraft merely to arouse love in an indifferent wife, in a maiden by her lover, or in a wife by her husband is no offence. But when it is injurious to others, the doer shall be punished with the middlemost amercement.

When a man performs witchcraft to win the sister of his own father or mother, the wife of a maternal uncle or of a preceptor, his own daughter-in-law, daughter, or sister, he shall have his limb cut off and also put to death, while any woman who yields herself to such an offender shall also receive similar punishment. Any woman who yields herself to a slave, a servant or a hired labourer shall be similarly punished.

A Kshatriya who commits adultery with an unguarded Brahman woman shall be punished with the highest amercement; a Vaisya doing the same shall be deprived of the whole of his property; and a Sudra shall be burnt alive wound round in mats.

Whoever commits adultery with the queen of the land shall be burnt alive in a vessel (*kumbhilpakah.*)

A man who commits adultery with a woman of low caste shall be banished with prescribed mark branded on his forehead, or shall be degraded to the same caste.

A Sudra or a *svapaka* who commits adultery with a woman of low caste shall be put to death, while the woman shall have her ears and nose cut off.

Adultery with a nun (*pravrajita*) shall be punishable with a fine of 24 *panas* while the nun who submits herself shall also pay a similar fine.

A man who forces his connection with a harlot shall be fined 12 *panas*.

When many persons perform witchcraft towards a single woman, each of them shall be punished with a fine of 24 *panas*.

When a man has connection with a woman against the order of nature (*a-yonau*), he shall be punished with the first amercement.

A man having sexual intercourse with another man shall also pay the first amercement.

• When a senseless man has sexual intercourse with beasts, he shall be fined 12 *panas*; when he comits the same act with idols (representatives) of goddesses (*daivatapratima*), he shall be fined twice as much.

• When the king punishes an innocent man, he shall throw into water dedicating to god Varuna a fine equal to thirty times the unjust imposition; and this amount shall afterwards be distributed among the Brahmans.

• By this act, the king will be free from the sin of unjust imposition; for king Varuna is the ruler of sinners among men.

[Thus ends Chapter 13, 'Punishment for violating justice', in Book IV, 'The Removal of Thorns', of the Arthashastra of Kautilya. End of the ninetieth chapter from the beginning. With this ends Book IV, 'The Removal of Thorns' of the Arthashastra of Kautilya.]

Book V

The Conduct of Courtiers

Chapter 1

CONCERNING THE AWARDS OF PUNISHMENTS

MEASURES necessary to remove the thorns of public peace both in fortified cities and country parts have been dealt with. We shall now proceed to treat of measures to suppress treason against the king and his kingdom.

With regard to those chiefs who, though living by service under the king, are inimically disposed towards him, or have taken the side of his enemy, a spy with secret mission or one in the guise of an ascetic and devoted to the king's cause shall set to work as described before; or a spy trained in the art of sowing the seeds of dissension may set to work, as will be described in connection with the 'Invasion of an enemy's villages'.

The king in the interests of righteousness may inflict punishment in secret on those courtiers or confederacy of chiefs who are dangerous to the safety of the kingdom and who cannot be put down in open daylight.

A spy may instigate the brother of a seditious minister and, with necessary inducements, take him to the king for an interview. The king, having conferred upon him the title to possess and enjoy the property of his seditious brother, may cause him to attack his brother; and when he murders his brother with a weapon or with poison, he shall be put to death in the same spot under the plea that he is a parricide.

The same measure will explain the proceedings to be taken against a seditious *parasava* (one who is begotten by a Brahman on Sudra wife), and a seditious son of a woman servant.

Or instigated by a spy, the brother of a seditious minister may put forward his claim for inheritance. While the claimant is lying at night at the door of the house of the seditious minister or elsewhere, a fiery spy (*tishna*) may murder him and declare: 'Alas! The claimant for inheritance is thus murdered (by his brother).' Then taking the side of the injured party, the king may punish the other (the seditious minister).

Spies in the presence of a seditious minister may threaten to beat his brother claiming inheritance. Then 'while the claimant is lying at the door of, etc,'... as before.

The same proceedings will explain the quarrel fraudulently caused to crop up between any two seditious ministers, in whose family a son or a father has had sexual intercourse with a daughter-in-law, or a brother with the wife of another brother.

A spy may flatter to the vanity of a seditious minister's son, of gentle manners and dignified conduct by telling him 'Though thou art the king's son, thou art kept here in fear of enemies'. The king may secretly honour this deluded person and tell him 'Apprehending danger from the minister, I have put off thy installation, though thou hast attained the age of heir apparent'. Then the spy may instigate him to murder the minister. The task being accomplished, he too may be put to death in the same spot under the plea that he is a parricide.

A mendicant woman, having captivated the wife of a seditious minister by administering such medicines as excite the feelings of love, may through that wife contrive to poison the minister.

Failing these measures, the king may send a seditious minister with an army of inefficient soldiers and fiery spies to put down a rebellious wild tribe or a village, or to set up a new superintendent of countries or of boundaries in a locality bordering upon a wilderness, or to bring under control a highly rebellious city, or to fetch a caravan bringing in the tribute due to the king from a neighbouring country. In an affray (that ensues in consequence of the above mission) either by day or at night, the fiery spies, or spies under the guise of robbers (*pratirodhaka*) may murder the minister and declare that he was killed in the battle.

While engaged in sports outside the city, the king may honour his seditious ministers with accommodation close to his own. A woman of bad character under the guise of the queen may be caught in the apartment of these ministers and steps may be taken against them as before.

A sauce maker or a sweetmeat maker may request of a seditious minister some sauce and sweetmeat by flattering him: 'Thou alone art worthy of such things.' Having mixed those two things and half a cup of water with poison, he may substitute those things in the luncheon (of the king) outside the city. Having made this event known to the public, the king may put them (the minister and the cook) to death under the plea that they are poisoners.

If a seditious minister is addicted to witchcraft, a spy under the guise of an accomplished wizard may make him believe that by manifesting (in witchcraft) anyone of the beautiful things—a pot containing an alligator, or a tortoise or crab—he can attain his desired end. While, with this belief, he is engaged in the act of witchcraft, a spy may murder him either by poisoning him or by striking him with an iron bar, and declare that he brought his own death by his proclivity to witchcraft.

A spy under the guise of a physician may make a seditious minister believe that he is suffering from a fatal or incurable disease and contrive to poison him while prescribing medicine and diet to him.

Spies under the guise of sauce makers and sweetmeat makers may, when opportunity occurs, contrive to poison him.

Such are the secret measures to get rid of seditious persons. As to measures to get rid of seditious persons conspiring against both the king and his kingdom:

When a seditious person is to be got rid of, another seditious person with an army of inefficient soldiers and fiery spies may be sent with the mission: 'Go out into this fort or country and raise an army or some revenue; deprive a courtier of his gold; bring by force the daughter of a courtier; build a fort; open a garden; construct a road for traffic; set up a new village; exploit a mine; form forest preserves for timber or elephants; set up a district or a boundary; and arrest and capture those who prevent your work or do not give you help'. Similarly the other party may be instructed to curb the spirit of the above person. When a quarrel arises between the two parties at work, fiery spies under cover may throw their weapons and murder the seditious person; and others are to be arrested and punished for the crime.

When with reference to boundaries, field produce, and boundaries of houses, or with reference to any damage done to things, instruments, crops, and beasts of burden, or on occasions of witnessing spectacles and processions, any dispute, real or caused by fiery spies, arises in seditious towns, villages or families, fiery spies may hurl weapons and say: 'This is what is done to them who quarrel with this man.' And for this offence others may be punished.

When there arises a quarrel among seditious persons, fiery spies may set fire to their fields, harvest grounds and houses, hurl weapons on their relatives, friends and beasts of burden, and say that they did so at the instigation of the seditious. And for this offence others may be punished.

Spies may induce seditious persons in forts or in country parts to be each other's guests at a dinner in which poisoners may administer poison. And for this offence others may be punished.

A mendicant woman may delude a seditious chief of a district into the belief that the wife, daughter or daughter-in-law of another seditious chief of another district loves the former. She may take the jewellery which the deluded chief gives her (for delivery to the wife, daughter, etc.), and, presenting it before the other chief, narrate that this chief in the pride of his youth makes love to the other's wife, daughter or daughter-in-law. When at night a duel arises between the two chiefs, etc., as before.

The prince or the commander of the army may confer some benefit upon such inimical persons as have been cowed down by a seditious army, and may declare his displeasure against them afterwards. And then some other persons, who are equally cowed down by another seditious army of the king, may be sent against the former along with an army of inefficient soldiers and fiery spies. Thus all the measures to get rid of seditious persons are of the same type.

Whoever among the sons of the seditious persons thus put down shows no perturbance of mind shall receive his father's property. It is only thus that the whole of the country will loyally follow the sons and grandsons of the king, and will be free from all troubles caused by men.

Possessed of forbearance and apprehending no disturbance either in the present or future, the king may award punishments in secret both upon his own subjects and those who uphold the enemy's cause.

[Thus ends Chapter 1, 'Concerning the Awards of Punishments', in Book V, 'The Conduct of Courtiers', of the Arthashastra of Kautilya. End of the ninety-first chapter from the beginning.]

Chapter 2

REPLENISHMENT OF THE TREASURY

THE king who finds himself in a great financial trouble and needs money, may collect (revenue by demand). In such parts of his country as depend solely upon rain for water and are rich in grain, he may demand of his subjects one-third or one-fourth of their grain according to their capacity. He shall never demand of such of his subjects as live in tracts of middle or low quality; nor of people who are of great help in the construction of fortifications, gardens, buildings, roads for traffic, colonization of wastelands, exploitation of mines, and formation of forest preserves for timber and elephants; nor of people who live on the border of his kingdom or who have not enough subsistence. He shall, on the other hand, supply with grain and cattle those who colonize wastelands. He may purchase for gold one-fourth of what remains, after deducting as much of the grain as is required for seeds and subsistence of his subjects. He shall avoid the property of forest tribes, as well as of Brahmans learned in the Vedas (*srotriya*). He may purchase this too, offering favourable price (to the owners). Failing these measures, the servants of the collector general may prevail upon the peasantry to raise summer crops. Saying that double the amount of fines will be levied from those who are guilty (among peasants), they (the king's employees) shall sow seeds in sowing seasons. When crops are ripe, they may beg a portion of vegetable and other ripe produce except what is gleaned in the form of vegetables and grains. They shall avoid the grains scattered in harvest fields, so that they may be utilized in making offerings to gods and ancestors on occasions of worship, in feeding cows, or for the subsistence of mendicants and village employees (*grâlmabhritaka*).

Whoever conceals his own grain shall pay a fine of eight times the amount in each kind; and whoever steals the crops of another person shall pay a fine of fifty times the amount, provided the robber belongs to the same community (*svavarga*); but if he is a foreigner, he shall be put to death. They (the king's employees) may demand of cultivators one-fourth of their grain, and one-sixth of forest produce (*vanya*) and of such commodities as cotton, wax, fabrics, barks of trees, hemp, wool, silk, medicines, sandal, flowers, fruits, vegetables, firewood, bamboos, flesh and dried flesh. They may also take one half of all ivory and skins of animals, and punish with the first amercement those who trade in any article without obtaining a licence from the king. So much for demands on cultivators.

Merchants dealing in gold, silver, diamonds, precious stones, pearls, coral, horses and elephants shall pay 50 *karas*. Those that trade in cotton threads, clothes, copper, brass, bronze, sandal, medicines and liquor shall pay 40 *karas*. Those that trade in grains, liquids, metals (*loha*), and deal with carts shall pay 30 *karas*. Those that carry on their trade in glass (*kâcha*); and also artisans of fine workmanship shall pay 20 *karas*. Articles of inferior workmanship, as well as those who keep prostitutes, shall pay 10 *karas*. Those that trade in firewood, bamboos, stones, earthen pots, cooked rice and vegetables shall pay 5 *karas*. Dramatists and prostitutes shall pay half of their wages. The entire property of goldsmiths shall be taken possession of; and no offence of theirs shall be forgiven; for they carry on their fraudulent trade while pretending at the same time to be honest and innocent. So much about demands on merchants.

Persons rearing cocks and pigs shall surrender to the government half of their stock of animals. Those that rear inferior animals shall give one-sixth. Those that keep cows, buffaloes, mules, asses and camels shall give one-tenth (of their livestock). Those who maintain prostitutes (*bandhakiposhaka*), shall, with the help of women noted for their beauty and youth in the service of the king, collect revenue. So much about demands on herdsmen.

Such demands shall be made only once and never twice. When such demands are not made, the collector general shall seek subscriptions from citizens and country people alike under false pretences of carrying this or that kind of business. Persons taken in concert shall publicly pay handsome donations and with this example, the king may demand of others among his subjects. Spies posing as citizens shall revile those who pay less. Wealthy persons may be requested to give as much of their gold as they can. Those who, of their own accord or with the intention of doing good, offer their wealth to the king shall be honoured with a rank in the court, an umbrella, or a turban or some ornaments in return for their gold.

Spies, under the guise of sorcerers, shall, under the pretence of ensuring safety, carry away the money, not only of the society of heretics and of temples but also of a dead man and of a man whose house is burnt, provided that it is not enjoyable by Brahmans.

The superintendent of religious institutions may collect in one place the various kinds of property of the gods of fortified cities and country parts and carry away the property (to the king's treasury).

Or having on some night set up a god or an altar, or having opened a sacred place of ascetics or having pointed out an evil omen, the king may collect subsistence under the pretence of holding processions and congregations (to avert calamities).

Or else he shall proclaim the arrival of gods, by pointing out to the people any of the sacred trees in the king's garden which has produced untimely flowers and fruits.

Or by causing a false panic owing to the arrival of an evil spirit on a tree in the city, wherein a man is hidden making all sorts of devilish noises, the king's spies, under the guise of ascetics, may collect money (with a view to propitiate the evil spirit and send it back).

Or spies may call upon spectators to see a serpent with numberless heads in a well connected with a subterranean passage and collect fees from them for the sight. Or they may place in a borehole made in the body of an image of a serpent, or in a hole in the corner of a temple, or in the hollow of an anthill, a cobra, which is, by diet, rendered unconscious, and call upon credulous spectators to see it (on payment of a certain amount of fee). As to persons who are not by nature credulous, spies may sprinkle over or give a drink of, such sacred water as is mixed with anasthetic ingredients and attribute their insensibility to the curse of gods. Or by causing an outcast person (*âbhityakta*) to be bitten by a cobra, spies may collect revenue under the pretext of undertaking remedial measures against ominous phenomena.

Or one of the king's spies in the garb of a merchant, may become a partner of a rich merchant and carry on trade in concert with him. As soon as a considerable amount of money has been gathered as sale proceeds, deposits and loans, he may cause himself to be robbed of the amount.

This will explain what the examiner of coins and the state goldsmith may also do.

Or else a spy, in the garb of a rich merchant, or a real rich merchant famous for his vast commerce, may borrow or take on pledge vast quantities of gold, silver and other commodities, or borrow from corporations gold bar gold, or coined gold for various kinds of merchandise to be procured from abroad. After having done this he may allow himself to be robbed of it the same night.

Prostitute spies under the garb of chaste women, may cause themselves to be enamoured of persons who are seditious. No sooner are the seditious persons seen within the abode of the female spies than they shall be seized and their property confiscated to the Government. Or whenever a quarrel arises between any two seditious parties of the same family, poisoners, previously engaged for the purpose, may administer poison to one party; and the other party may be accused of the offence and deprived of their property.

An outcast, under the guise of a high-born man, may claim from a seditious person a large amount of money professed to have been placed in the latter's custody by the claimant, or a large debt outstanding against the seditious person, or a share of parental property. (An outcast) may pretend to be the slave of a seditious person; and he may represent the wife, daughter or daughter-in-law of the seditious person as a slave woman or as his own wife;

and when the outcast is lying at the door of the seditious person's house at night or is living elsewhere, a fiery spy may murder him and declare: 'The claimant (of his own property or wife) has been thus killed'. And for this offence others (i.e., the seditious person and his followers) shall be deprived of their property.

Or a spy, under the garb of an ascetic, may offer inducements to a seditious person to acquire more wealth by taking in aid the art of witchcraft, and say: 'I am proficient in such witchcraft as brings inexhaustible wealth, or entitles a man to get admission into the king's palace, or can win the love of any woman, or can put an end to the life of one's enemy, or can lengthen the duration of one's life, or can give a son to anyone, if desired'. If the seditious person shows his desire to carry on the process of witchcraft securing wealth, the spy may make rich offerings, consisting of flesh, wine, and scent to the deity near an altar in a burial ground wherein a dead body of a man or of a child with a little quantity of money has been previously hidden. After the performance of worship is over, the hidden treasure may be dug out and the seditious person may be told that as the offerings fell short, the treasure is proportionately small; that the richest of offerings should be made to acquire vast amount of treasure, and that he may purchase rich offerings with the newly acquired wealth. Then he may be caught in the very act of purchasing commodities for offering.

A female spy, under the garb of a bereaved mother, may (in connection with the above case) raise an alarm, crying that her child was murdered (for the purposes of witchcraft).

When a seditious person is engaged in sorcery at night or in a sacrificial performance in a forest, or in sports in a park, fiery spies may murder him and carry away the corpse as that of an outcast.

Or a spy, under the garb of a servant of a seditious person, may mix counterfeit coins with the wages (he has received from his master), and pave the way for his arrest.

Or a spy, under the garb of a goldsmith, may undertake to do some work in the house of a seditious person, and gather in his employer's house such instruments as are necessary to manufacture counterfeit coins.

A spy, under the garb of a physician, may declare a healthy person of seditious character to be unhealthy (and administer poison). Or a spy, attending as a servant upon a seditious person, may not only call for an explanation from another fraudulent spy as to how certain articles necessary for the installation of a king and also the letters of an enemy came into the possession of his master, but also volunteer an explanation himself.

Measures such as the above shall be taken only against the seditious and the wicked and never against others.

Just as fruits are gathered from a garden as often as they become ripe, so revenue shall be collected as often as it becomes ripe. Collection of revenue or of fruits, when unripe, shall never be carried on, lest their source be injured, causing immense trouble.

[Thus ends Chapter 2, 'Replenishment of the Treasury', in Book V, 'The Conduct of Courtiers', of the Arthashastra of Kautilya. End of the ninety-second chapter from the beginning.]

Chapter 3

CONCERNING SUBSISTENCE TO GOVERNMENT SERVANTS

IN accordance with the requirements of his forts and country parts, the king should fix under one-fourth of the total revenue the charges of maintaining his servants. He should look to the bodily comforts of his servants by providing such emoluments as can infuse in them the spirit of enthusiasm to work. He should not violate the course of righteousness and wealth.

The sacrificial priest (*ritvik*), the teacher, the minister, the priest (*purohita*), the commander of the army, the heir apparent prince, the mother of the king, and the queen shall (each receive) 48,000 (*panas* per annum). With this amount of subsistence, they will scarcely yield themselves to temptation and hardly be discontented.

The doorkeeper, the superintendent of the harem (*antarvamsika*) the commander (*prasastri*), the collector general, and the chamberlain, 24,000. With this amount they become serviceable.

The prince (*kumara*), the nurse of the prince, the chief constable (*nayaka*), the officer in charge of the town (*paura*) the superintendent of law or commerce (*vyavaharika*), the superintendent of manufactories (*karmantika*), members of the council of ministers, the superintendents of country parts and of boundaries, 12,000. With this they will be loyal and powerful supporters of the king's cause.

The chiefs of military corporations, the chiefs of elephants, of horses, of chariots and of infantry, and commissioners (*pradeshtarah*), 8,000. With this amount they can have a good following in their own communities.

The superintendents of infantry, of cavalry, of chariots and of elephants, the guards of timber and elephant forests, 4,000.

The chariot driver, the physician of the army, the trainer of horses, the carpenter (*vardhaki*), and those who rear animals (*yoniposhaka*), 2,000.

The foreteller, the reader of omens, the astrologer, the reader of Puranas, the storyteller, the bard (*magadha*), the retinue of the priest, and all superintendents of departments, 1,000.

Trained soldiers, the staff of accountants and writers, 500.

Musicians (*kusilava*), 250. Of these, the trumpet blowers (*turyakara*) shall get twice as much wages as others. Artisans and carpenters, 120.

Servants in charge of quadrupeds and bipeds, workmen doing miscellaneous work, attendants upon the royal person, body-guards, and the procurer of free labourers shall receive a salary of 60 *panas*.

The honourable playmate of the king (*aryayukta*), the elephant driver, the sorcerer (*manavaka*), miners of mountains (*sailakhanaka*), all kinds of attendants, teachers and learned men shall have honorarium ranging from 500 to 1,000 (*panas*) according to their merit.

A messanger of middle quality shall receive 10 *panas* for each *yojana* he travels; and twice as much when he travels from 10 to 100 *yojanas*.

Whoever represents the king in the *rajasuya* and other sacrifices shall get three times as much as is paid to others who are equal to him in learning; and the charioteer of the king (in the sacrifices), 1,000.

Spies such as the fradulent (*kapatika*), the indifferent (*udasthita*), the householder, the merchant, and the ascetic 1,000.

The village servant (*gramabhritaka*), fiery spies, poisoners and mendicant women, 500 (*panas*).

Servants leading the spies, 250 or in proportion to the work done by them.

Superintendents of a hundred or a thousand communities (*varga*) shall regulate the subsistence, wages, profits, appointinent, and transference (*vikshepa*), of the men under them.

There shall be no transference of officers employed to guard the royal buildings, forts and country parts. The chief officers employed to superintend the above places shall be many and shall permanently hold the same office.

The sons and wives of those who die while on duty shall get subsistence and wages. Infants, aged persons, or deceased persons related to the deceased servants shall also be shown favour. On occasions of funerals, sickness, or childbirth, the king shall give presentations to his servants concerned therein.

When wanting in money, the king may give forest produce, cattle, or fields along with a small amount of money. If he is alone; and if he is desirous of regulating the affairs of all villages equally, he shall give no village to any (of his servants).

Thus the king shall not only maintain his servants, but also increase their subsistence and wages in consideration of their learning and work.

Substituting one *adhaka* for the salary of 60 *panas* payment in gold may be commuted for that in kind.

Footmen, horses, chariots and elephants shall be given necessary training in the art of war at sunrise, on all days but those of conjunction (of planets). On these occasions of training, the king shall ever be present and witness their exercise.

Weapons and armour shall be entered into the armoury only after they are marked with the king's seal.

Persons with weapons shall not be allowed to move anywhere unless they are permitted by a passport.

When weapons are either lost or spoilt, the superintendent shall pay double their value; an account of the weapons that are destroyed shall be kept up.

Boundary guards shall take away the weapons and armour possessed by caravans unless the latter are provided with a passport to travel with weapons.

When starting on a military tour, the king shall put his army in action. On such occasions, spies, under the garb of merchants, shall supply to military stations all kinds of merchandise for double the quantity of the same to be repaid in future. Thus not only is there afforded an opportunity for the sale of the king's merchandise but also is there a way opened for a good return for the wages paid.

Thus, when both the receipts and expenditure are properly cared for, the king will never find himself in financial or military difficulties.

Such are the alternatives with regard to subsistence and wages.

Spies, prostitutes, artisans, singers and aged military officers shall vigilantly examine the pure or impure conduct of military men.

[Thus ends Chapter 3, 'Concerning Subsistence to Government Servants', in Book V, 'The Conduct of Courtiers', of the Arthashastra of Kautilya. End of the 93rd chapter from the beginning.]

Chapter 4

THE CONDUCT OF A COURTIER

WHOEVER possesses enough experience of the world and its affairs may, through the influence of an interested friend, seek the favour of a king who is endowed with amiable qualities and is possessed of all the elements of sovereignty. He may court the favour of any king provided he thinks: *Just as I am in need of a patron, so is this king possessed of a taste for good advice and is of amiable character*. He may even court the favour of such a king as is poor and destitute of the elements of sovereignty, but never, of such a one as is of a depraved character; whoever, as a king, is destitute of good temper and amiable character cannot, by reason of his habitual hatred of the science of polity and an inborn proclivity to evil ways, maintain his sovereignty, though he is possessed of immense sovereign power.

Having obtained admittance to an amiable king, he shall give the king instructions in sciences. Absence of contradiction from the king will render his position secure. When his opinion is sought about present or future schemes needing much thought and consideration, he may boldly and sensibly, and with no fear of contradiction from the assembly of ministers, pronounce his opinion so as to be in harmony with the principles of righteousness and economy. When required, he may answer questions on points of righteousness and economy (and tell the king):

'Following the rule that there should be no delay in putting down by force even a strong confederacy of wicked people, you should apply force against the wicked, if they have a strong support; do not despise my advice, character and secrets; and by means of gestures, I shall prevent you from inflicting punishments on anyone, when you are going to do so either wilfully or under provocation.'

With such agreements with the king, he (a courtier) may enter on the duty assigned to him. He shall sit by the side of, and close to, the king and far from the seat of another courtier. He shall avoid speaking slyly against the opinion of any member of the assembly; he shall never make incredible or false statements; nor loud laughter with no cause for jest, and loud noise and spittle. He shall also avoid talking to another in secret, mutual conversation with another in the assembly (of ministers), appearing in royal dress in the public, haughtiness, buffoonery, open request for gems and promotions, seeing with one eye, biting the lips, brow-beating, interrupting the king while speaking, enmity with a strong party, association with women, pimps, messengers of foreign kings, enemies, inimical parties, dismissed officers, and wicked people, stubborn adherence to a single purpose, and contact with any confederacy of men.

• Without losing the opportune moments, he should speak of the king's interest; of his own interest when in company with persons friendly to him; and of others' interests in a suitable time and place, and in conformity with the principles of righteousness and economy.
• When asked, he should tell the king what is both good and pleasing, but not what is bad, though pleasing; if the king is pleased to listen, he may secretly tell what, though unpleasant, is good.
• He may even keep silence, but should never describe what is hateful; by abstaining from talking of what the king hates, even undesirable persons have become powerful when, seeing that the king likes only pleasant things without caring for their evil consequences, they have followed his will.
• While laughing in jest, he should avoid loud laughter; he shall avoid evil aspersions against others, nor ascribe evil to others; he shall forgive evil done to himself and have as much forbearance as the earth.
• Self-protection shall be the first and constant thought of a wise man; for the life of a man under the service of a king is aptly compared to life in fire; whereas fire burns a part or the whole of the body, if at all, the king has the power either to destroy or to advance the whole family, consisting of sons and wives, of his servants.

[Thus ends Chapter 4, 'The Conduct of a Courtier', in Book V, 'The Conduct of Courtiers', of the Arthashastra of Kautilya. End of the 94th chapter from the beginning.]

Chapter 5

TIME SERVING

WHEN employed as a minister, he (the courtier) shall show the net revenue that remains after all kinds of expenditure are met with. He shall also give the exact particulars—as this is thus—of whatever work is external, internal, secret, open, costly or negligible. He shall follow the king in his pursuits after hunting, gambling, drinking, and sexual pleasures. Ever attending upon the king, he shall, by flattery, endeavour to arrest his fall into evil habits and save him from the intrigues, plots and deceptions of enemies. He shall also endeavour to read the mind and appearance of the king.

By way of collecting his wandering thoughts into a resolve, the king exhibits in his appearance and movements his inclination, anger, pleasure, sorrow, determination, fear and change in the pairs of opposite feelings.

'By cognizing wisdom in others, he is pleased; he attends to the speech of others; he gives a seat; allows himself to be seen in private; does not suspect in places of suspicion; takes delight in conversation; spontaneously looks to things without being reminded; tolerates what is said agreeably to reason; orders with smiling face; touches with the hand; does not laugh at what is commendable; commends the qualities of another behind him; remembers (the courtier) while taking luncheon; engages himself in sports accompanied by (the courtier); consults (the courtier) when in trouble; honours the followers of the courtier; reveals the secret; honours the courtier more and more; gives him wealth; and averts his troubles—these are the signs of the king's satisfaction (with the courtier).'

The reverse of the above indicates his (the king's) displeasure. Still, we shall describe them in plain terms:

Angry appearance when the courtier is in sight; evading or refusal to hear his speech; no inclination to give him a seat or to see him; change in syllables and accents while talking to him; seeing with one eye; brow-beating; biting the lips; rise of sweat; hard breathing and smiling with no palpable cause; talking to himself; sudden bending or raising of the body; touching the body or the seat of another; molestation to another; contempt of learning, caste and country (of the courtier); condemnation of a colleague of equal defects; condemnation of a man of opposite defects; condemnation of his opponent; failure to acknowledge his good deeds; enumeration of his bad deeds; attention to whoever enters into the chamber; too much gift; uttering falsehood; change in the conduct and attitude of visitors to the king; nay, the courtier shall also note the change in the life of animals other than men.

Katyayana holds that this (king) showers his favours broadcast.

Kaninka Bharadvaja says that *krauncha* (a bird) has moved from right to left.

Dirgha Charayana says that this (king) is (like) a grass.

Ghotamukha says that (he is like) a wet cloth.

Kinjalka says that (he is like) an elephant pouring over water.

Pisuna is of opinion that one should declare him to be a chariot horse.

The son of Pisuna says that mortification ensues when his opponent is courted.

When wealth and honour are discontinued, such a king may be abandoned; or by recognizing the character of the king as well as his own defects, he may rectify himself; or he may seek the protection of one of the best friends of the king.

Living with the king's friend, the courtier has to endeavour to remove, through the medium of his own friends, the defects of his master, and then come back to his original place, no matter whether the king is alive or dead.

[Thus ends Chapter 5 'Time Serving', in Book V, 'The Conduct of Courtiers', of the Arthashastra of Kautilya. End of the 95th chapter from the beginning.]

Chapter 6

CONSOLIDATION OF THE KINGDOM AND ABSOLUTE SOVEREIGNTY

THE minister shall thus avert the calamities in which the king is involved; long before the apprehended death of the king, he shall, in concert with his friends and followers, allow visitors to the king once in a month or two (and avoid their visits on other occasions) under the plea that the king is engaged in performing such rites as are calculated to avert national calamities, or are destructive of enemies, or capable of prolonging life or of procuring a son.

On appropriate occasions, he may show a pseudo-king not only to the people but also to messengers coming from friends or enemies; and this (false) king shall make the minister his mouthpiece in conversing with them as deserved. And through the medium of the gatekeeper and the officer in charge of the harem, the minister shall (pretend to) receive the orders of the king. Displeasure or mercy to wrongdoers shall be shown only indirectly.

Both the treasury and the army shall be kept under the command of two reliable and confidential persons and in a single locality, either within the fort or at the boundary of the kingdom.

Cognates, princes and other chiefs of the royal family may be employed in works such as the capture of a chief who, employed as a commander of a fort or the tracts of wilderness, has turned inimical along with a strong band of supporters; or they may be sent on an expedition full of difficulties, or to visit the family of the king's friend.

Whoever, among the neighbouring kings, seems to threaten with an invasion may be invited for some festival, marriage, capture of elephants, purchase of horses or of merchandise, or for taking possession of some lands ceded to him, and captured; or such an enemy may be kept at bay by an ally till an agreement of not condemnable nature is made with him; or he may be made to incur the displeasure of wild tribes or of his enemies; or whoever among his nearest relatives is kept under guard may be promised a portion of his territory and set against him.

Or with the help of nobles and princes of the king's family, the minister may have the heir apparent installed and show him to the public.

Or having, as pointed out in the chapter concerning the awards of punishments, removed the thorns of the kingdom, he may conduct the administration.

Or if a chief among the neighbouring kings seems to give trouble, the minister may invite him, saying, 'Come here and I shall make thee king,' and then put him to death; or he may be kept at bay by taking such measures as can ward off dangers.

Or having gradually placed the burden of administration on the shoulders of the heir apparent, the minister may announce the death of the king to the public.

In case of the king's demise in an enemy's land, the minister, having brought about an agreement between the enemy and a friend pretending to be an enemy of the dead king, may withdraw himself; or having installed in the king's fort anyone of the neighbouring kings, he may withdraw himself; or having installed the heir apparent, he may set the army against the enemy; and when attacked by the enemy, he may take, as detailed elsewhere, such measures as can ward off dangers.

'Thus,' says Kautilya, 'the minister shall invest himself with the powers of sovereignty.'

'Not so,' says Bharadvaja, 'the king lying on his deathbed, the minister may set up the princes and other chiefs of the royal family against one another or against other chiefs. Whoever attacks the kingdom may be put to death under the plea of disturbance and annoyance to the people; or having secretly punished the chief rebels of the royal family and brought them under his control, the minister shall himself take possession of the kingdom, for on account of the kingdom the father hates his sons, and sons their father; why then should the minister who is the sole prop of the kingdom (be an exception to it)? Therefore he shall never discard what has, of its own accord, fallen into his hands; for it is a general talk among the people that a woman making love of her own accord will, when discarded, curse the man.

'An opportunity will only once offer itself to a man who is waiting for it, and will not come a second time when he may be desirous of accomplishing his work.'

'But it is,' says Kautilya, 'unrighteous to do an act which excites popular fury; nor is it an accepted rule. He shall, therefore, install in the kingdom such a son of the king as is possessed of amiable qualities. In the absence of a prince of good character, he may place before himself a wicked prince, or a princess, or the pregnant queen, and tell the other ministers: "This is your caste (*kshepa*); look to the father of this (boy) as well as to your own valour and descent; this (boy) is merely a flag; and yourselves are the lords; pray, how shall I act?"'

As he is saying this, others, taken in confidence before, shall say in reply: 'Who else than the one of your lead is capable of protecting the mass of the people of the four castes of the king?' Then the other ministers will certainly agree to it. Accordingly he shall install a prince, a princess or the pregnant queen, and show him or her to all the royal relations as well as to the messengers coming from friends or enemies. He shall provide the ministers and military officers with increased subsistence and salary, promising them that 'This (boy) will, after attaining full age, increase your emolument still more'. He shall likewise promise the chief officers in charge of the forts and country parts as well as the parties of both the friends and enemies. He shall then take necessary steps to educate and train the prince.

Or he may install a child begotten on the princess by a man of the same caste.

He shall keep as a representative of the prince one who is of the same family, of little valour and of beautiful appearance, lest the mother's mind be agitated with wild apprehensions. He shall justly protect her. He shall not provide himself with luxurious means of enjoyment. As to the king, he may provide him with new chariots, horses, jewels, dress, women and palaces.

• When the prince comes of age, he may request the prince to relieve him from the intellectual worry. He may abandon the king, if he (the king) is displeased; and follow him if he is pleased.

• If he is disgusted with the ministerial life, he may go to a forest or a long sacrifice, after having informed the queen of the safeguards and persons that are employed to bring up the prince.

• Even if the king is held by the chiefs under their influence, the minister may, through the medium of the king's favourites, teach him the principles of polity with illustrations, taken from the Itihasa and Purana.

• Having taken the garb of an accomplished ascetic, the minister may ingratiate himself with the king; and having brought the king under his influence, he may take coercive measure against the seditious.

[Thus ends Chapter 6 'Consolidation of the Kingdom and Absolute Sovereignty', in Book V, 'The Conduct of Courtiers', of the Arthashastra of Kautilya. End of the ninety-sixth chapter from the beginning. With this, ends Book V 'The Conduct of Courtiers' of the Arthashastra of Kautilya.]

Book VI

The Source of Sovereign States

Chapter 1

THE ELEMENTS OF SOVEREIGNTY

THE king, the minister, the country, the fort, the treasury, the army and the friend are the elements of sovereignty.

Of these, the best qualities of the king are:

Born of a high family, godly, possessed of valour, seeing through the medium of aged persons, virtuous, truthful, not of a contradictory nature, grateful, having large aims, highly enthusiastic, not addicted to procrastination, powerful to control his neighbouring kings, of resolute mind, having an assembly of ministers of no mean quality, and possessed of a taste for discipline. These are the qualities of an inviting nature.

Inquiry, hearing, perception, retention in memory, reflection, deliberation, inference and steadfast adherence to conclusions are the qualities of the intellect.

Valour, determination of purpose, quickness and probity are the aspects of enthusiasm.

Possessed of a sharp intellect, strong memory and keen mind, energetic, powerful, trained in all kinds of arts, free from vice, capable of paying in the same coin by way of awarding punishments or rewards, possessed of dignity, capable of taking remedial measures against dangers, possessed of foresight, ready to avail himself of opportunities when afforded in respect of place, time and manly efforts, clever enough to discern the causes necessitating the cessation of treaty or war with an enemy, or to lie in wait keeping treaties, obligations and pledges, or to avail himself of his enemy's weak points, making jokes with no loss of dignity or secrecy, never brow beating and casting haughty and stern looks, free from passion, anger, greed, obstinacy, fickleness, haste and backbiting habits, talking to others with a smiling face, and observing customs as taught by aged persons—such is the nature of self-possession.

The qualifications of a minister have been described in the beginning, middle and at the close of the work.

Possessed of capital cities both in the centre and the extremities of the kingdom, productive of subsistence not only to its own people but also to outsiders on occasions of calamities, repulsive to enemies, powerful enough to put down neighbouring kings, free from miry, rocky, uneven and desert tracts as well as from conspirators, tigers, wild beasts and large tracts of wilderness, beautiful to look at, containing fertile lands, mines, timber and elephant forests, and pasture grounds, artistic, containing hidden passages, full of cattle, not depending upon rain for water, possessed of land and waterways, rich in various kinds of commercial articles, capable of bearing the burden of a vast army and heavy taxation, inhabited by agriculturists of good and active character, full of intelligent masters and servants, and with a population noted for its loyalty and good character—these are the qualities of a good country.

The excellent qualities of forts have already been described.

Justly obtained either by inheritance or by self-acquisition, rich in gold and silver, filled with an abundance of big gems of various colours and of gold coins, and capable to withstand calamities of long duration is the best treasury.

Coming down directly from father and grandfather (of the king), ever strong, obedient, happy in keeping their sons and wives well contented, not averse to making a long sojourn, ever and everywhere invincible, endowed with the power of endurance, trained in fighting various kinds of battles, skilful in handling various forms of weapons, ready to share in the weal or woe of the king, and consequently not falling foul with him, and purely composed of soldiers of Kshatriya caste—these constitute the best army.

Coming down directly from father and grandfather, long-standing, open to conviction, never falling foul, and capable of making preparations for war quickly and on a large scale—these are the qualities of the best friend.

Not born of a royal family, greedy, possessed of a mean assembly of ministers, with disloyal subjects, ever doing unrighteous acts, of loose character, addicted to mean pleasures, devoid of enthusiasm, trusting to fate, indiscreet in action, powerless, helpless, impotent, and ever injurious—these are the signs of the worst enemy. Such an enemy is easily uprooted.

- Excepting the enemy, these seven elements, possessed of their excellent characteristics are said to be the limb-like elements of sovereignty.
- A wise king can make even the poor and miserable elements of his sovereignty happy and prosperous; but a wicked king will surely destroy the most prosperous and loyal elements of his kingdom.
- Hence a king of unrighteous character and of vicious habits will, though he is an emperor, fall a prey either to the fury of his own subjects or to that of his enemies.
- But a wise king, trained in politics, will, though he possesses a small territory, conquer the whole earth with the help of the best-fitted elements of his sovereignty, and will never be defeated.

[Thus ends Chapter 1 'The Elements of Sovereignty', in Book VI, 'The Source of Sovereign States', of the Arthashastra of Kautilya. End of the ninety-seventh chapter from the beginning.]

Chapter 2

CONCERNING PEACE AND EXERTION

ACQUISITION and security (of property) are dependent upon peace and industry.

Efforts to achieve the results of works undertaken is industry (*vyayama*).

Absence of disturbance to the enjoyment of the results achieved from works is peace.

The application of the sixfold royal policy is the source of peace and industry.

Deterioration, stagnation and progress are the three aspects of position.

Those causes of human make which affect position are policy and impolicy (*naya* and *apanaya*); fortune and misfortune (*aya* and *anaya*) are providential causes. Causes, both human and providential, govern the world and its affairs.

What is unforeseen is providential; here, the attainment of that desired end which seemed almost lost is (termed) fortune.

What is anticipated is human; and the attainment of a desired end as anticipated is (due to policy).

What produces unfavourable results is impolicy. This can be foreseen; but misfortune due to providence cannot be known.

The king who, being possessed of good character and best-fitted elements of sovereignty, is the fountain of policy, and is termed the conqueror.

The king who is situated anywhere immediately on the circumference of the conqueror's territory is termed the enemy.

The king who is likewise situated close to the enemy, but separated from the conqueror only by the enemy, is termed the friend (of the conqueror).

A neighbouring foe of considerable power is styled an enemy; and when he is involved in calamities or has taken himself to evil ways, he becomes assailable; and when he has little or no help, he becomes destructible; otherwise (i.e., when he is provided with some help), he deserves to be harassed or reduced. Such are the aspects of an enemy.

In front of the conqueror and close to his enemy, there happen to be situated kings such as the conqueror's friend, next to him, the enemy's friend, and next to the last, the conqueror's friend's friend, and next, the enemy's friend's friend.

In the rear of the conqueror, there happen to be situated a rearward enemy (*parshnigraha*), a rearward friend (*akranda*), an ally of the rearward enemy (*parshnigrahasara*), and an ally of the rearward friend (*akrandasara*).

That foe who is equally of high birth and occupies a territory close to that of the conqueror is a natural enemy; while he who is merely antagonistic and creates enemies to the conqueror is a factitious enemy.

He whose friendship is derived from father and grandfather, and who is situated close to the territory of the immediate enemy of the conqueror, is a natural friend; while he whose friendship is courted for self-maintenance is an acquired friend.

The king who occupies a territory close to both the conqueror and his immediate enemy in front and who is capable of helping both the kings, whether united or disunited, or of resisting either of them individually is termed a *madhyama* (mediatory) king.

He who is situated beyond the territory of any of the above kings and who is very powerful and capable of helping the enemy, the conqueror, and the *madhyama* king together or individually, or of resisting any of them individually, is a neutral king (*udasina*). These are the (twelve) primary kings.

The conqueror, his friend, and his friend's friend are the three primary kings constituting a circle of states. As each of these three kings possesses the five elements of sovereignty, such as the minister, the country, the fort, the treasury, and the army, a circle of states consists of eighteen elements. Thus, it needs no commentary to understand that the (three) circles of states having the enemy (of the conqueror), the *madhyama* king, or the neutral king at the centre of each of the three circles, are different from that of the conqueror. Thus there are four primary circles of states, twelve kings, sixty elements of sovereignty, and seventy-two elements of states.

Each of the twelve primary kings shall have their elements of sovereignty, power, and end. Strength is power, and happiness is the end.

Strength is of three kinds: power of deliberation is intellectual strength; the possession of a prosperous treasury and a strong army is the strength of sovereignty; and martial power is physical strength.

The end is also of three kinds: that which is attainable by deliberation is the end of deliberation; that which is attainable by the strength of sovereignty is the end of sovereignty; and that which is to be secured by perseverance is the end of martial power.

The possession of power and happiness in a greater degree makes a king superior to another; in a less degree, inferior; and in an equal degree, equal. Hence a king shall always endeavour to augment his own power and elevate his happiness.

A king who is equal to his enemy in the matter of his sovereign elements shall, by virtue of his own righteous conduct or with the help of those who are hostile or conspiring against his enemy, endeavour to throw his enemy's power into the shade; or if he thinks:

'That my enemy, possessed as he is of immense power, will yet in the near future hurt the elements of his own sovereignty, by using contumelious language, by inflicting severe punishments, and by squandering his wealth; that though attaining success for a time yet he will blindly take himself to hunting, gambling, drinking and women; that as his subjects are disaffected, himself powerless and haughty, I can overthrow him; that when attacked, he will take shelter with all his paraphernalia into a fort or elsewhere; that possessed as he is of a strong army, he will yet fall into my hands, as he has neither a friend nor a fort to help him; that a distant king is desirous to put down his own enemy, and also inclined to help me to put down my own assailable enemy when my resources are poor; or that I may be invited as a *madhyama* king'—for these reasons the conqueror may allow his enemy to grow in strength and to attain success for the time being.

• Throwing the circumference of the circle of states beyond his friend's territory, and making the kings of those states as the spokes of that circle, the conqueror shall make himself the nave of that circle.

• A reducible or a conquerable enemy will, when placed between a conqueror and the conqueror's friend, appear to be growing in strength.

[Thus ends Chapter 2 'Peace and Exertion', in Book VI, 'The Source of Sovereign States', of the Arthashastra of Kautilya. End of the ninety-eighth chapter from the beginning. With this ends Book VI, 'The Source of Sovereign States' of the Arthashastra of Kautilya.]

Book VII

The End of the Sixfold Policy

Chapter 1

THE SIX-FOLD POLICY, AND DETERMINATION OF DETERIORATION, STAGNATION AND PROGRESS

THE circle of states is the source of the sixfold policy.

My teacher says that peace (*sandhi*), war (*vigraha*), observance of neutrality (*asana*), marching (*yana*), alliance (*samsraya*), and making peace with one and waging war with another are the six forms of state policy.

But Vatavyadhi holds that there are only two forms of policy, peace and war, inasmuch as the six forms result from these two primary forms of policy.

While Kautilya holds that as their respective conditions differ, the forms of policy are six.

Of these, agreement with pledges is peace; offensive operation is war; indifference is neutrality; making preparations is marching; seeking the protection of another is alliance; and making peace with one while waging war with another is termed a double policy (*dvaidhibhava*). These are the six forms.

Whoever is inferior to another shall make peace with him; whoever is superior in power shall wage war; whoever thinks 'no enemy can hurt me, nor am I strong enough to destroy my enemy', shall observe neutrality; whoever is possessed of necessary means shall march against his enemy; whoever is devoid of necessary strength to defend himself shall seek the protection of another; whoever thinks that help is necessary to work out an end shall make peace with one and wage war with another. Such is the aspect of the six forms of policy.

Of these, a wise king shall observe that form of policy which, in his opinion, enables him to build forts, to construct buildings and commercial roads, to open new plantations and villages, to exploit mines and timber and elephant forests, and at the same time to harass similar works of his enemy.

Whoever thinks himself to be growing in power more rapidly both in quality and quantity (than his enemy), and the reverse of his enemy, may neglect his enemy's progress for the time.

If any two kings hostile to each other find the time of achieving the results of their respective works to be equal, they shall make peace with each other.

No king shall keep that form of policy, which causes him the loss of profit from his own works, but which entails no such loss on the enemy; for it is deterioration.

Whoever thinks that in the course of time his loss will be less than his acquisition as contrasted with that of his enemy, may neglect his temporary deterioration.

If any two kings hostile to each other and deteriorating, expect to acquire equal amount of wealth in equal time, they shall make peace with each other.

That position in which neither progress nor retrogression is seen is stagnation.

Whoever thinks his stagnancy to be of a shorter duration and his prosperity in the long run to be greater than his enemy's may neglect his temporary stagnation.

My teacher says that if any two kings, who are hostile to each other and are in a stationary condition expect to acquire equal amount of wealth and power in equal time, they shall make peace with each other.

'Of course,' says Kautilya, 'there is no other alternative.' Or if a king thinks:

'That keeping the agreement of peace, I can undertake productive works of considerable importance and destroy at the same time those of my enemy; or apart from enjoying the results of my own works, I shall also enjoy those of my enemy by virtue of the agreement of peace; or I can destroy the works of my enemy by employing spies and other secret means; or by holding out such inducements as a happy dwelling, rewards, remission of taxes, little work and large profits and wages, I can empty my enemy's country of its population, with which he has been able to carry his own works; or being allied with a king of considerable power, my enemy will have his own works destroyed; or I can prolong my enemy's hostility with another king whose threats have driven my enemy to seek my protection; or being allied with me, my enemy can harass the country of another king who hates me; or oppressed by another king, the subjects of my enemy will immigrate into my country, and I can, therefore, achieve the results of my own works very easily; or being in a precarious condition due to the destruction of his works, my enemy will not be so powerful as to attack me; or by exploiting my own resources in alliance with any two (friendly) kings, I can augment my resources; or if a circle of states is formed by my enemy as one of its members, I can divide them and combine with the others; or by threats or favour, I can catch hold of my enemy, and when he desires to be a member of my own circle of states, I can make him incur the displeasure of the other members and fall a victim to their own fury,'—if a king thinks thus, he may increase his resources by keeping peace.

Or if a king thinks:

'That as my country is full of born soldiers and of corporations of fighting men, and as it possesses such natural defensive positions as mountains, forests, rivers, and forts with only one entrance, it can easily repel the attack of my enemy; or having taken my stand in my impregnable fortress at the border of my country, I can harass the works of my enemy; or owing to internal troubles and loss of energy, my enemy will early suffer from the destruction of his works; or when my enemy is attacked by another king, I can induce his subjects to immigrate into my country,' then he may augment his own resources by keeping open hostility with such an enemy.

Or if a king thinks:

'That neither is my enemy strong enough to destroy my works, nor am I his; or if he comes to fight with me, like a dog with a boar, I can increase his afflictions without incurring any loss in my own works', he may observe neutrality and augment his own resources.

Or if a king thinks:

'That by marching my troops it is possible to destroy the works of my enemy; and as for myself, I have made proper arrangements to safeguard my own works,' he may increase his resources by marching.

Or if a king thinks:

'That I am strong enough neither to harass my enemy's works nor to defend my own against my enemy's attack,' he shall seek protection from a king of superior power and endeavour to pass from the stage of deterioration to that of stagnancy and from the latter to that of progress.

Or if a king thinks:

'That by making peace with one, I can work out my own resources, and by waging war with another, I can destroy the works of my enemy,' he may adopt that double policy and improve his resources.

Thus, a king in the circle of sovereign states shall, by adopting the sixfold policy, endeavour to pass from the state of deterioration to that of stagnation and from the latter to that of progress.

[Thus ends Chapter 1, 'The Sixfold Policy and Determination of Deterioration, Stagnation and Progress', in Book VII, 'The End of the Sixfold Policy', of the Arthashastra of Kautilya. End of the ninety-ninth chapter from the beginning.]

Chapter 2

THE NATURE OF ALLIANCE

WHEN the advantages derivable from peace and war are of equal character, one should prefer peace; for disadvantages, such as the loss of power and wealth, sojourning, and sin, are ever attending upon war.

The same holds good in the case of neutrality and war. Of the two (forms of policy), double policy and alliance, double policy (i.e., making peace with one and waging war with another) is preferable; for whoever adopts the double policy enriches himself, being ever attentive to his own works, whereas an allied king has to help his ally at his own expense.

One shall make an alliance with a king who is stronger than one's neighbouring enemy; in the absence of such a king, one should ingratiate oneself with one's neighbouring enemy, either by supplying money or army or by ceding a part of one's territory and by keeping oneself aloof; for there can be no greater evil to kings than alliance with a king of considerable power, unless one is actually attacked by one's enemy.

A powerless king should behave as a conquered king (towards his immediate enemy); but when he finds that the time of his own ascendancy is at hand due to a fatal disease, internal troubles, increase of enemies, or a friend's calamities that are vexing his enemy, then under the pretence of performing some expiatory rites to avert the danger of his enemy, he may get out (of the enemy's court); or if he is in his own territory, he should not go to see his suffering enemy; or if he is near to his enemy, he may murder the enemy when opportunity affords itself.

A king who is situated between two powerful kings shall seek protection from the stronger of the two; or from one of them on whom he can rely; or he may make peace with both of them on equal terms. Then he may begin to set one of them against the other by telling each that the other is a tyrant causing utter ruin to himself, and thus cause dissension between them. When they are divided, he may pat down each separately by secret or covert means. Or, throwing himself under the protection of any two immediate kings of considerable power, he may defend himself against an immediate enemy. Or, having made an alliance with a chief in a stronghold, he may adopt double policy (i.e., make peace with one of the two kings, and wage war with the other). Or, he may adapt himself to circumstances depending upon the causes of peace and war in order. Or, he may make friendship with traitors, enemies and wild chiefs who are conspiring against both the kings. Or, pretending to be a close friend of one of them, he may strike the other at the latter's weak point by employing enemies, and wild tribes. Or, having made friendship with both, he may form a circle of states. Or, he may make an alliance with the *madhyama* or the neutral king; and with this help he may put down one of them or both. Or when hurt by both, he may seek protection from a king of righteous character among the *madhyama* king, the neutral king, and their friends or equals, or from any other king whose subjects are so disposed as to increase his happiness and peace, with whose help he may be able to recover his lost position, with whom his ancestors were in close intimacy or had blood relationship, and in whose kingdom he can find a number of powerful friends.

Of two powerful kings who are on amicable terms with each other, a king shall make alliance with one of them who likes him and whom he likes; this is the best way of making alliance.

[Thus ends Chapter 2, 'The Nature of Alliance', in Book VII, 'The End of the Sixfold Policy', of the Arthashastra of Kautilya. End of the 100th chapter from the beginning.]

Chapter 3

THE CHARACTER OF EQUAL, INFERIOR AND SUPERIOR KINGS; AND FORMS OF AGREEMENT MADE BY AN INFERIOR KING

A KING desirous of expanding his own power shall make use of the sixfold policy.

Agreements of peace shall be made with equal and superior kings; and an inferior king shall be attacked.

Whoever goes to wage war with a superior king will be reduced to the same condition as that of a foot soldier opposing an elephant.

Just as the collision of an unbaked mud vessel with a similar vessel is destructive to both, so war with an equal king brings ruin to both.

Like a stone striking an earthen pot, a superior king attains decisive victory over an inferior king.

If a superior king discards the proposal of an inferior king for peace, the latter should take the attitude of a conquered king, or play the part of an inferior king towards a superior.

When a king of equal power does not like peace, the same amount of vexation as his opponent has received at his hands should be given to him in return; for it is power that brings about peace between any two kings: no piece of iron that is not made red-hot will combine with another piece of iron.

When an inferior king is all submissive, peace should be made with him; for when provoked by causing him troubles and anger, an inferior king, like a wildfire, will attack his enemy and will also be favoured by (his) circle of states.

When a king in peace with another finds that greedy, impoverished and oppressed as are the subjects of his ally, they do not yet immigrate into his own territory lest they be called back by their master, he should, though of inferior power, proclaim war against his ally.

When a king at war with another finds that greedy, impoverished and oppressed as are the subjects of his enemy, still they do not come to his side in consequence of the troubles of war, he should, though of superior power, make peace with his enemy or remove the troubles of war as far as possible.

When one of the two kings at war with each other and equally involved in trouble finds his own troubles to be greater than his enemy's, and thinks that by getting rid of his (enemy's) trouble his enemy can successfully wage war against him, he should, though possessing greater resources, sue for peace.

When, either in peace or war, a king finds neither loss to his enemy nor gain to himself, he should, though superior, observe neutrality.

When a king finds the troubles of his enemy irremediable, he should, though of inferior power, march against the enemy.

When a king finds himself threatened by imminent dangers or troubles, he should, though superior, seek the protection of another.

When a king is sure to achieve his desired ends by making peace with one and waging war against another, he should, though superior, adopt the double policy.

Thus it is that the six forms of policy are applied together. As to their special application:

• When a powerless king finds himself attacked by a powerful king, leading a circle of states, he should submissively sue for peace on the condition of offering treasure, army, himself or his territory.

• Agreement made on the condition that with a fixed number of troops or with the flower of his army, a king should present himself (when called for), is peace termed *atmamisha*, 'offering himself as flesh'.

• Agreement made on the condition that the commander of the army together with the heir apparent should present himself (when called for), is peace styled *purushantarasandhi,* 'peace with hostages other than the king himself'; and it is conducive to self-preservation, as it does not require the personal attendance of the king.

• Agreement made on the condition that the king himself or some one else should march with the army to some place, as required, is peace termed *adrishtapurusha,* 'peace with no specified person to serve'; and it is conducive to the safety of the king and the chiefs of his army.

• In the first two forms of the peace, a woman of rank should be given as hostage, and in the last, a secret attempt should be made to capture the enemy; these are the forms of peace concluded on the condition of supplying his army.

• When, by offering wealth, the rest of the elements of sovereignty are set free, that peace is termed *parikraya,* 'price'.

• Similarly, when peace is concluded by offering money capable of being taken on a man's shoulders, it is termed *upagraha*, 'subsidy'; and it is of various forms. Owing to distance and owing to its having been kept long, the amount of the tribute promised may sometimes fall in arrears.

• Yet as such a burden can tolerably be paid in future, this peace is better than the one with a woman given as hostage. When the parties making an agreement of peace are amicably united, it is termed *suvarnasandhi*, 'golden peace'.

• Quite reverse from the former is the peace called *kapala,* 'half of a pot', which is concluded on the condition of paying immense quantity of money.

• In the first two, one should send the supply of raw materials, elephants, horses and troops; in the third, money; and in the fourth, one should evade the payment under the plea of loss of results from works; these are the forms of peace concluded on the payment of money.

• When, by ceding a part of the territory, the rest of the kingdom with its subjects is kept safe, it is termed *adishta*, 'ceded', and is of advantage to one who is desirous of destroying thieves and other wicked persons (infesting the ceded part).

• When, with the exception of the capital, the whole of the territory impoverished by exploitation of its resources is ceded, it is termed *uchchhinnasandhi,* 'peace cut off from profit', and is of advantage to one who desires to involve the enemy in troubles.

• When, by the stipulation of paying the produce of the land, the kingdom is set free, it is termed *avakraya*, 'rent'. That which is concluded by the promise of paying more than the land yields is *paribhushana*, 'ornament'.

• One should prefer the first; but the last two based upon the payment of the produce should be made only when one is obliged to submit to power. These are the forms of peace made by ceding territory.

• These three kinds of peace are to be concluded by an inferior king in submission to the power of a superior king owing to the peculiar condition of his own works, circumstances and time.

[Thus ends Chapter 3, 'The Character of Equal, Inferior, and Superior Kings; and Forms of Agreement Made by an Inferior King', in Book VII, 'The End of the Sixfold Policy', of the Arthashastra of Kautilya. End of the 101st chapter from the beginning.]

Chapter 4

NEUTRALITY AFTER PROCLAIMING WAR OR AFTER CONCLUDING A TREATY OF PEACE; MARCHING AFTER PROCLAIMING WAR OR AFTER MAKING PEACE; AND THE MARCH OF COMBINED POWERS

NEUTRALITY or marching after proclaiming war or peace has been explained.

Sthana (keeping quiet), *asana* (withdrawal from hostility), and *upekshana* (negligence) are synonymous with the word '*asana*', 'neutrality'. As to the difference between three aspects of neutrality: Keeping quiet, maintaining a particular kind of policy is *sthana*; withdrawal from hostile actions for the sake of one's own interests is *asana*; and taking no steps (against an enemy) is *upekshana*.

When two kings, who, though bent on making conquests, are desirous of peace, are unable to proceed, one against the other, they may keep quiet after proclaiming war or after making peace.

When a king finds it possible to put down by means of his own army, or with the help of a friend, or of wild tribes, another king of equal or superior power, having set up proper defences against both internal and external enemies, he may keep quiet after proclaiming war.

When a king is convinced that his own subjects are brave, united, prosperous, and able not only to carry on their own works without interference but also to harass his enemy's works, he may keep quiet after proclaiming war.

When a king finds that as his enemy's subjects are ill-treated, impoverished and greedy and are ever being oppressed by the inroads of the army, thieves, and wild tribes, they can be made through intrigue to join his side; or that his own agriculture and commerce are flourishing while those of his enemy are waning; or that as the subjects of his enemy are suffering from famine, they will immigrate into his own territory; or that, though his own returns of agriculture and commerce are falling and those of his enemy increasing, his own subjects will never desert him in favour of his enemy; or that by proclaiming war, he can carry off, by force, the grains, cattle and gold of his enemy; or that he can prevent the import of his enemy's merchandise, which was destructive of his own commerce; or that valuable merchandise would come to his own territory, leaving that of his enemy; or that war being proclaimed, his enemy would be unable to put down traitors, enemies, and wild tribes and other rebels, and would be involved in war with them; or that his own friend would in a very short time accumulate wealth without much loss and would not fail to follow him in his march, since no friend would neglect the opportunity of acquiring a fertile land and a prosperous friend like himself in such cases, in view of inflicting injuries on his enemy and of exhibiting his own power, he may keep quiet after proclaiming war.

But my teacher says that turning against such a king, his enemy may swallow him.

'Not so', says Kautilya, 'impoverishment of the enemy who is free from troubles is all that is aimed at (when a king keeps quiet after proclaiming war). As soon as such a king acquires sufficient strength, he will undertake to destroy the enemy. To such a king, the enemy's enemy will send help to secure his own personal safety'. Hence, whoever is provided with necessary strength may keep quiet after proclaiming war.

When the policy of keeping quiet after proclaiming war is found productive of unfavourable results, one shall keep quiet after making peace.

Whoever has grown in strength in consequence of keeping quiet after proclaiming war should proceed to attack his enemy.

When a king finds that his enemy has fallen into troubles; that the troubles of his enemy's subjects can by no means be remedied; that as his enemy's subjects are oppressed, ill-treated, disaffected, impoverished, have become effiminate and disunited among themselves, they can be prevailed upon to desert their master; that his enemy's country has fallen a victim to the inroads of such calamities, as fire, floods, pestilence epidemics (*maraka*), and famine and is therefore losing the flower of its youth and its defensive power, then he should march after proclaiming war.

When a king is so fortunate as to have a powerful friend in front and a powerful ally (*akranda*) in the rear, both with brave and loyal subjects, while the reverse is the case with he enemies both in front and in the rear, and when he finds it possible for his friend to hold his frontal enemy in check, and for his rear ally to keep his rear enemy (*parshnigraha*) at bay, he may march after proclaiming war against his frontal enemy.

When a king finds it possible to achieve the results of victory single-handed in a very short time, he may march (against his frontal enemy) after proclaiming war against his rear enemies; otherwise he should march after making peace (with his rear enemies).

When a king finds himself unable to confront his enemy single-handed and when it is necessary that he should march, he should make the expedition in combination with kings of inferior, equal or superior powers.

When the object aimed at is of a definite nature, the share of spoils should be fixed; but when it is of a manifold or complex nature, there should be no fixity in the share of the spoils. When no such combination is possible, he may request a king either to supply him with the army for a fixed share, or to accompany him for an equal share of the spoils.

When profit is certain, they should march with fixed shares of profit; but when it is uncertain, with no fixity of shares.

Share of profit proportional to the strength of the army is of the first kind; that which is equal to the effort made is the best; shares may be allotted in proportion to the profit earned or to the capital invested.

[Thus ends Chapter 4, 'Neutrality after Proclaiming War or after Concluding a Treaty of Peace; Marching after Proclaiming War or after Making Peace; and the March of Combined Powers', in Book VII, 'The End of the Sixfold Policy' of the Arthashastra of Kautilya. End of the 102nd chapter from the beginning.]

Chapter 5

CONSIDERATIONS ABOUT MARCHING AGAINST AN ASSAILABLE ENEMY AND A STRONG ENEMY; CAUSES LEADING TO THE DWINDLING, GREED, AND DISLOYALTY OF THE ARMY; AND CONSIDERATIONS ABOUT THE COMBINATION OF POWERS

WHEN two enemies, one an assailable enemy and another a strong enemy, are equally involved in troubles, which of them is to be marched against first?

The strong enemy is to be marched against first; after a strong enemy has been vanquished, an assailable enemy will volunteer of his own accord to help the conqueror; but not so, a strong enemy.

Which is to be marched against—an assailable enemy involved in troubles to a greater degree or a strong enemy troubled to a lesser degree?

My teacher says that as a matter of easy conquest, the assailable enemy under worse troubles should be marched against first.

Not so, says Kautilya. The conqueror should march against the strong enemy under less troubles, for the troubles of the strong enemy, though less, will be augmented when attacked. True, that the worse troubles of the assailable enemy will be still worse when attacked. But when left to himself, the strong enemy under less troubles will endeavour to get rid of his troubles and unite with the assailable enemy or with another enemy in the rear of the conqueror.

When there are two assailable enemies, one of virtuous character and under worse troubles, and another of vicious character, under less troubles, and with disloyal subjects, which of them is to be marched against first?

When the enemy of virtuous character and under worse troubles is attacked, his subjects will help him; whereas, the subjects of the other of vicious character and under less troubles will be indifferent. Disloyal or indifferent subjects will endeavour to destroy even a strong king. Hence the conqueror should march against that enemy whose subjects are disloyal.

Which is to be marched against—an enemy whose subjects are impoverished and greedy or an enemy whose subjects are being oppressed?

My teacher says that the conqueror should march against that enemy whose subjects are impoverished and greedy, for impoverished and greedy subjects suffer themselves to be won over to the other side by intrigue, and are easily excited. But not so the oppressed subjects whose wrath can be pacified by punishing the chief men (of the state).

Not so, says Kautilya, for though impoverished and greedy, they are loyal to their master and are ready to stand for his cause and to defeat any intrigue against him; for it is in loyalty that all other good qualities have their strength. Hence the conqueror should march against the enemy whose subjects are oppressed.

Which enemy is to be marched against—a powerful enemy of wicked character or a powerless enemy of righteous character?

The strong enemy of wicked character should be marched against, for when he is attacked, his subjects will not help him, but rather put him down or go to the side of the conqueror. But when the enemy of virtuous character is attacked, his subjects will help him or die with him.

- By insulting the good and commending the wicked; by causing unnatural and unrighteous slaughter of life;
- by neglecting the observance of proper and righteous customs; by doing unrighteous acts and neglecting righteous ones;
- by doing what ought not to be done and not doing what ought to be done; by not paying what ought to be paid and exacting what ought not to be taken;
- by not punishing the guilty and severely punishing the less guilty; by arresting those who are not to be caught hold of and leaving those who are to be arrested;
- by undertaking risky works and destroying profitable ones; by not protecting the people against thieves and by robbing them of their wealth;
- by giving up manly enterprise and condemning good works; by hurting the leaders of the people and despising the worthy;

• by provoking the aged, by crooked conduct, and by untruthfulness; by not applying remedies against evils and neglecting works in hand;
• and by carelessness and negligence of himself in maintaining the security of person and property of his subjects, the king causes impoverishment, greed, and disaffection to appear among his subjects.
• When a people are impoverished, they become greedy; when they are greedy, they become disaffected; when disaffected, they voluntarily go to the side of the enemy or destroy their own master.

Hence, no king should give room to such causes as would bring about impoverishment, greed or disaffection among his people. If, however, they appear, he should at once take remedial measures against them.

Which (of the three) is the worst—an impoverished people, greedy people or disaffected people?

An impoverished people are ever apprehensive of oppression and destruction (by overtaxation, etc.), and are therefore desirous of getting rid of their impoverishment, or of waging war or of migrating elsewhere.

A greedy people are ever discontented and they yield themselves to the intrigues of an enemy.

A disaffected people rise against their master along with his enemy.

When the dwindling of the people is due to want of gold and grain, it is a calamity fraught with danger to the whole of the kingdom and can be remedied with difficulty. The dearth of efficient men can be made up by means of gold and grain. Greed (is) partial and is found among a few chief officers, and it can be got rid of or satisfied by allowing them to plunder an enemy's wealth. Disaffection or disloyalty (*viraga*) can be got rid of by putting down the leaders; for in the absence of a leader or leaders, the people are easily governed (*bhogya*) and they will not take part in the intrigues of enemies. When a people are too nervous to endure the calamities, they first become dispersed, when their leaders are put down; and when they are kept under restraint, they endure calamities.

Having well considered the causes which bring about peace or war, one should combine with kings of considerable power and righteous character and march against one's enemy.

'A king of considerable power', means one who is strong enough to put down or capture an enemy in the rear of his friend or to give sufficient help to his friend in his march.

'A king of righteous character', means one who does what one has promised to do, irrespective of good or bad results.

Having combined with one of superior power, or with two of equal power among such kings, should the conqueror march against his enemy?

It is better to march combined with two kings of equal power; for, if combined with a king of superior power, the ally appears to move, caught hold of by his superior, whereas in marching with two kings of equal power, the same will be the result, only when those two kings are experts in the art of intrigue; besides it is easy to separate them; and when one of them is wicked, he can be put down by the other two and made to suffer the consequence of dissension.

Combined with one of equal power or with two of lesser power, should a king march against his enemy?

Better to march with two kings of lesser power; for the conqueror can depute them to carry out any two different works and keep them under his control. When the desired end is achieved, the inferior king will quietly retire after the satisfaction of his superior.

- Till his discharge, the good conduct of an ally of usually bad character should be closely scrutinized either by suddenly coming out at a critical time from a covert position (*sattra*) to examine his conduct, or by having his wife as a pledge for his good conduct.
- Though actuated with feelings of true friendship, the conqueror has reason to fear his ally, though of equal power, when the latter attains success in his mission; having succeeded in his mission, an ally of equal power is likely to change his attitude even towards the conqueror of superior power.
- An ally of superior power should not be relied upon, for prosperity changes the mind. Even with little or no share in the spoils, an ally of superior power may go back, appearing contented; but some time afterwards, he may not fail to sit on the lap of the conqueror and carry off twice the amount of share due to him.
- Having been satisfied with mere victory, the leading conqueror should discharge his allies, having satisfied them with their shares he

may allow himself to be conquered by them instead of attempting to conquer them (in the matter of spoils); it is thus that a king can win the good graces of his circle of states.

[Thus ends Chapter 5, 'Considerations about Marching Against an Assailable Enemy and a Strong Enemy; Causes Leading to the Dwindling, Greed, and Disloyalty of the Army; and Considerations about the Combination of Powers' in Book VII, 'The End of the Sixfold Policy' of the Arthashastra of Kautilya. End of the 103rd chapter from the beginning.]

Chapter 6

THE MARCH OF COMBINED POWERS; AGREEMENT OF PEACE WITH OR WITHOUT DEFINITE TERMS; AND PEACE WITH RENEGADES

THE conqueror should thus overreach the second element (the enemy close to his territory): He should engage his neighbouring enemy to undertake a simultaneous march with him and tell the enemy: 'Thou march in that direction, and I shall march in this direction; and the share in the spoils is equal.'

If the booty is to be equally divided, it is an agreement of peace; if otherwise, it is overpowering the enemy.

An agreement of peace may be made with promise to carry out a definite work (*paripanita*) or with no such promise (*aparipanita*).

When the agreement is to the effect that 'Thou, march to that place, and I shall march to this place', it is termed an agreement of peace to carry out a work in definite locality.

When it is agreed upon that 'Thou, be engaged so long, I shall be engaged thus long', it is an agreement to attain an object in a fixed time.

When it is agreed upon that 'Thou, try to accomplish that work, and I shall try to finish this work', it is an agreement to achieve a definite end.

When the conqueror thinks that 'my enemy (now an ally) has to march through an unknown country, which is intersected with mountains, forests, rivers, forts and deserts; which is devoid of foodstuffs, people, pastoral grounds, fodder, firewood and water; and which is far away, different from other countries, and not affording suitable grounds for the exercise of his army; and I have to traverse a country of quite the reverse description', he should make an agreement to carry out a work in a definite locality.

When the conqueror thinks that 'my enemy has to work with foodstuffs falling short and with no comfort during the rainy, hot or cold season, giving rise to various kinds of diseases and obstructing the free exercise of his army during a shorter or longer period of time than necessary for the accomplishment of the work in hand; and I have to work during a time of quite the reverse nature', he should make time a factor of the agreement.

When the conqueror thinks that 'my enemy has to accomplish a work which, not lasting but trifling in its nature, enrages his subjects, which requires much expenditure of time and money, and which is productive of evil consequences, unrighteous, repugnant to the *madhyama* and neutral kings, and destructive of all friendship; whereas, I have to do the reverse', he should make an agreement to carry out a definite work.

Likewise with space and time, with time and work, with space and work, and with space, time and work, made as terms of an agreement, it resolves itself into seven forms.

Long before making such an agreement, the conqueror has to fix his own work and then attempt to overreach his enemy.

When, in order to destroy an enemy who has fallen into troubles and who is hasty, indolent, and not foresighted, an agreement of peace with no terms of time, space or work is made with an enemy merely for mutual peace, and when under cover of such an agreement, the enemy is caught hold of at his weak points and is struck, it is termed peace with no definite terms (*aparipanita*). With regard to this there is a saying as follows:

'Having kept a neighbouring enemy engaged with another neighbouring enemy, a wise king should proceed against a third king, and having conquered that enemy of equal power, take possession of his territory.'

Peace with no specific end (*akritachikirsha*), peace with binding terms (*kritasleshana*), the breaking of peace (*kritavidushana*), and restoration of peace broken (*apasirnakriya*) are other forms of peace.

Open battle, treacherous battle, and silent battle (i.e. killing an enemy by employing spies when there is no talk of battle at all), are the three forms of battle.

When, by making use of conciliation and other forms of stratagem and the like, a new agreement of peace is made and the rights of equal, inferior, and superior powers concerned in the agreement are defined according to their respective positions, it is termed an agreement of peace with no specific end (other than self-preservation).

When, by the employment of friends (at the courts of each other), the agreement of peace made is kept secure and the terms are invariably observed and strictly maintained so that no dissension may creep among the parties, it is termed peace with binding terms.

When, having proved through the agency of traitors and spies the treachery of a king, who has made an agreement of peace, the agreement is broken, it is termed the breaking of peace.

When reconciliation is made with a servant, or a friend, or any other renegade, it is termed the restoration of broken peace.

There are four persons who run away from, and return to, their master: one who had reason to run away and to return; one who had no reason either to run away or to return; one who had reason to run away, but none to return; and one who had no reason to run away, but had reason to come back.

He who runs away owing to his master's fault and returns in consideration of (his master's) good nature, or he who runs away attracted by the good nature of his master's enemy and returns finding fault with the enemy is to be reconciled as he had reason to run away and to return.

Whoever runs away owing to his own fault and returns without minding the good nature either of his old or new master is a fickle-minded person having no explanation to account for his conduct, and he should have no terms of reconciliation.

Whoever runs away owing to his master's fault and returns owing to his own defects, is a renegade who had reason to run away, but none to return, and his case is to be well considered (before he is taken back).

Whoever returns deputed by the enemy; or of his own accord, with the intention of hurting his old master, as is natural to persons of such bad character; or coming to know that his old master is attempting to put down the enemy, his new master, and apprehensive of danger to himself; or looking on the attempt of his new master to destroy his old master as cruelty—these should be examined; and if he is found to be actuated with good motives, he is to be taken back respectfully; otherwise, he should be kept at a distance.

Whoever runs away owing to his own fault and returns owing to his new master's wickedness is a renegade who had no reason to run away, but had reason to come back; such a person is to be examined.

When a king thinks that 'This renegade supplies me with full information about my enemy's weakness, and, therefore, he deserves to remain here; his own people with me are in friendship with my friends and at enmity with my enemies and are easily excited at the sight of greedy and cruel persons or of a band of enemies', he may treat such a renegade as deserved.

My teacher says that whoever has failed to achieve profit from his works, lost his strength, or made his learning a commercial article, or is very greedy, inquisitive to see different countries, dead to the feelings of friendship, or has strong enemies, deserves to be abandoned.

But Kautilya says that it is timidity, unprofessional business and lack of forbearance (to do so). Whoever is injurious to the king's interests should be abandoned, while he who is injurious to the interests of the enemy should be reconciled; and whoever is injurious to the interests of both the king and his enemy should be carefully examined.

When it is necessary to make peace with a king with whom no peace ought to be made, defensive measures should be taken against that point where he can show his power.

• In restoring broken peace, a renegade or a person inclined towards the enemy should be kept at such a distance that till the close of his life, he may be useful to the state.

• Or, he may be set against the enemy or may be employed as a captain of an army to guard wild tracts against enemies, or thrown somewhere on the boundary.

• Or, he may be employed to carry on a secret trade in new or old commodities in foreign countries and may accordingly be accused of conspiracy with the enemy.

• Or, in the interests of future peace, a renegade who must be put to death may at once be destroyed.

• That kind of wicked character which has from the beginning grown upon a man owing to his association with enemies is as ever fraught with danger as constant living in company with a snake;

• and is ever threatening with destruction just as a pigeon living on the seeds of *plaksha* (holy fig tree) is to the *salmali* (silk cotton) tree.

• When a battle is fought in daylight and in some locality, it is termed an open battle; threatening in one direction, assault in another, destruction of an enemy captured while he was careless or in troubles;

• and bribing a portion of the army and destroying another portion are forms of treacherous fight; and attempt to win over the chief officers of the enemy by intrigue is the characteristic of silent battle.

[Thus ends Chapter 6, 'The March of Combined Powers; Agreement of Peace with or Without Definite Terms; and Peace with Renegades', in Book VII, 'The End of the Sixfold Policy' of the Arthashastra of Kautilya. End of the 104th chapter from the beginning.]

Chapter 7

PEACE AND WAR BY ADOPTING THE DOUBLE POLICY

THE conqueror may overpower the second member (i.e., the immediate enemy) thus:

Having combined with a neighbouring king, the conqueror may march against another neighbouring king. Or if he thinks that '(my enemy) will neither capture my rear nor make an alliance with my assailable enemy against whom I am going to march; (for otherwise) I shall have to fight against great odds; (my ally) will not only facilitate the collection of my revenue and supplies and put down the internal enemies who are causing me immense trouble, but also punish wild tribes and their followers entrenched in their strongholds, reduce my assailable enemy to a precarious condition or compel him to accept the proffered peace, and having received as much profit as he desires, he will endeavour to endear my other enemies to me', the conqueror may proclaim war against one and make peace with another and endeavour to get an army for money or money for the supply of an army from among his neighbouring kings.

When the kings of superior, equal or inferior power make peace with the conqueror and agree to pay a greater, or equal, or less amount of profit in proportion to the army supplied, it is termed even peace; that which is of the reverse character is styled uneven peace; and when the profit is proportionally very high, it is termed deception (*atisandhi*).

When a king of superior power is involved in troubles, or has come to grief or is afflicted with misfortune, his enemy, though of inferior power, may request of him the help of his army in return for a share in the profit proportional to the strength of the army supplied. If the king to whom peace is offered on such terms is powerful enough to retaliate, he may declare war; and otherwise he may accept the terms.

In view of marching for the purpose of exacting some expected revenue to be utilized in recouping his own strength and resources, an inferior king may request of a superior the help of the latter's army for the purpose of guarding the base and the rear of his territory in return for the payment of a greater share in the profit than the strength of the army supplied deserves. The king to whom such a proposal is made may accept the proposal, if the proposer is of good intentions; but otherwise he may declare war.

When a king of inferior power or one who is provided with the aid of forts and friends has to make a short march in order to capture an enemy without waging war or to receive some expected profit, he may request a third king of superior power involved under various troubles and misfortunes the help of the latter's army in return for the payment of a share in the profit less than the strength of the army supplied deserves. If the king to whom this proposal is made is powerful enough to retaliate, he may declare war; but otherwise he may accept the proposal.

When a king of superior power and free from all troubles is desirous of causing to his enemy loss of men and money in the latter's ill-considered undertakings, or of sending his own treacherous army abroad, or bringing his enemy under the clutches of an inimical army, or of causing trouble to a reducible and tottering enemy by setting an inferior king against that enemy, or is desirous of having peace for the sake of peace itself and is possessed of good intentions, he may accept a less share in the profit (promise for the army supplied to another) and endeavour to make wealth by combining with an ally if the latter is equally of good intentions; but otherwise he may declare war (against that ally).

A king may deceive or help his equal as follows:

When a king proposes peace to another king of equal power on the condition of receiving the help of the latter army strong enough to oppose an enemy's army, or to guard the front, centre and rear of his territory, or to help his friend, or to protect any other wild tracts of his territory in return for the payment of a share in the profit proportionally equal to the strength of the army supplied, the latter may accept the terms if the proposer is of good intentions; but otherwise he may declare war.

When a king of equal power, capable of receiving the help of an army from another quarter requests of another king in troubles due to the diminished strength of the elements of sovereignty, and with many enemies, the help of the latter's army in return for the payment of a share in the profit less than the strength of the army supplied deserves, the latter, if powerful, may declare war or accept the terms otherwise.

When a king who is under troubles, who has his works at the mercy of his neighbouring kings, and who has yet to make an army, requests of another king of equal power the help of the latter's army in return for the payment of a share in the profit greater than the strength of the army supplied deserves, the latter may accept the terms if the proposer is of good intentions; but otherwise war may be declared.

When, with the desire of putting down a king in troubles due to the diminished strength of the elements of sovereignty, or with the desire of destroying his well-begun work of immense and unfailing profit, or with the intention of striking him in his own place or on the occasion of marching, one, though frequently getting immense (subsidy) from an assailable enemy of equal, inferior, or superior power, sends demands to him again and again, he may comply with the demands of the former if he is desirous of maintaining his own power by destroying with the army of the former an impregnable fortress of an enemy or a friend of that enemy or laying waste the wild tracts of that enemy, or if he is desirous of exposing the army of the ally to wear and tear even in good roads and good seasons, or if he is desirous of strengthening his own army with that of his ally and thereby putting down the ally or winning over the army of the ally.

When a king is desirous of keeping under his power another king of superior or inferior power as an assailable enemy and of destroying the latter after routing out another enemy with the help of the latter, or when he is desirous of getting back whatever he has paid (as subsidy), he may send a proposal of peace to another on the condition of paying more than the cost of the army supplied. If the king to whom this proposal is made is powerful enough to retaliate he may declare war; or if otherwise, he may accept the terms; or he may keep quiet allied with the assailable enemy; or he may supply the proposer of peace with his army full of traitors, enemies and wild tribes.

When a king of superior power falls into troubles owing to the weakness of the elements of his sovereignty, and requests of an inferior king the help of the latter's army in return for the payment of a share in the profit proportionally equal to the strength of the army supplied, the latter, if powerful enough to retaliate, may declare war, and if otherwise, accept the terms.

A king of superior power may request of an inferior the help of the latter's army in return for the payment of a share in the profit less than the cost of the army supplied; and the latter, if powerful enough to retaliate, may declare war, or accept the terms otherwise.

The king who is sued for peace and also the king who offers peace should both consider the motive with which the proposal of peace is made, and adopt that course of action which on consideration seems to be productive of good results.

[Thus ends Chapter 7 'Peace and War by Adopting the Double Policy' in Book VII, 'The End of the Sixfold Policy' of the Arthashastra of Kautilya. End of the 105th chapter from the beginning.]

Chapter 8

THE ATTITUDE OF AN ASSAILABLE ENEMY; AND FRIENDS THAT DESERVE HELP

WHEN an assailable enemy who is in danger of being attacked is desirous of taking upon himself the condition which led one king to combine with another against himself, or of splitting them from each other, he may propose peace to one of the kings on the condition of himself paying twice the amount of profit accruing from the combination. The agreement having been made, he may describe to that king the loss of men and money, the hardships of sojourning abroad, the commission of sinful deeds, and the misery and other personal troubles to which that king would have been subjected. When the king is convinced of the truth, the amount promised may be paid; or having made that king to incur enmity with other kings, the agreement itself may be broken off.

When a king is inclined to cause to another, loss of men and money in the ill-considered undertakings of the latter or to frustrate the latter in the attempt of achieving large profits from well-begun undertakings; or when he means to strike another at his (the other's) own place or while marching; or when he intends to exact subsidy again in combination with the latter's assailable enemy; or when he is in need of money and does not like to trust his ally, he may, for the time being, be satisfied with a small amount of profit.

When a king has in view the necessity of helping a friend or of destroying an enemy, or the possibility of acquiring much wealth (in return for the present help) or when he intends to utilize in future the services of the one now obliged by him, he may reject the offer of large profit at the present in preference of a small gain in future.

When a king means to help another from the clutches of traitors or enemies or of a superior king threatening the very existence of the latter, and intends thereby to set an example of rendering similar help to himself in future, he should receive no profit either at the present or in the future.

When a king means to harass the people of an enemy or to break the agreement of peace between a friend and a foe, or when he suspects of another's attack upon himself, and when owing to any of these causes, he wants to break peace with his ally, he may demand from the latter an enhanced amount of profit long before it is due. The latter under these circumstances may demand for a procedure (*krama*) either at the present or in the future. The same procedure explains the cases treated of before.

The conqueror and his enemy helping their respective friends differ according as their friends are such or are not such as undertaking possible, praiseworthy or productive works and as are resolute in their undertakings and are provided with loyal and devoted subjects.

Whoever undertakes tolerable work is a beginner of possible work; whoever undertakes an unblemished work is a beginner of praiseworthy work; whoever undertakes work of large profits is a beginner of a productive work; whoever takes no rest before the completion of the work undertaken is a resolute worker; and whoever has loyal and devoted subjects is in a position to command help and to bring to a successful termination any work without losing anything in the form of favour. When such friends are gratified by the enemy or the conqueror, they can be of immense help to him; friends of reverse character should never be helped.

Of the two, the conqueror and his enemy, both of whom may happen to have a friend in the same person, he who helps a true or a truer friend overreaches the other; for, by helping a true friend, he enriches himself, while the other not only incurs loss of men and money and the hardships of sojourning abroad, but also showers benefits on an enemy who hates the benefactor all the more for his gratification.

Whoever of the two, the conqueror and his enemy, who may happen to have a friend in the same *madhyama* king, helps a *madhyama* king of true or truer friendship overreaches the other; for, by helping a true friend, he enriches himself, while the other incurs loss of men and money and the difficulties of sojourning abroad. When a *madhyama* king thus helped is devoid of good qualities, the enemy overreaches the conqueror: for, such a *madhyama* king, spending his energies on useless undertakings and receiving help with no idea of returning it, withdraws himself away.

The same thing holds good with a neutral king under similar circumstances.

In case of helping with a portion of the army one of the two, a *madhyama* or a neutral king, whoever happens to help one who is brave, skilful in handling weapons, and possessed of endurance and friendly feelings will himself be deceived while his enemy, helping one of reverse character, will overreach him.

When a king achieves this or that object with the assistance of a friend who is to receive the help of his army in return later on, then he may send out of his various kinds of army—such as hereditary army, hired army, army formed of corporations of people, his friend's army and the army composed of wild tribes—either that kind of army which has the experience of all sorts of grounds and of seasons or the army of enemies or of wild tribes, which is far removed in space and time.

When a king thinks that 'though successful, my ally may cause my army to move in an enemy's territory or in wild tracts, and during unfavourable seasons, and thereby he may render it useless to me', under the excuse of having to employ his army otherwise, he may help his ally in any other way; but when he is obliged to lend his army, he may send that kind of his army, which is used to the weather of the time of operation, under the condition of employing it till the completion of the work and of protecting it from dangers. When the ally has finished his work, he should, under some excuse, try to get back his army or he may send to his ally that army which is composed of traitors, enemies, and wild tribes; or having made peace with the ally's assailable enemy, he may deceive the ally.

When the profit accruing to kings under an agreement, whether they be of equal, inferior or superior power, is equal to all, that agreement is termed peace (*sandhi*); when unequal, it is termed defeat (*vikrama*). Such is the nature of peace and war.

[Thus ends Chapter 8, 'The Attitude of an Assailable Enemy; and Friends that Deserve Help', in Book VII, 'The End of the Sixfold Policy' of the Arthashastra of Kautilya. End of the 106th chapter from the beginning.]

Chapter 9

AGREEMENT FOR THE ACQUISITION OF A FRIEND OR GOLD

OF the three gains, the acquisition of a friend, of gold, and of territory, accruing from the march of combined powers, that which is mentioned later is better than the one previously mentioned; for friends and gold can be acquired by means of territory; of the two gains, that of a friend and of gold, each can be a means to acquire the other.

Agreement under the condition, 'let us acquire a friend, etc.', is termed even peace; when one acquires a friend and the other makes an enemy, etc., it is termed uneven peace; and when one gains more than the other, it is deception.

In an even peace (i.e., agreement on equal terms) whoever acquires a friend of good character or relieves an old friend from troubles, overreaches the other; for help given in misfortune renders friendship very firm.

Which is better of the two: a friend of long standing, but unsubmissive nature, or a temporary friend of submissive nature, both being acquired by affording relief from their respective troubles?

My teacher says that a long-standing friend of unsubmissive nature is better inasmuch as such a friend, though not helpful, will not create harm.

Not so, says Kautilya, a temporary friend of submissive nature is better; for such a friend will be a true friend so long as he is helpful; for the real characteristic of friendship lies in giving help.

Which is the better of two submissive friends: a temporary friend of large prospects, or a long-standing friend of limited prospects?

My teacher says that a temporary friend of large prospects is better inasmuch as such a friend can, by virtue of his large prospects, render immense service in a very short time, and can stand undertakings of large outlay.

Not so, says Kautilya, a long-standing friend of limited prospects is better, inasmuch as a temporary friend of large prospects is likely to withdraw his friendship on account of material loss in the shape of help given, or is likely to expect similar kind of help in return; but a long-standing friend of limited prospects can, by virtue of his long-standing nature, render immense service in the long run.

Which is better, a big friend, difficult to be roused, or a small friend, easy to be roused?

My teacher says that a big friend, though difficult to be roused, is of imposing nature, and when he rises up, he can accomplish the work undertaken.

Not so, says Kautilya, a small friend easy to be roused is better, for such a friend will not, by virtue of his ready preparations, be behind the opportune moment of work, and can, by virtue of his weakness in power, be used in any way the conqueror may like; but not so the other of vast territorial power.

Which is better, scattered troops, or an unsubmissive standing army?

My teacher says that scattered troops can be collected in time as they are of submissive nature.

Not so, says Kautilya, an unsubmissive standing army is better as it can be made submissive by conciliation and other strategic means; but it is not so easy to collect in time scattered troops as they are engaged in their individual avocations.

Which is better, a friend of vast population, or a friend of immense gold?

My teacher says that a friend of vast population is better inasmuch as such a friend will be of imposing power and can, when he rises up, accomplish any work undertaken.

Not so, says Kautilya, a friend possessing immense gold is better; for possession of gold is ever desirable; but an army is not always required. Moreover, armies and other desired objects can be purchased for gold.

Which is better, a friend possessing gold, or a friend possessing vast territory?

My teacher says that a friend possessing gold can stand any heavy expenditure made with discretion.

Not so, says Kautilya, for it has already been stated that both friends and gold can be acquired by means of territory. Hence a friend of vast territory is far better.

When the friend of the conqueror and his enemy happen to possess equal population, their people may yet differ in possession of qualities such as bravery, power of endurance, amicableness, and qualification for the formation of any kind of army.

When the friends are equally rich in gold, they may yet differ in qualities such as readiness to comply with requests, magnanimous and munificent help, and accessibility at any time and always.

About this topic, the following sayings are current:

• Long-standing, submissive, easy to be roused, coming from fathers and grandfathers, powerful, and never of a contradictory nature is a good friend; and these are said to be the six qualities of a good friend;

• that friend who maintains friendship with disinterested motives and merely for the sake of friendship and by whom the relationship acquired of old is kept intact is a long-standing friend;
• that friend whose munificence is enjoyable in various ways is a submissive friend, and is said to be of three forms: one who is enjoyable only by one, one who is enjoyable by two (the enemy and the conqueror), and one who is enjoyable by all is the third;
• that friend who, whether as receiving help or as giving help, lives with an oppressive hand over his enemies, and who possesses a number of forts and a vast army of wild tribes is said to be a long-standing friend of unsubmissive nature;
• that friend who, either when attacked or when in trouble, makes friendship for the security of his own existence is temporary and submissive friend;
• that friend who contracts friendship with a single aim in view and who is helpful, immutable, and amicable is a friend never falling foul even in adversity;
• whoever is of an amicable nature is a true friend; whoever sides also with the enemy is a mutable friend and whoever is indifferent to neither (the conqueror and his enemy) is a friend to both;
• that friend who is inimical to the conqueror or who is equally friendly to the conqueror's enemy is a harmful friend, whether he is giving help or is capable of helping;
• whoever helps the enemy's friend, protege, or any vulnerable person or a relation of the enemy is a friend common to (both) the enemy (and the conqueror);
• whoever possesses extensive and fertile territory and is contented, strong, but indolent, will be indifferent (towards his ally) when the latter becomes despicable under troubles;
• whoever, owing to his own weakness, follows the ascendancy of both the conqueror and his enemy, not incurring enmity with either, is known as a common friend;
• whoever neglects a friend who is being hurt with or without reason and who seeks help with or without reason despises his own danger.

Which is better, an immediate small gain, or a distant large gain? My teacher says that an immediate small gain is better, as it is useful to carry out immediate undertakings.

Not so, says Kautilya, a large gain, as continuous as a productive seed, is better; otherwise an immediate small gain.

Thus, having taken into consideration the good aspects of a permanent gain or of a share in a permanent gain, should a king, desirous of strengthening himself, march combined with others.

[Thus ends Chapter 9, 'Agreement for the Acquisition of a Friend or Gold' in Book VII, 'The End of the Sixfold Policy' of the Arthashastra of Kautilya. End of the 107th chapter from the beginning.]

Chapter 10

AGREEMENT OF PEACE FOR THE ACQUISITION OF LAND

THE agreement made under the condition, 'Let us acquire land', is an agreement of peace for the acquisition of land.

Of the two kings thus entering into an agreement whoever acquires a rich and fertile land withstanding crops overreaches the other.

The acquisition of rich land being equal, whoever acquires such land by putting down a powerful enemy overreaches the other; for not only does he acquire territory, but also destroys an enemy and thereby augments his own power. True, there is beauty in acquiring land by putting down a weak enemy; but the land acquired will also be poor, and the king in the neighbourhood who has hitherto been a friend, will now become an enemy.

The enemies being equally strong, he who acquires territory after beating a fortified enemy overreaches the other; for the capture of a fort is conducive to the protection of territory and to the destruction of wild tribes.

As to the acquisition of land from a wandering enemy, there is the difference of having a powerful or powerless enemy close to the acquired territory; for the land which is close to a powerless enemy is easily maintained while that bordering upon the territory of a powerful enemy has to be kept at the expense of men and money.

Which is better, the acquisition of a rich land close to a constant enemy, or that of sterile land near to a temporary enemy?

My teacher says that a rich land with a constant enemy is better, inasmuch as it yields much wealth to maintain a strong army, by which the enemy can be put down.

Not so, says Kautilya, for a rich land creates many enemies, and the constant enemy will ever be an enemy, whether or not he is helped (with men and money to conciliate him); but a temporary enemy will be quiet either from fear or favour. That land, on the border of which there are a number of forts giving shelter to bands of thieves, *mlecchas*, and wild tribes is a land with a constant enemy; and that which is of reverse character is one with a temporary enemy.

Which is better, a small piece of land, not far, or an extensive piece of land, very far?

A small piece of land, not far, is better, inasmuch as it can be easily acquired, protected, and defended, whereas the other is of a reverse nature.

Of the above two kinds of land, which is better, that which can be maintained by itself, or that which requires external armed force to maintain?

The former is better, as it can be maintained with the army and money produced by itself, whereas the latter is of a reverse character as a military station.

Which is better, acquisition of land from a stupid or a wise king?

That acquired from a stupid king is better, as it can be easily acquired and secured, and cannot be taken back, whereas that obtained from a wise king, beloved of his subjects, is of a reverse nature.

Of two enemies, of whom one can only be harassed and another is reducible, acquisition of land from the latter is better; for when the latter is attacked, he, having little or no help, begins to run away, taking his army and treasure with him, and he is deserted by his subjects; whereas the former does not do so, as he has the help of his forts and friends.

Of two fortified kings, one who has his forts on a plain is more easily reduced than the other owning a fort in the centre of a river; for a fort in a plain can be easily assailed, destroyed or captured along with the enemy in it, whereas a fort, surrounded by a river requires twice as much effort to capture and supplies the enemy with water and other necessaries of life.

Of two kings, one owning a fort surrounded by a river, and another having mountainous fortifications, seizing the former's land is better, for a fort in the centre of a river can be assailed by a bridge formed of elephants made to stand in a row in the river or by wooden bridges, or by means of boats; and the river will not always be deep and can be emptied of its water, whereas a fort on a mountain is of a self-defensive nature, and not easy to besiege or to ascend; and when one portion of the army defending it is routed out, the other portions can escape unhurt and such a fort is of immense service, as it affords facilities to throw down heaps of stone and trees over the enemy.

Which is easier, seizing land from those who fight on plains, or from those who fight from low grounds?

Seizing the land from the latter is easier, inasmuch as they have to fight in time and space of adverse nature whereas the former can fight anywhere and at any time.

Of the two enemies, one fighting from ditches and another from heights (*khanakakasayodhibhyam*), seizing land from the former is better; for they can be serviceable inasmuch as they fight from ditches and with weapons in hand, whereas the latter can only fight with weapons in hand.

Whoever, well versed in the science of polity, wrests land from such and other enemies will outshine both his allies in combination with him and enemies out of combination.

[Thus ends Chapter 10, 'Agreement of Peace for the Acquisition of Land' in Book VII, 'The End of the Sixfold Policy' of the Arthashastra of Kautilya. End of the 108th chapter from the beginning.]

Chapter 11

INTERMINABLE AGREEMENT

THE agreement made under the condition, 'Let us colonize wasteland', is termed an interminable agreement.

Whoever of the two parties of the agreement colonizes a fertile land, reaping the harvest earlier, overreaches the other.

Which is better for colonization: a plain or watery land?

A limited tract of land with water is far better than a vast plain, inasmuch as the former is conducive to the growth of crops and fruits throughout the year.

Of plains, that which is conducive to the growth of both early and late crops and which requires less labour and less rain for cultivation is better than the other of reverse character.

Of watery lands, that which is conducive to the growth of grains is better than another productive of crops other than grains.

Of two watery tracts, one of limited area and conducive to the growth of grains, and another, vast and productive of crops other than grains, the latter is better, inasmuch as it affords vast area not only to grow spices and other medicinal crops, but also to construct forts and other defensive works in plenty: for fertility and other qualities of lands are artificial (*kritrimah*).

Of the two tracts of land, one rich in grains and another in mines, the latter helps the treasury, while the former can fill both the treasury and the storehouse; and besides this, the construction of forts and other buildings requires grains. Still, that kind of land containing mines and which yields precious metals to purchase large tracts of land is far better.

My teacher says that of two forests, one productive of timber, and another of elephants, the former is the source of all kinds of works and is of immense help in forming a storehouse, while the latter is of reverse character.

Not so, says Kautilya, for it is possible to plant any of timber forests in many places, but not an elephant forest; yet it is on elephants that the destruction of an enemy's army depends.

Of the two, communication by water and by land, the former is not long-standing, while the latter can ever be enjoyed.

Which is better, the land with scattered people or that with a corporation of people?

The former is better inasmuch as it can be kept under control and is not susceptible to the intrigues of enemys while the latter is intolerant of calamities and susceptible anger and other passions.

In colonizing a land with four castes, colonization with the lowest caste is better, inasmuch as it is serviceable in various ways, plentiful and permanent.

Of cultivated and uncultivated tracts, the uncultivated tract may be suitable for various kinds of agricultural operations; and when it is fertile, adapted for pasture grounds, manufacture of merchandise, mercantile transactions of borrowing and lending, and attractive to rich merchants, it is still far better (than a cultivated tract).

Which is better of the two, the tract of land with forts or that which is thickly populated?

The latter is better; for that which is thickly populated is a kingdom in all its senses. What can a depopulated country like a barren cow be productive of?

The king who is desirous of getting back the land sold for colonization to another when the latter has lost his men and money in colonizing it, should first make an agreement with such a purchaser as is weak, base-born, devoid of energy, helpless, of unrighteous character, addicted to evil ways, trusting to fate, and indiscreet in his actions. When the colonization of a land entails much expenditure of men and money, and when a weak and base-born man attempts to colonize it, he will perish along with his people in consequence of his loss of men and money. Though strong, a base-born man will be deserted by his people who do not like him lest they come to grief under him; though possessing an army, he cannot employ it if he is devoid of energy; and such an army will perish in consequence of the loss incurred by its master; though possessing wealth, a man who hesitates to part with his money and shows favour to none, cannot find help in any quarter; and when it is easy to drive out a man of unrighteous character from the colony in which he has firmly established himself, none can expect that a man of unrighteous character would be capable of colonizing a tract of wasteland and keeping it secure; the same fact explains the fate of such a colonizer as is addicted to evil ways; whoever, trusting to fate and putting no reliance on manliness, withdraws himself from energetic work, will perish without undertaking anything or without achieving anything from his undertakings; and whoever is indiscreet in his actions will achieve nothing, and is the worst of the set of the colonizers.

My teacher says that an indiscreet colonizer may sometimes betray the weak points of his employer, the conqueror.

But Kautilya says that, just as he betrays the weak points, so also does he facilitate his destruction by the conqueror.

In the absence of such persons to colonize wastelands, the conqueror may arrange for the colonization of wasteland in the same way as we shall treat of later on in connection with the 'Considerations about an enemy in the rear'.

The above is what is termed verbal agreement (*abhihitasandhih*).

When a king of immense power compels another to sell a portion of the latter's fertile territory of which the former is very fond, the latter may make an agreement with the former and sell the land. This is what is termed 'unconcealed peace' (*anibhritasandhih*).

When a king of equal power demands land from another as above, the latter may sell it after considering 'whether the land can be recovered by me, or can be kept under my control; whether my enemy can be brought under my power in consequence of his taking possession of the land; and whether I can acquire by the sale of the land friends and wealth, enough to help me in my undertakings'.

This explains the case of a king of inferior power, who purchases lands.

Whoever, well versed in the science of polity, thus acquires friends, wealth, and territory with or without population will overreach other kings in combination with him.

[Thus ends Chapter 11, 'Interminable Agreement' in Book VII, 'The End of the Sixfold Policy' of the Arthashastra of Kautilya. End of the 109th chapter from the beginning.]

Chapter 12

AGREEMENT FOR UNDERTAKING A WORK

WHEN an agreement is made on the condition 'Let us have a fort built', it is termed agreement for undertaking a work.

Whoever of the two kings builds an impregnable fortress on a spot naturally best fitted for the purpose with less labour and expenditure overreaches the other.

Of forts such as a fort on a plain, in the centre of a river, and on a mountain, that which is mentioned later is of more advantage than the one previously mentioned; of irrigational works (*setubandha*), that which is of perennial water is better than that which is fed with water drawn from other sources; and of works containing perennial water, that which can irrigate an extensive area is better.

Of timber forests, whoever plants a forest which produces valuable articles, which expands into wild tracts, and which possesses a river on its border overreaches the other, for a forest containing a river is self-dependent and can afford shelter in calamities.

Of gameforests, whoever plants a forest full of cruel beasts, close to an enemy's forest containing wild animals, causing therefore much harm to the enemy, and extending into an elephant forest at the country's border, overreaches the other.

My teacher says that of the two countries, one with a large number of effete persons, and another with a small number of brave persons, the latter is better inasmuch as a few brave persons can destroy a large mass of effete persons whose slaughter brings about the destruction of the entire army of their master.

Not so, says Kautilya, a large number of effete persons is better, inasmuch as they can be employed to do other kinds of works in the camp—to serve the soldiers fighting in battlefields, and to terrify the enemy by its number. It is also possible to infuse spirit and enthusiasm in the timid by means of discipline and training.

Of mines, whoever exploits with less labour and expenditure a mine of valuable output and of easy communication overreaches the other.

Which is better of the two, a small mine of valuable yield, or a big mine productive of commodities of inferior value?

My teacher says that the former is better inasmuch as valuable products, such as diamonds, precious stones, pearls, corals, gold and silver, can swallow vast quantities of inferior commodities.

Not so, says Kautilya, for there is the possibility of purchasing valuable commodities by a mass of accumulated articles of inferior value, collected from a vast and long-standing mine of inferior commodities.

This explains the selection of trade routes:

My teacher says that of the two trade routes, one by water and another by land, the former is better, inasmuch as it is less expensive, but productive of large profit.

Not so, says Kautilya, for water route is liable to obstruction, not permanent, a source of imminent dangers, and incapable of defence, whereas a land route is of reverse nature.

Of water routes, one along the shore and another in mid-ocean, the route along, and close to the shore is better, as it touches at many trading port towns; likewise river navigation is better, as it is uninterrupted and is of avoidable or endurable dangers.

My teacher says that of land routes, that which leads to the Himalayas is better than that which leads to the south.

Not so, says Kautilya, for with the exception of blankets, skins and horses, other articles of merchandise such as, conch shells, diamonds, precious stones, pearls and gold are available in plenty in the south.

Of routes leading to the south, either that trade route which traverses a large number of mines which is frequented by people, and which is less expensive or troublesome, or that route by taking which plenty of merchandise of various kinds can be obtained is better.

This explains the selection of trade routes leading either to the east or to the west.

Of a cart track and a foot path, a cart track is better as it affords facilities for preparations on a large scale.

Routes that can be traversed by asses or camels, irrespective of countries and seasons are also good.

This explains the selection of trade routes traversed by men alone (*amsa-patha*, shoulder path, i.e., a path traversed by men carrying merchandise on their shoulders).

• It is a loss for the conqueror to undertake that kind of work which is productive of benefits to the enemy, while a work of reverse nature is a gain. When the benefits are equal, the conqueror has to consider that his condition is stagnant.

• Likewise it is a loss to undertake a work of less output and of a greater outlay, while a work of reverse nature is a gain. If the output and outlay of a work are at par, the conqueror has to consider that his condition is stagnant.

• Hence the conqueror should find out such fort-building and other works as, instead of being expensive, are productive of greater profit and power. Such is the nature of agreements for undertaking works.

[Thus ends Chapter 12, 'Agreement for Undertaking a Work', in Book VII, 'The End of the Sixfold Policy' of the Arthashastra of Kautilya. End of the 110th chapter from the beginning.]

Chapter 13

CONSIDERATIONS ABOUT AN ENEMY IN THE REAR

WHEN the conqueror and his enemy simultaneously proceeded to capture the rear of their respective enemies who are engaged in an attack against others, he who captures the rear of one who is possessed of vast resources gains more advantages (*atisandhatte*); for one who is possessed of vast resources has to put down the rear enemy only after doing away with one's frontal enemy already attacked, but not one who is poor in resources and who has not realized the desired profits.

Resources being equal, he who captures the rear of one who has made vast preparations gains more advantages, for one who has made vast preparations has to put down the enemy in the rear only after destroying the frontal enemy, but not one whose preparations are made on a small scale and whose movements are, therefore, obstructed by the circle of states.

Preparations being equal, he who captures the rear of one who has marched out with all the resources gains more advantages; for one whose base is undefended is easy to be subdued, but not one who has marched out with a part of the army after having made arrangements to defend the rear.

Troops taken being of equal strength, he who captures the rear of one who has gone against a wandering enemy gains more advantages; for one who has marched out against a wandering enemy has to put down the rear enemy only after obtaining an easy victory over the wandering enemy; but not one who has marched out against an entrenched enemy, for one who has marched out against an entrenched enemy will be repelled in his attack against the enemy's forts, and will, after his return, find himself between the rear enemy, and the frontal enemy who is possessed of strong forts.

This explains the cases of other enemies described before.

Enemies being of equal description, he who attacks the rear of one who has gone against a virtuous king gains more advantages, for one who has gone against a virtuous king will incur the displeasure of even his own people, whereas one who has attacked a wicked king will endear himself to all.

This explains the consequences of capturing the rear of those who have marched against an extravagant king or a king living from hand to mouth, or a niggardly king.

The same reasons hold good in the case of those who have marched against their own friends.

When there are two enemies, one engaged in attacking a friend and another an enemy, he who attacks the rear of the latter gains more advantages, for one who has attacked a friend will, after easily making peace with the friend, proceed against the rear enemy; for it is easier to make peace with a friend than with an enemy.

When there are two kings, one engaged in destroying a friend, and another an enemy, he who attacks the rear of the former gains more advantages; for one who is engaged in destroying an enemy will have the support of his friends and will thereby put down the rear enemy, but not the former who is engaged in destroying his own side.

When the conqueror and his enemy in their attack against the rear of an enemy mean to enforce the payment of what is not due to them, he whose enemy has lost considerable profits and has sustained a great loss of men and money gains more advantages; when they mean to enforce the payment of what is due to them, he, whose enemy has lost profits and army, gains more advantages.

When the assailable enemy is capable of retaliation and when the assailant's rear enemy, capable of augmenting his army and other resources, has entrenched himself on one of the assailant's flanks, the rear enemy gains more advantages; for a rear enemy on one of the assailant's flanks will not only become a friend of the assailable enemy but also attack the base of the assailant, whereas a rear enemy behind the assailant can only harass the rear.

Kings, capable of harassing the rear of an enemy and of obstructing his movements are three: the group of kings situated behind the enemy, and the group of kings on both of his flanks.

He who is situated between a conqueror and his enemy is called an *antardhi* (one between two kings); when such a king is possessed of forts, wild tribes, and other kinds of help, he proves an impediment in the way of the strong.

When the conqueror and his enemy are desirous of catching hold of a *madhyama* king and attack the latter's rear, he who in his attempt to enforce the promised payment separates the *madhyama* king from the latter's friend and obtains, thereby, an enemy as a friend, gains more advantages; for an enemy compelled to sue for peace will be of greater help than a friend compelled to maintain the abandoned friendship.

This explains the attempt to catch hold of a neutral king.

Of attacks from the rear and front, that which affords opportunities of carrying on a treacherous fight (*mantrayuddha*) is preferable.

My teacher says that in an open war, both sides suffer by sustaining a heavy loss of men and money; and that even the king who wins a victory will appear as defeated in consequence of the loss of men and money.

No, says Kautilya, even at considerable loss of men and money, the destruction of an enemy is desirable.

Loss of men and money being equal, he who entirely destroys first his frontal enemy, and next attacks his rear enemy gains more advantages; when both the conqueror and his enemy are severally engaged in destroying their respective frontal enemies, he who destroys a frontal enemy of deep-rooted enmity and of vast resources, gains more advantages.

This explains the destruction of other enemies and wild tribes.

When an enemy in the rear and in the front, and an assailable enemy to be marched against happen together, the conqueror should adopt the following policy:

• The rear enemy will usually lead the conqueror's frontal enemy to attack the conqueror's friend; then having set the *akranda* (the enemy of the rear enemy) against the rear enemy's ally,

• and, having caused war between them, the conqueror should frustrate the rear enemy's designs; likewise he should provoke hostilities between, the allies of the *akranda* and of the rear enemy;

• he should also keep his frontal enemy's friend engaged in war with his own friend; and with the help of his friend's friend, he should avert the attack, threatened by the friend of his enemy's friend;

• he should, with his friend's help, hold his rear enemy at bay; and with the help of his friend's friend, he should prevent his rear enemy attacking the *akranda* (his rear ally);

• thus the conqueror should, through the aid of his friends, bring the circle of states under his own sway both in his rear and front;

• he should send messengers and spies to reside in each of the states composing the circle and having again and again destroyed the strength of his enemies he should keep his counsels concealed, being friendly with his friends;

• the works of him, whose counsels are not kept concealed, will, though they may prosper for a time, perish as undoubtedly as a broken raft on the sea.

[Thus ends Chapter 13, 'Considerations about an Enemy in the Rear', in Book VII, 'The End of the Sixfold Policy' of the Arthashastra of Kautilya. End of the 111th chapter from the beginning.]

Chapter 14

RECRUITMENT OF LOST POWER

WHEN the conqueror is thus attacked by the combined army of his enemies, he may tell their leader: 'I shall make peace with you; this is the gold, and I am the friend; your gain is doubled; it is not worthy of you to augment at your own expense the power of your enemies who keep a friendly appearance now; for gaining in power, they will put you down in the long run.'

Or he may tell the leader so as to break the combination: 'Just as an innocent person like myself is now attacked by the combined army of these kings, so the very same kings in combination will attack you in weal or woe; for power intoxicates the mind; hence break their combination.'

The combination being broken, he may set the leader against the weak among his enemies; or offering inducements, he may set the combined power of the weak against the leader; or in whatever way he may find it to be conducive to his own prosperity, in that way he may make the leader incur the displeasure of others, and thus frustrate their attempts; or showing the prospect of a larger profit, he may, through intrigue, make peace with their leader. Then the recipients of salaries from two states, exhibiting the acquisition of large profits (to the leader), may satirize the kings, saying, 'You are all very well combined'.

If some of the kings of the combination are wicked, they may be made to break the treaty; then the recipients of salaries from two states may again tell them so as to break the combination entirely: 'This is just what we have already pointed out.'

When the enemies are separated, the conqueror may move forward by catching hold of any of the kings (as an ally).

In the absence of a leader, the conqueror may win him over who is the inciter of the combination; or who is of a resolute mind, or who has endeared himself to his people, or who, from greed or fear, joined the combination, or who is afraid of the conqueror, or whose friendship with the conqueror is based upon some consanguinity of royalty, or who is a friend, or who is a wandering enemy—in the order of enumeration.

Of these, one has to please the inciter by surrendering oneself; by conciliation and salutation; him who is of a resolute mind; by giving a daughter in marriage or by availing oneself of his youth (to beget a son on one's wife?); him who is the beloved of his people, by giving twice the amount of profits; him who is greedy, by helping with men and money; him who is afraid of the combination, by giving a hostage to him who is naturally timid; by entering into a closer union with him whose friendship is based upon some consanguinity of royalty; by doing what is pleasing and beneficial to both or by abandoning hostilities against him who is a friend; and by offering help and abandoning hostilities against him who is a wandering enemy; one has to win over the confidence of any of the above kings by adopting suitable means or by means of conciliation, gifts, dissension, or threats, as will be explained in Chapter 2, Book VII, under the heading 'Considerations about the Troubles of the King and of His Kingdom'.

He who is in troubles and is apprehensive of an attack from his enemy, should, on the condition of supplying the enemy with army and money, make peace with the enemy on definite terms with reference to place, time and work; he should also set right any offence he might have given by the violation of a treaty; if he has no supporters, he should find them among his relatives and friends; or he may build an impregnable fortress, for he who is defended by forts and friends will be respected both by his own and his enemy's people.

Whoever is wanting in the power of deliberation should collect wise men around himself, and associate with old men of considerable learning; thus he would attain his desired ends.

He who is devoid of a good treasury and army should direct his attention towards the strengthening of the safety and security of the elements of his sovereignty; for the country is the source of all those works which are conducive to treasury and army; the haven of the king and of his army is a strong fort.

Irrigational works (*setubandha*) are the source of crops; the results of a good shower of rain are ever attained in the case of crops below irrigational works.

The roads of traffic are a means to overreach an enemy; for it is through the roads of traffic that armies and spies are led (from one country to another); and that weapons, armour, chariots and draught animals are purchased; and that entrance and exit (in travelling) are facilitated.

Mines are the source of whatever is useful in battle.

Timber forests are the source of such materials as are necessary for building forts, conveyances and chariots.

Elephant forests are the source of elephants.

Pasture lands are the source of cows, horses and camels to draw chariots. In the absence of such sources of his own, he should acquire them from someone among his relatives and friends. If he is destitute of an army, he should, as far as possible, attract to himself the brave men of corporations, of thieves, of wild tribes, of *mlecchas*, and of spies who are capable of inflicting injuries upon enemies.

He should also adopt the policy of a weak king towards powerful king in view of averting danger from enemies or friends.

Thus with the aid of one's own party, the power of deliberation, the treasury, and the army, one should get rid of the clutches of one's enemies.

[Thus ends Chapter 14, 'Recruitment of Lost Power', in Book VII, 'The End of the Sixfold Policy' of the Arthashastra of Kautilya. End of the 112th chapter from the beginning.]

Chapter 15

MEASURES CONDUCIVE TO PEACE WITH A STRONG AND PROVOKED ENEMY; AND THE ATTITUDE OF A CONQUERED ENEMY

WHEN a weak king is attacked by a powerful enemy, the former should seek the protection of one who is superior to his enemy and whom his enemy's power of deliberation for intrigue cannot affect. Of kings who are equal in the power of deliberation, difference should be sought in unchangeable prosperity and in association with the aged.

In the absence of a superior king, he should combine with a number of his equals who are equal in power to his enemy and whom his enemy's power of purse, army and intrigue cannot reach. Of kings who are equally possessed of the power of purse, army and intrigue, difference should be sought in their capacity for making vast preparations.

In the absence of equals, he should combine with a number of inferior kings who are pure and enthusiastic, who can oppose the enemy, and whom his enemy's power of purse, army and intrigue cannot reach. Of kings who are equally possessed of enthusiasm and capacity for action, a difference should be sought in the opportunity of securing favourable battlefields. Of kings who are equally possessed of favourable battlefields, difference should be sought in their ever being ready for war. Of kings who are equal possessed of favourable battlefields and who are equally ready for war, difference should be sought in their possession of weapons and armour necessary for war.

In the absence of any such help, he should seek shelter inside a fort in which his enemy with a large army can offer no obstruction to the supply of foodstuff, grass, firewood and water, but would sustain a heavy loss of men and money. When there are many forts, difference should be sought in their affording facility for the collection of stores and supplies. Kautilya is of opinion that one should entrench oneself in a fort inhabited by men and provided with stores and supplies. Also for the following reasons, one should shelter oneself in such a fort:

'I shall oppose him (the enemy) with his rear enemy's ally or with a *madhyama* king, or with a neutral king; I shall either capture or devastate his kingdom with the aid of a neighbouring king, a wild tribe, a scion of his family, or an imprisoned prince; by the help of my partisans with him, I shall create troubles in his fort, country or camp; when he is near, I shall murder him with weapons, fire or poison, or any other secret means at my pleasure; I shall, cause him to sustain a heavy loss of men and money in works undertaken by himself or made to be undertaken at the instance of my spies; I shall easily sow the seeds of dissension among his friends or his army when they have suffered from loss of men and money; I shall catch hold of his camp by cutting off supplies and stores going to it; or by surrendering myself (to him), I shall create some weak points in him and put him down with all my resources; or having curbed his spirit, I shall compel him to make peace with me on my own terms; when I obstruct his movements troubles arise to him from all sides; when he is helpless, I shall slay him with the help of my hereditary army or with his enemy's army; or with wild tribes; I shall maintain the safety and security of my vast country by entrenching myself within my fort; the army of myself and of my friends will be invincible when collected together in this fort; my army which is trained to fight from valleys, pits, or at night, will bring him into difficulties on his way, when he is engaged in an immediate work; owing to loss of men and money, he will make himself powerless when he arrives here at a bad place and in a bad time; owing to the existence of forts and of wild tribes (on the way), he will find this country accessible only at considerable cost of men and money; being unable to find positions favourable for the exercise of the armies of himself and of his friends, suffering from disease, he will arrive here in distress; or having arrived here, he will not return.'

In the absence of such circumstances, or when the enemy's army is very strong, one may run away abandoning one's fort.

My teacher says that one may rush against the enemy like a moth against a flame; success in one way or other (i.e., death or victory) is certain for one who is reckless of life.

No, says Kautilya, having observed the conditions conducive to peace between himself and his enemy, he may make peace; in the absence of such conditions, he may, by taking recourse to threats, secure peace or a friend; or he may send a messenger to one who is likely to accept peace; or having pleased with wealth and honour the messenger sent by his enemy, he may tell the latter: 'This is the king's manufactory; this is the residence of the queen and the princes; this kingdom and I myself are at your disposal, as approved of by the queen and the princes.'

Having secured his enemy's protection, he should behave himself like a servant to his master by serving the protector's occasional needs.

Forts and other defensive works, acquisition of things, celebration of marriages, installation of the heir apparent, commercial undertakings, capture of elephants, construction of covert places for battle (*sattra*), marching against an enemy, and holding sports—all these he should undertake only at the permission of his protector. He should also obtain his protector's permission before making any agreement with people settled in his country or before punishing those who may run away from his country. If the citizens and country people living in his kingdom prove disloyal or inimical to him, he may request of his protector another good country; or he may get rid of wicked people by making use of such secret means as are employed against traitors. He should not accept the offer of a good country even from a friend. Unknown to his protector, he may see the protector's minister, high priest, commander of the army or heir apparent. He should also help his protector as much as he can. On all occasions of worshipping gods and of making prayers, be should cause his people to pray for the long life of his protector; and he should always proclaim his readiness to place himself at the disposal of his protector.

Serving him who is strong and combined with others, and being far away from the society of suspected persons, a conquered king should thus always behave himself towards his protector.

[Thus ends Chapter 15, 'Measures Conducive to Peace with a Strong And Provoked Enemy; and the Attitude of a Conquered Enemy', in Book VII, 'The End of the Sixfold Policy' of the Arthashastra of Kautilya. End of the 113th chapter from the beginning.]

Chapter 16

THE ATTITUDE OF A CONQUERED KING

IN view of causing financial trouble to his protector, a powerful vassal king, desirous of making conquests, may, under the permission of his protector, march on countries where the formation of the ground and the climate are favourable for the manouvre of his army, his enemy having neither forts, nor any other defensive works, and the conqueror himself having no enemies in the rear. Otherwise (in case of enemies in the rear), he should march after making provisions for the defence of his rear.

By means of conciliation and gifts, he should subdue weak kings; and by means of sowing the seeds of dissension and by threats, strong kings. By adopting a particular, or an alternative, or all of the strategic means, he should subdue his immediate and distant enemies.

He should observe the policy of conciliation by promising the protection of villages, of those who live in forests, of flocks of cattle, and of the roads of traffic as well as the restoration of those who have been banished or who have run away or who have done some harm.

Gifts of land, of things, and of girls in marriage and absence of fear—by declaring these, he should observe the policy of gifts.

By instigating any one of the neighbouring kings, a wild chief, a scion of the enemy's family, or an imprisoned prince, he should sow the seeds of dissension.

By capturing the enemy in an open battle, or in a treacherous fight, or through a conspiracy, or in the tumult of seizing the enemy's fort by strategic means, he should punish the enemy.

He may reinstate kings who are spirited and who can strengthen his army; likewise he may reinstate those who are possessed of a good treasury and army and who can therefore help him with money; as well as those who are wise and who can therefore provide him with lands.

Whoever among his friends helps him with gems, precious things, raw materials acquired from commercial towns, villages and mines, or with conveyances and draught animals acquired from timber and elephant forests, and herds of cattle, is a friend affording a variety of enjoyment (*chitrabhoga*); whoever supplies him with wealth and army is a friend affording vast enjoyment (*mahabhoga*); whoever supplies him with army, wealth and lands is a friend affording all enjoyments (*sarvabhoga*); whoever safeguards him against a side enemy is a friend affording enjoyments on one side (*ekatobhogi*); whoever helps also his enemy and his enemy's allies is a friend affording enjoyment to both sides (*ubhayatobhogi*); and whoever helps him against his enemy, his enemy's ally, his neighbour and wild tribes is a friend affording enjoyment on all sides (*sarvatobhogi*).

If he happens to have an enemy in the rear, or a wild chief, or an enemy, or a chief enemy capable of being propitiated with the gift of lands, he should provide such an enemy with a useless piece of land,; an enemy possessed of forts with a piece of land not connected with his (conqueror's) own territory; a wild chief with a piece of land yielding no livelihood; a scion of the enemy's family with a piece of land that can be taken back; an enemy's prisoner with a piece of land which is (not?) snatched from the enemy; a corporation of armed men with a piece of land, constantly under troubles from an enemy; the combination of corporations with a piece of land close to the territory of a powerful king; a corporation invincible in war with a piece of land under both the above troubles; a spirited king desirous of war with a piece of land which affords no advantageous positions for the manoeuvre of the army; an enemy's partisan with wastelands; a banished prince with a piece of land exhausted of its resources; a king who has renewed the observance of a treaty of peace after breaking it, with a piece of land which can be colonized at considerable cost of men and money; a deserted prince with a piece of land which affords no protection; and his own protector with an uninhabitable piece of land.

(The king who is desirous of making conquests) should continue in following the same policy towards him, who, among the above kings, is most helpful and keeps the same attitude; should by secret means bring him round who is opposed; should favour the helpful with facilities for giving further help, besides bestowing rewards and honour at all costs upon him; should give relief to him who is under troubles; should receive visitors at their own choice and afford satisfaction to them; should avoid using contemptuous, threatening, defamatory or harsh words towards them; should like a father protect those who are promised security from fear; should punish the guilty after publishing their guilt; and in order to avoid causing suspicion to the protector, the vassal king should adopt the procedure of inflicting secret punishments upon offenders.

He should never covet the land, things, and sons and wives of the king slain by him; he should reinstate in their own estates the relatives of the kings slain. He should install in the kingdom the heir apparent of the king who has died while working (with the conqueror); all conquered kings will, if thus treated, loyally follow the sons and grandsons of the conqueror.

Whoever covets the lands, things, and sons and wives of the kings whom he has either slain or bound in chains will cause provocation to the circle of states and make it rise against himself; also his own ministers employed in his own territory will be provoked and will seek shelter under the circle of states, having an eye upon his life and kingdom.

Hence conquered kings preserved in their own lands in accordance with the policy of conciliation will be loyal to the conqueror and follow his sons and grandsons.

[Thus ends Chapter 16, 'The Attitude of a Conquered King', in Book VII, 'The End of the Six-fold Policy', of the Arthashastra of Kautilya. End of the 114th chapter from the beginning.]

Chapter 17

MAKING PEACE AND BREAKING IT

THE words *sama* (quiet), *sandhi* (agreement of peace), and *samadhi* (reconcilement) are synonymous. That which is conducive to mutual faith among kings is termed *sama*, *sandhi* or *samadhi*.

My teacher says that peace, depended upon honesty or oath, is mutable, while peace with a security or a hostage is immutable.

No, says Kautilya, peace, dependent upon honesty or oath, is immutable both in this and the next world. It is for this world only that a security or a hostage is required for strengthening the agreement.

Honest kings of old made their agreement of peace with this declaration: 'We have joined in peace'.

In case of any apprehension of breach of honesty, they made their agreement by swearing by fire, water, plough, the brick of a fort wall, the shoulder of an elephant, the hips of a horse, the front of a chariot, a weapon, seeds, scents, juice (*rasa*), wrought gold (*suvarna*) or bullion gold (*hiranya*), and by declaring that these things will destroy and desert him who violates the oath.

In order to avoid the contingency of violation of oath, peace is made with the security of such persons as ascetics engaged in penance, or nobles is peace with a security. In such a peace, whoever takes as security a person capable of controlling the enemy gains more advantages, while he who acts to the contrary is deceived.

In peace made with children as hostages, and in the case of giving a princess or a prince as a hostage, whoever gives a princess gains advantages; for a princess, when taken as a hostage, causes troubles to the receiver, while a prince is of reverse nature.

With regard to two sons, whoever hands over a high-born, brave and wise son, trained in military art, or an only son, is deceived, while he who acts otherwise gains advantages. It is better to give a base-born son as a hostage than a high-born one, inasmuch as the former has neither heirship nor the right to beget heirs; it is better to give a stupid son than a wise one, inasmuch as the former is destitute of the power of deliberation; better to give a timid son than a brave one, inasmuch as the former is destitute of martial spirit; better, a son who is not trained in military art than one who is trained, inasmuch as the former is devoid of the capacity for striking an enemy; and better one of many sons than an only son, since many sons are not wanted.

With regard to a high-born and a wise son, people will continue to be loyal to a high-born son though he is not wise; a wise son, though base-born, is characterized with capacity to consider state matters; but so far as capacity to consider state matters is concerned, a high-born prince associating himself with the aged, has more advantages than a wise but base-born prince.

With regard to a wise and a brave prince, a wise prince, though timid, is characterized with capacity for intellectual works; and a brave prince though not wise, possesses warlike spirit. So far as warlike spirit is concerned, a wise prince overreaches a brave one just as a hunter does an elephant.

With regard to a brave and a trained prince, a brave prince, though untrained, is characterized with capacity for war; and a trained prince, though timid, is capable of hitting objects aright. Notwithstanding the capacity for hitting objects aright, a brave prince excels a trained prince in determination and firm adherence to his policy.

With regard to a king having many sons and another an only son, the former, giving one of his sons as a hostage and being contented with the rest, is able to break the peace but not the latter.

When peace is made by handing over the whole lot of sons, advantage is to be sought in capacity to beget additional sons; capacity to beget additional sons being common, he who can beget able sons will have more advantages than another king (who is not so fortunate); capacity to beget able sons being common, he by whom the birth of a son is early expected will have more advantages than another (who is not so fortunate).

In the case of an only son who is also brave, he who has lost capacity to beget any more sons should surrender himself as an hostage, but not the only son.

Whoever is rising in power may break the agreement of peace. Carpenters, artisans and other spies, attending upon the prince (kept as a hostage) and doing work under the enemy, may take away the prince at night through an underground tunnel dug for the purpose. Dancers, actors, singers, players on musical instruments, buffoons, court bards, swimmers, and *saubhika*s (?), previously set about the enemy, may continue under his service and may indirectly serve the prince. They should have the privilege of entering into, staying in and going out of the palace at any time without rule. The prince may therefore get out at night disguized as anyone of the above spies.

This explains the work of prostitutes and other women spies under the garb of wives; the prince may get out, carrying their pipes, utensils or vessels.

Or the prince may be removed concealed under things, clothes, commodities, vessels, beds, seats and other articles by cooks, confectioners, servants employed to serve the king while bathing, servants employed for carrying conveyances, for spreading the bed, toilet making, dressing, and procuring water; or taking something in pitch-dark, he may get out, disguized as a servant.

Or he may (pretend to) be in communion with god Varuna in a reservoir (which is seen) through a tunnel or to which he is taken at night; spies under the guise of traders dealing in cooked rice and fruits may (poison those things and) distribute among the sentinels.

Or having served the sentinels with cooked rice and beverage mixed with the juice of madana plant on occasions of making offerings to gods or of performing an ancestral ceremony or some sacrificial rite, the prince may get out; or by bribing the sentinels; or spies disguized as a *nagaraka* (officer in charge of the city), a court bard, or a physician may set fire to a building filled with valuable articles; or sentinels or spies disguized as merchants may set fire to the store of commercial articles; or in view of avoiding the fear of pursuit, the prince may, after putting some human body in the house occupied by him, set fire to it and escape by breaking open some house joints, or a window, or through a tunnel; or having disguized himself as a carrier of glass beads, pots and other commodities, he may set out at night; or having entered the residence of ascetics with shaven heads or with twisted hair, he may set out at night, disguized as anyone of them; or having disguized himself as one suffering from a peculiar disease or as a forest man, he may get out; or spies may carry him away as a corpse; or disguized as a widowed wife, he may follow a corpse that is being carried away. Spies disguized as forest people, should mislead the pursuers of the prince by pointing out another direction, and the prince himself may take a different direction.

Or he may escape, hiding himself in the midst of carts of cart drivers; if he is closely followed, he may lead the pursuers to an ambuscade (*sattra*); in the absence of an ambuscade he may leave here and there gold or morsels of poisoned food on both sides of a road and take a different road.

If he is captured, he should try to win over the pursuers by conciliation and other means, or serve them with poisoned food; and having caused another body to be put in a sacrifice performed to please god Varuna or in a fire that has broken out (the prince's father) may accuse the enemy of the murder of his son and attack the enemy.

Or taking out a concealed sword, and falling upon the sentinels, he may quickly run away together with the spies concealed before.

[Thus ends Chapter 17, 'Making Peace and Breaking It', in Book VII, 'The End of the Sixfold Policy' of the Arthashastra of Kautilya. End of the 115th chapter from the beginning.]

Chapter 18

THE CONDUCT OF A MADHYAMA KING, A NEUTRAL KING, AND OF A CIRCLE OF STATES

THE third and the fifth states from a *madhyama* king are states friendly to him; while the second, the fourth and the sixth are unfriendly. If the *madhyama* king shows favour to both of these states, the conqueror should be friendly with him; if he does not favour them, the conqueror should be friendly with those states.

If the *madhyama* king is desirous of securing the friendship of the conqueor's would-be friend, having set his own and his friend's friends against the *madhyama*, and having separated the *madhyama* from the latter's friends, the conqueror should preserve his own friend; or the conqueror may incite the circle of states against the *madhyama* by telling them: 'This *madhyama* king has grown haughty, and is aiming at our destruction: let us therefore combine and interrupt his march.'

If the circle of states is favourable to his cause, he may aggrandise himself by putting down the *madhyama*; if not favourable, having helped his friend with men and money, he should, by means of conciliation and gifts, win over either the leader or a neigbbouring king among the kings who hate the *madhyama*, or who have been living with mutual support, or who will follow the one that is won over (by the conqueror), or who do not rise owing to mutual suspicion; thus by winning over a second (king), he should double his own power; by securing a third, he should treble his own power; thus gaining in strength, he should put down the *madhyama* king.

When place and time are found unsuitable for success in the above attempt, he should, by peace, seek the friendship of one of the enemies of the *madhyama* king, or cause some traitors to combine against the *madhyama*; if the *madhyama* king is desirous of reducing the conqueror's friend, the conqueror should prevent it, and tell the friend: 'I shall protect you as long as you are weak', and should accordingly protect him when he is poor in resources; if the *madhyama* king desires to rout out a friend of the conqueror, the latter should protect him in his difficulties; or having removed him from the fear of the madhyama king, the conqueror should provide him with new lands and keep him under his (the conqueror's) protection, lest he go elsewhere.

If, among the conqueror's friends who are either reducible or assailable enemies of the *madhyama* king, some undertake to help the *madhyama*, the conqueror should make peace with a third king; and if among the *madhyama* king's friends who are either reducible or assailable enemies of the conqueror, some are capable of offence and defence and become friendly to the conqueror, he should make peace with them; thus the conqueror cannot only attain his own ends but also please the *madhyama* king.

If the *madhyama* king is desirous of securing a would-be friend of the conqueror as a friend, the conqueror may make peace with another king, or prevent the friend from going to the madhyama, telling him: 'It is unworthy of you to forsake a friend who is desirous of your friendship', or the conqueror may keep quiet, if the conqueror thinks that the circle of states would be enraged against the friend for deserting his own party. If the *madhyama* king is desirous of securing the conqueror's enemy as his friend, the conqueror should indirectly (i.e., without being known to the *madhyama*) help the enemy with wealth and army.

If the *madhyama* king desires to win the neutral king, the conqueror should sow the seeds of dissension between them. Whoever of the *madhyama* and the neutral kings is esteemed by the circle of states, his protection should the conqueror seek.

The conduct of the *madhyama* king explains that of the neutral king. If the neutral king is desirous of combining with the *madhyama* king, the conqueror should so attempt as to frustrate the desire of the neutral king to overreach an enemy or to help a friend or to secure the services of the army of another neutral king. Having thus strengthened himself, the conqueror should reduce his enemies and help his friends, though their position is inimical towards him.

Those who may be inimical to the conqueror are a king who is of wicked character and who is therefore always harmful, a rear enemy in combination with a frontal enemy, a reducible enemy under troubles, and one who is watching the troubles of the conqueror to invade him.

Those who may be friendly with the conqueror are one who marches with him with the same end in view, one who marches with him with a different end in view, one who wants to combine with the conqueror to march (against a common enemy), one who marches under an agreement for peace, one who marches with a set purpose of his own, one who rises along with others, one who is ready to purchase or to sell either the army or the treasury, and one who adopts the double policy (i.e., making peace with one and waging war with another).

Those neighbouring kings who can be servants to the conqueror are a neighbouring king under the apprehension of an attack from a powerful king, one who is situated between the conqueror and his enemy, the rear enemy of a powerful king, one who has voluntarily surrendered oneself to the conqueror, one who has surrendered oneself under fear, and one who has been subdued. The same is the case with those kings who are next to the territory of the immediate enemies of the conqueror.

• Of these kings, the conqueror should, as far as possible, help that friend who has the same end in view as the conqueror in his conflict with the enemy, and thus hold the enemy at bay.

• When, after having put down the enemy, and after having grown in power, a friend becomes unsubmissive, the conqueror should cause the friend to incur the displeasure of a neighbour and of the king who is next to the neighbour.

• Or the conqueror may employ a scion of the friend's family or an imprisoned prince to seize his lands; or the conqueror may so act that his friend, desirous of further help, may continue to be obedient.

• The conqueror should never help his friend when the latter is more and more deteriorating; a politician should so keep his friend that the latter neither deteriorates nor grows in power.

• When, with the desire of getting wealth, a wandering friend (i.e., a nomadic king) makes an agreement with the conqueror, the latter should so remove the cause of the friend's flight that he never flies again.
• When a friend is as accessible to the conqueror as to the latter's enemy, the conqueror should first separate that obstinate friend from the enemy, and then destroy him, and afterwards the enemy also.
• When a friend remains neutral, the conqueror should cause him to incur the displeasure of his immediate enemies; and when he is worried in his wars with them, the conqueror should oblige him with help.
• When, owing to his own weakness, a friend seeks protection both from the conqueror and the latter's enemy, the conqueror should help him with the army, so that he never turns his attention elsewhere.
• Or having, removed him from his own lands, the conqueror may keep him in another tract of land, having made some previous arrangements to punish or favour the friend.
• Or the conqueror may harm him when he has grown powerful, or destroy him when he does not help the conqueror in danger and when he lies on the conqueror's lap in good faith.
• When an enemy furiously rises against his own enemy (i.e., the conqueror's friend) under troubles, the former should be put down by the latter himself with troubles concealed.
• When a friend keeps quiet after rising against an enemy under troubles, that friend will be subdued by the enemy himself after getting rid of his troubles.
• Whoever is acquainted with the science of polity should clearly observe the conditions of progress, deterioration, stagnation, reduction and destruction, as well as the use of all kinds of strategic means.
• Whoever thus knows the interdependence of the six kinds of policy plays at his pleasure with kings, bound round, as it were, in chains skilfully devised by himself.

[Thus ends Chapter 18, 'The Conduct of a *Madhyama* King, a Neutral King and of a Circle of States', in Book VII, 'The End of the Sixfold Policy' of the Arthashastra of Kautilya. End of the 116th chapter from the beginning. With this ends Book VII, 'The End of the Sixfold Policy' of the Arthashastra of Kautilya.]

Book VIII

Concerning Vices and Calamities

Chapter 1

THE AGGREGATE OF THE CALAMITIES OF THE ELEMENTS OF SOVEREIGNTY

WHEN calamities happen together, the form of consideration should be whether it is easier to take an offensive or defensive attitude. National calamities, coming from Providence or from man happen from one's misfortune or bad policy. The word *vyasana* (vices or calamities), means the reverse or absence of virtue, the preponderance of vices, and occasional troubles. That which deprives (*vyasyati*) a person of his happiness is termed *vyasana* (vices or calamities).

My teacher says that of the calamities, viz., the king in distress, the minister in distress, the people in distress, distress due to bad fortifications, financial distress, the army in distress, and an ally in distress—that which is first mentioned is more serious than the one, coming later in the order of enumeration.

No, says Bharadvaja, of the distress of the king and of his minister, ministerial distress is more serious; deliberations in council, the attainment of results as anticipated while deliberating in council, the accomplishment of works, the business of revenue collection and its expenditure, recruiting the army, the driving out of the enemy and of wild tribes, the protection of the kingdom, taking remedial measures against calamities, the protection of the heir apparent, and the installation of princes constitute the duties of ministers. In the absence of ministers; the above works are ill-done; and like a bird, deprived of its feathers, the king loses his active capacity. In such calamities, the intrigues of the enemy find a ready scope. In ministerial distress, the king's life itself comes into danger, for a minister is the mainstay of the security of the king's life.

No, says Kautilya, it is verily the king who attends to the business of appointing ministers, priests and other servants, including the superintendents of several departments, the application of remedies against the troubles of his people, and of his kingdom, and the adoption of progressive measures; when his ministers fall into troubles, he employs others; he is ever ready to bestow rewards on the worthy and inflict punishments on the wicked; when the king is well off, by his welfare and prosperity, he pleases the people; of what kind the king's character is, of the same kind will be the character of his people; for their progress or downfall, the people depend upon the king; the king is, as it were, the aggregate of the people.

Visalaksha says that of the troubles of the minister and of the people; the troubles of the people are more serious; finance, army, raw products, free labour, carriage of things, and collection (of necessaries) are all secured from the people. There will be no such things in the absence of people, next to the king and his minister.

No, says Kautilya, all activities proceed from the minister—activities such as the successful accomplishment of the works of the people, security of person and property from internal and external enemies, remedial measures against calamities, colonization and improvement of wild tracts of land, recruiting the army, collection of revenue, and bestowal of favour.

The school of Parasara says that of the distress of the people and distress due to bad fortifications, the latter is a more serious evil; for it is in fortified towns that the treasury and the army are secured; they (fortified towns) are a secure place for the people; they are a stronger power than the citizens or country people; and they are a powerful defensive instrument in times of danger for the king. As to the people, they are common both to the king and his enemy.

No, says Kautilya, for forts, finance and the army depend upon the people; likewise buildings, trade, agricu1ture, cattle rearing, bravery, stability, power and abundance (of things). In countries inhabited by people, there are mountains and islands (as natural forts); in the absence of an expansive country, forts are resorted to. When a country consists purely of cultivators, troubles due to the absence of fortifications (are apparent); while in a country which consists purely of warlike people, troubles that may appear are due to the absence of (an expansive and cultivated) territory.

Pisuna says that of the troubles due to the absence of forts and to want of finance, troubles due to want of finance are more serious; the repair of fortifications and their maintenance depend upon finance; by means of wealth, intrigue to capture an enemy's fort may be carried on; by means of wealth, the people, friends and enemies can be kept under control; by means of it, outsiders can be encouraged and the establishment of the army and its operations conducted. It is possible to remove the treasure in times of danger, but not the fort.

No, says Kautilya, for it is in the fort that the treasury and the army are safely kept, and it is from the fort that secret war (intrigue), control over one's partisans, the upkeep of the army, the reception of allies and the driving out of enemies and of wild tribes are successfully practized. In the absence of forts, the treasury is to the enemy, for it seems that for those who own forts, there is no destruction.

Kaunapadanta says that of distress due to want of finance or to an inefficient army, that which is due to the want of an efficient army is more serious; for control over one's own friends and enemies, the winning over the army of an enemy, and the business of administration are all dependent upon the army. In the absence of the army, it is certain that the treasury will be lost, whereas lack of finance can be made up by procuring raw products and lands or by seizing an enemy's territory.

The army may go to the enemy, or murder the king himself, and bring about all kinds of troubles. But finance is the chief means of observing virtuous acts and of enjoying desires. Owing to a change in place, time and policy, either finance or the army may be a superior power; for the army is (sometimes) the means of securing the wealth acquired; but wealth is (always) the means of securing both the treasury and the army. Since all activities are dependent upon finance, financial troubles are more serious.

Vatavyadhi says that of the distress of the army and of an ally, the distress of an ally is more serious—an ally, though he is not fed and is far off, is still serviceable; he drives off not only the rear enemy and the friends of the rear enemy but also the frontal enemy and wild tribes; he also helps his friend with money, army and lands on occasions of troubles.

No, says Kautilya, the ally of him who has a powerful army keeps the alliance; and even the enemy assumes a friendly attitude; when there is a work that can be equally accomplished either by the army or by an ally, preference to the army or to the ally should depend on the advantages of securing the appropriate place and time for war and the expected profit. In times of sudden expedition and on occasions of troubles from an enemy, a wild tribe, or local rebels, no friend can be trusted. When calamities happen together, or when an enemy has grown strong, a friend keeps up his friendship as long as money is forthcoming. Thus the determination of the comparative seriousness of the calamities of the various elements of sovereignty.

- When a part of one of the elements of sovereignty is under troubles, the extent, affection and strength of the serviceable part can be the means of accomplishing a work.
- When any two elements of sovereignty are equally under troubles, they should be distinguished in respect of their progressive or declining tendency, provided that the good condition of the rest of the elements needs no description.
- When the calamities of a single element tend to destroy the rest of the elements, those calamities, whether they be of the fundamental or any other element, are verily serious.

[Thus ends Chapter 1, 'The Aggregate of the Calamities of the Elements of Sovereignty', in Book VIII, 'Concerning Vices and Calamities' of the Arthashastra of Kautilya. End of the 117th chapter from the beginning.]

Chapter 2

CONSIDERATIONS ABOUT THE TROUBLES OF THE KING AND OF HIS KINGDOM

THE king and his kingdom are the primary elements of the state.

The troubles of the king may be either internal or external. Internal troubles are more serious than external troubles which are like the danger arising from a lurking snake. Troubles due to a minister are more serious than other kinds of internal troubles. Hence, the king should keep under his own control the powers of finance and the army.

Of divided rule and foreign rule, divided rule or rule of a country by two kings perishes owing to mutual hatred, partiality and rivalry. Foreign rule, which comes into existence by seizing the country from its king still alive, thinks that the country is not its own, impoverishes it, and carries off its wealth, or treats it as a commercial article; and when the country ceases to love it, it retires abandoning the country.

Which is better, a blind king or a king erring against the science?

My teacher says that a blind king, i.e., a king who is not possessed of an eye in sciences, is indiscriminate in doing works, very obstinate, and is led by others; such a king destroys the kingdom by his own maladministration. But an erring king can be easily brought round when and where his mind goes astray from the procedure laid down in sciences.

No, says Kautilya, a blind king can be made by his supporters to adhere to whatever line of policy he ought to. But an erring king, who is bent upon doing what is against the science, brings about destruction to himself and his kingdom by maladministration.

Which is better, a diseased or a new king?

My teacher says that a diseased king loses his kingdom owing to the intrigue of his ministers, or loses his life on account of the kingdom; but a new king pleases the people by such popular deeds as the observance of his own duties and the act of bestowing favours, remissions (of taxes), gifts and presents upon others.

No, says Kautilya, a diseased king continues to observe his duties as usual. But a new king begins to act as he pleases under the impression that the country, acquired by his own might, belongs to himself; when pressed by combined kings (for plunder), he tolerates their oppression of the country. Or having no firm control over the elements of the state, he is easily removed. There is this difference among diseased kings: a king who is morally diseased, and a king who is suffering from physical disease; there is also this difference among new kings: a high-born king and a base-born king.

Which is better, a weak but high-born king, or a strong but low-born king?

My teacher says that a people, even if interested in having a weak king, will hardly allow room for the intrigues of a weak but high-born person to rule over them; but that if they desire power, they will easily yield themselves to the intrigues of a strong but base-born person to do so.

No, says Kautilya, a people will naturally obey a high-born king though he is weak, for the tendency of a prosperous people is to follow a high-born king. Also they render the intrigues of a strong but base-born person, unavailing, as the saying is, that possession of virtues makes for friendship.

The destruction of crops is worse than the destruction of handfuls (of grains), since it is the labour that is destroyed thereby; absence of rain is worse than too much rain.

The comparative seriousness or insignificance of any two kinds of troubles affecting the elements of sovereignty, in the order of enumeration of the several kinds of distress, is the cause of adopting offensive or defensive operations.

[Thus ends Chapter 2, 'Considerations about the Troubles of the King and of his Kingdom', in Book VIII, 'Concerning Vices and Calamities', of the Arthashastra of Kautilya. End of the 118th chapter from the beginning.]

Chapter 3

THE AGGREGATE OF THE TROUBLE OF MEN

IGNORANCE and absence of discipline are the causes of a man's troubles. An untrained man does not perceive the injuries arising from vices. We are going to treat of them (vices):–

Vice's due to anger form a triad; and those due to desire are fourfold. Of these two, anger is worse, for anger proceeds against all. In a majority of cases, kings given to anger are said to have fallen a prey to popular fury. But kings addicted to pleasures have perished in consequence of serious diseases brought about by deterioration and improverishment.

No, says Bharadvaja, anger is the characteristic of a righteous man. It is the foundation of bravery; it puts an end to despicable (persons); and it keeps the people under fear. Anger is always a necessary quality for the prevention of sin. But desire (accompanies) the enjoyment of results, reconciliation, generosity and the act of endearing oneself to all. Possession of desire is always necessary for him who is inclined to enjoy the fruits of what he has accomplished.

No, says Kautilya, anger brings about enmity with, and troubles from, an enemy, and is always associated with pain. Addiction to pleasure (*kama*) occasions contempt and loss of wealth, and throws the addicted person into the company of thieves, gamblers, hunters, singers, players on musical instruments, and other undesirable persons. Of these, enmity is more serious than contempt, for a despised person is caught hold of by his own people and by his enemies, whereas a hated person is destroyed. Troubles from an enemy are more serious than loss of wealth, for loss of wealth causes financial troubles, whereas troubles from an enemy are injurious to life. Suffering on account of vices is more serious than keeping company with undesirable persons, for the company of undesirable persons can be got rid of in a moment, whereas suffering from vices causes injury for a long time. Hence, anger is a more serious evil.

Which is worse: abuse of language, or of money, or oppressive punishment?

Visalaksha says that of abuse of language and of money, abuse of language is worse; for when harshly spoken to, a brave man retaliates; and bad language, like a nail piercing the heart, excites anger and gives pain to the senses.

No, says Kautilya, gift of money palliates the fury occasioned by abusive language, whereas abuse of money causes the loss of livelihood itself. Abuse of money means gifts, exaction, loss or abandonment of money.

The school of Parasara says that of abuse of money and oppressive punishment, abuse of money is worse; for good deeds and enjoyments depend upon wealth; the world itself is bound by wealth. Hence, its abuse is a more serious evil.

No, says Kautilya, in preference to a large amount of wealth, no man desires the loss of his own life. Owing to oppressive punishment, one is liable to the same punishment at the hands of one's enemies.

Such is the nature of the triad of evils due to anger.

The fourfold vices due to desire are hunting, gambling, women and drinking.

Pisuna says that of hunting and gambling, hunting is a worse vice; for falling into the hand of robbers, enemies and elephants, getting into wild fire, fear, inability to distinguish between the cardinal points, hunger, thirst and loss of life are evils consequent upon hunting, whereas in gambling, the expert gambler wins a victory like Jayatsena and Duryodhana.

No, says Kautilya, of the two parties, one has to suffer from defeat, as is well known from the history of Nala and Yudhishthira; the same wealth that is won like a piece of flesh in gambling, causes enmity. Lack of recognition of wealth properly acquired, acquisition of ill-gotten wealth, loss of wealth without enjoyment, staying away from answering the calls of nature, and contracting diseases from not taking timely meals, are the evils of gambling, whereas in hunting, exercise, the disappearance of phlegm, bile, fat and sweat, the acquisition of skill in aiming at stationary and moving bodies, the ascertainment of the appearance of beasts when provoked, and occasional march (are its good characteristics).

Kaunapadanta says that of addiction to gambling and to women, gambling is a more serious evil; for gamblers always play, even at night by lamplight, and even when the mother (of one of the players) is dead; the gambler exhibits anger when spoken to in times of trouble; whereas in the case of addiction to women, it is possible to hold conversation about virtue and wealth, at the time of bathing, dressing and eating. Also it is possible to make, by means of secret punishment, a woman to be so good as to secure the welfare of the king, or to get rid of her, or drive her out, under the plea of disease.

No, says Kautilya, it is possible to divert the attention from gambling, but not so from women. (The evils of the latter are) failure to see (what ought to be seen), violation of duty, the evil of postponing works that are to be immediately done, incapacity to deal with politics, and contracting the evil of drinking.

Vatavyadhi says that of addiction to women and to drinking, addiction to women is a more serious evil: there are various kinds of childishness among women, as explained in Book I, Chapter 20: 'Duty Towards the Harem', whereas in drinking, the enjoyment of sound and other objects of the senses, pleasing other people, honouring the followers, and relaxation from the fatigue of work (are the advantages).

No, says Kautilya, in the case of addiction to women, the consequences are the birth of children, self-protection, change of wives in the harem, and absence of such consequences in the case of unworthy outside women. Both the above consequences follow from drinking. The auspicious effects of drinking are loss of money, lunacy in a sensate man, corpse-like appearance while living, nakedness, the loss of the knowledge of the Vedas, loss of life, wealth and friends, disassociation with the good, suffering from pain, and indulgence in playing on musical instruments and in singing at the expense of wealth.

Of gambling and drinking, gambling causes gain or loss of the stakes to one party or other. Even among dumb animals, it splits them into factions and causes provocation. It is specially due to gambling that assemblies and royal confederacies possessing the characteristics of assemblies are split into factions, and are consequently destroyed. The reception of what is condemned is the worst of all evils since it causes incapacity to deal with politics.

• The reception of what is condemned is (due to) desire; and anger consists in oppressing the good; since both these are productive of many evils, both of them are held to be the worst evils.

• Hence he who is possessed of discretion should associate with the aged and, after controlling his passions, abandon both anger and desire which are productive of other evils and destructive of the very basis (of life).

[Thus ends Chapter 3, 'The Aggregate of the Troubles of Men', in Book VIII. 'Concerning Vices and Calamities' of the Arthashastra of Kautilya. End of the 119th chapter from the beginning.]

Chapter 4

THE GROUP OF MOLESTATIONS, THE GROUP OF OBSTRUCTIONS, AND THE GROUP OF FINANCIAL TROUBLES

PROVIDENTIAL calamities are fire, floods, pestilence, famine and (the epidemic disease called) *maraka*.

My teacher says that of fire and floods, destruction due to fire is irremediable; all kinds of troubles, except those due to fire, can be alleviated, and troubles due to floods can be passed over.

No, says Kautilya, fire destroys a village, or part of a village whereas floods carry off hundreds of villages.

My teacher says that of pestilence and famine, pestilence brings all kinds of business to a stop by causing obstruction to work on account of disease and death among men and owing to the flight of servants, whereas famine stops no work, but is productive of gold, cattle and taxes.

No, says Kautilya, pestilence devastates only a part (of the country) and can be remedied, whereas famine causes troubles to the whole (of the country) and occasions dearth of livelihood to all creatures.

This explains the consequences of *maraka*.

My teacher says that of the loss of chief and vulgar men, the loss of vulgar men causes obstruction to work.

No, says Kautilya, it is possible to recruit vulgar men, since they form the majority of people; for the sake of vulgar men, nobles should not be allowed to perish; one in a thousand may or may not be a noble man; he it is who is possessed of excessive courage and wisdom and is the refuge of vulgar people.

My teacher says that of the troubles arising from one's own or one's enemy's circle of states, those due to one's own circle are doubly injurious and are irremediable, whereas an inimical circle of states can be fought out or kept away by the intervention of an ally or by making peace.

No, says Kautilya, troubles due to one's own circle can be got rid of by arresting or destroying the leaders among the subjective people; or they may be injurious to a part of the country, whereas troubles due to an enemy's circle of states cause oppression by inflicting loss and destruction and by burning, devastation and plunder.

My teacher says that of the quarrels among the people and among kings, quarrel among the people brings about disunion and thereby enables an enemy to invade the country, whereas quarrel among kings is productive of double pay and wages and of remission of taxes to the people.

No, says Kautilya, it is possible to end the quarrel among the people by arresting the leaders, or by removing the cause of quarrel; and people quarrelling among themselves vie with each other and thereby help the country, whereas quarrel among kings causes trouble and destruction to the people and requires double the energy for its settlement.

My teacher says that of a sportive king and a sportive country, a sportive country is always ruinous to the results of work, whereas a sportive king is beneficial to artisans, carpenters, musicians, buffoons and traders.

No, says Kautilya, a sportive country, taking to sports for relaxation from labour, causes only a trifling loss; and after enjoyment, it resumes work, whereas a sportive king causes oppression by showing indulgence to his courtiers, by seizing and begging, and by obstructing work in the manufactories.

My teacher says that of a favourite wife and a prince, the prince causes oppression by showing indulgence to his followers, by seizing and begging, and by obstructing the work in manufactories whereas the favourite wife is addicted to her amorous sports.

No, says Kautilya, it is possible to prevent through the minister and the priest, the oppression caused by the prince, but not the oppression caused by the favourite wife, since she is usually stubborn and keeps company with wicked persons.

My teacher says that of the troubles due to a corporation of people and to a leader (a chief), the corporation of people cannot be put down since it consists of a number of men and causes oppression by theft and violence, whereas a leader causes troubles by obstruction to, and destruction of, work.

No, says Kautilya, it is very easy to get rid of (the troubles from) a corporation; since it has to rise or fall with the king; or it can be put down by arresting its leader or a part of the corporation itself, whereas a leader backed up with support causes oppression by injuring the life and property of others.

My teacher says that of the chamberlain and the collector of revenue, the chamberlain causes oppression by spoiling works and by inflicting fines, whereas the collector of revenue makes use of the ascertained revenue in the department over which he presides.

No, says Kautilya, the chamberlain takes to himself what is presented by others to be entered into the treasury whereas the collector makes his own revenue first and then the king's; or he destroys the king's revenue and proceeds as he pleases to seize the property of others.

My teacher says that of the superintendent of the boundary and a trader, the superintendent of the boundary destroys traffic by allowing thieves and taking taxes more than he ought to, whereas a trader renders the country prosperous by a favourable barter of commercial articles.

No, says Kautilya, the superintendent of the boundary increases commercial traffic by welcoming the arrival of merchandise, whereas traders unite in causing rise and fall in the value of articles, and live by making profits cent per cent in *pana*s or *kumbha*s (measures of grain).

Which is more desirable, land occupied by a high-born person or land reserved for grazing a flock of cattle?

My teacher says that the land occupied by a high-born person is very productive; and it supplies men to the army; hence it does not deserve to be confiscated lest the owner cause troubles, whereas the land occupied for grazing a flock of cattle is cultivable and deserves therefore to be freed, for cultivable land is preferred to pastureland.

No, says Kautilya, though immensely useful, the land occupied by a high-born person deserves to be freed, lest he cause troubles (otherwise), whereas the land held for grazing a flock of cattle is productive of money and beasts, and does not therefore deserve to be confiscated unless cultivation of crops is impeded thereby.

My teacher says that of robbers and wild tribes, robbers are ever bent on carrying off women at night, make assaults on persons, and take away hundreds and thousands of *pana*s, whereas wild tribes, living under a leader and moving in the neighbouring forests can be seen here and there causing destruction only to a part.

No, says Kautilya, robbers carry off the property of the careless and can be put down as they are easily recognized and caught hold of, whereas wild tribes have their own strongholds, being numerous and brave, ready to fight in broad daylight, and seizing and destroying countries like kings.

Of the forests of beasts and of elephants, beasts are numerous and productive of plenty of flesh and skins; they arrest the growth of the grass and are easily controlled, whereas elephants are of the reverse nature and are seen to be destructive of countries even when they are captured and tamed.

Of benefits derived from one's own or a foreign country, benefits derived from one's own country consists of grains, cattle, gold and raw products, and are useful for the maintenance of the people in calamities, whereas benefits derived from a foreign country are of the reverse nature.

Such is the group of molestations.

Obstruction to movements caused by a chief is internal obstruction; and obstruction to movements caused by an enemy or a wild tribe is external obstruction.

Such is the group of obstructions.

Financial troubles due to the two kinds of obstruction and to the molestations described above are stagnation of financial position, loss of wealth due to the allowance of remission of taxes in favour of leaders, scattered revenue, false account of revenue collected, and revenue left in the custody of a neighbouring king or of a wild tribe.

Thus the group of financial troubles.

In the interests of the prosperity of the country, one should attempt to avoid the cause of troubles, remedy them when they happen, and avert obstructions and financial troubles.

[Thus ends Chapter 4, 'The Group of Molestations, the Group of Obstructions, and the Group of Financial Troubles', in Book VIII, 'Concerning Vices and Calamities', of the Arthashastra of Kautilya. End of the 120th chapter from the beginning.]

Chapter 5

THE GROUP OF TROUBLES OF THE ARMY, AND THE GROUP OF TROUBLES OF A FRIEND

The troubles of the army are: That which is disrespected; that which is mortified; that which is not paid for; that which is diseased; that which has freshly arrived; that which has made a long journey; that which is tired; that which has sustained loss; that which has been repelled; that of which the front portion is destroyed; that which is suffering from inclemency of weather; that which has found itself in an unsuitable ground; that which is displeased from disappointment; that which has run away; that of which the men are fond of their wives; that which contains traitors; that of which the prime portion is provoked; that which has dissensions; that which has come from a foreign state; that which has served in many states; that which is specially trained to a particular kind of manoeuvre and encampment; that which is trained to a particular movement in a particular place; that which is obstructed; that which is surrounded; that which has its supply of grains cut off; that which has its men and stores cut off; that which is kept in one's own country; that which is under the protection of an ally; that which contains inimical persons; that which is afraid of an enemy in the rear; that which has lost its communication; that which has lost its commander; that which has lost its leader; and that which is blind (i.e., untrained).

Of the disrespected and the mortified among these, that which is disrespected may be taken to fight after being honoured, but not that which is suffering from its own mortification.

Of unpaid and diseased armies, the unpaid may be taken to fight after making full payment but not the diseased, which is unfit for work.

Of freshly arrived and long-travelled armies, that which has freshly arrived may be taken to fight after it has taken its position without mingling with any other new army, but not that which is tired from its long journey.

Of tired and reduced armies, the army that is tired may be taken to fight after it has refreshed itself from bathing, eating, and sleeping, but not the reduced army, i.e., the army, the leaders of which have been killed.

Of armies which have either been repelled or have their front destroyed, that which has been repelled may be taken to fight together with fresh men attached to it, but not the army which has lost many of its brave men in its frontal attack.

Of armies, either suffering from inclemency of weather or driven to an unsuitable ground, that which is suffering from inclemency of weather may be taken to fight after providing it with weapons and dress appropriate for the season, but not the army on an unfavourable ground obstructing its movements.

Of disappointed and renegade armies, that which is disappointed may be taken to fight after satisfying it but not the army which has (once) run away.

Of soldiers who are either fond of their wives or are under an enemy, those who are fond of their wives may be taken to fight after separating them from their wives; but not those who are under an enemy, and are, therefore, like internal enemies.

Of provoked and disunited armies, that, of which a part is provoked, may be taken to fight after pacifying it by conciliation and other strategic means but not the disunited army, the members of which are estranged from each other.

Of armies which have left service either in one state or in many states, that whose resignation of service in a foreign state is not due to instigation or conspiracy may be taken to fight under the leadership of spies and friends, but not the army which has resigned its service in many states and is, therefore, dangerous.

Of armies which are trained either to a particular kind of manoeuvre and encampment or to a particular movement in a particular place, that which is taught a special kind of manoeuvre and encampment may be taken to fight, but not the army whose way of making encampments and marches is only suited for a particular place.

Of obstructed and surrounded armies, that which is prevented from its movements in one direction may be taken to fight against the obstructor in another direction, but not the army whose movements are obstructed on all sides.

Of troops whose supply of grain is cut off or whose supply of men and stores is cut off, that which has lost its supply of grain may be taken to fight after providing it with grain brought from another quarter or after supplying to it moveable and immoveable foodstuffs (animal and vegetable foodstuffs) but not the army to which men and provisions cannot be supplied.

Of armies kept in one's own country or under the protection of an ally, that which is kept in one's own country can possibly be disbanded in time of danger, but not the army under the protection of an ally, as it is far removed in place and time.

Of armies either filled with traitors, or frightened by an enemy in the rear, that which is full of traitors may be taken to fight apart under the leadership of a trusted commander, but not the army which is afraid of an attack from the rear.

Of armies without communication or without leaders, that which has lost its communication with the base of operations may be taken to fight after restoring the communication and placing it under the protection of citizens and country people, but not the army which is without a leader such as the king or any other persons.

Of troops which have lost their leader or which are not trained, those that have lost their leader may be taken to fight under the leadership of a different person but not the troops which are not trained.

Removal of vices and troubles, recruitment (of new men), keeping away from places of an enemy's ambush, and harmony among the officers of the army, are the means of protecting the army from troubles.

• He (the king) should ever carefully guard his army from the troubles caused by an enemy, and should ever be ready to strike his enemy's army when the latter is under troubles;

• Whatever he may come to know as the source of trouble to his people, he should quickly and carefully apply antidotes against that cause.

• A friend who, by himself, or in combination with others or under the influence of another king, has marched against his own ally, a friend who is abandoned owing to inability to retain his friendship, or owing to greediness or indifference;

• A friend who is bought by another and who has withdrawn himself from fighting;

• A friend who, following the policy of making peace with one and marching against another, has contracted friendship with one, who is going to march either singly or in combination with others against an ally;

• A friend who is not relieved from his troubles owing to fear, contempt or indifference; a friend who is surrounded in his own place or who has run away owing to fear;

• A friend who is displeased owing to his having to pay much, or owing to his not having received his due, or owing to his dissatisfaction even after the receipt of his due;

• A friend who has voluntarily paid much or who is made by another to pay much (to his ally); a friend who is kept under pressure, or who, having broken the bond of friendship, sought friendship with another;

• A friend who is neglected owing to inability to retain his friendship; and a friend who has become an enemy in spite of his ally's entreaties to the contrary—such friends are hardly acquired; and if acquired at all, they turn away.

• A friend who has realized the responsibilities of friendship, or who is honourable; or whose disappointment is due to want of information, or who, though excited, is unequal (to the task), or who is made to turn back owing to fear from another;

• Or who is frightened at the destruction of another friend, or who is apprehensive of danger from the combination of enemies, or who is made by traitors to give up his friendship—it is possible to acquire such a friend; and if acquired, he keeps up his friendship.

• Hence one should not give rise to those causes which are destructive of friendship; and when they arise, one should get rid of them by adopting such friendly attitude as can remove those causes.

[Thus ends Chapter 5, 'The Group of Troubles of the Army, and the Group of Troubles of a Friend', in Book VIII 'Concerning Vices and Calamities', of the Arthashastra of Kautilya. End of the 121st chapter from the beginning. With this ends Book VIII, 'Concerning Vices and Calamities', of the Arthashastra of Kautilya.]

Book IX

The Work of an Invader

Chapter 1

THE KNOWLEDGE OF POWER, PLACE, TIME, STRENGTH, AND WEAKNESS; THE TIME OF INVASION

THE conqueror should know the comparative strength and weakness of himself and of his enemy; and having ascertained the power, place, time, the time of marching and of recruiting the army, the consequences, the loss of men and money, and profits and danger, he should march with his full force; otherwise, he should keep quiet.

My teacher says that of enthusiasm and power, enthusiasm is better: a king, himself energetic, brave, strong, free from disease, and skilful in wielding weapons is able with his army as a secondary power to subdue a powerful king; his army, though small, will, when led by him, be capable of turning out any work. But a king who has no enthusiasm in himself, will perish though possessed of a strong army.

No, says Kautilya, he who is possessed of power overreaches, by the sheer force of his power, another who is merely enthusiastic. Having acquired, captured, or bought another enthusiastic king as well as brave soldiers, he can make his enthusiastic army of horses, elephants, chariots and others to move anywhere without obstruction. Powerful kings, whether women, young men, lame or blind, conquered the earth by winning over or purchasing the aid of enthusiastic persons.

My teacher says that of power (money and army) and skill in intrigue, power is better; for a king, though possessed of skill for intrigue (*mantrasakti*) becomes a man of barren mind if he has no power; for the work of intrigue is well defined. He who has no power loses his kingdom as sprouts of seeds in drought vomit their sap.

No, says Kautilya, skill for intrigue is better; he who has the eye of knowledge and is acquainted with the science of polity can with little effort make use of his skill for intrigue and can succeed by means of conciliation and other strategic means and by spies and chemical appliances in overreaching even those kings who are possessed of enthusiasm and power. Thus of the three acquirements, viz., enthusiasm, power and skill for intrigue, he who posesses more of the quality mentioned later than the one mentioned first in the order of enumeration will be successful in overreaching others.

Country (space) means the earth; in it the thousand *yojana*s of the northern portion of the country that stretches between the Himalayas and the ocean form the dominion of no insignificant emperor; in it there are such varieties of land, as forests, villages, waterfalls, level plains and uneven grounds. In such lands, he should undertake such works as he considers to be conducive to his power and prosperity. That part of the country, in which his army finds a convenient place for its manoeuvre and which proves unfavourable to his enemy, is the best; that part of the country which is of the reverse nature, is the worst; and that which partakes of both the characteristics is a country of middling quality.

Time consists of cold, hot and rainy periods. The divisions of time are the night, the day, the fortnight, the month, the season, solstices, the year, and the yuga (cycle of five years). In these divisions of time he should undertake such works as are conducive to the growth of his power and prosperity. That time which is congenial for the manoeuvre of his army but which is of the reverse nature for his enemy is the best; that which is of the reverse nature is the worst; and that which possesses both the characteristics is of middling quality.

My teacher says that of strength, place and time, strength is the best; for a man who is possessed of strength can overcome the difficulties due either to the unevenness of the ground or to the cold, hot or rainy periods of time. Some say that place is the best for the reason that a dog, seated in a convenient place, can drag a crocodile and that a crocodile in low ground can drag a dog.

Others say that time is the best for the reason that during the daytime the crow kills the owl, and that at night the owl the crow.

No, says Kautilya, of strength, place and time, each is helpful to the other; whoever is possessed of these three things should, after having placed one-third or one-fourth of his army to protect his base of operations against his rear enemy and wild tribes in his vicinity and after having taken with him as much army and treasure as is sufficient to accomplish his work, march during the month of *Margasirsha* (November–December) against his enemy whose collection of foodstuff is old and insipid and who has not only not gathered fresh foodstuff, but also not repaired his fortifications, in order to destroy the enemy's rainy crops and autumnal handfuls (*mushti*). He should march during the month of *Chaitra* (March–April), if he means to destroy the enemy's autumnal crops and vernal handfuls. He should march during the month of *Jyaishtha* (May–June) against one whose storage of fodder, firewood and water has diminished and who has not repaired his fortifications, if he means to destroy the enemy's vernal crops and handfuls of the rainy season. Or he may march during the dewy season against a country which is of hot climate and in which fodder and water are obtained in little quantities. Or he may march during the summer against a country in which the sun is enshrouded by mist and which is full of deep valleys and thickets of trees and grass, or he may march during the rains against a country which is suitable for the manoeuvre of his own army and which is of the reverse nature for his enemy's army. He has to undertake a long march between the months of *Margasirsha* (November–December) and *Pausha* (December–January), a march of mean length between March and April, and a short march between May and June; and one, afflicted with troubles, should keep quiet.

Marching against an enemy under troubles has been explained in connection with 'Marching After Proclaiming War' in Chapter 4 of Book VII.

My teacher says that one should almost invariably march against an enemy in troubles.

But Kautilya says that when one's resources are sufficient one should march, since the troubles of an enemy cannot be properly recognized; or whenever one finds it possible to reduce or destroy an enemy by marching against him, one may undertake a march.

When the weather is free from heat, one should march with an army mostly composed of elephants. Elephants with profuse sweat in hot weather are attacked by leprosy; and when they have no water for bathing and drinking, they lose their quickness and become obstinate. Hence, against a country containing plenty of water and during the rainy season, one should march with an army mostly composed of elephants. Against a country of the reverse description, i.e., which has little rain and muddy water, one should march with an army mostly composed of asses, camels and horses.

Against a desert, one should march during the rainy season with all the four constituents of the army (elephants , horses, chariots, and men). One should prepare a programme of short and long distances to be marched in accordance with the nature of the ground to be traversed, viz., even ground, uneven ground, valleys and plains.

When the work to be accomplished is small, march against all kinds of enemies should be of short duration; and when it is great, it should also be of long duration; during the rains, encampment should be made abroad.

[Thus ends Chapter 1, 'The Knowledge of Power, Place, Time, Strength, and Weakness; the Time of Invasion', in Book IX, 'The Work of an Invader', of the Arthashastra of Kautilya. End of the 122nd chapter from the beginning.]

Chapter 2

THE TIME OF RECRUITING THE ARMY; THE FORM OF EQUIPMENT; AND THE WORK OF ARRAYING A RIVAL FORCE

THE time of recruiting troops, such as hereditary troops (*maula*), hired troops, corporation of soldiers (*sreni*), troops belonging to a friend or to an enemy, and wild tribes.

When he (a king) thinks that his hereditary army is more than he requires for the defence of his own possessions or when he thinks that as his hereditary army consists of more men than he requires, some of them may be disaffected; or when he thinks that his enemy has a strong hereditary army famous for its attachment, and is, therefore, to be fought out with much skill on his part; or when he thinks that though the roads are good and the weather favourable, it is still the hereditary army that can endure wear and tear; or when he thinks that though they are famous for their attachment, hired soldiers and other kinds of troops cannot be relied upon lest they lend their ears to the intrigues of the enemy to be invaded; or when he thinks that other kinds of force are wanting in strength, that is the time for taking the hereditary army.

When he thinks that the army he has hired is greater than his hereditary army; that his enemy's hereditary army is small and disaffected, while the army his enemy has hired is insignificant and weak; that actual fight is less than treacherous fight; that the place to be traversed and the time required do not entail much loss; that his own army is little given to stupor, is beyond the fear of intrigue, and is reliable; or that little is the enemy's power which he has to put down, that is the time for leading the hired army.

When he thinks that the immense corporation of soldiers he possesses can be trusted both to defend his country and to march against his enemy; that he has to be absent only for a short time; or that his enemy's army consists mostly of soldiers of corporations, and consequently the enemy is desirous of carrying on treacherous fight rather than an actual war, that is the time for the enlistment of corporations of soldiers (*sreni*).

When he thinks that the strong help he has in his friend can be made use of both in his own country and in his marches; that he has to be absent only for a short time, and actual fight is more than treacherous fight; that having made his friend's army to occupy wild tracts, cities or plains, and to fight with the enemy's ally, he, himself, would lead his own army to fight with the enemy's army; that his work can be accomplished by his friend as well; that his success depends on his friend; that he has a friend near and deserving of obligation; or that he has to utilize the excessive force of his friend, that is the time for the enlistment of a friend's army.

When he thinks that he will have to make his strong enemy to fight against another enemy on account of a city, a plain or a wild tract of land, and that in that fight he will achieve one or the other of his objects, just like an outcast person in the fight between a dog and a pig; that through the battle, he will have the mischievous power of his enemy's allies or of wild tribes destroyed; that he will have to make his immediate and powerful enemy to march elsewhere and thus get rid of internal rebellion which his enemy might have occasioned; and that the time of battle between enemies or between inferior kings has arrived, then is the time for the exercise of an enemy's forces.

This explains the time for the engagement of wild tribes. When he thinks that the army of wild tribes is living by the same road (that his enemy has to traverse); that the road is unfavourable for the march of his enemy's army; that his enemy's army consists mostly of wild tribes; that just as a wood apple (*bilva*) is broken by means of another wood apple, the small army of his enemy is to be destroyed, that is the time for engaging the army of wild tribes.

That army which is vast and is composed of various kinds of men and is so enthusiastic as to rise even without provision and wages for plunder when told or untold; that which is capable of applying its own remedies against unfavourable rains; that which can be disbanded and which is invincible for enemies; and that, of which all the men are of the same country, same caste, and same training, is (to be considered as) a compact body of vast power.

Such are the periods of time for recruiting the army.

Of these armies, one has to pay the army of wild tribes either with raw produce or with allowance for plunder.

When the time for the march of one's enemy's army has approached, one has to obstruct the enemy or send him far away, or make his movements fruitless, or, by false promise, cause him to delay the march, and then deceive him after the time for his march has passed away. One should ever be vigilant to increase one's own resources and frustrate the attempts of one's enemy to gain in strength.

Of these armies, that which is mentioned first is better than the one subsequently mentioned in the order of enumeration.

Hereditary army is better than hired army inasmuch as the former has its existence dependent on that of its master, and is constantly drilled.

That kind of hired army which is ever near, ready to rise quickly, and obedient, is better than a corporation of soldiers.

That corporation of soldiers which is native, which has the same end in view (as the king), and which is actuated with similar feelings of rivalry, anger and expectation of success and gain, is better than the army of a friend. Even that corporation of soldiers which is further removed in place and time is, by virtue of its having the same end in view, better than the army of a friend.

The army of an enemy under the leadership of an Arya is better than the army of wild tribes. Both of them (the army of an enemy and of wild tribes) are anxious for plunder. In the absence of plunder and under troubles, they prove as dangerous as a lurking snake.

My teacher says that of the armies composed of Brahman*s*, Kshatriyas, Vaisyas, or Sudras, that which is mentioned first is, on account of bravery, better to be enlisted than the one subsequently mentioned in the order of enumeration.

No, says Kautilya, the enemy may win over to himself the army of Brahman*s* by means of prostration. Hence, the army of Kshatriyas trained in the art of wielding weapons is better; or the army of Vaisyas or Sudras having great numerical strength (is better).

Hence one should recruit one's army, reflecting that 'such is the army of my enemy; and this is my army to oppose it'.

The army which possesses elephants, machines, *sakatagarbha* (?), *kunta* (a wooden rod), *prasa* (a weapon, 24 inches long, with two handles), *kharvataka* (?), bamboo sticks, and iron sticks is the army to oppose an army of elephants.

The same possessed of stones, clubs, armour, hooks and spears in plenty is the army to oppose an army of chariots.

The same is the army to oppose cavalry. Men, clad in armour, can oppose elephants. Horses can oppose men, clad in armour.

Men, clad in armour, chariots, men possessing defensive weapons, and infantry can oppose an army consisting of all the four constituents (elephants, chariots, cavalry and infantry).

Thus considering the strength of the constituents of one's own quadripartite army, one should recruit men to it so as to oppose an enemy's army successfully.

[Thus ends Chapter 2, 'The Time of Recruiting the Army; the Form of Equipment; and the Work of Arraying a Rival Force', in Book IX, 'The Work of an Invader', of the Arthashastra of Kautilya. End of the 123rd chapter from the beginning.]

Chapter 3

CONSIDERATION OF ANNOYANCE IN THE REAR; AND REMEDIES AGAINST INTERNAL AND EXTERNAL TROUBLES

OF the two things, slight annoyance in the rear, and considerable profit in the front, slight annoyance in the rear is more serious; for traitors, enemies and wild tribes augment on all sides the slight annoyance which one may have in the rear. The members of one's own state may be provoked about the acquisition of considerable profit in the front.

When one under the protection of another has come to such a condition (i.e., slight annoyance in the rear and considerable profit in the front), one should endeavour so as to cause to the rear enemy the loss and impoverishment of his servants and friends; and in order to fetch the profit in the front, one should also employ the commander of the army or the heir apparent to lead the army.

Or the king himself may go in person to receive the profit in the front, if he is able to ward off the annoyance in the rear. If he is apprehensive of internal troubles, he may take with him the suspected leaders. If he is apprehensive of external troubles, he should march after keeping inside his capital as hostages the sons and wives of suspected enemies and after having split into a number of divisions the troops of the officer in charge of wastelands (*sunyapala*) and having placed those divisions under the command of several chiefs, or he may abandon his march, for it has been already stated that internal troubles are more serious than external troubles.

The provocation of anyone of the minister the priest, the commander-in-chief and the heir apparent is what is termed internal trouble. The king should get rid of such an internal enemy either by giving up his own fault or by pointing out the danger arising from an external enemy. When the priest is guilty of the gravest treason, relief should be found either by confining him or by banishing him; when the heir apparent is so, confinement or death (*nigraha*), provided that there is another son of good character. From these, the case of the minister and the commander-in-chief is explained.

When a son, or a brother, or any other person of the royal family attempts to seize the kingdom, he should be won over by holding out hopes; when this is not possible, he should be conciliated by allowing him to enjoy what he has already seized, or by making an agreement with him, or by means of intrigue through an enemy, or by securing to him land from an enemy, or any other person of inimical character. Or he may be sent out on a mission with an inimical force to receive the only punishment he deserves; or a conspiracy may be made with a frontier king or wild tribes whose displeasure he has incurred; or the same policy that is employed in securing an imprisoned prince or in seizing an enemy's villages may be resorted to.

The provocation of ministers other than the prime minister is what is called the internal ministerial trouble. Even in this case, necessary strategic means should be employed.

The provocation of the chief of a district (*rashtramukhya*), the officer in charge of the boundary, the chief of wild tribes, and a conquered king is what is termed external trouble. This should be overcome by setting one against the other. Whoever among these has strongly fortified himself should be caught hold of through the agency of a frontier king, or the chief of wild tribes, or a scion of his family, or an imprisoned prince; or he may be captured through the agency of a friend, so that he may not combine with an enemy; or a spy may prevent him from combining with an enemy by saying: 'This enemy makes a cat's-paw of you and causes you to fall upon your own lord; When his aim is realized, he makes you to lead an army against enemies or wild tribes, or to sojourn in a troublesome place; or he causes you to reside at a frontier station far from the company of your sons and wife. When you have lost all your strength, he sells you to your own lord; or having made peace with you, he will please your own lord. Hence it is advisable for you to go to the best friend of your lord.' When he agrees to the proposal, he is to be honoured; but when he refuses to listen, he is to be told: 'I am specially sent to separate you from the enemy'. The spy should however appoint some persons to murder him; or he may be killed by some concealed persons; or some persons pretending to be brave soldiers may be made to accompany him and may be told by a spy (to murder him). Thus the end of troubles. One should cause such troubles to one's enemy and ward off those of one's own.

In the case of a person who is capable of causing or alleviating troubles, intrigue should be made use of; and in the case of a person who is of reliable character, able to undertake works, and to favour his ally in his success; and to afford protection against calamities, counter-intrigue (*pratijapa*) should be made use of (to keep his friendship secure). It should also be considered whether the person is of good disposition or of obstinate temper (*satha*).

The intrigue carried on by a foreigner of obstinate temper with local persons is of the following form: 'If after killing his own master, he comes to me, I will secure these two objects, the destruction of my enemy and the acquisition of the enemy's lands; or else my enemy kills him, with the consequence that the partisans of the relations killed, and other persons who are equally guilty and are therefore apprehensive of similar punishment to themselves will perturb my enemy's peace when my enemy has no friends to count; or when my enemy falls to suspect any other person who is equally guilty, I shall be able to cause the death of this or that officer under my enemy's own command.'

The intrigue carried on by a local person of obstinate temper with a foreigner is of the following form: 'I shall either plunder the treasury of this king or destroy his army; I shall murder my master by employing this man; if my master consents, I shall cause him to march against an external enemy or a wild tribe; let his circle of states be brought to confusion, let him incur enmity with them; then it is easy to keep him under my power, and conciliate him; or I myself shall seize the kingdom; or, having bound him in chains, I shall obtain both my master's land and outside land; or having caused the enemy (of my master) to march out, I shall cause the enemy to be murdered in good faith; or I shall seize the enemy's capital when it is empty (of soldiers).'

When a person of good disposition makes a conspiracy for the purpose of acquiring what is to be enjoyed by both, an agreement should be made with him. But when a person of obstinate temper so conspires, he should be allowed to have his own way and then deceived. Thus the form of policy to be adopted should be considered. Enemies from enemies, subjects from subjects, subjects from enemies, and enemies from subjects should ever be guarded; and both from his subjects and enemies, a learned man should ever guard his own person.

[Thus ends Chapter 3, 'Consideration of Annoyance in the Rear, and Remedies Against Internal and External Troubles', in Book IX, 'The Work of an Invader', of the Arthashastra of Kautilya. End of the 124th chapter from the beginning.]

Chapter 4

Consideration About Loss Of Men, Wealth, And Profit

LOSS of trained men is what is called *kshaya*, loss of men. Diminution of gold and grains is loss of wealth.

When the expected profit overweighs both these; one should march (against an enemy).

The characteristics of an expected profit are: that which is receivable, that which is to be returned, that which pleases all, that which excites hatred, that which is realized in a short time, that which entails little loss of men to earn, that which entails little loss of wealth to earn, that which is vast, that which is productive, that which is harmless, that which is just, and that which comes first.

When a profit is easily acquired and secured without the necessity of returning it to others, it is termed 'receivable'; that which is of the reverse nature is 'repayable'; whoever goes to receive a repayable profit or is enjoying it gets destruction.

When he, however, thinks that 'by taking a repayable profit I shall cause my enemy's treasury, army, and other defensive resources to dwindle; I shall exploit to impoverishment the mines, timber and elephant forests, irrigational works and roads of traffic of my enemy; I shall impoverish his subjects, or cause them to migrate, or conspire against him; when they are reduced to this condition, my enemy inflames their hatred (by punishing them); or I shall set my enemy against another enemy; my enemy will give up his hopes and run away to one who has some blood relationship with him; or having improved his lands, I shall return them to him, and when he is thus brought to ascendancy, he will be a lasting friend of mine', then he may take even a repayable profit. Thus receivable and repayable profits are explained.

That profit which a virtuous king receives from a wicked king pleases both his own and other people; that which is of the reverse nature excites hatred; that profit which is received at the advice of ministers excites hatred, for they think: 'This king has reduced our party and impoverished us'. That profit which is received without caring for the opinion of treacherous ministers excites hatred, for they think: 'Having made the profit, this king destroys us'. But that which is of the reverse nature pleases. Thus pleasing and provoking profits are explained.

That which is acquired by mere marching is what is acquired soon.

That which is to be realized by negotiation (*mantrasaddhya*) entails little loss of men.

That which requires merely the expenditure of provisions (for servants employed to earn it) entails little loss of wealth.

That which is immediately of considerable value is vast.

That which is the source of wealth is productive. That which is attained with no troubles is harmless. That which is acquired best is just.

That which is acquired without any hindrance from allies is profit coming first.

When profits (from two sources) are equal, he should consider the place and time, the strength and means (required to acquire it), affection and disaffection (caused by it), intrigue and absence of intrigue (involving it), its nearness and distance, its present and future effects, its constant worth or worthlessness, and its plentifulness and usefulness; and he should accept only that profit which is possessed of most of the above good characteristics.

Obstructions to profit are: passion, anger, timidity, mercy, bashfulness, living like one who is not an *Arya*, haughtiness, pity, desire for the other world, strict adherence to virtuous life, deception, neediness, envy, negligence of what is at hand, generosity, want of faith, fear, inability to endure cold, heat, and rain, and faith in the auspiciousness of lunar days and stars.

- Wealth will pass away from that childish man who inquires most after the stars; for wealth is the star for wealth; what will the stars do?
- Capable men will certainly secure wealth at least after a hundred trials; and wealth is bound by wealth just as elephants are bound by counter-elephants.

[Thus ends Chapter 4, 'Consideration about Loss of Men, Wealth and Profit', in Book IX, 'The Work of an Invader', of the Arthashastra of Kautilya. End of the 125th chapter from the beginning.]

Chapter 5

EXTERNAL AND INTERNAL DANGERS

THE formation of a treaty and other settlements otherwise than they ought to have been made is against policy. From it arise dangers.

The various kinds of dangers are: that which is of external origin and of internal abetment; that which is of internal origin and of external abetment; that which is of external origin and of external abetment; and that which is of internal origin and of internal abetment.

Where foreigners carry on an intrigue with local men or local men with foreigners, the consequence of the intrigue carried on by the combination of local and foreign persons will be very serious. Abettors of an intrigue have a better chance of success than its originators; for when the originators of an intrigue are put down, others will hardly succeed in undertaking any other intrigue. Foreigners can hardly win over local persons by intrigue; nor can local men seduce foreigners. Foreigners will find their vast efforts after all unavailing, and only conducive to the prosperity of the king (against whom they want to conspire).

When local persons are abetting (with foreigners), the means to be employed to suppress them are conciliation (*sama*) and gifts (*dana*).

The act of pleasing a man with a high rank and honour is conciliation; favour and remission of taxes or employment to conduct state-works is what is termed gifts.

When foreigners are abetting, the king should employ the policy of dissension and coercion. Spies under the guise of friends may inform foreigners: 'Mind, this man is desirous of deceiving you with the help of his own spies who are disguised as traitors.' Spies under the garb of traitors may mix with traitors and separate them from foreigners, or foreigners from local traitors. Fiery spies may make friendship with traitors and kill them with weapons or poison; or having invited the plotting foreigners, they may murder the latter.

Where foreigners carry on an intrigue with foreigners, or local men with local men, there the consequences of the intrigue, unanimously carried on with a set purpose, will be very serious. When guilt is got rid of, there will be no guilty persons; but when a guilty person is got rid of, the guilt will contaminate others. Hence, when foreigners carry on an intrigue, the king should employ the policy of dissension and coercion. Spies under the guise of friends may inform foreign conspirators: 'Mind, this your king, with the desire of enriching himself, is naturally provoked against you all.' Then fiery spies may mix with the servants and soldiers of the abettor (of foreign conspirators) and kill them with weapons, poison and other means. Other spies may then expose or betray the abettor.

When local men carry on an intrigue with local men, the king should employ necessary strategic means to put it down. He may employ the policy of conciliation with regard to those who keep the appearance of contentment, or who are naturally discontented or otherwise. Gifts may be given under the pretext of having been satisfied with a favoured man's steadfastness in maintaining the purity of his character, or under the plea of anxious care about his weal or woe. A spy under the garb of a friend may tell the local persons: 'Your king is attempting to find your heart; you should tell him the truth.' Or local men may be separated from each other, by telling them: 'This man carries such a tale to the king against you.' And coercive measures may be employed as described in the chapter 'Concerning the Awards of Punishments', Book V, Chapter 1.

Of these four kinds of danger, internal danger should first be got rid of; for it has been already stated that internal troubles like the fear from a lurking snake are more serious than external troubles.

One must consider that of these four kinds of danger, that which is mentioned first is less grave than the one subsequently mentioned, whether or not it is caused by powerful persons; otherwise (i.e., when the danger is caused by insignificant persons), simple means may be used to get rid of it.

[Thus ends Chapter V, 'External and Internal Dangers' in Book IX, 'The Work of an Invader', of the Arthashastra of Kautilya. End of the 126th chapter from the beginning.]

Chapter 6

PERSONS ASSOCIATED WITH TRAITORS AND ENEMIES

THERE are two kinds of innocent persons, those who have disassociated themselves from traitors and those who have kept themselves away from enemies.

In order to separate citizens and country-people from traitors, the king should employ all the strategic means, except coercion. It is very difficult to inflict punishment on an assembly of influential men; and if inflicted at all, it may not produce the desired effect, but may give rise to undesirable consequences. He may, however, take steps against the leaders of the seditious as shown in the chapter 'Concerning the Awards of Punishments', Book V, Chapter 1.

In order to separate his people from an enemy, he should employ conciliation and other strategic means to frustrate the attempt of those who are the enemy's principal agents or by whom the enemy's work is to be carried out.

Success in securing the services of capable agents depends upon the king; success of efforts depends upon ministers; and success to be achieved through capable agents is, therefore, dependent both upon the king and his ministers.

When, in spite of the combination of traitors and loyal persons, success is achieved, it is mixed success; when people are thus mixed, success is to be achieved through the agency of loyal persons; for in the absence of a support, nothing that requires a support for its existence can exist. When success is involved in the union of friends and enemies it is termed a success contaminated by an enemy; when success is contaminated by an enemy, it is to be achieved through the agency of a friend; for it is easy to attain success through a friend but not through an enemy.

When a friend does not come to terms, intrigue should be frequently resorted to. Through the agency of spies, the friend should be won over after separating him from the enemy. Or attempts may be made to win him over who is the last among combined friends; for when he who is the last among combined friends is secured, those who occupy the middle rank will be separated from each other; or attempts may be made to win over a friend who occupies middle rank; for when a friend occupying middle rank among combined kings is secured, friends, occupying the extreme ranks cannot keep the union. (In brief) all those measures which tend to break their combination should be employed.

A virtuous king may be conciliated by praising his birth, family, learning and character, and by pointing out the relationship which his ancestors had (with the proposer of peace), or by describing the benefits and absence of enmity shown to him.

Or a king who is of good intentions, or who has lost his enthusiastic spirits, or whose strategic means are all exhausted and thwarted in a number of wars, or who has lost his men and wealth, or who has suffered from sojourning abroad, or who is desirous of gaining a friend in good faith, or who is apprehensive of danger from another, or who cares more for friendship than anything else, may be won over by conciliation.

Or a king who is greedy or who has lost his men may be won over by giving gifts through the medium of ascetics and chiefs who have been previously kept with him for the purpose.

Gifts are of five kinds: abandonment of what is to be paid; continuance of what is being given; repayment of what is received; payment of one's own wealth; and help for a voluntary raid on the property of others.

When any two kings are apprehensive of enmity and seizure of land from each other, seeds of dissension may be sown between them. The timid of the two may be threatened with destruction and may be told: 'Having made peace with you, this king works against you; the friend of this other king is permitted to make an open peace.'

When from one's own country or from another's country merchandise or commodities for manufacture in a manufactory are going to an enemy's country, spies may spread the information that those commodities are obtained from one whom the enemy wanted to march against. When commodities are thus gathered in abundance (the owner of the articles) may send a message to the enemy: 'These commodities and merchandise are sent by me to you; please declare war against the combined kings or desert them; you will then get the rest of the tribute'. Then spies may inform the other kings of the combination; 'These articles are given to him by your enemy.'

The conqueror may gather some merchandise peculiar to his enemy's country and unknown elsewhere. Spies, under the garb of merchants, may sell that merchandise to other important enemies and tell them that that merchandise was given (to the conqueror) by the enemy (whose country's product it is).

Or having pleased with wealth and honour those who are highly treacherous (among an enemy's people), the conqueror may cause them to live with the enemy, armed with weapons, poison and fire. One of the ministers of the enemy may be killed. His sons and wife may be induced to say that the minister was killed at night (by such and such a person). Then the enemy's minister may ask every one of the family of the murdered minister (as to the cause of the death). If they say in reply as they are told, they may be caused to be set free; if they do not do so, they may be caused to be caught hold of. Whoever has gained the confidence of the king may tell the king (the enemy) that he (the enemy) has to guard his own person from such and such a minister. Then the recipient of salaries from the two states (the conqueror's and the enemy's state) may inform the suspected minister to destroy (the king).

Or such kings as are possessed of enthusiasm and power may be told: 'Seize the country of this king, our treaty of peace standing as before.' Then spies should inform the particular king of the attempt of these kings and cause the destruction of the commissariat and of the followers of one of these kings. Other spies, pretending to be friends, should inform these kings of the necessity of destroying the particular king.

When an enemy's brave soldier, elephant or horse dies, or is killed, or carried off by spies, other spies may tell the enemy that the death is due to mutual conflict among his followers. The man who is employed to commit such murders may be asked to repeat his work again on the condition of his receiving the balance due to him. He should receive the amount from the recipient of salaries from two states; when the king's party is thus divided, some may be won over (to the side of the conqueror).

This explains the case of the commander-in-chief, the prince and the officers of the army (of the enemy).

Likewise seeds of dissension may be sown among combined states. Thus the work of sowing the seeds of dissension.

Spies under concealment may, without the help of a fiery spy, murder by means of weapons, poison or other things a fortified enemy who is of mean character or who is under troubles; anyone of hidden spies may do the work when it is found easy; or a fiery spy alone may do the work by means of weapons, poison or fire; for a fiery spy can do what others require all the necessary aids to do.

Thus the four forms of strategic means.

Of these means, that which comes first in the order of enumeration is, as stated in connection with 'invaders', easier than the rest. Conciliation is of single quality; gift is twofold, since conciliation precedes it; dissension is threefold, since conciliation and gift precede it; and conciliatory coercion is fourfold, since conciliation, gift, and dissension precede it.

The same means are employed in the case of local enemies too; the difference is this: the chief messengers known to the manufactories may be sent to anyone of the local enemies in order to employ him for the purpose of making a treaty or for the purpose of destroying another person. When he agrees to the proposal, the messengers should inform (their master) of their success. Then recipients of salaries from two states should inform the people or enemies concerned in the local enemy's work: 'This person (the local enemy) is your wicked king.' When a person has reason to fear or hate another, spies may augment dissension between them by telling one of them: 'This man is making an agreement with your enemy, and will soon deceive you; hence make peace (with the king) soon and attempt to put down this man.' Or by bringing about friendship or marriage connection between persons who have not been hitherto connected, spies may separate them from others; or through the aid of a neighbouring king, a wild chief, a scion of an enemy's family, or an imprisoned prince, local enemies may be destroyed outside the kingdom; or through the agency of a caravan or wild tribes, a local enemy may be killed along with his army; or persons, pretending to be the supporters of a local enemy and who are of the same caste, may under favourable opportunities kill him; or spies under concealment may kill local enemies with fire, poison, and weapons.

When the country is full of local enemies, they may be got rid of by making them drink poisonous (liquids); an obstinate (clever) enemy may be destroyed by spies or by means of (poisoned) flesh given to him in good faith.

[Thus ends Chapter 6, 'Persons Associated with Traitors and Enemies', in Book IX, 'The Work of an Invader', of the Arthashastra of Kautilya. End of the 127th chapter from the beginning,]

Chapter 7

DOUBTS ABOUT WEALTH AND HARM; AND SUCCESS TO BE OBTAINED BY THE EMPLOYMENT OF ALTERNATIVE STRATEGIC MEANS

INTENSITY of desire and other passions provoke one's own people; policy provokes external enemies. Both these are the characteristics of demoniac life. Anger disturbs the feelings of one's own men. Those causes which are conducive to the prosperity of one's enemy are dangerous wealth, provocative wealth, and wealth of doubtful consequences.

Wealth which, when obtained, increases the enemy's prosperity, or which, though obtained, is repayable to the enemy, or which causes loss of men and money, is dangerous wealth; for example, wealth which is enjoyed in common by neighbouring kings and which is acquired at their expense; or wealth which is asked for by an enemy; or wealth which is seized like one's own property; or wealth which is acquired in the front and which causes future troubles or provokes an enemy in the rear; or wealth which is obtained by destroying a friend or by breaking a treaty and which is therefore detested by the circle of states–all these are the varieties of dangerous wealth.

Wealth which causes fear from one's own people or from an enemy is provocative wealth.

When, in connection with these two kinds of wealth, there arise doubts, such as: 'Is it provocative wealth or not? Harmless wealth or provocative wealth? First provocative and then harmless? Is it profitable to encourage an enemy or a friend? Would the bestowal of wealth and honour on an enemy's army excite hatred or not?'—of these doubts, doubt regarding the acquirement of wealth is preferable to (doubts regarding harm or provocation).

Wealth productive of wealth; wealth productive of nothing; wealth productive of harm; loss or harm productive of wealth; sustenance of harm for no profit; harm productive of harm—these are the six varieties of harmful wealth.

Destruction of an enemy in the front resulting in the destruction of an enemy in the rear is what is termed 'wealth productive of wealth'.

Wealth acquired by helping a neutral king with the army is what is called 'wealth productive of nothing'.

The reduction of the internal strength of an enemy is 'wealth productive of harm'.

Helping the neighbouring king of an enemy with men and money is 'harm productive of wealth'. Withdrawal after encouraging or setting a king of poor resources (against another) is 'harm productive of nothing'.

Inactivity after causing excitement to a superior king is 'harm productive of harm'.

Of these, it is better to pursue that which is mentioned first in the order of enumeration than that which is subsequently mentioned. Thus the procedure of setting to work.

When the surrounding circumstances are conducive to wealth, it is known as wealth from all sides.

When the acquirement of wealth from all sides is obstructed by an enemy in the rear, it takes the form of dangerous wealth involved in doubts.

In these two cases, success can be achieved by securing the help of a friend and the enemy of the rear enemy. When there is reason to apprehend fear from enemies on all sides, it is a dangerous trouble; when a friend comes forward to avert this fear, that trouble becomes involved in doubt. In these two cases, success can be achieved by securing the support of a nomadic enemy and the enemy of the rear enemy.

When the prospect of acquiring profit from one or the other side is irremediably obstructed by enemies, it is called 'dangerous wealth'. In this case as well as in the case of profit from all sides, one should undertake to march for acquiring profitable wealth. When the prospects of getting wealth (from two sides) are equal, one should march to secure that which is important, near, unfailing, and obtainable by easy means.

When there is the apprehension of harm from one quarter as well as from another, it is wealth beset with danger from two sides. In this case as well as in the case of wealth involved in danger from all sides, success is to be desired with the help of friends. In the absence of friends, he should attempt to ward off harm from one side with the help of an ally who can be easily won over; he should ward off harm from two sides with help of an ally of superior power; and he should ward off harm from all sides with all the resources he can command. When it is impossible to do this, he should run away, leaving all that belongs to him; for if he lives, his return to power is certain as in the case of *Suyatra* and *Udayana*.

When there is the prospect of wealth from one side and the apprehension of an attack from another, it is termed a situation beset with wealth and harm. In this case, he should march to acquire that wealth which will enable him to ward off the attack; otherwise he should attempt to avert the attack. This explains the situation which is beset with wealth and harm on all sides.

When there is the apprehension of harm from one side and when the prospect of acquiring wealth from another side is involved in doubt, it is termed doubt of harm and wealth from two sides. In this, he should ward off the harm first; when this is done, he should attempt to acquire the doubtful wealth. This explains the doubtful situation of harm and wealth from all sides.

When there is the prospect of wealth from one side and the apprehension of doubtful harm from another, it is a doubtful situation of harm and wealth from two sides. This explains the situation of doubtful harm and wealth from all sides. In this, he should attempt to ward off the doubts of harm against each of the elements of his sovereignty in order; for it is better to leave a friend under circumstances of doubtful harm, than the army; also the army may be left under circumstances of doubtful harm, but not the treasury. When all the elements of his sovereignty cannot be relieved from harm, he should attempt to relieve some of them at least. Among the elements, he should attempt to relieve first those animate elements which are most loyal, and free from firebrands and greedy men; of inanimate elements (he should relieve) that which is most precious and useful. Such elements as are capable of easy relief may be relieved by such means as an agreement of peace, observance of neutrality, and making peace with one and waging war with another. Those which require greater efforts may be relieved by other means.

Of deterioration, stagnation and progress, he should attempt to secure that which is mentioned later in the order of enumeration; or in the reverse order, if he finds that deterioration and other stages are conducive to future prosperity. Thus the determination of situations. This explains the situation of doubtful harm and wealth in the middle or at the close of a march.

Since doubts of wealth and harm are constantly associated with all expeditions, it is better to secure wealth by which it is easy to destroy an enemy in the rear and his allies, to recoup the loss of men and money, to make provisions during the time of sojourning abroad, to make good what is repayable, and to defend the state. Also harm or doubtful prospects of wealth in one's own state are always intolerable.

This explains the situation of doubtful harm in the middle of an expedition. But at the close of an expedition, it is better to acquire wealth either by reducing or destroying a reducible or assailable enemy than to get into a situation of doubtful harm, lest enemies might cause troubles. But, for one who is not the leader of combination of states, it is better to risk the situation of doubtful wealth or harm in the middle or at the close of an expedition, since one is not obliged to continue the expedition.

Wealth, virtue and enjoyment form the aggregate of the three kinds of wealth. Of these, it is better to secure that which is mentioned first than that which is subsequently mentioned in the order of enumeration.

Harm, sin and grief form the aggregate of the three kinds of harm. Of these, it is better to provide against that which is mentioned first, than that which is subsequently mentioned.

Wealth or harm, virtue or sin, and enjoyment or grief, are the aggregate of the three kinds of doubts. Of these, it is better to try that which is mentioned first than that which is mentioned later in the order of enumeration, and which it is certain to shake off. Thus the determination of opportunities. Thus ends the discourse on danger.

Regarding success in these dangerous situations and times: in the case of troubles from sons, brothers or relatives, it is better to secure relief by means of conciliation and gifts; in the case of troubles from citizens, country people, or chiefs of the army, it is by means of gifts and sowing the seeds of dissension; in the case of troubles from a neighbouring king or wild tribes, it is by means of sowing the seeds of dissension and coercion. This is following the order of the means. In other kinds of situations, the same means may be employed in the reverse order.

Success against friends and enemies is always achieved by complicated means; for strategic means help each other. In the case of suspected ministers of an enemy, the employment of conciliation does not need the use of the other means; in the case of treacherous ministers it is by means of gifts; in the case of combination of states, it is by means of sowing the seeds of dissension; and in the case of the powerful, it is by means of coercion.

When grave and light dangers are together apprehended, a particular means, or alternative means, or all the means may be employed.

By this alone, but not by any other means, is what is meant by a particular means.

By this or that, is what is meant by alternative means.

By this as well as by that, is what is meant by all the means.

Of these, the single means as well as the combination of any three means are four; the combinations of any two means are six; and the combination of all the four is one. Thus there are fifteen kinds of strategic means. Of the same number are the means in the reverse order.

When a king attains success by only one means among these various means, he is called one of single success; when by two, one of double success; when by three, one of treble success; and when by four, one of fourfold success.

As virtue is the basis of wealth and as enjoyment is the end of wealth, success in achieving that kind of wealth which promotes virtue, wealth and enjoyment is termed success in all (*sarvarthasiddhi*). Thus varieties of success.

Such providential visitations as fire, floods, disease, pestilence (*pramara*), fever (*vidrava*), famine, and demoniac troubles are dangerous.

Success in averting these is to be sought by worshipping gods and Brahmans.

Whether demoniacal troubles are absent, or are too many, or normal, the rites prescribed in the *Atharvaveda* as well as the rites undertaken by accomplished ascetics are to be performed for success.

[Thus ends Chapter 7, 'Doubts about Wealth and Harm; and Success to Be Obtained by the Employment of Alternative Strategic Means' in Book IX, 'The Work of an Invader', of the Arthashastra of Kautilya. End of the 128th chapter from the beginning. With this, ends the ninth Book 'The Work of an Invader' of the *Arthashastra* of Kautilya.]

Book X

Relating to War

Chapter 1

ENCAMPMENT

ON a site declared to be the best according to the science of buildings, the leader (*nayaka*), the carpenter (*vardhaki*), and the astrologer (*mauhurtika*) should measure a circular, rectangular, or square spot for the camp which should, in accordance with the available space, consist of four gates, six roads and nine divisions.

Provided with ditches, parapets, walls, doors, and watchtowers for defence against fear, the quarters of the king, 1,000 bows long and half as broad, should be situated in one of the nine divisions to the north from the centre, while to the west of it his harem, and at its extremity the army of the harem are to be situated. In his front, the place for worshipping gods; to his right the departments of finance and accounts; and to his left the quarters of elephants and horses mounted by the king himself. Outside this and at a distance of 100 bows from each other, there should be fixed four cart-poles (*sakatamedhi*), pillars and walls. In the first (of these four divisions), the prime minister and the priest (should have their quarters); to its right the storehouse and the kitchen: to its left the store of raw products and weapons; in the second division the quarters of the hereditary army and of horses and chariots; outside this, hunters and keepers of dogs with their trumpets and with fire; also spies and sentinels; also, to prevent the attack of enemies, wells, mounds and thorns should be arranged. The eighteen divisions of sentinels employed for the purpose of securing the safety of the king should be changing their watches in turn. In order to ascertain the movements of spies, a timetable of business should also be prepared during the day. Disputes, drinking, social gatherings and gambling should also be prohibited. The system of passports should also be observed. The officer in charge of the boundary (of the camp) should supervise the conduct of the commander-in-chief and the observance of the instructions given to the army.

The instructor (*prasasta*) with his retinue and with carpenters and free labourers should carefully march in front on the road, and should dig wells of water.

[Thus ends Chapter I, 'Encampment', in Book X, 'Relating to War', of the Arthashastra of Kautilya. End of the 129th chapter from the beginning.]

Chapter 2

MARCH OF THE CAMP; AND PROTECTION OF THE ARMY IN TIMES OF DISTRESS AND ATTACK

HAVING prepared a list of the villages and forests situated on the road with reference to their capacity to supply grass, firewood and water, march of the army should be regulated according to the programme of short and long halts. Foodstuffs and provisions should be carried in double the quantity that may be required in any emergency. In the absence of separate means to carry foodstuffs, the army itself should be entrusted with the business of carrying them; or they may be stored in a central place.

In front the leader (*nayaka*); in the centre the harem and the master (the king); on the sides horses and bodyguards (*bahutsara*); at the extremity of the (marching) circular array, elephants and the surplus army; on all sides the army habituated to forest life; and other troops following the camp, the commissariat, the army of an ally, and his followers should select their own road; for armies who have secured suitable positions will prove superior in fight to those who are in bad positions.

The army of the lowest quality can march a *yojana* (5 5⁄44 miles a day); that of the middle quality a *yojana* and a half and the best army two *yojanas*. Hence, it is easy to ascertain the rate of march. The commander should march behind and put up his camp in the front.

In case of any obstruction, the army should march in crocodile array in the front, in cart-like array behind, and on the sides in diamond-like array (i.e., in four or five rows, each having its front, rear and sides) and in a compact array on all sides. When the army is marching on a path passable by a single man, it should march in pin-like array. When peace is made with one and war is to be waged with another, steps should be taken to protect the friends who are bringing help against enemies, such as an enemy in the rear, his ally, a *madhyama* king, or a neutral king. Roads with obstructions should be examined and cleared. Finance, the army, the strength of the armies of friends, enemies, and wild tribes, the prospect of rains, and the seasons should be thoroughly examined.

When the protective power of fortifications and stores (of the enemies) is on its decay, when it is thought that distress of the hired army or of a friend's army (of the enemy) is impending; when intriguers are not for a quick march; or when the enemy is likely to come to terms (with the invader), slow march should be made; otherwise quick march should be made.

Waters may be crossed by means of elephants, planks spread over pillars erected, bridges, boats, timber and mass of bamboos, as well as by means of dry sour gourds, big baskets covered with skins, rafts, *gandika* (i), and *venika* (i).

When the crossing of a river is obstructed by the enemy, the invader may cross it elsewhere together with his elephants and horses, and entangle the enemy in an ambuscade (*sattra*).

He should protect his army when it has to pass a long desert without water; when it is without grass, firewood and water; when it has to traverse a difficult road; when it is harassed by an enemy's attacks; when it is suffering from hunger and thirst after a journey;

when it is ascending or descending a mountainous country full of mire, pools of water, rivers and cataracts; when it finds itself crowded in a narrow and difficult path; when it is halting, starting or eating; when it is tired from a long march; when it is sleepy; when it is suffering from a disease, pestilence or famine; when a great portion of its infantry, cavalry and elephants is diseased; when it is not sufficiently strong; or when it is under troubles. He should destroy the enemy's army under such circumstances.

When the enemy's army is marching through a path traversable by a single man, the commander (of the invader's army) should ascertain its strength by estimating the quantity of foodstuffs, grass, bedding, and other requisites, fire pots (*agninidhana*), flags and weapons. He should also conceal those of his own army.

Keeping a mountainous or river fortress with all its resources at his back in his own country he should fight or put up his camp.

[Thus ends Chapter 2, 'March of the Camp; and Protection of the Army in Times of Distress and Attack' in Book X, 'Relating to War' of the Arthashastra of Kautilya. End of the 130th chapter from the beginning.]

Chapter 3

FORMS OF TREACHEROUS FIGHTS; ENCOURAGEMENT TO ONE'S OWN ARMY AND FIGHT BETWEEN ONE'S OWN AND ENEMY'S ARMIES

HE who is possessed of a strong army, who has succeeded in his intrigues, and who has applied remedies against dangers may undertake an open fight, if he has secured a position favourable to himself; otherwise a treacherous fight.

He should strike the enemy when the latter's army is under troubles or is furiously attacked; or he who has secured a favourable position may strike the enemy entangled in an unfavourable position. Or he who possesses control over the elements of his own state may, through the aid of the enemy's traitors, enemies and inimical wild tribes, make a false impression of his own defeat on the mind of the enemy who is entrenched in a favourable position, and having thus dragged the enemy into an unfavourable position, he may strike the latter. When the enemy's army is in a compact body, he should break it by means of his elephants; when the enemy has come down from its favourable position, following the false impression of the invader's defeat, the invader may turn back and strike the enemy's army, broken or unbroken. Having struck the front of the enemy's army, he may strike it again by means of his elephants and horses when it has shown its back and is running away. When frontal attack is unfavourable, he should strike it from behind; when attack on the rear is unfavourable, he should strike it in front; when attack on one side is unfavourable, he should strike it on the other.

Or having caused the enemy to fight with his own army of traitors, enemies and wild tribes, the invader should, with his fresh army, strike the enemy when tired. Or having through the aid of the army of traitors given to the enemy the impression of defeat, the invader with full confidence in his own strength may allure and strike the over-confident enemy. Or the invader, if he is vigilant, may strike the careless enemy when the latter is deluded with the thought that the invader's merchants, camp and carriers have been destroyed. Or having made his strong force look like a weak force, he may strike the enemy's brave men when falling against him. Or having captured the enemy's cattle or having destroyed the enemy's dogs (*svapadavadha*?), he may induce the enemy's brave men to come out and may slay them. Or having made the enemy's men sleepless by harassing them at night, he may strike them during the day, when they are weary from want of sleep and are parched by heat, himself being under the shade. Or with his army of elephants enshrouded with cotton and leather dress, he may offer a night-battle to his enemy. Or he may strike the enemy's men during the afternoon when they are tired by making preparations during the forenoon; or he may strike the whole of the enemy's army when it is facing the sun.

A desert, a dangerous spot, marshy places, mountains, valleys, uneven boats, cows, cart-like array of the army, mist, and night are *sattras* (temptations alluring the enemy against the invader).

The beginning of an attack is the time for treacherous fights. As to an open or fair fight, a virtuous king should call his army together, and, specifying the place and time of battle, address them thus: 'I am a paid servant like yourselves; this country is to be enjoyed (by me) together with you; you have to strike the enemy specified by me'.

His minister and priest should encourage the army by saying thus:

'It is declared in the Vedas that the goal which is reached by sacrificers after performing the final ablutions in sacrifices in which the priests have been duly paid for is the very goal which brave men are destined to attain.' About this there are the two verses–

• Beyond those places which Brahmans, desirous of getting into heaven, attain together with their sacrificial instruments by performing a number of sacrifices, or by practising penance are the places which brave men, losing life in good battles, are destined to attain immediately.

• Let not a new vessel filled with water, consecrated and covered over with *darbha* grass be the acquisition of that man who does not fight in return for the subsistence received by him from his master, and who is therefore destined to go to hell.

Astrologers and other followers of the king should infuse spirit into his army by pointing out the impregnable nature of the array of his army, his power to associate with gods, and his omniscience; and they should at the same time frighten the enemy. The day before the battle, the king should fast and lie down on his chariot with weapons. He should also make oblations into the fire pronouncing the *mantra*s of the Atharvaveda, and cause prayers to be offered for the good of the victors as well as of those who attain heaven by dying in the battlefield. He should also submit his person to Brahmans; he should make the central portion of his army consist of such men as are noted for their bravery, skill, high birth and loyalty, and as are not displeased with the rewards and honours bestowed on them. The place that is to be occupied by the king is that portion of the army which is composed of his father, sons, brothers, and other men, skilled in using weapons, and having no flags and headdress. He should mount an elephant or a chariot, if the army consists mostly of horses; or he may mount that kind of animal, of which the army is mostly composed or which is the most skilfully trained. One who is disguised like the king should attend to the work of arraying the army.

Soothsayers and court bards should describe heaven as the goal for the brave and hell for the timid; and also extol the caste, corporation, family, deeds and character of his men. The followers of the priest should proclaim the auspicious aspects of the witchcraft performed. Spies, carpenters and astrologers should also declare the success of their own operations and the failure of those of the enemy.

After having pleased the army with rewards and honours, the commander-in-chief should address it and say:

A hundred thousand (*panas*) for slaying the king (the enemy); fifty thousand for slaying the commander-in-chief, and the heir apparent; ten thousand for slaying the chief of the brave; five thousand for destroying an elephant, or a chariot; a thousand for killing a horse, a hundred (*panas*) for slaying the chief of the infantry; twenty for bringing a head; and twice the pay in addition to whatever is seized. This information should be made known to the leaders of every group of ten (men).

Physicians with surgical instruments (*sastra*), machines, remedial oils and cloth in their hands; and women with prepared food and beverage should stand behind, uttering encouraging words to fighting men.

The army should be arrayed on a favourable position, facing other than the south quarter, with its back turned to the sun, and capable to rush as it stands. If the array is made on an unfavourable spot, horses should be run. If the army arrayed on an unfavourable position is confined or is made to run away from it (by the enemy), it will be subjugated either as standing or running away; otherwise it will conquer the enemy when standing or running away. The even, uneven and complex nature of the ground in the front or on the sides or in the rear should be examined. On an even site, staff-like or circular array should be made; and on an uneven ground, arrays of compact movement or of detached bodies should be made.

Having broken the whole army (of the enemy), (the invader) should seek for peace; if the armies are of equal strength, he should make peace when requested for it; and if the enemy's army is inferior, he should attempt to destroy it, but not that which has secured a favourable position and is reckless of life.

When a broken army, reckless of life, resumes its attack, its fury becomes irresistible; hence he should not harass a broken army (of the enemy).

[Thus ends Chapter 3, 'Forms of Treacherous Fights; Encouragement to One's Own Army and Fight Between One's Own and Enemy's Armies', in Book X, 'Relating to War', of the Arthashastra of Kautilya. End of the 131st chapter from the beginning.]

Chapter 4

BATTLEFIELDS; THE WORK OF INFANTRY, CAVALRY, CHARIOTS, AND ELEPHANTS

FAVOURABLE positions for infantry, cavalry, chariots and elephants are desirable both for war and camp.

For men who are trained to fight in desert tracts, forests, valleys or plains, and for those who are trained to fight from ditches or heights, during the day or night, and for elephants which are bred in countries with rivers, mountains, marshy lands or lakes, as well as for horses, such battlefields as they would find suitable (are to be secured).

That which is even, splendidly firm, free from mounds and pits made by wheels and footprints of beasts, not offering obstructions to the axle, free from trees, plants, creepers and trunks of trees, not wet, and free from pits, anthills, sand and thorns is the ground for chariots.

For elephants, horses and men, even or uneven grounds are good, either for war or for camp.

That which contains small stones, trees and pits that can be jumped over and which is almost free from thorns is the ground for horses.

That which contains big stones, dry or green trees, and anthills is the ground for the infantry.

That which is uneven with assailable hills and valleys, which has trees that can be pulled down and plants that can be torn, and which is full of muddy soil free from thorns is the ground for elephants.

That which is free from thorns, not very uneven, but very expansive, is an excellent ground for the infantry.

That which is doubly expansive, free from mud, water and roots of trees, and which is devoid of piercing gravel is an excellent ground for horses.

That which possesses dust, muddy soil, water, grass and weeds, and which is free from thorns (known as dog's teeth) and obstructions from the branches of big trees is an excellent ground for elephants.

That which contains lakes, which is free from mounds and wetlands, and which affords space for turning is an excellent ground for chariots.

Positions suitable for all the constituents of the army have been treated of. This explains the nature of the ground which is fit for the camp or battle of all kinds of the army.

Concentration on occupied positions, in camps and forests; holding the ropes (of beasts and other things) while crossing the rivers or when the wind is blowing hard; destruction or protection of the commissariat and of troops arriving afresh; supervision of the discipline of the army; lengthening the line of the army; protecting the sides of the army; first attack; dispersion (of the enemy's army); trampling it down; defence; seizing; letting it out; causing the army to take a different direction; carrying the treasury and the princes; falling against the rear of the enemy; chasing the timid; pursuit; and concentration—these constitute the work of horses.

Marching in the front; preparing the roads, camping grounds and path for bringing water; protecting the sides; firm standing, fording and entering into water while crossing pools of water and ascending from them; forced entrance into impregnable places; setting or quenching the fire; the subjugation of one of the four constituents of the army; gathering the dispersed army; breaking a compact army; protection against dangers; trampling down (the enemy's army); frightening and driving it; magnificence; seizing; abandoning; destruction of walls, gates and towers; and carrying the treasury—these constitute the work of elephants.

Protection of the army; repelling the attack made by all the four constituents of the enemy's army; seizing and abandoning (positions) during the time of battle; gathering a dispersed army; breaking the compact array of the enemy's army; frightening it; magnificence; and fearful noise—these constitute the work of chariots.

Always carrying the weapons to all places; and fighting—these constitute the work of the infantry.

The examination of camps, roads, bridges, wells and rivers; carrying the machines, weapons, armours, instruments and provisions; carrying away the men that are knocked down, along with their weapons and armours—these constitute the work of free labourers.

The king who has a small number of horses may combine bulls with horses; likewise when he is deficient in elephants, he may fill up the centre of his army with mules, camels and carts.

[Thus ends Chapter 4, 'Battlefields; the Work of Infantry, Cavalry, Chariots, and Elephants', in Book X, 'Relating to War', of the Arthashastra of Kautilya. End of the 132nd chapter from the beginning.]

Chapter 5

THE DISTINCTIVE ARRAY OF TROOPS IN RESPECT OF WINGS, FLANKS, AND FRONT; DISTINCTION BETWEEN STRONG AND WEAK TROOPS; AND BATTLE WITH INFANTRY, CAVALRY, CHARIOTS AND ELEPHANTS

HAVING fortified a camp at the distance of five hundred bows he should begin to fight. Having detached the flower of the army and kept it on a favourable position not visible (to the enemy), the commander-in-chief and the leader should array the rest of the army. The infantry should be arrayed such that the space between any two men is a *sama* (14 *angulas*); cavalry with three *samas*; chariots with four *samas;* and elephants with twice or thrice as much space (as between any two chariots). With such an array free to move and having no confusion, one should fight. A bow means five *aratni*s (5 × 54, i.e., 120 *angula*s). Archers should be stationed at the distance of five bows (from one line to another); the cavalry at the distance of three bows; and chariots or elephants at the distance of five bows.

The intervening space (*anikasandhi*) between wings, flanks and front of the army should be five bows. There must be three men to oppose a horse (*pratiyoddha*); fifteen men or five horses to oppose a chariot or an elephant; and as many (fifteen) servants (*padagopa)* for a horse, a chariot and an elephant should be maintained.

Three groups (*anika*) of three chariots each should be stationed in front; the same number on the two flanks and the two wings. Thus, in an array of chariots, the number of chariots amounts to forty-five, 225 horses, 675 men, and as many servants to attend upon the horses, chariots and elephants—this is called an even array of troops. The number of chariots in this array (of three groups of three chariots each) may be increased by two and two till the increased number amounts to twenty-one. Thus, this array of odd numbers of chariots gives rise to ten odd varieties. Thus the surplus of the army may therefore be distributed in the above manner. Two-thirds of the (surplus) chariots may be added to the flanks and the wings, the rest being put in front. Thus the added surplus of chariots should be one-third less (than the number added to the flanks and wings). This explains the distribution of surplus elephants and horses. As many horses, chariots and elephants may be added as occasion no confusion in fighting.

Excess of the army is called surplus (*avapa*); deficiency in infantry is called absence of surplus (*pratyavapa*); excess of anyone of the four constituents of the army is akin to surplus (*anvavapa*); excess of traitors is far from surplus (*atyavapa*); in accordance with one's own resources, one should increase one's army from four to eight times the excess of the enemy's army or the deficiency in the enemy's infantry.

The array of elephants is explained by the array of chariots. An array of elephants, chariots and horses mixed together may also be made: at the extremities of the circle (array), elephants; and on the flanks, horses and principal chariots. The array in which the front is occupied by elephants, the flanks by chariots, and the wings by horses is an array which can break the centre of the enemy's army; the reverse of this can harass the extremities of the enemy's army. An array of elephants may also be made: the front by such elephants as are trained for war; the flanks by such as are trained for riding; and the wings by rogue elephants. In an array of horses, the front by horses with mail armour; and the flanks and wings by horses without armour. In an array of infantry, men dressed in mail armour in front, archers in the rear, and men without armour on the wings; or horses on the wings, elephants on the flanks, and chariots in front; other changes may also be made so as to oppose the enemy's army successfully.

The best army is that which consists of strong infantry and of such elephants and horses as are noted for their breed, birth, strength, youth, vitality, capacity to run even in old age, fury, skill, firmness, magnanimity, obedience and good habits.

One-third of the best of infantry, cavalry and elephants should be kept in front; two-thirds on both the flanks and wings; the array of the army according to the strength of its constituents is in the direct order; that which is arrayed mixing one-third of strong and weak troops is in the reverse order. Thus, one should know all the varieties of arraying the array.

Having stationed the weak troops at the extremities, one would be liable to the force of the enemy's onslaught. Having stationed the flower of the army in front, one should make the wings equally strong. One-third of the best in the rear, and weak troops in the centre—this array is able to resist the enemy; having made an array, he should strike the enemy with one or two of the divisions on the wings, flanks and front, and capture the enemy by means of the rest of the troops.

When the enemy's force is weak, with few horses and elephants, and is contaminated with the intrigue of treacherous ministers, the conqueror should strike it with most of his best troops. He should increase the numerical strength of that constituent of the army which is physically weak. He should array his troops on that side on which the enemy is weak or from which danger is apprehended.

Running against; running round; running beyond; running back; disturbing the enemy's halt; gathering the troops; curving, circling, miscellaneous operations; removal of the rear; pursuit of the line from the front, flanks and rear; protection of the broken army; and falling upon the broken army—these are the forms of waging war with horses.

The same varieties with the exception of (what is called) miscellaneous operations; the destruction of the four constituents of the army, either single or combined; the dispersion of the flanks, wings and front trampling down; and attacking the army when it is asleep—these are the varieties of waging war with elephants.

The same varieties with the exception of disturbing the enemy's halt; running against; running back; and fighting from where it stands on its own ground—these are the varieties of waging war with chariots.

Striking in all places and at all times, and striking by surprise are varieties of waging war with infantry.

• In this way, he should make odd or even arrays, keeping the strength of the four constituents of the army equal.

• Having gone to a distance of 200 bows, the king should take his position together with the reserve of his army; and without a reserve, he should never attempt to fight, for it is by the reserved force that dispersed troops are collected together.

[Thus ends Chapter 5, 'The Distinctive Array of Troops in Respect of Wings, Flanks, and Front; Distinction Between Strong and Weak Troops; and Battle with Infantry, Cavalry, Chariots and Elephants', in Book X, 'Relating to War', of the Arthashastra of Kautilya. End of the 133rd chapter from the beginning.]

Chapter 6

THE ARRAY OF THE ARMY LIKE A STAFF, A SNAKE, A CIRCLE, OR IN DETACHED ORDER; THE ARRAY OF THE ARMY AGAINST THAT OF AN ENEMY

WINGS and front, capable to turn (against an enemy is what is called) a snake-like array (*bhoga*); the two wings, the two flanks, the front and the reserve (form an array) according to the school of Brihaspati. The principal forms of the array of the army, such as that like a staff, like a snake, like a circle, and in detached order, are varieties of the above two forms of the array consisting of wings, flanks and front.

Stationing the army so as to stand abreast, is called a staff-like array (*danda*).

Stationing the army in a line so that one may follow the other, is called a snake-like array (*bhoga*).

Stationing the army so as to face all the directions, is called a circle-like array (*mandala*).

Detached arrangement of the army into small bodies so as to enable each to act for itself, is termed an array in detached order (*asamhata*).

That which is of equal strength on its wings, flanks and front is a staff-like array.

The same array is called *pradara* (breaking the enemy's array) when its flanks are made to project in front.

The same is called *dridhaka* (firm) when its wings and flanks are stretched back.

The same is called *asahya* (irresistible) when its wings are lengthened.

When, having formed the wings, the front is made to bulge out, it is called an eagle-like array.

The same four varieties are called 'a bow', 'the centre of a bow', 'a hold', and 'a strong hold', when they are arranged in a reverse form.

That, of which the wings are arrayed like a bow, is called *sanjaya* (victory).

The same with projected front is called *vijaya* (conqueror); that which has its flanks and wings formed like a staff is called *sthulakarna* (big ear); the same with its front made twice as strong as the conqueror is called *visalavijaya* (vast victory); that which has its wings stretched forward is called *chamumukha* (face of the army); and the same is called *ghashasya* (face of the fish) when it is arrayed in the reverse form.

The staff-like array in which one (constituent of the army) is made to stand behind the other is called a pin-like array.

When this array consists of two such lines, it is called an aggregate (*valaya*); and when of four lines, it is called an invincible array—these are the varieties of the staff-like array.

The snake-like array in which the wings, flanks and front are of unequal depth is called *sarpasari* (serpentine movement), or *gomutrika* (the course of a cow's urine).

When it consists of two lines in front and has its wings arranged as in the staff-like array, it is called a cart-like array; the reverse of this is called a crocodile-like array; the cart-like array which consists of elephants, horses and chariots is called *varipatantaka* (?)—these are the varieties of the snake-like array.

The circle-like array in which the distinction of wings, flanks and front is lost is called *sarvatomukha* (facing all directions), or *sarvatobhadra* (all auspicious), *ashtanika* (one of eight divisions), or *vijaya* (victory)—these are the varieties of the circle-like array.

That, of which the wings, flanks and front are stationed apart is called an array in detached order; when five divisions of the army are arranged in detached order, it is called *vajra* (diamond), or *godha* (alligator); when four divisions, it is called *udyanaka* (park), or *kakapadi* (crow's foot); when three divisions, it is called a*rdhachandrika* (half moon), or *karkatakasringi* (?)—these are the varieties of the array in detached-order.

The array in which chariots form the front, elephants the wings, and horses the rear, is called *arishta* (auspicious).

The array in which infantry, cavalry, chariots and elephants stand one behind the other is called *achala* (immovable).

The array in which elephants, horses, chariots and infantry stand in order one behind the other is called *apratihata* (invincible).

Of these, the conqueror should assail the *pradara* by means of the *dridhaka*; *dridhaka* by means of the *asahya*; *syena* (eagle-like array) by means of *chapa* (an array like a bow); a hold by means of a stronghold; *sanjaya* by means of *vijaya*; *sthulakarna* by means of *visalavijaya; varipatantaka* by means of *sarvatobhadra.* He may assail all kinds of arrays by means of the *durjaya.*

Of infantry, cavalry, chariots and elephants, he should strike the first-mentioned with that which is subsequently mentioned; and a small constituent of the army with a big one.

For every ten members of each of the constituents of the army, there must be one commander, called *padika*; ten *padika*s under a *senapati*; ten *senapati*s under a *nayaka* (leader).

The constituents of the array of the army should be called after the names of trumpet sounds, flags and ensigns. Achievement of success in arranging the constituents of the army, in gathering the forces, in camping, in marching, in turning back, in making onslaughts, and in the array of equal strength depends upon the place and time of action.

• By the display of the army, by secret contrivances, by fiery spies employed to strike the enemy engaged otherwise, by witchcraft, by proclaiming the conqueror's association with gods, by carts, by the ornaments of elephants;

• By inciting traitors, by herds of cattle, by setting fire to the camp, by destroying the wings and the rear of the enemy's army, by sowing the seeds of dissension through the agency of men under the guise of servants;

• Or by telling the enemy that his fort was burnt, stormed, or that some one of his family, or an enemy or a wild chief rose in rebellion—by these and other means the conqueror should cause excitement to the enemy.

• The arrow shot by an archer may or may not kill a single man; but skilful intrigue devised by wise men can kill even those who are in the womb.

[Thus ends Chapter 6, 'The Array of the Army Like a Staff, a Snake, a Circle, or in Detached Order; The Array of the Army Against that of an Enemy', in Book X, 'Relating to War', of the Arthashastra of Kautilya. End of the 134h chapter from the beginning. With this ends the tenth Book 'Relating to War' of the Arthashastra of Kautilya.]

Book XI

The Conduct of Corporations

Chapter 1

CAUSES OF DISSENSION; AND SECRET PUNISHMENT

THE acquisition of the help of corporations is better than the acquisition of an army, a friend or profits. By means of conciliation and gifts, the conqueror should secure and enjoy the services of such corporations as are invincible to the enemy and are favourably disposed towards himself. But those who are opposed to him, he should put down by sowing the seeds of dissension among them and by secretly punishing them.

The corporations of warriors (*kshattriyasreni*) of Kambhoja, and Surashtra, and other countries live by agriculture, trade and wielding weapons.

The corporations of Lichchhivika,Vrijika, Mallaka, Mudraka, Kukura, Kuru, Panchala and others live by the title of a Raja.

Spies, gaining access to all these corporations and finding out jealousy, hatred and other causes of quarrel among them, should sow the seeds of a well-planned dissension among them, and tell one of them: 'This man decries you.' Spies, under the guise of teachers (*acharya*) should cause childish embroils among those of mutual enmity on occasions of disputations about certain points of science, arts, gambling or sports. Fiery spies may occasion quarrel among the leaders of corporations by praising inferior leaders in taverns and theatres; or pretending to be friends, they may excite ambition in the minds of princes by praising their high birth, though they (the princes) are low-born; they may prevent the superiors from interdining and intermarriage with others; they may persuade the superiors to interdine or to intermarry with inferiors; or they may give publicity to the consideration of priority shown to inferior persons in social intercourse in the face of the established custom of recognizing the status of other persons by birth, bravery and social position; or fiery spies may bring about quarrel among them at night by destroying the things, beasts or persons concerned in some legal disputes. In all these disputes, the conqueror should help the inferior party with men and money and set them against the superior party. When they are divided, he should remove them (from their country); or he may gather them together and cause them to settle in a cultivable part of their own country, under the designation of 'five households' and 'ten households'; for when living together, they can be trained in the art of wielding weapons. Specified fines should also be prescribed against any treacherous combinations among them. He may install as the heir apparent a prince born of a high family, but dethroned or imprisoned. Spies, under the guise of astrologers and others, should bring to the notice of the corporations the royal characteristics of the prince, and should induce the virtuous leaders of the corporations to acknowledge their duty to the prince who is the son of such and such a king, and who is the hearer of their complaints. To those who are thus prevailed upon, the conqueror should send men and money for the purpose of winning over other partisans. On occasions of any affray, spies under the guise of vintners, should, under the plea of the birth of a son, of marriage or of the death of a man, distribute as toast (*naishechanika*) hundreds of vessels of liquor adulterated with the juice of *madana* plant. Near the gates of altars (*chaitya*), temples and other places under the watch of sentinels, spies should pretend to declare their agreement (with the enemy of the corporations), their mission, their rewards, and bags of money with the golden seals of the enemy; when the corporations appear before the spies, they may tell the corporations that they (the spies) have sold themselves to the enemy, and challenge the corporations for war. Or having seized the draught animals and golden articles belonging to the corporations, they may give the most important of those animals and articles to the chief of the corporations, and tell the corporations, when asked for, that it was given to the chief (for the purpose of causing quarrel among them).

This explains the method of sowing the seeds of dissension in camps and among wild tribes.

Or a spy may tell a self-confident son of the chief of corporations: 'You are the son of such and such a king and are kept here under the apprehension of danger from enemies.' When he is deluded with this belief, the conqueror may help him with men and money and set him against the corporations. When the object in view is realized, the conqueror may also banish him.

Keepers of harlots or dancers, players and actors may, after gaining access, excite love in the minds of the chiefs of corporations by exhibiting women endowed with bewitching youth and beauty. By causing the woman to go to another person or by pretending that another person has violently carried her off, they may bring about quarrel among those who love that woman; in the ensuing affray, fiery spies may do their work and declare: 'Thus has he been killed in consequence of his love.'

A woman who has disappointed her lover and has been forgiven, may approach a chief and say: 'This chief is troubling me when my mind is set upon you; when he is alive, I cannot stay here,' and thus induce the former to slay the latter.

A woman who has been violently carried off at night may cause the death of her violator in the vicinity of a park or in a pleasure house, by means of fiery spies or with poison administered by herself. Then she may declare: 'This beloved person of mine has been killed by such and such a person.'

A spy, under the garb of an ascetic, may apply to a lover such medical ointments as are declared to be capable of captivating the beloved woman and as are adulterated with poison; and then he may disappear. Other spies may ascribe the incident to an enemy's action.

Widows or women, employed as spies with secret instructions, may dispute among themselves about the claim for a deposit kept with the king, and attract the chiefs of the corporations (by their beauty when they present themselves before the king).

Harlots, or a dancing woman, or a songstress may make an appointment to meet a lover in some secret house; and when the lover comes to the house with the desire of meeting her there, fiery spies may kill him or carry him off bound (in chains).

A spy may tell the chief of a corporation who is fond of women: 'In this village, the family of a poor man is bereaved (of the householder); his wife deserves to be the wife of a king; seize her'. Half a month after she has been seized, an ascetic spy may accuse the chief in the midst of the corporation by saying: 'This man has illegally kept my chief wife, or sister-in-law, or sister, or daughter.' If the corporation punishes the chief, the conqueror may take the side of the corporation and set it against wicked persons. Fiery spies should always cause an ascetic spy to go abroad at night. Spies, selected suitably, should accuse (the chiefs) by saying: 'This man is the slayer of a Brahman and also the adulterer of a Brahman woman.'

A spy, under the guise of an astrologer, may describe to a chief the destiny of a maiden who is at the point of being married to another, and say: 'This man's daughter deserves to be the wife of a king and will bring forth a son, destined to be a king; purchase her with all your wealth, or seize her by force'. When it is not possible to secure her, spies should enrage the parties; but when she is secured, quarrel will necessarily ensue.

A mendicant woman may tell a chief who is fond of his wife: 'This (another) chief, proud of his youth, has sent me to entice your wife; being afraid of him, I have taken with me his letter and jewellery (for your wife); your wife is free from sin; secret steps should be taken against him; and I am very anxious (about your success)'.

Thus in these and other kinds of brawls which have originated of themselves or which have been brought about by spies, the conqueror should help the inferior party with men and money and set them against the wicked or cause them to migrate (to other parts of the country).

Thus he should live as the only monarch of all the corporations; the corporations also, under the protection of such a single monarch, should guard themselves against all kinds of treachery.

The chief of corporations should endear himself to all the people by leading a virtuous life, by controlling his passions, and by pursuing that course of action which is liked by all those who are his followers.

[Thus ends Chapter 1, 'Causes of Dissension and Secret Punishment', in Book XI, 'The Conduct of Corporations', of the Arthashastra of Kautilya. End of the 135th chapter from the beginning. With this ends, 'The Conduct of Corporations', of the Arthashastra of Kautilya.]

Book XII

Concerning a Powerful Enemy

Chapter 1

THE DUTIES OF A MESSENGER

WHEN a king of poor resources is attacked by a powerful enemy, he should surrender himself together with his sons to the enemy and live like a reed (in the midst of a current of water).

Bharadvaja says that he, who surrenders himself to the strong, bows down before Indra (the god of rain).

But Visalaksha says that a weak king should rather fight with all his resources, for bravery destroys all troubles; this (fighting) is the natural duty of a Kshatriya, no matter whether he achieves victory or sustains defeat in battle.

No, says Kautilya, he who bows down to all like a crab on the banks (of a river) lives in despair; whoever goes with his small army to fight perishes like a man attempting to cross the sea without a boat. Hence, a weak king should either seek the protection of a powerful king or maintain himself in an impregnable fort.

Invaders are of three kinds: a just conqueror, a demon-like conqueror, and a greedy conqueror.

Of these, the just conqueror is satisfied with mere obeisance. Hence, a weak king should seek his protection.

Fearing his own enemies, the greedy conqueror is satisfied with what he can safely gain in land or money. Hence, a weak king should satisfy such a conqueror with wealth.

The demon-like conqueror satisfies himself not merely by seizing the land, treasure, sons and wives of the conquered, but by taking the life of the latter. Hence, a weak king should keep such a conqueror at a distance by offering him land and wealth.

When anyone of these is on the point of rising against a weak king, the latter should avert the invasion by making a treaty of peace, or by taking recourse to the battle of intrigue (*mantrayuddha*), or by a treacherous fight in the battlefield. He may seduce the enemy's men either by conciliation or by giving gifts, and should prevent the treacherous proceedings of his own men either by sowing the seeds of dissension among them or by punishing them. Spies, under concealment, may capture the enemy's fort, country, or camp with the aid of weapons, poison or fire. He may harass the enemy's rear on all sides; and he may devastate the enemy's country through the help of wild tribes. Or he may set up a scion of the enemy's family or an imprisoned prince to seize the enemy's territory. When all this mischief has been perpetrated, a messenger may be sent to the enemy (to sue for peace); or he may make peace with the enemy without offending the latter. If the enemy still continues the march, the weak king may sue for peace by offering more than one-fourth of his wealth and army, the payment being made after the lapse of a day and night.

If the enemy desires to make peace on condition of the weak king surrendering a portion of his army, he may give the enemy such of his elephants and cavalry as are uncontrollable or as are provided with poison; if the enemy desires to make peace on condition of his surrendering his chief men, he may send over to the enemy such portion of his army as is full of traitors, enemies and wild tribes under the command of a trusted officer, so that both his enemy and his own undesirable army may perish; or he may provide the enemy with an army composed of fiery spies, taking care to satisfy his own disappointed men (before sending them over to the enemy); or he may transfer to the enemy his own faithful and hereditary army that is capable to hurt the enemy on occasions of trouble; if the enemy desires to make peace on condition of his paying certain amount of wealth, he may give the enemy such precious articles as do not find a purchaser or such raw products as are of no use in war; if the enemy desires to make peace on condition of his ceding a part of his land, he should provide the enemy with that kind of land which he can recover, which is always at the mercy of another enemy, which possesses no protective defences, or which can be colonized at considerable cost of men and money; or he may make peace, surrendering his whole state except his capital.

He should so contrive as to make the enemy accept that which another enemy is likely to carry off by force; and he should take care more of his person than of his wealth, for of what interest is perishing wealth?

[Thus ends Chapter 1, 'The Duties of a Messenger', in Book XII, 'Concerning a Powerful Enemy', of the Arthashastra of Kautilya. End of the 136th chapter from the beginning.]

Chapter 2

BATTLE OF INTRIGUE

IF the enemy does not keep peace, he should be told: 'These kings perished by surrendering themselves to the aggregate of the six enemies; it is not worthy of you to follow the lead of these unwise kings; be mindful of virtue and wealth; those who advise you to brave danger, sin and violation of wealth are enemies under the guise of friends; it is danger to fight with men who are reckless of their own lives; it is sin to cause the loss of life on both sides; it is violation of wealth to abandon the wealth at hand and the friend of no mean character (meaning the addresser himself); that king has many friends whom he will set against you with the same wealth (that is acquired with your help at my expense), and who will fall upon you from all sides; that king has not lost his influence over the circle of the *madhyama* and neutral states; but you have lost that power over them who are, therefore, waiting for an opportunity to fall upon you; patiently bear the loss of men and money again; break peace with that friend; then we shall be able to remove him from that stronghold over which he has lost his influence. Hence, it is not worthy of you to lend your ear to those enemies with the face of friends, to expose your real friends to trouble, to help your enemies to attain success, and to involve yourself in dangers costing life and wealth.'

If without caring for the advice, the enemy proceeds on his own way, the weak king should create disaffection among the enemy's people by adopting such measures as are explained in the chapters, 'The Causes of Dissension; and Secret Punishment'(Book VI, Chapter 1) and 'Enticement of kings by Secret Contrivances' (Book XIII, Chapter 2). He should also make use of fiery spies and poison. Against what is described as deserving protection in the chapter, 'Personal Safety' (Book I, Chapter 21), fiery spies and poisoners should be employed (in the enemy's court). Keepers of harlots should excite love in the minds of the leaders of the enemy's army by exhibiting women endowed with youth and beauty. Fiery spies should bring about quarrels among them when one or two of them have fallen in love. In the affray that ensues they should prevail upon the defeated party to migrate elsewhere or to proceed to help the master (of the spies) in the invasion undertaken by the latter.

Or to those who have follow in love, spies under the guise of ascetics, may administer poison under the plea that the medical drugs given to them are capable of securing the object of love.

A spy, under the guise of a merchant, may, under the plea of winning the love of an immediate maidservant of the beautiful queen (of the enemy), shower wealth upon her and then give her up. A spy in the service of the merchant may give to another spy, employed as a servant of the maidservant, some medical drug, telling the latter that (in order to regain the love of the merchant), the drug may be applied to the person of the merchant (by the maidservant). On her attaining success (the maidservant) may inform the queen that the same drug may be applied to the person of the king (to secure his love), and then change the drug for poison.

A spy, under the guise of an astrologer, may gradually delude the enemy's prime minister with the belief that he is possessed of all the physiognomical characteristics of a king; a mendicant woman may tell the minister's wife that she has the characteristics of a queen and that she will bring forth a prince; or a woman, disguised as the minister's wife, may tell him, 'The king is troubling me; and an ascetic woman has brought to me this letter and jewellery.'

Spies, under the guise of cooks, may, under the pretence of the king's (the enemy's) order, take some covetable wealth (to the minister) meant for use in an immediate expedition. A spy under the guise of a merchant may, by some contrivance or other, take possession of that wealth and inform the minister of the readiness of all the preparations (for the expedition). Thus by the employment of one, two or three of the strategic means, the ministers of each of the combined enemies may be induced to set out on the expedition and thus to be away from the inimical kings.

Spies, under the service of the officer in charge of the enemy's wastelands, may inform the citizens and country people residing in the enemy's fortified towns of the condition of the officer's friendship with the people, and say: 'The officer in charge of the wastelands tells the warriors and departmental officers thus: 'The king has hardly escaped from danger and scarcely returns with life. Do not hoard up your wealth and thereby create enemies; if so, you will all be put to death.' When all the people are collected together, fiery spies may take the citizens out of the town and kill their leaders, saying: 'Thus will be treated those who do not hear the officer in charge of the wastelands'. On the wastelands under the charge of the officer, the spies may throw down weapons, money and ropes bespattered with blood. Then other spies may spread the news that the officer in charge of the wastelands destroys the people and plunders them. Similarly, spies may cause disagreement between the enemy's collector general and the people. Addressing the servants of the collector general in the centre of the village at night, fiery spies may say: 'Thus will be treated those who subject the people to unjust oppression'. When the fault of the collector general or of the officer in charge of the wastelands is widely known, the spies may cause the people to slay either of them, and employ in his place one of his family or one who is imprisoned.

Spreading the false news of the danger of the enemy, they (spies) may set fire to the harem, the gates of the town and the storehouse of grains and other things, and slay the sentinels who are kept to guard them.

[Thus ends Chapter 3, 'Battle of Intrigue', in Book XII, 'Concerning a Powerful Enemy', of the Arthashastra of Kautilya. End of the 137th chapter from the beginning.]

Chapter 3

SLAYING THE COMMANDER-IN-CHIEF AND INCITING A CIRCLE OF STATES

SPIES in the service of the king (the enemy) or of his courtiers may, under the pretence of friendship, say in the presence of other friends that the king is angry with the chiefs of infantry, cavalry, chariots and elephants. When their men are collected together, fiery spies, having guarded themselves against night watches, may, under the pretence of the king's (the enemy's) order, invite the chiefs to a certain house and slay the chiefs when returning from the house. Other spies in the vicinity may say that it has been the king's (the enemy's) order to slay them. Spies may also tell those who have been banished from the country: 'This is just what we foretold; for personal safety, you may go elsewhere.'

Spies may also tell those who have not received what they requested of the king (the enemy) that the officer in charge of wastelands has been told by the king: 'Such and such a person has begged of me what he should not demand; I refused to grant his request; he is in conspiracy with my enemy. So make attempts to put him down.' Then the spies may proceed in their usual way.

Spies may also tell those who have been granted their request by the king (the enemy) that the officer in charge of wastelands has been told by the king: 'Such and such persons have demanded their due from me; I have granted them all their requests in order to gain their confidence. But they are conspiring with my enemy. So make attempts to put them down'. Then the spies may proceed in their usual way.

Spies may also tell those who do not demand their due from the king that the officer in charge of wastelands has been told: 'Such and such persons do not demand their due from me. What else can be the reason than their suspicion about my knowledge of their guilt? So make attempts to put them down'. Then the spies may proceed in their usual way.

This explains the treatment of partisans.

A spy employed as the personal servant of the king (the enemy) may inform him that such and such ministers of his are being interviewed by the enemy's servants. When he comes to believe this, some treacherous persons may be represented as the messengers of the enemy, specifying as 'this is that'.

The chief officers of the army may be induced by offering land and gold to fall against their own men and secede from the enemy (their king). If one of the sons of the commander-in-chief is living near or inside the fort, a spy may tell him: 'You are the most worthy son; still you are neglected; why are you indifferent? Seize your position by force; otherwise the heir apparent will destroy you.'

Or some one of the family (of the commander-in-chief or the king), or one who is imprisoned may be bribed in gold and told: 'Destroy the internal strength of the enemy, or a portion of his force in the border of his country.'

Or having seduced wild tribes with rewards of wealth and honour, they may be incited to devastate the enemy's country. Or the enemy's rear enemy may be told: 'I am, as it were, a bridge to you all; if I am broken like a rafter, this king will drown you all; let us, therefore, combine and thwart the enemy in his march.' Accordingly, a message may be sent to individual or combined states to the effect: 'After having done with me, this king will do his work of you: Beware of it. I am the best man to be relied upon.'

In order to escape from the danger from an immediate enemy, a king should frequently send to a *madhyama* or a neutral king (whatever would please him); or one may put one's whole property at the enemy's disposal.

[Thus ends Chapter 3, 'Slaying the Commander-in-Chief and Inciting a Circle of States', in Book XII, 'Concerning a Powerful Enemy', of the Arthashastra of Kautilya. End of the 138th chapter from the beginning.]

Chapter 4

SPIES WITH WEAPONS, FIRE, AND POISON; AND DESTRUCTION OF SUPPLY, STORES AND GRANARIES

THE conqueror's spies who are residing as traders in the enemy's forts, and those who are living as cultivators in the enemy's villages, as well as those who are living as cowherds or ascetics in the district borders of the enemy's country may send through merchants, information to another neighbouring enemy, or a wild chief, or a scion of the enemy's family, or an imprisoned prince that the enemy's country is to be captured. When their secret emissaries come as invited, they are to be pleased with rewards of wealth and honour and shown the enemy's weak points; and with the help of the emissaries, the spies should strike the enemy at his weak points.

Or having put a banished prince in the enemy's camp; a spy disguised as a vintner in the service of the enemy, may distribute as a toast hundreds of vessels of liquor mixed with the juice of the *madana* plant; or, for the first day, he may distribute a mild or intoxicating variety of liquor, and on the following days such liquor as is mixed with poison; or having given pure liquor to the officers of the enemy's army, he may give them poisoned liquor when they are in intoxication.

A spy, employed as a chief officer of the enemy's army, may adopt the same measures as those employed by the vintner.

Spies, disguised as experts in trading in cooked flesh, cooked rice, liquor, and cakes, may vie with each other in proclaiming in public the sale of a fresh supply of their special articles at cheap price and may sell the articles mixed with poison to the attracted customers of the enemy.

Women and children may receive in their poisoned vessels, liquor, milk, curd, ghee or oil from traders in those articles, and pour those fluids back into the vessels of the traders, saying that at a specified rate the whole may be sold to them. Spies, disguised as merchants, may purchase the above articles, and may so contrive that servants, attending upon the elephants and horses of the enemy, may make use of the same articles in giving rations and grass to those animals. Spies, under the garb of servants, may sell poisoned grass and water. Spies, let off as traders in cattle for a long time, may leave herds of cattle, sheep, or goats in tempting places so as to divert the attention of the enemy from the attack which they (the enemy) intend to make; spies as cowherds may let off such animals as are ferocious among horses, mules, camels, buffaloes and others beasts, having smeared the eyes of those animals with the blood of a muskrat (*chuchundari*); spies as hunters may let off cruel beasts from traps; spies as snake charmers may let off highly poisonous snakes; those who keep elephants may let off elephants (near the enemy's camp); those who live by making use of fire may set fire (to the camp, etc.). Secret spies may slay from behind the chiefs of infantry, cavalry, chariots and elephants, or they may set fire to the chief residences of the enemy. Traitors, enemies and wild tribes, employed for the purpose, may destroy the enemy's rear or obstruct his reinforcement; or spies, concealed in forests, may enter into the border of the enemy's country, and devastate it; or they may destroy the enemy's supply, stores, and other things, when those things are being conveyed on a narrow path passable by a single man.

Or in accordance with a preconcerted plan, they may, on the occasion of a night-battle, go to the enemy's capital, and blowing a large number of trumpets, cry aloud: 'We have entered into the capital, and the country has been conquered.' After entering into the king's (the enemy's) palace, they may kill the king in the tumult; when the king begins to run from one direction to another, *mlechchhas*, wild tribes, or chiefs of the army, lying in ambush (*sattra*), or concealed near a pillar or a fence, may slay him; or spies, under the guise of hunters, may slay the king when he is directing his attack, or in the tumult of attack following the plan of treacherous fights. Or occupying an advantageous position, they may slay the enemy when he is marching in a narrow path passable by a single man, or on a mountain, or near the trunk of a tree, or under the branches of a banian tree, or in water; or they may cause him to be carried off by the force of a current of water let off by the destruction of a dam across a river, or of a lake or pond; or they may destroy him by means of an explosive fire or poisonous snake when he has entrenched himself in a fort, in a desert, in a forest, or in a valley. He should be destroyed with fire when he is under a thicket; with smoke when he is in a desert; with poison when he is in a comfortable place; with crocodile and other cruel beasts when he is in water; or they may slay him when he is going out of his burning house.

By means of such measures as are narrated in the chapter, 'Enticement of the Enemy by Secret Means' or by any other measures, the enemy should be caught hold of in places to which he is confined or from which he is attempting to escape.

[Thus ends Chapter 6, 'Spies with Weapons, Fire and Poison; and Destruction of Supply, Stores and Granaries', in Book XII, 'Concerning a Powerful Enemy', of the Arthashastra of Kautilya. End of the 139th chapter from the beginning.]

Chapter 5

CAPTURE OF THE ENEMY BY MEANS OF SECRET CONTRIVANCES OR BY MEANS OF THE ARMY; AND COMPLETE VICTORY

CONTRIVANCES to kill the enemy may be formed in those places of worship and visit, which the enemy, under the influence of faith, frequents on occasions of worshipping gods, and of pilgrimage.

A wall or a stone, kept by mechanical contrivance, may, by loosening the fastenings, be let to fall on the head of the enemy when he has entered into a temple; stones and weapons may be showered over his head from the topmost storey; or a door-panel may be let to fall; or a huge rod kept over a wall or partly attached to a wall may be made to fall over him; or weapons kept inside the body of an idol may be thrown over his head; or the floor of those places where he usually stands, sits, or walks may be be sprinkled with poison mixed with cow-dung or with pure water; or under the plea of giving him flowers, scented powders, or of causing scented smoke, he may be poisoned; or by removing the fastenings made under a cot or a seat, he may be made to fall into a pit containing pointed spears; or when he is eager to escape from impending imprisonment in his own country, he may be led away to fall into the hands of a wild tribe or an enemy waiting for him not far from his country; or when he is eager to get out of his castle he may be likewise misled or made to enter an enemy's country which is to be restored (to the conqueror); the enemy's people should also be kept under the protection of sons and brothers (of the conqueror) in some forts on a mountain, or in a forest, or in the midst of a river separated from the enemy's country by wild tracts of lands.

Measures to obstruct the movements of the enemy are explained in the chapter, 'The Attitude of a Conquered King', Book VII, Chapter 16.

Grass and firewood should be set on fire as far as a *yojana* (5⁵⁄₄₄ miles); water should be vitiated and caused to flow away; mounds, wells, pits and thorns (outside the fort wall) should be destroyed; having widened the mouth of the underground tunnel of the enemy's fort, his stores and leaders may be removed; the enemy may also be likewise carried off; when the underground tunnel has been made by the enemy for his own use, the water in the ditch outside the fort may be made to flow into it; in suspicious places along the parapet (of the enemy's fort) and in the house containing a well outside the fort, empty pots or bronze vessels may be placed in order to find out the direction of the wind (blowing from the underground tunnel); when the direction of the tunnel is found out, a counter tunnel may be formed; or having opened the tunnel, it may be filled with smoke or water.

Having arranged for the defence of the fort by a scion of his family, the enemy may run in an opposite direction where it is possible for him to meet with friends, relatives or wild tribes, or with his enemy's treacherous friends of vast resources, or where he may separate his enemy from the latter's friends, or where he may capture the enemy's rear, or country, or where he may prevent the transport of supplies to his enemy, or whence he may strike his enemy by throwing down trees at hand, or where he can find means to defend his own country or to gather reinforcements for his hereditary army; or he may go to any other country whence he can obtain peace on his own terms.

His enemy's (the conqueror's) allies may send a mission to him, saying: 'This man, your enemy, has fallen into our hands; under the plea of merchandise or some presentation, send gold and a strong force; we shall either hand over to you your enemy bound in chains, or banish him.' If he approves of it, the gold and the army he may send may be received (by the conqueror).

Having access to the enemy's castle, the officer in charge of the boundaries (of the enemy's country) may lead a part of his force and slay the enemy in good faith under the plea of destroying a people in some place, he may take the enemy to an inimical army; and having led the enemy to the surrounded place, he may slay the enemy in good faith.

A pretending friend may send information to an outsider: 'Grains, oil and jaggery and salt stored in the fort (of the enemy) have been exhausted; a fresh supply of them is expected to reach the fort at such and such a place and time; seize it by force.' Then traitors, enemies, or wild tribes, or some other persons, specially appointed for the purpose, may send a supply of poisoned grains, oil, jaggery and salt to the fort. This explains the seizure of all kinds of supply.

Having made peace with the conqueror, he may give the conqueror part of the gold promised and the rest gradually. Thus he may cause the conqueror's defensive force to be slackened and then strike them down with fire, poison or sword; or he may win the confidence of the conqueror's courtiers deputed to take the tribute.

Or if his resources are exhausted, he may run away abandoning his fort; he may escape through a tunnel or through a hole newly made or by breaking the parapet.

Or having challenged the conqueror at night, he may successfully confront the attack; if he cannot do this, he may run away by a side path; or disguised as a heretic, he may escape with a small retinue; or he may be carried off by spies as a corpse; or disguised as a woman, he may follow a corpse (as it were, of her husband to the cremation ground); or on the occasion of feeding the people in honour of gods or of ancestors or in some festival, he may make use of poisoned rice and water, and having conspired with his enemy's traitors, he may strike the enemy with his concealed army; or when he is surrounded in his fort, he may lie concealed in a hole bored into the body of an idol after eating sacramental food and setting up an altar; or he may lie in a secret hole in a wall, or in a hole made in the body of an idol in an underground chamber; and when he is forgotten, he may get out of his concealment through a tunnel, and, entering into the palace, slay his enemy while sleeping, or loosening the fastenings of a machine (*yantra*), he may let it fall on his enemy; or when his enemy is lying in a chamber which is besmeared with poisonous and explosive substances or which is made of lac, he may set fire to it. Fiery spies, hidden in an underground chamber, or in a tunnel, or inside a secret wall, may slay the enemy when the latter is carelessly amusing himself in a pleasure park or any other place of recreation; or spies under concealment may poison him; or women under concealment may throw a snake, or poison, or fire or poisonous smoke over his person when he is asleep in confined place; or spies, having access to the enemy's harem, may, when opportunities occur, do to the enemy whatever is found possible on the occasion, and then get out unknown. On such occasions, they should make use of the signs indicative of the purpose of their society.

Having by means of trumpet sounds called together the sentinels at the gate as well as aged men and other spies stationed by others, the enemy may completely carry out the rest of his work.

[Thus ends Chapter 5, 'Capture of the Enemy by Means of Secret Contrivances or by Means of the Army; and Complete Victory', in Book XII, 'Concerning a Powerful Enemy', of the Arthashastra of Kautilya. End of the 140th chapter from the beginning. With this ends Book XII, 'Concerning a Powerful Enemy', of the Arthashastra of Kautilya.]

Book XIII

Strategic Means to Capture a Fortress

Chapter 1

SOWING THE SEEDS OF DISSENSION

WHEN the conqueror is desirous of seizing an enemy's village, he should infuse enthusiastic spirit among his own men and frighten his enemy's people by giving publicity to his power of omniscience and close association with gods.

Proclamation of his omniscience is as follows: Rejection of his chief officers when their secret, domestic and other private affairs are known; revealing the names of traitors after receiving information from spies specially employed to find out such men; pointing out the impolitic aspect of any course of action suggested to him; and pretensions to the knowledge of foreign affairs by means of his power to read omens and signs invisible to others when information about foreign affairs is just received through a domestic pigeon which has brought a sealed letter.

Proclamation of his association with gods is as follows: Holding conversation with and worshipping the spies who pretend to be the gods of fire or altar when through a tunnel they come to stand in the midst of fire, altar, or in the interior of a hollow image; holding conversation with and worshipping the spies who rise up from water and pretend to be the gods and goddesses of *naga*s (snakes); placing under water at night a mass of sea foam mixed with burning oil, and exhibiting it as the spontaneous outbreak of fire, when it is burning in a line; sitting on a raft in water which is secretly fastened by a rope to a rock; such magical performance in water as is usually done at night by bands of magicians, using the sack of abdomen or womb of water animals to hide the head and the nose, and applying to the nose the oil, prepared from the entrails of red spotted deer and the serum of the flesh of the crab, crocodile, porpoise and otter; holding conversation as though with women of Varuna (the god of water), or of Naga (the snake god) when they are performing magical tricks in water; and sending out volumes of smoke from the mouth on occasions of anger.

Astrologers, soothsayers, horologists, storytellers (*pauranika*), as well as those who read the forebodings of every moment, together with spies and their disciples, inclusive of those who have witnessed the wonderful performances of the conqueror should give wide publicity to the power of the king to associate with gods throughout his territory. Likewise in foreign countries, they should spread the news of gods appearing before the conqueror and of his having received from heaven weapons and treasure. Those who are well versed in horary and astrology and the science of omens should proclaim abroad that the conqueror is a successful expert in explaining the indications of dreams and in understanding the language of beasts and birds. They should not only attribute the contrary to his enemy, but also show to the enemy's people the shower of firebrand (*ulka*) with the noise of drums (from the sky) on the day of the birth star of the enemy.

The conqueror's chief messengers, pretending to be friendly towards the enemy, should highly speak of the conqueror's respectful treatment of visitors, of the strength of his army, and of the likelihood of impending destruction of his enemy's men. They should also make it known to the enemy that under their master, both ministers and soldiers are equally safe and happy, and that their master treats his servants with parental care in their weal or woe.

By these and other means, they should win over the enemy's men as pointed out above, and as we are going to treat of them again at length:

They should characterize the enemy as an ordinary donkey towards skilful persons; as the branch of *lakucha* (*Artocarpus lacucha*) broken to the officers of his army; as a crab on the shore to anxious persons; as a downpour of lightnings to those who are treated with contempt; as a reed, a barren tree, or an iron ball, or as false clouds to those who are disappointed; as the ornaments of an ugly woman to those who are disappointed in spite of their worshipful service; as a tiger's skin, or as a trap of death to his favourites; and as eating a piece of the wood of *pilu* (*Careya arborea*), or as churning the milk of a she-camel or a she-donkey (for butter) to those who are rendering to him valuable help.

When the people of the enemy are convinced of this, they may be sent to the conqueror to receive wealth and honour. Those of the enemy who are in need of money and food should be supplied with an abundance of those things. Those who do not like to receive such things may be presented with ornaments for their wives and children.

When the people of the enemy are suffering from famine and the oppression of thieves and wild tribes, the conqueror's spies should sow the seeds of dissension among them, saying: 'Let us request the king for favour and go elsewhere if not favoured'.

When they agree to such proposals, they should be supplied with money, grains and other necessary help. Thus, much can be done by sowing the seeds of dissension.

[Thus ends Chapter 1, 'Sowing the Seeds of Dissension', in Book XIII, 'Strategic Means to Capture a Fortress', of the Arthashastra, of Kautilya. End of the 141st chapter from the beginning.]

Chapter 2

ENTICEMENT OF KINGS BY SECRET CONTRIVANCES

AN ascetic, with shaved head or braided hair and living in the cave of a mountain, may pretend to be four hundred years old, and, followed by a number of disciples with braided hair, halt in the vicinity of the capital city of the enemy. The disciples of the ascetic may make presentations of roots and fruits to the king and his ministers and invite them to pay a visit to the venerable ascetic. On the arrival of the king on the spot, the ascetic may acquaint him with the history of ancient kings and their states, and tell him: 'Every time when I complete the course of a hundred years, I enter into the fire and come out of it as a fresh youth (*bala*). Now, here in your presence, I am going to enter into the fire for the fourth time. It is highly necessary that you may be pleased to honour me with your presence at the time. Please request three boons.' When the king agrees to do so, he may be requested to come and remain at the spot with his wives and children for seven nights to witness the sacrificial performance. When he does so, he may be caught hold of.

An ascetic, with shaved head or braided hair, and followed by a number of disciples with shaved heads or braided hair, and pretending to be aware of whatever is contained in the interior of the earth, may put in the interior of an anthill either a bamboo stick wound round with a piece of cloth drenched in blood and painted with gold dust, or a hollow golden tube into which a snake can enter and remain. One of the disciples may tell the king: 'This ascetic can discover blooming treasure trove.' When he asks the ascetic (as to the veracity of the statement), the latter should acknowledge it, and produce a confirmatory evidence (by pulling out the bamboo stick); or having kept some more gold in the interior of the anthill, the ascetic may tell the king: 'This treasure trove is guarded by a snake and can possibly be taken out by performing necessary sacrifice. When the king agrees to do so, he may be requested to come and remain. . . (as before).

When an ascetic, pretending to be able to find out hidden treasure trove, is seated with his body burning with magical fire at night in a lonely place, his disciples may bring the king to see him and inform the king that the ascetic can find out treasure trove. While engaged in performing some work at the request of the king, the latter may be requested to come and remain at the spot for seven nights . . . (as before).

An accomplished ascetic may beguile a king by his knowledge of the science of magic known as *jambhaka*, and request him to come and remain . . . (as before).

An accomplished ascetic, pretending to have secured the favour of the powerful guardian deity of the country, may often beguile the king's chief ministers with his wonderful performance and gradually impose upon the king.

Any person, disguised as an ascetic and living underwater or in the interior of an idol entered into through a tunnel or an underground chamber, may be said by his disciples to be Varuna, the god of water, or the king of snakes, and shown to the king. While going to accomplish whatever the king may desire, the latter may be requested to come and remain . . . (as before.)

An accomplished ascetic, halting in the vicinity of the capital city, may invite the king to witness the person (of his enemy) when he comes to witness the invocation of his enemy's life in the image to be destroyed, he may be murdered in an unguarded place.

Spies, under the guise of merchants come to sell horses, may invite the king to examine and purchase any of the animals. While attentively examining the horses, he may be murdered in the tumult or trampled down by horses.

Getting into an altar at night in the vicinity of the capital city of the enemy and blowing through tubes or hollow reeds the fire contained in a few pots, some fiery spies may shout aloud: 'We are going to eat the flesh of the king or of his ministers; let the worship of the gods go on'. Spies, under the guise of soothsayers and horologists may spread the news abroad.

Spies, disguised as Nagas (snake gods and with their body besmeared with burning oil (*tejanataila*), may stand in the centre of a sacred pool of water or of a lake at night, and sharpening their iron swords or spikes, may shout aloud as before.

Spies, wearing coats formed of the skins of bears and sending out volumes of smoke from their mouth, may pretend to be demons, and after circumambulating the city thrice from right to left, may shout aloud as before at a place full of the horrid noise of antelopes and jackals; or spies may set fire to an altar or an image of a god covered with a layer of mica besmeared with burning oil at night, and shout aloud as before. Others may spread this news abroad; or they may cause (by some contrivance or other) blood to flow out in floods from revered images of gods. Others may spread this news abroad and challenge any bold or brave man to come out to witness this flow of divine blood. Whoever accepts the challenge may be beaten to death by others with rods, making the people believe that he was killed by demons. Spies and other witnesses may inform the king of this wonder. Then spies, disguised as soothsayers and astrologers may prescribe auspicious and expiatory rites to avert the evil consequences which would otherwise overtake the king and his country. When the king agrees to the proposal he may be asked to perform in person special sacrifices and offerings with special *mantras* every night for seven days. Then (while doing this, he may be slain) as before.

In order to delude other kings, the conqueror may himself undertake the performance of expiatory rites to avert such evil consequences as the above and thus set an example to others.

In view of averting the evil consequences of unnatural occurrences, he (the conqueror) may collect money (from his subjects).

When the enemy is fond of elephants, spies may delude him with the sight of a beautiful elephant reared by the officer in charge of elephant forests. When he desires to capture the elephant, he may be taken to a remote desolate part of the forest, and killed or carried off as a prisoner. This explains the fate of kings addicted to hunting.

When the enemy is fond of wealth or women, he may be beguiled at the sight of rich and beautiful widows brought before him with a plaint for the recovery of a deposit kept by them in the custody of one of their kinsmen; and when he comes to meet with a woman at night as arranged, hidden spies may kill him with weapons or poison.

When the enemy is in the habit of paying frequent visits to ascetics, altars, sacred pillars (*stupa*), and images of gods, spies hidden in underground chambers or in subterranean passages, or inside the walls, may strike him down.

• Whatever may be the sights or spectacles which the king goes in person to witness; wherever he may engage himself in sports or in swimming in water;

• Wherever he may be careless in uttering such words of rebuke as '*Tut*' or on the occasions of sacrificial performance or during the accouchement of women or at the time of death or disease (of some person in the palace), or at the time of love, sorrow or fear;

• Whatever may be the festivities of his own men, which the king goes to attend, wherever he is unguarded or during a cloudy day, or in the tumultuous concourse of people;
• Or in an assembly of Brahmans, or whenever he may go in person to see the outbreak of fire, or when, he is in a lonely place, or when he is putting on dress or ornaments, or garlands of flower, or when he is lying in his bed or sitting on a seat;
• Or when he is eating or drinking, on these and other occasions, spies, together with other persons previously hidden at those places, may strike him down at the sound of trumpets.
• And they may get out as secretly as they came there with the pretemce of witnessing the sights; thus it is that kings and other persons are entired to come out and be captured.

[Thus ends Chapter 2, 'Enticement of Kings by Secret Contrivances', in Book XIII, 'Strategic means to Capture a Fortress', of the Arthashastra of Kautilya. End of the 142nd chapter from the beginning.]

Chapter 3

THE WORK OF SPIES IN A SIEGE

THE conqueror may dismiss a confidential chief of a corporation. The chief may go over to the enemy as a friend and offer to supply him with recruits and other help collected from the conqueror's territory or followed by a band of spies, the chief may please the enemy by destroying a disloyal village or a regiment or an ally of the conqueror and by sending as a present the elephants, horses and disaffected persons of the conqueror's army or of the latter's ally; or a confidential chief officer of the conqueror may solicit help from a portion of the territory (of the enemy), or from a corporation of people (*sreni*) or from wild tribes; and when he has gained their confidence, he may send them down to the conqueror to be routed down on the occasion of a farcical attempt to capture elephants or wild tribes.

This explains the work of ministers and wild chiefs under the mission of the conqueror.

After making peace with the enemy, the conqueror may dismiss his own confidential ministers. They may request the enemy to reconcile them to their master. When the enemy sends a messenger for this purpose, the conqueror may rebuke him and say: 'Thy master attempts to sow the seeds of dissension between myself and my ministers; so thou should not come here again.' Then one of the dismissed ministers may go over to the enemy, taking with him a band of spies, disaffected people, traitors, brave thieves and wild tribes who make no distinction between a friend and a foe. Having secured the good graces of the enemy, the minister may propose to him the destruction of his officers, such as the boundary guard, wild chief, and commander of his army, telling him: 'These and other persons are in concert with your enemy.' Then these persons may be put to death under the unequivocal orders of the enemy.

The conqueror may tell his enemy: 'A chief with a powerful army means to offend us, so let us combine and put him down; you may take possession of his treasury or territory.' When the enemy agrees to the proposal and comes out honoured by the conqueror, he may be slain in a tumult or in an open battle with the chief (in concert with the conqueror). Or having invited the enemy to be present as a thick friend on the occasion of a pretended gift of territory, or the installation of the heir apparent, or the performance of some expiatory rites, the conqueror may capture the enemy. Whoever withstands such inducements may be slain by secret means. If the enemy refuses to meet any man in person, attempts may then also be made to kill him by employing his enemy. If the enemy likes to march alone with his army, but not in company with the conqueror, he may be hemmed in between two forces and destroyed. If, trusting to none, he wants to march alone in order to capture a portion of the territory of an assailable enemy, he may be slain by employing one of his enemies or any other person provided with all necessary help. When he goes to his subdued enemy for the purpose of collecting an army, his capital may be captured. Or he may be asked to take possession of the territory of another enemy or a friend of the conqueror; and when he goes to seize the territory, the conqueror may ask his (the conqueror's) friend to offend him (the conqueror), and then enable the friend to catch hold of the enemy. These and other contrivances lead to the same end.

When the enemy is desirous of taking possession of the territory of the conqueror's friend, the conqueror may, under the pretence of compliance, supply the enemy with army. Then having entered into a secret concert with the friend, the conqueror may pretend to be under troubles and allow himself to be attacked by the enemy combined with the neglected friend. Then, hemmed from two sides, the enemy may be killed or captured alive to distribute his territory among the conqueror and his friend.

If the enemy, helped by his friend, shuts himself in an impregnable fort, his neighbouring enemies may be employed to lay waste his territory. If he attempts to defend his territory by his army, that army may be annihilated. If the enemy and his ally cannot be separated, each of these may be openly asked to come to an agreement with the conqueror to seize the territory of the other. Then they will, of course, send such of their messengers as are termed friends and recipients of salaries from two states to each other with information: 'This king (the conqueror), allied with my army, desires to seize thy territory'. Then one of them may, with enragement and suspicion, act as before (i.e., fall upon the conqueror or the friend).

The conqueror may dismiss his chief officers in charge of his forests, country parts, and army, under the pretence of their intrigue with the enemy. Then going over to the enemy, they may catch hold of him on occasions of war, siege or any other troubles; or they may sow the seeds of dissension between the enemy and his party, corroborating the causes of dissension by producing witnesses specially tutored.

Spies, disguised as hunters, may take a stand near the gate of the enemy's fort to sell flesh, and make friendship with the sentinels at the gate. Having informed the enemy of the arrival of thieves on two or three occasions, they may prove themselves to be of reliable character and cause him to split his army into two divisions and to station them in two different parts of his territory. When his villages are being plundered or besieged, they may tell him that thieves are come very near, that the tumult is very great, and that a large army is required. They may take the army supplied, and surrendering it to the commander laying waste the villages, return at night with a part of the commander's army, and cry aloud at the gate of the fort that the thieves are slain, that the army has returned victorious, and that the gate may be opened. When the gate is opened by the watchmen under the enemy's order or by others in confidence, they may strike the enemy with the help of the army.

Painters, carpenters, heretics, actors, merchants and other disguised spies belonging to the conqueror's army may also reside inside the fort of the enemy. Spies, disguised as agriculturists, may supply them with weapons taken in carts loaded with firewood, grass, grains and other commodities of commerce, or disguised as images and flags of gods. Then spies, disguised as priests, may announce to the enemy, blowing their conch shells and beating their drums, that a besieging army, eager to destroy all, and armed with weapons, is coming closely behind them. Then in the ensuing tumult, they may surrender the fort-gate and the towers of the fort to the army of the conqueror or disperse the enemy's army and bring about his fall.

Or taking advantage of peace and friendship with the enemy, army and weapons may be collected inside the enemy's fort by spies disguised as merchants, caravans, processions leading a bride, merchants selling horses, peddlers trading in miscellaneous articles, purchasers or sellers of grains, and as ascetics. These and others are the spies aiming on the life of a king.

The same spies, together with those described in Book IV: 'The Removal of Thorns' may, by employing thieves, destroy the flock of the enemy's cattle or merchandise in the vicinity of wild tracts. They may poison with the juice of the *madana* plant, the foodstuffs and beverage kept, as previously arranged, in a definite place for the enemy's cowherds, and go out unknown. When the cowherds show signs of intoxication in consequence of their eating the above foodstuffs, spies, disguised as cowherds, merchants, and thieves, may fall upon the enemy's cowherds, and carry off the cattle.

Spies disguised as ascetics with shaved head or braided hair and pretending to be the worshippers of God Sankarshana, may mix their sacrificial beverage with the juice of the *madana* plant (and give it to the cowherds), and carry off the cattle.

A spy, under the guise of a vintner, may, on the occasion of procession of gods, funeral rites, festivals, and other congregations of people, go to sell liquor and present the cowherds with some liquor mixed with the juice of the *madana* plant. Then others may fall upon the intoxicated cowherds (and carry off the cattle).

Those spies, who enter into the wild tracts of the enemy with the intention of plundering his villages, and who, leaving that work, set themselves to destroy the enemy, are termed spies under the garb of thieves.

[Thus ends Chapter 3, 'The Work of Spies in a Siege', in Book XIII, 'The Strategic Means to Capture a Fortress', of the Arthashastra of Kautilya. End of the 143rd chapter from the beginning.]

Chapter 4

THE OPERATION OF A SIEGE

REDUCTION (of the enemy) must precede a siege. The territory that has been conquered should be kept so peacefully that it might sleep without any fear. When it is in rebellion, it is to be pacified by bestowing rewards and remitting taxes, unless the conqueror means to quit it. Or he may select his battlefields in a remote part of the enemy's territory, far from the populous centres; for, in the opinion of Kautilya, no territory deserves the name of a kingdom or country unless it is full of people. When a people resist the attempt of the conqueror, he may destroy their stores, crops and granaries, and trade.

By the destruction of trade, agricultural produce and standing crops, by causing the people to run away, and by slaying their leaders in secret, the country will be denuded of its people.

When the conqueror thinks: 'My army is provided with abundance of staple corn, raw materials, machines, weapons, dress, labourers, ropes and the like, and has a favourable season to act, whereas my enemy has an unfavourable season and is suffering from disease, famine and loss of stores and defencive force, while his hired troops as well as the army of his friend are in a miserable condition,' he may begin the siege.

Having well guarded his camp, transports, supplies and also the roads of communication, and having dug up a ditch and raised a rampart round his camp, he may vitiate the water in the ditches round the enemy's fort, or empty the ditches of their water or fill them with water if empty, and then he may assail the rampart and the parapets by making use of underground tunnels and iron rods. If the ditch (*dvaram*) is very deep, he may fill it up with soil. If it is defended by a number of men, he may destroy it by means of machines. Horse soldiers may force their passage through the gate into the fort and smite the enemy. Now and then in the midst of tumult, he may offer terms to the enemy by taking recourse to one, two, three or all of the strategic means.

Having captured the birds such as the vulture, crow, naptri, bhasa, parrot, *maina* and pigeon which have their nests in the fort walls, and having tied to their tails inflammable powders (*agniyoga*), he may let them fly to the forts. If the camp is situated at a distance from the fort and is provided with an elevated post for archers and their flags, the enemy's fort may be set on fire. Spies, living as watchmen of the fort, may tie inflammable powder to the tails of mongooses, monkeys, cats and dogs, and let them go over the thatched roofs of the houses. A splinter of fire kept in the body of a dried fish may be caused to be carried off by a monkey, or a crow, or any other bird (to the thatched roofs of the houses).

Small balls prepared from the mixture of *sarala* (*Pinus longifolia*), *devadaru* (deodar), *putitrina* (stinking grass), *guggulu* (bdellium), *sriveshtaka* (turpentine), the juice of *sarja* (*Vatica robusta*), and *laksha* (lac) combined with dungs of an ass, camel, sheep and goat are inflammable (*agnidharanah*, i.e., such as keep fire.)

The mixture of the powder of *priyala* (*Chironjia sapida*), the charcoal of *avalguja* (*oanyza, Serratula, Baecharoides anthelmintica*), *madhuchchhishta* (wax), and the dung of a horse, ass, camel and cow is an inflammable powder to be hurled against the enemy.

The powder of all the metals (*sarvaloha*) as red as fire, or the mixture of the powder of *kumbhi* (*Gmelia arberea*, *sisa* (lead), *trapu* (zinc), mixed with the charcoal powder of the flowers of *paribhadraka* (deodar), *palasa* (*Butea frondosa*), and hair, and with oil, wax and turpentine, is also an inflammable powder.

A stick of *visvasaghati* painted with the above mixture and wound round with a bark made of hemp, zinc and lead, is a fire arrow (to be hurled against the enemy).

When a fort can be captured by other means, no attempt should be made to set fire to it; for fire cannot be trusted; it not only offends gods, but also destroys the people, grains, cattle, gold, raw materials and the like. Also the acquisition of a fort with its property all destroyed is a source of further loss. Such is the aspect of a siege.

When the conqueror thinks: 'I am well provided with all necessary means and with workmen whereas my enemy is diseased with officers proved to be impure under temptations, with unfinished forts and deficient stores, allied with no friends, or with friends inimical at heart', he should consider it as an opportune moment to take up arms and storm the fort.

When fire, accidental or intentionally kindled, breaks out; when the enemy's people are engaged in a sacrificial performance, or in witnessing spectacles or the troops, or in a quarrel due to the drinking of liquor; or when the enemy's army is too much tired by daily engagements in battles and is reduced in strength in consequence of the slaughter of a number of its men in a number of battles; when the enemy's people wearied from sleeplessness have fallen asleep; or on the occasion of a cloudy day, of floods, or of a thick fog or snow, general assault should be made.

Or having concealed himself in a forest after abandoning the camp, the conqueror may strike the enemy when the latter comes out.

A king pretending to be the enemy's chief friend or ally, may make the friendship closer with the besieged, and send a messenger to say: 'This is thy weak point; these are thy internal enemies; that is the weak point of the besieger; and this person (who, deserting the conqueror, is now coming to thee) is thy partisan.' When this partisan is returning with another messenger from the enemy, the conqueror should catch hold of him and, having published the partisan's guilt, should banish him, and retire from the siege operations. Then the pretending friend may tell the besieged: 'Come out to help me, or let us combine and strike the besieger.' Accordingly, when the enemy comes out, he may be hemmed between the two forces (the conqueror's force and the pretending friend's force) and killed or captured alive to distribute his territory (between the conqueror and the friend). His capital city may be razed to the ground; and the flower of his army made to come out and destroyed.

This explains the treatment of a conquered enemy or wild chief.

Either a conquered enemy or the chief of a wild tribe (in conspiracy with the conqueror) may inform the besieged: 'With the intention of escaping from a disease, or from the attack in his weak point by his enemy in the rear, or from a rebellion in his army, the conqueror seems to be thinking of going elsewhere, abandoning the siege.' When the enemy is made to believe this, the conqueror may set fire to his camp and retire. Then the enemy coming out may be hemmed . . . as before.

Or having collected merchandise mixed with poison, the conqueror may deceive the enemy by sending that merchandise to the latter.

Or a pretending ally of the enemy may send a messenger to the enemy, asking him: 'Come out to smite the conqueror already struck by me'. When he does so, he may be hemmed . . . as before.

Spies, disguised as friends or relatives and with passports and orders in their hands, may enter the enemy's fort and help to its capture.

Or a pretending ally of the enemy may send information to the besieged: 'I am going to strike the besieging camp at such a time and place; then you should also fight along with me.' When the enemy does so, or when he comes out of his fort after witnessing the tumult and uproar of the besieging army in danger, he may be slain as before.

Or a friend or a wild chief in friendship with the enemy may be induced and encouraged to seize the land of the enemy when the latter is besieged by the conqueror. When accordingly anyone of them attempts to seize the enemy's territory, the enemy's people or the leaders of the enemy's traitors may be employed to murder him (the friend or the wild chief); or the conqueror himself may administer poison to him. Then another pretending friend may inform the enemy that the murdered person was a fratricide (as he attempted to seize the territory of his friend in troubles). After strengthening his intimacy with the enemy, the pretending friend may sow the seeds of dissension between the enemy and his officers and have the latter hanged. Causing the peaceful people of the enemy to rebel, he may put them down, unknown to the enemy. Then having taken with him a portion of his army composed of furious wild tribes, he may enter the enemy's fort and allow it to be captured by the conqueror. Or traitors, enemies, wild tribes and other persons who have deserted the enemy, may, under the plea of having been reconciled, honoured and rewarded, go back to the enemy and allow the fort to be captured by the conqueror.

Having captured the fort or having returned to the camp after its capture, he should give quarter to those of the enemy's army who, whether as lying prostrate in the field, or as standing with their back turned to the conqueror, or with their hair dishevelled, with their weapons thrown down or with their body disfigured and shivering under fear, surrender themselves. After the captured fort is cleared of the enemy's partisans and is well guarded by the conqueror's men both within and without, he should make his victorious entry into it.

Having thus seized the territory of the enemy close to his country, the conqueror should direct his attention to that of the *madhyama* king; this being taken, he should catch hold of that of the neutral king. This is the first way to conquer the world. In the absence of the *madhyama* and neutral kings, he should, by virtue of his own excellent qualities, win the hearts of his enemy's subjects, and then direct his attention to other remote enemies. This is the second way. In the absence of a circle of states (to be conquered), he should conquer his friend or his enemy by hemming each between his own force and that of his enemy or that of his friend respectively. This is the third way.

Or he may first put down an almost invincible immediate enemy. Having doubled his power by this victory, he may go against a second enemy; having trebled his power by this victory, he may attack a third. This is the fourth way to conquer the world.

Having conquered the earth with its people of distinct castes and divisions of religious life, he should enjoy it by governing it in accordance with the duties prescribed to kings.

Intrigue, spies, winning over the enemy's people, siege and assault are the five means to capture a fort.

[Thus ends Chapter 4, 'The Operation of a Siege', in Book XIII, 'Strategic Means to Capture a Fortress', of the Arthashastra of Kautilya. End of the 144th chapter from the beginning.]

Chapter 5

RESTORATION OF PEACE IN A CONQUERED COUNTRY

THE expedition which the conqueror has to undertake may be of two kinds: in wild tracts or in single villages and the like.

The territory which he acquires may be of three kinds: that which is newly acquired, that which is recovered (from an usurper) and that which is inherited.

Having acquired a new territory, he should cover the enemy's vices with his own virtues, and the enemy's virtues by doubling his own virtues, by strict observance of his own duties, by attending to his works, by bestowing rewards, by remitting taxes, by giving gifts, and by bestowing honours. He should follow the friends and leaders of the people. He should give rewards, as promised, to those who deserted the enemy for his cause; he should also offer rewards to them as often as they render help to him; for whoever fails to fullfil his promises becomes untrustworthy both to his own and his enemy's people. Whoever acts against the will of the people will also become unreliable. He should adopt the same mode of life, the same dress, language, and customs as those of the people. He should follow the people in their faith with which they celebrate their national, religious and congregational festivals or amusements. His spies should often bring home to the mind of the leaders of provinces, villages, castes and corporations the hurt inflicted on the enemies in contrast with the high esteem and favour with which they are treated by the conqueror, who finds his own prosperity in theirs. He should please them by giving gifts, remitting taxes, and providing for their security. He should always hold religious life in high esteem. Learned men, orators, charitable and brave persons should be favoured with gifts of land and money and with remission of taxes. He should release all the prisoners, and afford help to miserable, helpless, and diseased persons. He should prohibit the slaughter of animals for half a month during the period of *chaturmasya*, for four nights during the full moon, and for a night on the day of the birth star of the conqueror or of the national star. He should also prohibit the slaughter of females and young ones (*yonibalavadham*) as well as castration. Having abolished those customs or transactions which he might consider either as injurious to the growth of his revenue and army or as unrighteous, he should establish righteous transactions. He should compel born thieves as well as the *mlechchhas* to change their habitations often and reside in many places. Such of his chief officers in charge of the forts, country parts and the army, and ministers and priests as are found to have been in conspiracy with the enemy should also be compelled to have their habitations in different places on the borders of the enemy's country. Such of his men as are capable to hurt him, but are convinced of their own fall with that of their master, should be pacified by secret remonstrance. Such renegades of his own country as are captured along with the enemy should be made to reside in remote corners. Whoever of the enemy's family is capable to wrest the conquered territory and is taking shelter in a wild tract on the border, often harassing the conqueror, should be provided with a sterile portion of territory or with a fourth part of a fertile tract on the condition of supplying to the conqueror a fixed amount of money and a fixed number of troops, in raising which he may incur the displeasure of the people and may be destroyed by them. Whoever has caused excitement to the people or incurred their displeasure should be removed and placed in a dangerous locality.

Having recovered a lost territory, he should hide those vices of his, owing to which he lost it, and increase those virtues by which he recovered it.

With regard to the inherited territory, he should cover the vices of his father and display his own virtues.

He should initiate the observance of all those customs, which, though righteous and practised by others, are not observed in his own country, and give no room for the practice of whatever is unrighteous, though observed by others.

[Thus ends Chapter 5, 'Restoration of Peace in a Conquered Country', in Book XIII, 'Strategic Means to Capture a Fortress', of the Arthashastra of Kautilya. End of the 145th chapter from the beginning. With this end Book XIII, 'Strategic Means to Capture a Fortress', of the Arthashastra of Kautilya]

Book XIV

Secret Means

Chapter 1

MEANS TO INJURE AN ENEMY

IN order to protect the institution of the four castes, such measures as are treated of in secret science shall be applied against the wicked. Through the instrumentality of such men or women of *mleccha* class as can put on disguises, appropriate to different countries, arts or professions, or as can put on the appearance of a humpbacked, dwarfish or short-sized person, or of a dumb, deaf, idiot or blind person, *kalakata* and other manifold poisons should be administered in the diet and other physical enjoyments of the wicked. Spies lying in wait or living as inmates (in the same house) may make use of weapons on occasions of royal sports or musical and other entertainments. Spies, under the disguise of night-walkers (*ratrichari*) or of fire keepers (*agni-jivi*) may set fire (to the houses of the wicked).

The powder (prepared from the carcass) of animals such as chitra (?), *bheka* (frog), *kaundinyaka* (?), *krikana* (*Perdix sylvatika*), *panchakushtha* (?) and *satapadi* (centipede); or of animals such as *uchchitinga* (crab), *kambali* (?), *krikalasa* (lizard) with the powder of the bark of *satakanda* (*Phyalis flexuosa*); or of animals such as *grihagaulika* (a small house lizard), *andhahika* (a blind snake), *krakanthaka* (a kind of partridge), *putikita* (a stinking insect), and *gomarika* (?) combined with the juice of *bhallataka* (*Semecarpus anacardium*) and *valgaka* (?)—the smoke caused by burning the above powders causes instantaneous death.

Any of the (above) insects may be heated with a black snake and *priyangu* (panic seed) and reduced to powder. This mixture, when burnt, causes instantaneous death.

The powder prepared from the roots of *dhamargava* (*Lufta foetida*) and *yatudhana* (?) mixed with the powder of the flower of *bhallataka* (*Semecarpus anacardium*) causes, when administered, death in the course of half a month. The root of *vyaghata* (*Casia fistula*) reduced to powder with the flower of *bhallataka* (*Semecarpus anacardium*) mixed with the essence of an insect (*kita*) causes, when administered, death in the course of a month.

As much as a *kala* (one-sixteenth of a *tola*) to men; twice as much to mules and horses; and four times as much to elephants and camels.

The smoke caused by burning the powder of *satakardama*(?), *uchchitinga* (crab), *karavira* (*Nerium odorum*), *katutumbi* (a kind of bitter gourd) and fish, together with the chaff of the grains of *madana* (?) and *kodrava* (*Paspalam scrobiculatum*), or with the chaff of the seeds of *hastikarna* (castor oil tree) and *palasa* (*Butea frondosa*) destroys animal life as far as it is carried off by the wind.

The smoke caused by burning the powder of *putikita* (a stinking insect), fish, *katutumbi* (a kind of bitter gourd), the bark of *satakardama* (?), and *indragopa* (the insect cochineal), or the powder of *putikita*, *kshudrarala* (the resin of the plant *Shorea robusta*), and *hemavidari* (?) mixed with the powder of the hoof and horn of a goat causes blindness.

The smoke caused by burning the leaves of *putikaranja* (*Guilandina bonducella*), yellow arsenic, realgar, the seeds of *gunja* (*Abrus precatorius*), the chaff of the seeds of red cotton, *asphota* (a plant, *Careya arborea*), *khacha* (salt?), and the dung and urine of a cow causes blindness.

The smoke caused by burning the skin of a snake, the dung of a cow and a horse, and the head of a blind snake causes blindness.

The smoke caused by burning the powder made of the mixture of the dung and urine of pigeons, frogs, flesh-eating animals, elephants, men, and boars, the chaff and powder of barley mixed with *kasisa* (green sulphate of iron), rice, the seeds of cotton, *kutaja* (*Nerium antidysentericum*), and *kosataki* (*Lufta pentandra*), cow's urine, the root of *bhandi* (*Hydroeotyle asiatica*), the powder of *nimba* (*Nimba meria*), *sigru* (*Hyperanthera morunga*), *phanirjaka* (a kind of *tulasi* plant), *kshibapiluka* (ripe *Coreya arborea*), and bhanga (a common intoxicating drug), the skin of a snake and fish, and the powder of the nails and tusk of an elephant, all mixed with the chaff of *madana* and *kodrava* (*Paspalam scrobiculatum*), or with the chaff of the seeds of *hastikarna* (castor oil tree) and *palasa* (*Butea frondosa*), causes instantaneous death wherever the smoke is carried off by the wind.

When a man who has kept his eyes secure with the application of ointment and medicinal water burns, on the occasion of the commencement of a battle and the assailing of forts, the roots of *kali (Tragia involucrata), kushtha* (*costus*), *nada* (a kind of reed) and *satavari (Asperagus racemosus),* or the powder of (the skin of) a snake, the tail of a peacock, *krikana* (a kind of partridge), and *panchakushtha*(?), together with the chaff as previously described or with wet or dry chaff, the smoke caused thereby destroys the eyes of all animals.

The ointment prepared by mixing the excretion of *sarika* (*maina*), *kapota* (pigeon), *baka* (crane), and *balaka* (a kind of small crane) with the milk of *kakshiva* (*Hyperanthera morunga*), *piluka* (a species of *Careya arborea*) and *snuhi* (*Euphorbia*) causes blindness and poisons water.

The mixture of *yavaka* (a kind of barley), the root of *sala* (*Achyrantes triandria*), the fruit of *madana* (*dattura* plant?), the powder of the root of *plaksha* (fig tree), and *vidari* (liquorice), as well as the essence of the decoction of *musta* (a kind of poison), *udumbara* (glomerous fig tree), and *kodrava* (*Paspalam scrobiculatum*) or with the decoction of *hastikarna* (castor oil tree) and *palasa* (*Butea frondosa*) is termed the juice of *madana* (*madanayoga*).

The mixture of the powders of *sringi* (*Atis betula*), *gaumevriksha* (?), *kantakara* (*Solanum xanthocarpum*), and *mayurapadi* (?), the powder of *gunja* seeds, *languli* (*Jusseina repens*), *vishamulika* (?), and *ingudi* (heart pea), and the powder of *karavira* (oleander), *akshipiluka* (*Careya arborea*), *arka* plant, and *mrigamarini* (?) combined with the decoction of *madana* and *kodrava* or with that of *hastikarna* and *palasa* is termed *madana* mixture (*madanayoga*).

The combination of (the above two) mixtures poisons grass and water when applied to them.

The smoke caused by burning the mixture of the powders of *krikana* (a kind of partridge), krikalasa (lizard), *grihagaulika* (a small house lizard) and *andhahika* (a blind snake) destroys the eyes and causes madness.

The (smoke caused by burning the) mixture of *krikalasa* and *grihagaulika* causes leprosy.

The smoke caused by burning the same mixture together with the entrails of *chitrabheka* (a kind of frog of variegated colour), and *madhu* (*Celtis orientalis*?) causes gonorrhœa.

The same mixture, wetted with human blood causes consumption. *Kodrava* (*Paspalam scrobiculatum*) destroys the tongue.

The mixture of the powder of *matrivahaka* (?), jaluka (leech), the tail of a peacock, the eyes of a frog, and *piluka* (*Careya arborea*) causes the disease known as *vishuchika*.

The mixture of *panchakushtha* (?), *kaundinyaka* (?), *rajavriksha* (*Cassia fistula*), and *madhupushpa* (*Bassia latifolia*) and *madhu* (honey?) causes fever.

The mixture prepared from the powder of the knot of the tongue of *bhaja* (?), and *nakula* (mongoose) reduced to a paste with the milk of a she-donkey causes both dumbness and deafness.

The proportion of a dose to bring on the desired deformities in men and animals in the course of a fortnight or a month is as laid down before.

Mixtures become very powerful when, in the case of drugs, they are prepared by the process of decoction; and in the case of animals, by the process of making powders; or in all cases by the process of decoction.

Whoever is pierced by the arrow prepared from the grains of *salmali* (*Bombax heptaphyllum*) and *vidari* (liquorice) reduced to powder and mixed with the powder of *mulavatsanabha* (a kind of poison) and smeared over with the blood of *chuchundari* (muskrat) bites some ten other persons who in their turn bite others.

The mixture prepared from the flowers of *bhallataka* (*Semecarpus anacardium*), *yatudhana* (?), *dhamargava* (*Achyranthes aspera*), and *bana* (sal tree) mixed with the powder of *ela* (large cardamom), *kakshi* (red aluminous earth), *guggulu* (bdellium), and *halahala* (a kind of poison) together with the blood of a goat and a man causes biting madness.

When half a *dharana* of this mixture together with flour and oil-cakes is thrown into water of a reservoir measuring a hundred bows in length, it vitiates the whole mass of water; all the fish swallowing or touching this mixture become poisonous; and whoever drinks or touches this water will be poisoned.

No sooner does a person condemned to death pull out from the earth an alligator or iguana (*godha*) which, with three or five handfuls of both red and white mustard seeds, is entered into the earth than he dies at its sight.

When, on the days of the stars of *krittika* or *bharani* and following the method of performing fearful rites, an oblation with a black cobra emitting froth at the shock of lightning or caught hold of by means of the sticks of a tree struck by lightning and perfumed is made into the fire, that fire continues to burn unquenchably.

• An oblation of honey shall be made into the fire fetched from the house of a blacksmith; of spirituous liquor into the fire brought from the house of a vintner; of clarified butter into the fire of a sacrificer (?);

• Of a garland into the fire kept by a sacrificer with one wife; of mustard seeds into the fire kept by an adulterous woman; of curds into the fire kept during the birth of a child; of rice grain into the fire of a sacrificer;

• Of flesh into the fire kept by a *chandala*; of human flesh into the fire burning in cremation grounds; an oblation of the serum of the flesh of a goat and a man shall be made by means of a sacrificial ladle into the fire which is made of all the above fires;

• Repeating the *mantra*s addressed to the fire, an oblation of the wooden pieces of *rajavriksha* (*Cassia fistula*) into the same fire. This fire will unquenchably burn deluding the eyes of the enemies.

• Salutation to Aditi, salutation to Anumati, salutation to Sarasvati and salutation to Sun; oblation to Agni, oblation to soma, oblation to the earth, and oblation to the atmosphere.

[Thus ends Chapter 1, 'Means to Injure an Enemy', in Book XIV, 'Secret Means', of the Arthashastra of Kautilya. End of the 146th chapter from the beginning.]

Chapter 2

WONDERFUL AND DELUSIVE CONTRIVANCES

A DOSE of the powder of *sirisha* (*Mimosa sirisa*), *udumbara* (glomerous fig tree), and *sami* (*Acacia suma*) mixed with clarified butter, renders fasting possible for half a month; the scum prepared from the mixture of the root of *kaseruka* (a kind of water creeper), *utpala* (*Costus*), and sugar cane mixed with *bisa* (water lily), *durva* (grass), milk, and clarified butter enables a man to fast for a month.

The powder of *masha* (*Phraseolus radiatus*), *yava* (barley), *kuluttha* (horse gram) and the root of *darbha* (sacrificial grass) mixed with milk and clarified butter; the milk of *valli* (a kind of creeper) and clarified butter derived from it and mixed in equal proportions and combined with the paste prepared from the root of *sala* (*Shorea robusta*) and *prisniparni* (*Hedysarum lagopodio*i.e.), when drunk with milk; or a dose of milk mixed with clarified butter and spirituous liquor, both prepared from the above substances, enables one to fast for a month.

The oil prepared from mustard seeds previously kept for seven nights in the urine of a white goat will, when used (externally) after keeping the oil inside a large bitter gourd for a month and a half, alter the colour of both biped and quadruped animals.

The oil extracted from white mustard seeds mixed with the barley corns contained in the dung of a white donkey, which has been living for more than seven nights on a diet of butter, milk and barley, causes alteration in colour.

The oil prepared from mustard seeds which have been previously kept in the urine and fluid dung of any of the two animals, a white goat and a white donkey, causes (when applied) such white colour as that of the fibre of *arka* plant or the down of a (white) bird.

The mixture of the dung of a white cock and *ajagara* (boa constrictor) causes white colour.

The pastry made from white mustard seeds kept for seven nights in the urine of a white goat mixed with butter milk, the milk of *arka* plant, salt and grains (*dhanya*), causes, when applied for a fortnight, white colour.

The paste, prepared from white mustard seeds which have been previously kept within a large bitter gourd and with clarified butter prepared from the milk of *valli* (a creeper) for half a month, makes the hair white.

A bitter gourd, a stinking insect (*putikita*), and a white house lizard, when a paste prepared from these is applied to the hair, the latter becomes as white as a conch shell.

When any part of the body of a man is rubbed over with the pastry (*kalka*) prepared from *tinduka* (*glutinosa*) and *arishta* (soap berry), together with the dung of a cow, the part of the body being also smeared over with the juice of *bhallataka* (*Semecarpus anacardium*), he will catch leprosy in the course of a month.

(The application of the paste prepared from) *gunja* seeds kept previously for seven nights in the mouth of a white cobra or in the mouth of a house lizard brings on leprosy.

External application of the liquid essence of the egg of a parrot and a cuckoo brings on leprosy.

The pastry or decoction prepared from *priyala* (*Chironjia sapida* or *Vitis vinifera* ?) is a remedy for leprosy.

Whoever eats the mixture of the powders of the roots of *kukkuta* (*Marsilia dentata*), *kosataki* (*Duffa pentandra*), and *satavari* (*Asparagus racemosus*) for a month will become white.

Whoever bathes in the decoction of *vata* (banyan tree) and rubs his body with the paste prepared from *sahachara* (yellow *Barleria*) becomes black.

Sulphurate of arsenic and red arsenic mixed with the oil extracted from *sakuna* (a kind of bird) and *kanka* (a vulture) causes blackness.

The powder of *khadyota* (firefly) mixed with the oil of mustard seeds emits light at night.

The powder of *khadyota* (firefly) and *gandupada* (earthworm) or the powder of ocean animals mixed with the powder of *bhringa* (*malabathrum*), *kapala* (a pot herb), and *khadira* (*Mimosa catechu*), and *karnikara* (*Pentapetes acerifolia*), combined with the oil of *sakuna* (a bird) and *kanka* (vulture), is *tejanachurna* (ignition powder).

When the body of a man is rubbed over with the powder of the charcoal of the bark of *paribhadraka* (*Erythrina indica*) mixed with the serum of the flesh of *manduka* (a frog), it can be burnt with fire (without causing hurt).

The body which is painted with the pastry (*kalka*) prepared from the bark of *paribhadraka* (*Erythrina indica*) and sesamum seeds burns with fire.

The ball prepared from the powder of the charcoal of the bark of *pilu* (*Careya arborea*) can be held in hand and burnt with fire.

When the body of a man is smeared over with the serum of the flesh of a frog, it burns with fire (with no hurt).

When the body of a man is smeared over with the above serum as well as with the oil extracted from the fruits of *kusa* (*Ficus religiosa*), and *amra* (mango tree), and when the powder prepared from an ocean frog (*samdura manduki*), *phenaka* (sea foam), and *sarjarasa* (the juice of *Vatica robusta*) is sprinkled over the body, it burns with fire (without being hurt).

When the body of a man is smeared over with sesamum oil mixed with equal quantities of the serum of the flesh of a frog, crab and other animals, it can burn with fire (without hurt).

The body which is smeared over with the serum of the flesh of a frog burns with fire.

The body of a man, which is rubbed over with the powder of the root of bamboo (*venu*) and *saivala* (aquatic plant), and is smeared over with the serum of the flesh of a frog, burns with fire.

Whoever has anointed his legs with the oil extracted from the paste prepared from the roots of *paribhadraka* (*Erythrina indica*), *pratibala* (?), *vanjula* (a kind of *ratan* or tree), *vajra* (*Andropogon muricatum* or *Euphorbia*), and *kadali* (banana), mixed with the serum of the flesh of a frog, can walk over fire (without hurt).

Oil should be extracted from the paste prepared from the roots of *pratibala*, *vanjula* and *paribhadraka*, all growing near water, the paste being mixed with the serum of the flesh of a frog.

Having anointed one's legs with this oil, one can walk over a white-hot mass of fire as though on a bed of roses.

When birds such as a *hamsa* (goose), *krauncha* (heron), *mayura* (peacock) and other large swimming birds are let to fly at night with a burning reed attached to their tail it presents the appearance of a firebrand falling from the sky (*ulka*).

Ashes caused by lightning quench the fire.

When, in a fireplace, kidney beans (*masha*) wetted with the menstrual fluid of a woman, as well as the roots of *vajra* (*Andropogon muricatum*) and *kadali* (banana), wetted with the serum of the flesh of a frog are kept, no grains can be cooked there.

Cleansing the fireplace is its remedy.

By keeping in the mouth a ball-like piece of *pilu* (*Careya arberea*) or a knot of the root of linseed tree (*suvarchala*) with fire inserted within the mass of the ball and wound round with threads and cotton (*pichu*), volumes of smoke and fire can be breathed out.

When the oil extracted from the fruits of *kusa* (*Ficus religiosa*) and *amra* (mango) is poured over the fire, it burns even in the storm.

Sea foam wetted with oil and ignited keeps burning when floating on water.

The fire generated by churning the bone of a monkey by means of a bamboo stick of white and black colour (*kalmashavenu*) burns in water instead of being quenched.

There will burn no other fire where the fire generated by churning, by means of a bamboo stick of white and black colour, the left side rib bone of a man killed by a weapon or put to the gallows; or the fire generated by churning the bone of a man or woman by means of the bone of another man is circumambulated thrice from right to left.

When the paste prepared from the animals such as *chuchundari* (muskrat), *khanjarita* (?) and *kharakita* (?), with the urine of a horse is applied to the chains with which the legs of a man are bound, they will be broken to pieces.

The sun stone (*ayaskanta*) or any other stone (will break to pieces) when wetted with the serum of the flesh of the animals *kulinda* (?), *dardura* (?) and *kharakita* (?).

The paste prepared from the powder of the rib bone of *naraka* (?), a donkey, *kanka* (a kind of vulture), and *bhasa* (a bird), mixed with the juice of water lily, is applied to the legs of bipeds and quadrupeds (while making a journey).

When a man makes a journey, wearing the shoes made of the skin of a camel, smeared over with the serum of the flesh of an owl and a vulture and covered over with the leaves of the banyan tree, he can walk fifty *yojana*s without any fatigue.

(When the shoes are smeared over with) the pith, marrow or sperm of the birds, *syena, kanka, kaka, gridhra, hamsa, krauncha*, and *vichiralla*, (the traveller wearing them) can walk a hundred *yojana*s (without any fatigue).

The fat or serum derived from roasting a pregnant camel together with *saptaparna* (*Lechites scholaris*) or from roasting dead children in cremation grounds is applied to render a journey of a hundred *yojana*s easy.

Terror should be caused to the enemy by exhibiting these and other wonderful and delusive performances; while anger-causing terror is common to all, terrification by such wonders is held as a means to consolidate peace.

[Thus ends Chapter 2, 'Wonderful and Delusive Contrivances', in Book XIV, 'Secret Means', of the Arthashastra of Kautilya. End of the 147th chapter from the beginning.]

Chapter 3

THE APPLICATION OF MEDICINES AND MANTRAS

HAVING pulled out both the right and the left eyeballs of a cat, camel, wolf, boar, porcupine, *vaguli* (?), *naptri* (?), crow and owl, or of anyone, two, or three, or many of such animals as roam at nights, one should reduce them to two kinds of powder. Whoever anoints his own right eye with the powder of the left eye and his left eye with the powder of the right eyeball can clearly see things even in pitch-dark at night.

One is the eye of a boar; another is that of a *khadyota* (firefly), or a crow, or a *maina* bird. Having anointed one's own eyes with the above, one can clearly see things at night.

Having fasted for three nights, one should, on the day of the star *Pushya*, catch hold of the skull of a man who has been killed with a weapon or put to the gallows. Having filled the skull with soil and barley seeds, one should irrigate them with the milk of goats and sheep. Putting on the garland formed of the sprouts of the above barley crop, one can walk invisible to others.

Having fasted for three nights and having afterwards pulled out on the day of the star of *Pushya* both the right and the left eyes of a dog, a cat, an owl, and a *vaguli* (?), one should reduce them to two kinds of powder. Then having anointed one's own eyes with this ointment as usual, one can walk invisible to others.

Having fasted for three nights, one should, on the day of the star of *Pushya*, prepare a round-headed pin (*salaka*) from the branch of *purushaghati* (*punnaga* tree). Then having filled with ointment (*anjana*) the skull of any of the animals which roam at nights, and having inserted that skull in the organ of procreation of a dead woman, one should burn it. Having taken it out on the day of the star of *Pushya* and having anointed one's own eyes with that ointment, one can walk invisible to others.

Wherever one may happen to see the corpse burnt or just being burnt of a Brahman who kept sacrificial fire (while alive), there one should fast for three nights; and having on the day of the star of *Pushya* formed a sack from the garment of the corpse of a man who has died from natural causes, and having filled the sack with the ashes of the Brahman's corpse, one may put on the sack on one's back, and walk invisible to others.

The slough of a snake filled with the powder of the bones and marrow or fat of the cow sacrificed during the funeral rites of a Brahman, can, when put on the back of cattle, render them invisible.

The slough of *prachalaka* (a bird?) filled with the ashes of the corpse of a man dead from snake bite, can render beasts (*mriga*) invisible.

The slough of a snake (*ahi*) filled with the powder of the bone of the knee-joint mixed with that of the tail and dung (*purisha*) of an owl and a *vaguli* (?), can render birds invisible.

Such are the eight kinds of the contrivances causing invisibility.

• I bow to Bali, son of Virochana; to Sambara acquainted with a hundred kinds of magic; to Bhandirapaka, Naraka, Nikumbha, and Kumbha.

• I bow to Devala and Narada; I bow to Savarnigalava; with the permission of these I cause deep slumber to thee.

• Just as the snakes, known as *ajagara* (boa constrictor) fall into deep slumber, so may the rogues of the army who are very anxious to keep watch over the village;

• With their thousands of dogs (*bhandaka*) and hundreds of ruddy geese and donkeys, fall into deep slumber; I shall enter this house, and may the dogs be quiet.

• Having bowed to Manu, and having tethered the roguish dogs (*sunakaphelaka*), and having also bowed to those gods who are in heaven, and to Brahmans among mankind;

• To those who are well versed in their Vedic studies, those who have attained to Kailasa (a mountain of God Siva) by observing penance, and to all prophets, I do cause deep slumber to thee.

The fan (*chamari*) comes out; may all combinations retire. Oblation to Manu, O *Aliti* and *Paliti*.

The application of the above *mantra* is as follows:

Having fasted for three nights, one should, on the fourteenth day of the dark half of the month, the day being assigned to the star of *Pushya*, purchase from a low-caste woman (*svapaki*) *vilikhavalekhana* (finger nails?). Having kept them in a basket (*kandolika*), one should bury them apart in cremation grounds. Having unearthed them on the next fourteenth day, one should reduce them to a paste with *kumari* (aloe ?) and prepare small pills out of the paste. Wherever one of the pills is thrown, chanting the above *mantra*, there the whole animal life falls into deep slumber.

Following the same procedure, one should separately bury in cremation grounds three white and three black dart-like hairs (*salyaka*) of a porcupine. When, having on the next fourteenth day taken them out, one throws them together with the ashes of a burnt corpse, chanting the above *mantra*, the whole animal life in that place falls into deep slumber.

• I bow to Goddess Suvarnapushpi and to Brahmani, to god Brahma, and to Kusadhvaja; I bow to all serpents and goddesses; I bow to all ascetics.

• May all Brahmans and Kshattriyas come under my power; may all Vaisyas and, Sudras be at my beck and call.

• Oblation to thee, O. *Amile*, *Kimile*, *Vayujare*, *Prayoge*, *Phake*, *Kavayusve*, *Vihale*, and *Dantakatake*, oblation to thee.

• May the dogs which are anxiously keeping watch over the village fall into deep and happy slumber; these three white dart-like hairs of the porcupine are the creation of Brahma.

• All prophets (*siddha*) have fallen into deep slumber. I do cause sleep to the whole village as far as its boundary till the sun rises. Oblation!

The application of the above *mantra* is as follows:

When a man, having fasted for seven nights and secured three white dart-like hairs of a porcupine, makes on the fourteenth day of the dark half of the month oblations into the fire with 108 pieces of the sacrificial firewood of *khadira* (*Mimosa catechu*) and other trees together with honey and clarified butter chanting the above *mantra*, and when, chanting the same *mantra*, he buries one of the hairs at the entrance of either a village or a house within it, he causes the whole animal life therein to fall into deep slumber.

• I bow to *Bali*, the son of Vairochana, to Satamaya, Sambara, Nikumbha, Naraka, Kumbha, Tantukachchha, the great demon;

• To Armalava, Pramila, Mandoluka, Ghatodbala, to Krishna with his followers, and to the famous woman, Paulomi.

• Chanting the sacred *mantras*, I do take the pith or the bone of the corpse (*savasarika*) productive of my desired ends—may Salaka demons be victorious; salutation to them; oblation!—May the dogs which are anxiously keeping watch over the village fall into deep and happy slumber.

• May all prophets (*siddharthah*) fall into happy sleep about the object which we are seeking from sunset to sunrise and till the attainment of my desired end. Oblation!

The application of the above *mantra* is as follows:

Having fasted for four nights and having on the fourteenth day of the dark half of the month performed animal sacrifice (*bali*) in cremation grounds, one should, repeating the above *mantra*, collect the pith of a corpse (*savasarika*) and keep it in a basket made of leaves (*pattrapauttalika*). When this basket, being pierced in the centre by a dart-like hair of a porcupine, is buried, chanting the above *mantra*, the whole animal life therein falls into deep slumber.

I take refuge with the god of fire and with all the goddesses in the ten quarters; may all obstructions vanish and may all things come under my power. Oblation.

The application of the above *mantra* is as follows:

Having fasted for three nights and having on the day of the star of *Pushya* prepared twenty-one pieces of sugar candy, one should make oblation into the fire with honey and clarified butter; and having worshipped the pieces of sugar candy with scents and garlands of flowers, one should bury them. When, having on the next day of the star of *Pushya* unearthed the pieces of sugar candy, and chanting the above *mantra*, one strikes the door panel of a house with one piece and throws four pieces in the interior, the door will open itself.

Having fasted for four nights, one should on the fourteenth day of the dark half of the month get a figure of a bull prepared from the bone of a man, and worship it, repeating the above *mantra*. Then a cart drawn by two bulls will be brought before the worshipper who can (mount it and) drive in the sky and tell all that is connected with the sun and other planets of the sky.

O, *Chandali Kumbhi*, *Tumba Katuka*, and *Sarigha*, thou art possessed of the *bhaga* of a woman, oblation to thee.

When this *mantra* is repeated, the door will open and the inmates fall into sleep.

Having fasted for three nights, one should on the day of the star of *Pushya* fill with soil the skull of a man killed with weapons or put to the gallows, and, planting in it *valli* (*vallari* ?) plants, should irrigate them with water. Having taken up the grown-up plants on the next day of the star of *Pushya* (i.e., after twenty seven lunar days), one should manufacture a rope from them. When this rope is cut into two pieces before a drawn bow or any other shooting machine, the string of those machines will be suddenly cut into two pieces.

When the slough of a water snake (*udakahi*) is filled with the breathed-out dirt (*uchchhvasamrittika?*) of a man or woman (and is held before the face and nose of any person), it causes those organs to swell.

When the sack-like skin of the abdomen of a dog or a boar is filled with the breathed-out dirt (*uchchhvasamrittika*) of a man or woman and is bound (to the body of a man) with the ligaments of a monkey, it causes the man's body to grow in width and length (*anaha*),

When the figure of an enemy carved out of *rajavriksha* (*Cassia fistula*) is besmeared with the bile of a brown cow killed with a weapon on the fourteenth day of the dark half of the month, it causes blindness (to the enemy).

Having fasted for four nights and offered animal sacrifice (*bali*) on the fourteenth day of the dark half of the month, one should get a few bolt-like pieces prepared from the bone of a man put to the gallows. When one of these pieces is put in the faeces or urine (of an enemy), it causes (his) body to grow in size (*anaha*); and when the same piece is buried under the feet or seat (of an enemy), it causes death by consumption; and when it is buried in the shop, fields or the house (of an enemy), it causes him loss of livelihood.

The same process of smearing and burying holds good with the bolt-like pieces (*kilaka*) prepared from *vidyuddanda* tree.

• When the nail of the little finger (*punarnavam avachinam* ?) *nimba* (*Nimba melia*), *kama* (*bdellium*), *madhu* (*Celtis orientalis*), the hair of a monkey, and the bone of a man, all wound round with the garment of a dead man

• is buried in the house of, or is trodden down by, a man, that man with his wife, children and wealth will not survive three fortnights.

• When the nail of the little finger, *nimba* (*Nimba melia*), *kama* (*bdellium*), *madhu* (*Celtis orientalis*), and the bone of a man dead from natural causes are buried under the feet of,

• or near the house of, a man or in the vicinity of the camp of an army, of a village, or of a city, that man (or the body of men) with wife, children and wealth will not survive three fortnights.

• When the hair of a sheep and a monkey, of a cat and mongoose, of Brahmans, of low-caste men (*svapaka*), and of a crow and an owl is collected,

• and is made into a paste with faeces (*vishtavakshunna*), its application brings on instantaneous death. When a flower garland of a dead body, the ferment derived from burning corpse, the hair of a mangoose,

• and the skin of scorpion, a bee, and a snake are buried under the feet of a man, that man will lose all human appearance so long as they are not removed.

Having fasted for three nights and having on the day of the star of *Pushya* planted *gunja* seeds in the skull, filled with soil, of a man killed with weapons or put to the gallows, one should irrigate it with water. On the new or full moon day with the star of *Pushya*, one should take out the plants when grown, and prepare out of them circular pedestals (*mandalika*). When vessels containing food and water are placed on these pedestals, the foodstuff will never decrease in quantity.

When a grand procession is being celebrated at night, one should cut off the nipples of the udder of a dead cow and burn them in a torchlight flame. A fresh vessel should be plastered in the interior with the paste prepared from these burnt nipples, mixed with the urine of a bull. When this vessel, taken round the village in circumambulation from right to left, is placed below, the whole quantity of the butter produced by all the cows (of the village) will collect itself in the vessel.

On the fourteenth day of the dark half of the month combined with the star of *Pushya*, one should thrust into the organ of procreation of a dog or heat an iron seal (*katalayasam mudrikam*) and take it up when it falls down of itself. When, with this seal in hand, a collection of fruits is called out, it will come of itself (before the magician).

By the power of *mantras*, drugs and other magical performances, one should protect one's own people and hurt those of the enemy.

[Thus ends Chapter 3, 'The Application of Medicine and Mantras', in Book XIV, 'Secret Means', of the Arthashastra of Kautilya. End of the148th chapter from the beginning.]

Chapter 4

REMEDIES AGAINST THE INJURIES OF ONE'S OWN ARMY

WITH regard to remedies against poisons and poisonous compounds applied by an enemy against one's own army or people:

When the things that are meant for the king's use, inclusive of the limbs of women, as well as the things of the army are washed in the tepid water prepared from the decoction of *sleshmataki* (*sebesten* or *Cordia myxa*), *kapi* (*Emblica officinalis*), *madanti* (?), *danta* (ivory), *satha* (citron tree), *gojigi* (*gojihva* ?—*Elephantophus scaber*), *visha* (*Aconitum ferox*), *patali* (*Bignonia suave olens*), *bala* (*Lida cardifolia et rombifolia*), *syonaka* (*Bignonia indica*), *punarnava* (?), *sveta* (*Andropogon aciculatum*), and *tagara* (*Tabernaemontana coronaria*), mixed with *chandana* (sandal) and the blood of *salavriki* (jackal), it removes the bad effects of poison.

The mixture prepared from the biles of *prishata* (red-spotted deer), *nakula* (mongoose), *nilakantha* (peacock), and *godha* (alligator), with charcoal powder (*mashiraji*), combined with the sprouts (*agra*) of *sinduvara* (*Vitex trifolia*), *tagara* (*Tabernaemontana coronaria),* *varuna* (*Teriandium indicum*), *tanduliyaka* (*Amaranthus polygamus*), and *sataparva* (*Convolvulus repens*) together with *pinditaka* (*Vangueria spinosa*) removes the effects of the mixture of *madana.*

Among the decoctions of the roots of *srigāla* (*Bignonia indica*), *vinna* (?), *madana*, *sinduvara* (*Vitex trifolia*), *tagara* (*Tabernaemontana coronaria*), and *valli* (a creeper?), anyone or all mixed with milk, removes, when drunk, the effects of the mixture of *madana*.

The stinking oil extracted from *kaidarya* (*Vangueria spinosa*) removes madness.

The mixture prepared from *priyangu* (panic seed) and *naktamala* (*Galedupa arborea*) removes, when applied through the nose, leprosy.

The mixture prepared from *kushtha* (*Costus*) and *lodhra* (*Symplocus*) removes consumption.

The mixture prepared from *katuphala* (*Glelina arborea*), *dravanti* (*Anthericum tuberosum*), and *vilanga* (a kind of seed) removes, when applied through the nose, headache and other diseases of the head.

The application of the mixture prepared from *priyangu* (panic seed), *manjishtha (Rubia manjit*), *tagara* (*Tabernaemontana coronaria*), *laksharasa* (the juice or essence of lac) *madhuka* (?), *haridra* (turmeric), and *kshaudra* (honey) to persons who have fallen senseless by being beaten by a rope, by falling into water, or by eating poison, or by being whipped, or by falling, resuscitates them.

The proportion of a dose is as much as an *aksha* (?) to men; twice as much to cows and horses; and four times as much to elephants and camels.

A round ball (*mani*) prepared from the above mixture and containing gold (*rukma*) in its centre, removes the the effects due to any kind of poison.

A round ball (*mani*) prepared from the wood of *asvattha* (holy fig tree) growing wound round with the plants such as *jivanti* (a medicinal plant), *sveta* (*Andropogan aciculatum*), the flower of *mushkaka* (a species of tree), and *vanadaka* (*Epidendrum tesseloides*), removes the effects due to any kind of poison.

• The sound of trumpets painted with the above mixture destroys poison; whoever looks at a flag or banner besmeared with the above mixture will get rid of poison.

• Having applied these remedies to secure the safety of himself and his army, a king should make use of poisonous smokes and other mixtures to vitiate water against his enemy.

[Thus ends Chapter 4, 'Remedies Against the Injuries of One's Own Army', in Book XIV, 'Secret Means', of the Arthashastra of Kautilya. End of the 149th chapter from the beginning. With this, ends Book XIV, 'Secret Means', of the Arthashastra of Kautilya.]

Book XV

The Plan of a Treatise

Chapter 1

PARAGRAPHICAL DIVISIONS OF THIS TREATISE

THE subsistence of mankind is termed *artha*, wealth; the earth which contains mankind is also termed *artha*, wealth; that science which treats of the means of acquiring and maintaining the earth is the *Arthashastra*, Science of Polity.

It contains thirty-two paragraphical divisions; the book (*adhikarana*), contents (*vidhana*), suggestion of similar facts (*yoga*), the meaning of a word (*padartha*), the purport of reason (*hetvartha*), mention of a fact in brief (*uddesa*), mention of a fact in detail (*nirdesa*), guidance (*upadesa*), quotation, (*apadesa*), application (*atidesa*), the place of reference (*pradesa*), simile (*upamana*), implication (*arthapatti*), doubt (*samsaya*), reference to similar procedure (*presanga*), contrariety (*viparyaya*), ellipsis (*vakyasesha*), acceptance (*anumata*), explanation (*vyakhyana*), derivation (*nirvachana*), illustration (*nidarsana*), exception (*apavarga*), the author's own technical terms (*svasanja*), prima facie view (*purva paksha*), rejoinder (*uttarapaksha*), conclusion (*ekanta*), reference to a subsequent portion (*anagatavekshana*), reference to a previous portion (*atikrantavekshana*), command (*niyoga*), alternative (*vikalpa*), compounding together (*samuchchaya*), and determinable fact (*uhya*).

That portion of a work in which a subject or topic is treated of is a book, as for example: 'This Arthashastra or Science of Polity has been made as a compendium of all those Arthashastras which, as a guidance to kings in acquiring and maintaining the earth, have been written by ancient teachers.'

A brief description of the matter contained in a book is its contents, as: 'the end of learning; association with the aged; control of the organs of sense; the creation of ministers, and the like'.

Pointing out similar facts by the use of such words as 'These and the like', is suggestion of similar facts; for example: 'The world consisting of the four castes and the four religious divisions and the like.'

The sense which a word has to convey is its meaning; for example, with regard to the word *mulahara*: 'Whoever squanders the wealth acquired for him by his father and grandfather is a *mulahara*, prodigal son'.

What is meant to prove an assertion is the purport of reason; for example: 'For charity and enjoyment of life depend upon wealth'.

Saying in one word is mentioning a fact in brief; for example: 'It is the control of the organs of sense on which success in learning and discipline depends.'

Explanation in detached words is the mentioning of a fact in detail; for example: 'Absence of discrepancy in the perception of sound, touch, colour, flavour and scent, by means of the ear, the skin, the eyes, the tongue and the nose, is what is meant by restraint of the organs of sense'.

Such statement as 'Thus one should live', is guidance; for example: 'Not violating the laws of righteousness and economy, he should live.'

Such statement, as 'he says thus', is a quotation; for example: 'The school of Manu says that a king should make his assembly of ministers consist of twelve ministers; the school of Brihaspati says that it should consist of sixteen ministers; the school of Usanas says it should contain twenty members; but Kautilya holds that it should contain as many ministers as the need of the kingdom requires.'

When a rule dwelt upon in connection with a question is said to apply to another question also, it is termed application; for example: 'What is said of a debt not repaid holds good with failure to make good a promised gift'.

Establishing a fact by what is to be treated of later on is 'place of reference'; for example: 'By making use of such strategic means as conciliation, bribery, dissension and coercion, as we shall explain in connection with calamities.'

Proving an unseen thing or course of circumstances by what has been seen is simile; for example: 'Like a father his son, he should protect those of his subjects who have passed the period of the remission of taxes.'

What naturally follows from a statement of facts, though not spoken of in plain terms, is implication; for example, 'Whoever has full experience of the affairs of this world should, through the medium of the courtiers and other friends, win the favour of a king who is of good character and worthy sovereign. It follows from this that no one should seek the favour of a king through the medium of the king's enemies.'

When the statement of a reason is equally applicable to two cases of circumstances, it is termed doubt; for example: 'Which of the two should a conqueror march against: one whose subjects are impoverished and greedy, or one whose subjects are oppressed?'

When the nature of procedure to be specified in connection with a thing is said to be equal to what has already been specified in connection with another, it is termed reference to similar procedure; for example: 'On the lands allotted to him for the purpose of carrying on agricultural operations, he should do as before.'

The inference of a reverse statement from a positive statement is termed contrariety; for example: 'The reverse will be the appearance of a king who is not pleased with the messenger.'

That portion of a sentence which is omitted, though necessary to convey a complete sense, is ellipsis; for example: 'With his feathers plucked off, he will lose his power to move.' Here 'like a bird' is omitted.

When the opinion of another person is stated but not refuted, it is acceptance of that opinion; for example: 'Wings, front and reserve are the form of an array of the army according to the school of Usanas.'

Description in detail is explanation; for example: 'Especially amongst assemblies and confederacies of kings possessing the characteristics of assemblies, quarrel is due to gambling; and destruction of persons due to the quarrel. Hence, among evil propensities, gambling is the worst evil, since it renders the king powerless for activity.'

Stating the derivative sense of a word, is derivation; for example: 'That which throws off (*vyasyati*) a king from his prosperous career is propensity (*vyasana*).

The mentioning of a fact to illustrate a statement is illustration; for example: 'In war with a superior, the inferior will be reduced to the same condition as that of a foot soldier fighting with an elephant'.

Removal of an undesired implication from a statement is exception; for example: 'A king may allow his enemy's army to be present close to his territory, unless he suspects of the existence of any internal trouble.'

Words which are not used by others in the special sense in which they are used by the author are his own technical terms; for example: 'He who is close to the conqueror's territory is the first member; next to him comes the second member; and next to the second comes the third.'

The citation of another's opinion to be refuted, is prima facie view; for example: 'Of the two evils, the distress of the king and that of his minister, the latter is worse.'

Settled opinion is rejoinder; for example: 'The distress of the king is worse, since everything depends upon him; for the king is the central pivot, as it were'.

That which is universal in its application is conclusion or an established fact: for example: 'A king should ever be ready for manly effort.'

Drawing attention to a later chapter is reference to a subsequent portion; for example: 'We shall explain balance and weights in the chapter, 'The superintendent of Weights and Measures.'

The statement that it has been already spoken of is reference to a previous portion: for example, 'The qualifications of a minister have already been described.'

'Thus and not otherwise' is command; for example: 'Hence he should be taught the laws of righteousness and wealth, but not unrighteousness and non-wealth.'

'This or that' is alternative; for example: 'or daughters born of approved marriage (*dharmavivaha*)'.

'Both with this and that' is compounding together; for example: 'Whoever is begotten by a man on his wife is agnatic both to the father and the father's relatives.'

That which is to be determined after consideration is determinable fact; for example: 'Experts shall determine the validity or invalidity of gifts so that neither the giver nor the receiver is likely to be hurt thereby.'

- Thus this *Sastra*, conforming to these paragraphic divisions is composed as a guide to acquire and secure this and the other world.
- In the light of this *Sastra* one cannot only set on foot righteous, economical and aesthetical acts and maintain them, but also put down unrighteous, uneconomical and displeasing acts.
- This *Sastra* has been made by him who from intolerance (of misrule) quickly rescued the scriptures and the science of weapons and the earth which had passed to the Nanda king.

[Thus ends the Chapter 1, 'Paragraphic Divisions of the Treatise', in the Book XV, 'Plan of Treatise'. This is the 150th chapter from the first chapter of the entire work. Book XV 'The Plan of a Treatise', of the Arthashastra of Kautilya is thus brought to a close.]

Having seen discrepancies in many ways on the part of the writers of commentaries on the *Sastras*, Vishnugupta himself has made (this) *Sutra* and commentary.